Public Record Office Handbook No 19

Tracing Your Ancestors
in the
Public Record Office

Fifth revised edition

Edited by Amanda Bevan

PUBLIC RECORD OFFICE
The National Archives

Public Record Office
Kew
Richmond
Surrey TW9 4DU

First published 1981
Fifth edition 1999

ISBN 1 873162 61 8

A catalogue card for this book
is available from the British Library.

Typeset by Textype Typesetters, Cambridge
Printed by The Cromwell Press Ltd, Trowbridge, Wilts.

Contents

7 Welsh genealogy 88

8 Scottish genealogy 90

9 Irish genealogy 92

10 Isle of Man genealogy 95

11 Channel Isles genealogy 97

Foreword to the Fifth Edition

It is difficult to add to what previous writers have said about *Tracing Your Ancestors in the Public Record Office*, which first appeared to a general welcome in 1981. But I will try.

For a start this edition includes a comprehensive index, more guidance to fifteenth and sixteenth century records and more advice on legal records. There are also illustrations of the documents: one of particular interest to me shows the inventory of Richard Tyacke (a Cornish relation) after his early death, signed by his widow, Sibella Tyacke.

More records have flowed into the PRO since the last edition in 1990, in particular the 1891 census and the First World War service records for the armed services and the merchant marine. Many of the First World War service records were damaged by fire in enemy action during the Second World War, but thanks to a grant from the National Lottery Fund we are microfilming these records to preserve them and make them available to you over the next few years.

Our readers will also know of the establishment of the new family history service at the Family Records Centre, where you may now consult finding aids to records of births, marriages and deaths held by the Office for National Statistics (which shares the building with us), as well as looking at the censuses on microfilm. Original records are now all seen at Kew, where our services to readers have been revitalised and improved. Still to come are the catalogues and lists on-line for searching from home, local record office or library, and various database projects. Our web site, which gives further guidance to archival resources, is already much visited.

This is the first edition to be published under the PRO imprint, and, like its forebears, it is no doubt destined to be used until it falls apart.

Sarah Tyacke
Keeper of Public Records
September 1998

Preface

This is the fifth edition of a handbook originally written in 1981 by Mrs J Cox and Mr T Padfield. It was extensively revised and enlarged in the fourth edition in 1990 by Dr A Bevan and Miss A Duncan.

In this, the fifth edition, it has been revised and enlarged again by Dr Bevan, to take into account the closure of the Public Record Office's Chancery Lane site, the opening of the Family Records Centre, and the development of Kew, as well as the natural increase in the number of records available to the public – in particular, the service records of the First World War. Other chapters too have been added or considerably expanded.

The chapters on military records have been revised and expanded by Mr W Spencer, on legal records by Dr R Paley, on early records by Dr M Mercer, on records of merchant seamen and shipping by Mr C Watts, on enclosure records by Dr P Carter, and on prisoners of war by Dr K Bartlett, all of the Public Record Office. The chapter on wills is based on work by Mr G Hood, and that on the Royal Household on work by the Mrs V Carr. In addition, those parts of the text which relate to the Office for National Statistics (ONS) at the Family Records Centre have been approved by Mrs M Troyano of the ONS.

For this edition, the editor has received help from many people, both Public Record Office staff and others. Particular mention should be made of Dr T Brass, Miss M Brennand, Mr J Cassidy, Mrs N Chandrashekar, Miss S Colwell, Mr N Coney, Mrs J Cox, Dr S Cunningham, Mrs J Day, Mrs C Doidge Ripper, Mrs M Edwards, Mrs P Faithfull, Mr S Fowler, Mrs K Grannum, Mr D Hawkings, Mr C Heather, Mr G Hood, Professor H Horwitz, Mrs H Jones, Mr R Kershaw, Ms S Knight, Mr J Lappin, Mr A Lawes, Mr M Leyden, Mrs S Lumas, Mrs A Morton, Mr L Oliver, Mr B Pappalardo, Mr M Parker, Mr M Pearsall, Miss S Phillips, Mr K Smith, Mr M Smith, Mr N Taylor, Dr D Thomas, Mr G Toop, Dr M Wallace and Mr J Wood. In addition, several readers have supplied corrections and suggested improvements, which have been incorporated with gratitude. Thanks are specially due to the members of the Repository staff, who produce documents so quickly and efficiently.

Many thanks are owed to

- Tom, Anna, Edmund and Miles Brass: for putting up with a considerable diminution in their own family life during the preparation of this edition.
- Kate, Lucy and Alice Spencer: for helping to get the military chapters completed to time, despite the early arrival of Alice.

This book, a compilation of some of the collective knowledge of the Public Record Office, is dedicated to all those members of the staff, past and present, who gave and give help and advice to all-comers.

Amanda Bevan
September 1998

1 Introduction

1.1 The public records

The Public Record Office (PRO) at Kew, in south-west London, houses one of the finest, most complete archives in the world, running unbroken from the Domesday Book in 1086 to the present century. It holds the records for the central government of the United Kingdom (primarily of England and Wales, as Scotland and Northern Ireland have their own central record offices), as well as the records of the law courts of England. In addition, it is also a major international archive, because of its vast holdings on the former British colonies, and on foreign relations over eight centuries.

Public records are not normally made available for reading until thirty years after the date of their final creation; thus a file opened in 1960 and closed in 1965 became available in 1996. Exceptions to this rule are noted in the text. Many documents which refer to individuals have much longer closure periods, to safeguard personal confidentiality: an obvious example is the census, which is closed for 100 years.

These records were produced in the course of government and the dispensing of justice. Many people now use them for the wholly different purpose of historical research. Whether your field is family history or economic history, gender history or the history of crime, remember that the people who wrote down these records did so because there was an administrative need to do so. As a result, to find the answers we want, we often have to know something of how government and the courts operated, in order to better understand the surviving information. We hope this book will help you find out more, both about your own family history, and about all those people in the past whose lives appear so briefly in the spotlight of the record.

1.2 Family history research: starting out

The best place to begin family history research is at home, gathering as much factual information, memories and memorabilia as you can from members of your family. You may be surprised at how much you can accumulate. Putting it together will bring out all kinds of queries, as you realise that there are unexplained gaps. Answering those queries may lead to more questions, and so on until you find that you need to start looking outside the family for information. You will find that you probably have to keep going back to revisit family memories as you find out more.

Record offices are not necessarily the best place to start family history research, because neither local nor central government has ever had much interest in recording family history. We sometimes get questions from people who expect to find a government file kept on their family over the centuries. This was not the case. Records were only kept when people came into contact with government at some point – when their birth, marriage or death was registered; when they completed a census return; when they entered one of the armed services; when they committed a crime; when they were supposed to pay taxes. Because government had no interest in individuals, there are no official indexes to records which will give all the references to John Smith of Little Puddington. You really do need to have a list of defined questions, and as much information as you can, before you go to the trouble and expense of visiting a record office.

To help you work out what questions you can expect to get answers for, try your local library for books on researching family history. There are very many of these, mostly published over the last twenty years. These may be out-of-date in some respects: institutions move (as we have just done, from Chancery Lane) and records become open that were previously closed (like the service records from the First World War). However, the general advice on how to conduct family history, which this book does not give, will still be helpful: the principles of family history research don't change that much, after all.

Three books which are particularly interesting are Hey's *Oxford Guide to Family History* (especially the chapter showing how many surnames and families remain local to their placc of origin); Herber' s *Ancestral Trails*, which gives an overview of all the records that can be used by family historians, both locally and nationally; and Colwell' s *Family Roots: Discovering the Past in the Public Record Office* (which gives several case studies of family histories, illustrating the use that can be made of all kinds of records in the PRO).

The PRO bookshop, which runs a mail order service, currently holds about 250 publications on family history: for more information write to it or check the PRO web site (see section **1.5**). The bibliographies in this book contain, besides works for further reading, information on various aids to finding and understanding records. Many of the books cited are available in the PRO, either in the Library, the Research Enquiries Room, or the reading rooms. Some can be bought in the shops at Kew and at the Family Records Centre (FRC). Most can be read in the Guildhall Library (a public library with an excellent genealogical collection), the library of the Society of Genealogists and in good reference libraries. If it is more convenient, you could try inter-library loan, through your local lending library.

Next, contact your local family history society. There is a national network of these throughout the British Isles, most of which publish journals. These organisations can be extremely helpful in providing professional guidance and contact between family historians. A list of family history societies and like bodies appears in the journal of the Federation of Family History Societies, the *Family History News and Digest*, published twice yearly. The address of the Federation of Family History Societies (FFHS) is in Chapter **48** 'Useful addresses'. They publish an excellent series of brief and inexpensive guides to records. You will find among their members people from all walks of life, who have turned their various skills and unvaried enthusiasm and energy into the hunt for their own family history, and to the task of making sources for family history known and available. Many index records of no direct interest to themselves, on the understanding that someone, somewhere else, is indexing just the set of records they always needed and never knew existed. You will have plugged into a network of interesting and interested people: family historians seem to discover new friends at an even greater rate than 'new' ancestors!

Something you should do at some point is to make sure that you are not duplicating research someone else has already done. Try the *Register of One Name Studies*, an alphabetical listing of surnames that have been registered with the Guild of One Name Studies by researchers. Other sources are the *National Genealogical Directory*, produced annually by Burchall, and the *British Isles Genealogical Register*, produced on microfiche by the FFHS. You may also want to check Gibson's guide to *Unpublished Personal Name Indexes*.

You may find that you live reasonably near one of the excellent Family History Centres run by the Church of Jesus Christ of Latter-day Saints (LDS). To find out the nearest centre, write with a stamped addressed envelope to The Genealogical Society of Utah, British Isles Family History Service Centre (address in **48**). The LDS has filmed and indexed vast runs of records vital to the pursuit of family history; and these films can be seen at their local centres, for a small monthly fee. Most have to be ordered from the LDS headquarters in Utah, and take about a month to come.

All centres have a copy of the *International Genealogical Index* (see **3.3**), the index to parish registers, and other sources, and many have the CD-ROM *FamilySearch*, based on the parish registers, which can be a wonderful source for family history before 1837. This can also be seen at the Family Records Centre. The LDS also maintains a Family Registry on microfiche.

Another source for centralised genealogical information is the Society of Genealogists in central London (address in **48**). They have an incomparable library of published and unpublished source material, including transcripts of many parish registers, listed by county in *Parish Register Copies in the Library of the Society of Genealogists*. You can pay an annual fee to join the Society, or you can pay a daily or hourly charge to use the library.

If you have sound reasons for believing that your family is armigerous (entitled to bear a coat of arms), enquire of the officer-in-waiting at the College of Arms (address in **48**). The College has many pedigrees among its collections, and officers will undertake research into these. Scotland and Ireland have their own heraldic authorities.

Once you know what questions you want to ask, and where you can reasonably expect to get them answered, you will need to find out how to get there. Invest in Gibson and Peskett's inexpensive pamphlet, *Record Offices and How to Find Them*, which is a typically practical and helpful guide, and includes maps, or try your library again, for *British Archives*, by Foster and Sheppard which lists record offices, other archives, and museums or libraries holding records. As well as giving brief details of their collections, this gives opening times, addresses, phone numbers and conditions of access. A brief guide to the same type of information (but not the collection details) is given by the Royal Commission on Historical Manuscripts, *Record Repositories in Great Britain*. The Royal Commission can also provide information on the whereabouts of private papers and manorial documents: a link to their database is available on the PRO web site.

1.3 The Public Record Office and the Family Records Centre

If you are starting your family history research, and don't have all the certificates you need from the family papers, you will probably need to go to the Family Records Centre, in central London, where most of the main collections of birth, marriage, death and census records are held. Don't forget to consult our specialist guide to the FRC, *Never Been Here Before?* by Cox and Colwell, two renowned family historians, which will get you off to the best possible start.

The Family Records Centre is a new venture, opened in 1997, on the closure of the Census Rooms at the PRO's former central London site in Chancery Lane, and of the General Register Office public searchroom at St Catherine's House. In this book, these institutions are referred to as follows:

PRO	Public Record Office, Kew	Includes early and legal records previously held at Chancery Lane.
FRC (PRO)	Family Records Centre – the first floor searchroom, run by the PRO	Holdings include census records previously seen at the Census Rooms, Portugal Street or Chancery Lane.
FRC (ONS)	Family Records Centre – the ground floor searchroom, run by the General Register Office of England and Wales, part of the Office for National Statistics (ONS)	Holdings include indexes to birth, marriage and death records from 1837. Previously at St Catherine's House

At the FRC are housed the main genealogical records held by the PRO (the censuses from 1841–1891; the major archive of wills before 1858; and non-parochial registers of births, marriages and deaths (before 1837)) and by the General Register Office of England and Wales (civil birth, marriage and death indexes, 1837 to date, and adoption records, 1927 to date). The other main genealogical sources are the parish registers of births, marriages and deaths before 1837, held locally, usually in county record offices; wills proved in local church courts before 1858, also usually in county record offices; and the wills after 1858, held at the Probate Searchroom of the Supreme Court, in central London (address in **48**).

1.4 Practical details: Kew and the FRC

The staff at the PRO and the FRC can help you with advice and guidance, but we cannot actually do research for the public. The PRO and the FRC are open reference institutions, where readers have to come to the searchrooms to conduct their own research. If this is not possible, then we can supply lists of professional researchers or record agents, who will undertake research for a fee. The arrangement between you and the agent will be of a purely private nature, and the PRO and FRC can accept no responsibility for any aspect of the arrangements made between record agents and their clients. The Association of Genealogists and Record Agents (see **48**) can also put you in touch with a researcher accredited by the Association.

If you know the exact document reference, photocopies can be ordered by post: there is a minimum charge for this service (£10 at the time of writing). See Figure 1 for details.

The PRO has a very popular web site, at http://www.pro.gov.uk/ where you will find the latest information about the PRO's holdings, opening times, new accessions, publications, bookshop, etc., as well as the current e-mail address. It also contains copies of information leaflets which are sometimes more detailed in their instructions than the information given in this book. They are designed to be used in the reading rooms, and can be picked up when you arrive, or printed off the web site (download from http://www.pro.gov.uk/leaflets/default.htm). A full set can also be bought by institutions for about £20. The web site will eventually provide access to our catalogue on computer, when it is ready.

Neither the FRC nor the PRO are suitable places for small children. Even older children are often not as interested in your research as you might wish, and get bored. There are shops at both sites which sell a range of 'historic' items: some of these might appeal to children, if you need to bribe your way to a day at the PRO!

1.5 More practical details: Kew

The reading rooms at Kew are open to the public until 5 p.m., Monday to Saturday, with late night opening on Tuesday and Thursday until 7 p.m. They open at 9 a.m. except on Tuesdays (10 a.m.) and Saturdays (9.30 a.m.). Documents cannot be ordered until 9.30 a.m. Kew is closed on Sundays, public holidays, and during stock-taking (one week, normally in December). There is a restaurant on site, where you can also eat your own food, and a shop.

You will need to get a reader's ticket at the PRO at Kew in order to see original records. This will be issued at Reception when you arrive, on production of some positive means of identification, such as a passport, banker's card, or driving licence or, for foreign nationals, a passport

Your Ref:

Our Ref: SL/RORD 2

Date as postmark

PUBLIC
RECORD
OFFICE

Kew
Richmond
Surrey TW9 4DU

Telephone: 0181 876 3444
Extension: 2461 or 2438
Dept fax: 0181 392 5282

Dear Sir or Madam

YOUR REQUEST FOR COPIES OF PUBLIC RECORDS

Thank you for your recent enquiry. We are able to process orders for copying up to five documents (or parts of them) at a time. Our minimum order charge is £10.00.

If you wish us to begin work on your order, please complete this form and the enclosed address label and send them together with a cheque or postal order for £10.00 (made payable to the Public Record Office) or credit card details to the following address: The Finance Department, Public Record Office, Kew, Richmond, Surrey TW9 4DU (*a business reply envelope is enclosed for U.K. customers only*). Your copies will be posted to you.

Should your order come to more than £10.00, including handling and despatch charges, you will be sent an estimate of the cost of the balance within ten working days of receipt of your initial payment. We will begin making your copies upon receipt of the balance. Please note that if we send you an estimate and you do not place an order, the £10.00 minimum order charge is non-refundable.

If you requested copies of more than five documents (or parts of them) please specify the references of the five you would like to be copied. Additional orders for up to five documents (or parts of them) can be processed by sending details accompanied by a payment of £10.00 for each order. Further supplies of this form may be requested from the Reprographic Ordering Section by post, fax or telephone.

Your attention is drawn to the 'Conditions for Providing Copies and Estimates at Sections 3 and 4.

Yours faithfully

Reprographic Ordering Section

Figure 1 The PRO can supply copies of documents by post, if you can provide an exact reference. This is part of the estimate form, showing the initial charges that apply for postal estimates (as at December 1998).

or some other form of national identification document. Children over the age of 14 can be issued with a reader's ticket if they are either accompanied and vouched for by their parents (who have been able to produce their own identification to get a reader's ticket), or if they come with a letter of recommendation from their school, on headed notepaper and signed by the head teacher.

Large bags and coats are not allowed in the research areas at Kew. Lockable hangers are provided for coats, and there are lockers for other belongings. These take a £1 coin, which is returned after use. Pens and coloured pencils are not allowed in the reading rooms, but graphite pencils and laptop computers are – power points are available. Supplies of paper, tracing paper and pencils can be bought in the shop, which also sells magnifying sheets. If you want to trace anything, ask in the Reading Rooms for an acetate sheet to put over the document first. To help preserve the documents, please make use of the foam wedges and covered weights which are supplied – instructions for their use are on display.

The PRO welcomes readers with disabilities. There is a lift to all floors, and the facilities are wheelchair friendly. We have aids to help readers with impaired vision, but the totally blind are advised to come with a sighted friend. Equally, if you have mobility difficulties, it may be a good idea to come with a friend, as the PRO is a very large building, and there can be distances to cover between different sources of information. If you contact us in advance, we can provide wheelchair assistance for the 100 metres plus from the car park. You can look at our leaflet on *Physical Access to the Public Record Office and its Services* on our web site, or you can contact the PRO to ask for a copy to be sent to you.

The PRO's address is:

Post	Public Record Office, Ruskin Avenue, Kew, Richmond, Surrey TW9 4DU
Telephone	0181 876 3444
E-mail	look at our web site at http://www.pro.gov.uk/
Fax	0181 878 8905
Minicom	0181 392 9198

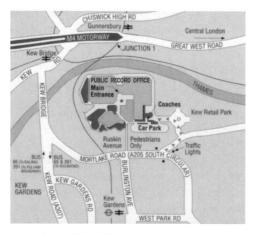

Location of the PRO

Location of the FRC

1.6 More practical details: the FRC

The FRC is open from 10 a.m. on Tuesdays, 9.30 a.m. on Saturdays, and 9 a.m. every other weekday. It closes at 7 p.m. on Tuesday and Thursday, and 5 p.m. on the other days. The FRC is closed on Sundays and public holidays. A reader's ticket is not needed. Pens can be used, and there are power points for laptop computers in the PRO searchroom. There is a shop and an eating area in the building, and several places sell meals and sandwiches nearby. There are lockers if you wish to use them: a £1 coin is needed, but is returned after use.

The FRC has ramp access for wheelchairs and a lift to both floors. It also has three parking spaces reserved for disabled readers, which you have to book in advance by ringing 0171 533 6436. There are some motorized microfilm readers with zoom facilities, for disabled readers, and magnifiers are available for printed sources or copies. If you are totally blind or have limited mobility, try to come with a sighted or more mobile friend. Once in the building, there is still a considerable amount of walking backwards and forwards during the course of a visit.

The Family Records Centre's address is:

Post	Family Records Centre, 1 Myddelton Street, London EC1R 1UW
Telephone	0181 392 5300 – census enquiries 0151 471 4800 – birth, death and marriage certificate enquiries
E-mail	look at the PRO web site at http://www.pro.gov.uk/ or look at the ONS web site at http://www.ons.gov.uk/
Fax	0181 392 5307
Minicom	0181 392 5308

Postal enquiries for certificates should be sent to GRO, PO Box 2, Southport, Merseyside PR8 2JD. For telephone enquires about certificates, ring 0151 471 4816, or for overseas registers only, 01704 69824 or 01704 63563. The ONS has a popular web site at http://www.ons.gov.uk/ where you can look under 'Services' for information about ordering certificates, as well as finding out about new services.

1.7 Finding your way round the FRC

The FRC is a very busy and popular place. It has an extensive range of leaflets giving you up-to-date guidance on how to use the records and finding aids there, which you will find on your arrival. If you want to be forearmed, or if you are planning several trips, the best thing to do is beg, borrow, steal or even buy a copy of Cox and Colwell's *Never Been Here Before?* It is fully illustrated with examples of the various certificates, census returns and other records that can be seen there, and will give you helpful and experienced guidance so that you can carry out your research most effectively.

If you want to take copies, there are self-service reader-printers. However, you may not take copies of the birth, marriage and death indexes.

1.8 Finding your way round Kew

Kew is a very large building, with several reading rooms and advice points, and an excellent library which is at last open to the public (see **1.12**). It is quite easy to lose your bearings, so be prepared to ask.

The first thing to say is that there is no simple way into the records occupying over 167 km of shelving at the Public Record Office at Kew. There is, unfortunately, no easy index of personal names to tap into, although there are some publications and records which may be worth checking to start with, and returning to every now and then as you pick up more information (see **1.13**). Expect to feel some confusion: be prepared to read and use any leaflets available for your guidance, and be ready to ask if you need to.

You will probably want to start off by using the Microfilm Reading Room, where there are explanatory panels and simple leaflets guiding you through the process for many of the more frequent genealogical searches (army ancestry, finding a will, etc.). From there, you may move into the Document Reading Room, to read original documents; or the Research Enquiries Room, for more complex modern enquiries; or to the Map and Large Document Room for maps and early record enquiries. If you find you want to look at an original document, you must ask at the Document Production Counters in the Document Reading Room or the Map Room for a pager. This assigns you a seat number, which you need when you order documents on a document ordering computer. Make sure you take a note of the seat number: it disappears from the pager display as soon as you are paged to tell you that your document has arrived. When you go up to the counter to collect it, you will be asked for the seat number.

This book concentrates on the main sources for genealogy in the public records. Nearly all these subjects have, at the PRO, a leaflet which gives detailed and specific instructions on what to do in searching for a particular record. They can also be seen (and printed) from our web site. These leaflets are not usually mentioned in each chapter's bibliography, as they are constantly under revision, but please remember to look for and use them.

In addition, the PRO has also produced many specialist guides, for example to records on foreign affairs, or Tudor taxation records, which will take you deeper into the records than this book can. If you want to use these, they should be available in each room, as well as being for sale in the shop.

If you want to explore the records on your own (and in general we find that family historians are often far more adventurous than many academic historians) you will need to learn how they are arranged, and how to use the *PRO Guide* and the class lists (see **1.9** and **1.10**).

If you want to take copies, ask at the Document Copying Counter in the Document Reading Room or Map Room. In the Microfilm Reading Room you can use the self-service reader-printer.

1.9 Understanding how the records are arranged and identified

'When I was first interviewed for my job at the PRO, I was asked if I knew the difference between a library and an archive. "Yes", I replied (in rather a foolhardy way) "– a library is arranged for the convenience of its users, and an archive isn't". It raised a laugh and I still got the job – because the answer was, unfortunately for readers, all too true.'

An archive, such as the PRO, does not arrange its holdings by subject, but by the original institutional author – the supposed creator of the records. This means that to really get the best out of the sources, you have to have some idea of how the government and courts worked, who was responsible for what kinds of affairs, who is likely to have written to whom, and what kind of information might have been collected or retained. You don't need to have a degree in English Constitutional History; you just need to know that the PRO holdings are divided up according to the government department or court that created them, or to whom they were sent in the course of everyday business, and that the publications of the PRO are there to help you find out likely and unlikely places to look. You will soon come to know that ADM means Admiralty, for the Navy, and KB means Court of King's Bench, and so on.

Records in the Public Record Office are divided into 'classes', reflecting as far as possible what they were created for, and how they were used at the time. Each class has its own name and code, and each consists of individual 'pieces', which is what you order to be produced from the storage areas, or what you get yourself from a microfilm or microfiche cabinet. Each piece has a unique reference. This is made up of a lettercode, a class number, and a piece number.

lettercode	e.g. WO	War Office
+ class number	e.g. WO 97	War Office, Royal Hospital Chelsea, Soldiers' Documents
+ piece number	e.g. WO 97/341	War Office, Royal Hospital Chelsea, Soldier's Documents, 13th Foot, Abb-Car, 1760–1854

These references can be discovered from the various finding aids in the Public Record Office.

The *PRO Guide* gives an overview of the history and content of all the records in its care. It is updated at regular intervals to include the latest accessions and discoveries. Because it is so large (over 5,500 pages) and is updated so frequently, it is sold in microfiche only. A new microfiche edition will be published in early 1999 and should be available at your local reference library or record office. At the PRO several printed copies are available so you can sit and browse at leisure. Copies can also be seen at the FRC (PRO).

The *Guide* occupies several loose-leaf volumes, and is divided into three parts. Part 1 contains the history of government. Part 2 contains class descriptions in alphabetical order of class code for each class. Part 3 is the index to the other two parts. The main kinds of finding aid, below the *Guide*, are:

Finding Aids Location Index	See MORIS.
MORIS	Means of Reference Information System – a computer index to finding aids at class level. Often referred to in Introductory Notes as the Finding Aids Location Index. Can contain references to published transcripts, etc.
list	A list of the pieces comprising a class of records, with dates and simple descriptions (a *descriptive list* gives fuller indications of the contents of each document).

	Lists in the Standard Set of class lists are filed in A4 binders, in alphabetical order: there are several (colour-coded) sets of the full sequence from A to ZSPC – you are welcome to browse among them.
	Other lists will be found in the Non-Standard Sets, in the Research Enquiries Room and the Map Room. These are often original or older finding aids, or published works. They each bear a small label on the spine saying which class they refer to.
	To make sure you have found all the works referring to a particular class, check for that class in MORIS.
introductory note	An introduction to the contents of a class, explaining why the records were created, and what they contain. These exist for all medieval, early modern and legal classes, for most very modern classes, and for some other classes.
	They are usually printed on green paper, and are filed with the class lists in what is known as the Standard Set of class lists.
calendar	A précis, usually in English, full enough to replace the original documents for most purposes. The documents have been published in date order in many, but not all, calendars.
publications	The PRO publishes reader's guides and handbooks. These are the specialist guides to particular records, referred to in this book.
transcript	A full text.
index	Alphabetically arranged references to people, places or subjects mentioned in the records. Many indexes are mentioned in this book: to find them, check in MORIS, using the class as the query.

1.10 Traditional searches of the records at Kew: the *PRO Guide* and the lists

Suppose you want to trace an ancestor who may have nursed at the Royal Greenwich Hospital. Start with the *PRO Guide* Part 3, the index. There are several index entries for Greenwich Hospital, some followed by class code (e.g. ADM 72), others by a string of numbers. The numbers (e.g. 703/6/3) are references to Part 1, in which each department has its own three figure number, with further sub-divisions for different parts of its organisation.

Public Record Office PRO Guide Part 3: Index

GREENWICH HOSPITAL

703/6/3

school ledgers, ADM 72

service records of candidates, ADM 29

staff pensions, ADM 165

staff records, ADM 73

In the Part 1 entry for 703/6/3, you will find a brief history of Greenwich Hospital.

Admiralty   703.6.3

703.6.3 ROYAL GREENWICH HOSPITAL

The Royal Greenwich Hospital was founded by Queen Mary, who in 1694 gave the royal estate at Greenwich for a home for superannuated seamen and marines. The foundation stone was laid in 1696 and the first pensioners were admitted in 1705. In 1716 the forfeited estates of Lord Derwentwater were added to the hospital's endowments (the Northern Estates). In addition to the in-pensioners, the hospital also maintained out-pensioners and provided pensions and allowances for widows and orphans of seamen and marines. It also provided for a limited number of officers. A school for the sons of seamen was attached to the hospital. In 1829 this school absorbed the Royal Naval Asylum for the children of seamen, originally established by the Patriotic Fund of Lloyds, but managed by commissioners since 1805. In 1803 the hospital took over the administration of the Chatham Chest (6.1), which was thereupon renamed the Greenwich Chest. It ceased to house in-pensioners in 1869 and since 1873 the building has become the home of the Royal Naval College (6.4); but the hospital has continued to administer the school, which moved to Holbrook in 1933, and to provide out-pensions and allowances of various kinds.

Records relating to pensioners are in ADM 6, ADM 73, ADM 165, PMG 24, PMG 69-71, WO 22, WO 23; records of widows' and orphans' pensions, etc. are in ADM 73, ADM 162-164, ADM 166. Records relating to staff of the hospital are in ADM 73 and ADM 165. Records of Greenwich Hospital School are in ADM 72, ADM 73, ADM 80, ADM 161. Registers of births, baptisms, marriages and burials for the hospital and school are in RG 4/1669-1679, further registers of baptisms and burials in RG 8/16-18 and burials in ADM 73. See also PRO 30/26.

This provides a description of the Hospital's history, and a very brief guide to its records, with references to the various classes involved, but little indication of dates covered.

To find out more, you need to look at Part 2, the class descriptions. In fact, you could have gone there directly from Part 3, where the entries followed by letters and numbers are to classes described in Part 2. Neither Part 3 nor Part 1 made any references to nurses at Greenwich Hospital, but both mentioned staff records as being in ADM 73. The class description of ADM 73 in Part 2 is more helpful: nurses' records are mentioned at last.

Public Record Office PRO Guide Part 2: Class Descriptions

ADM 73 Greenwich Hospital Miscellaneous Registers, etc.

1704 to 1981 465 volumes

PRO, Kew

These include the following:

Establishment and muster books, 1704 to 1809. Nurses, labourers, servants, etc. Out-pension pay books, 1781 to 1809. Artificers' wages lists, etc, 1845 to 1866. Burial Registers, 1844 to 1981.

School admission papers, 1728 to 1870. These contain baptismal or birth certificates of the children, with marriage certificates of the parents, fathers' naval services, etc. Arranged under first letters.

See *PRO Guide Part 1: 703/6/3*

Having identified the class you want to look at, you then have to find the class list to discover which particular document you want to order. You will need to do this when you get references to classes from this book, to identify exactly which piece you want.

There may be several lists in one volume, or one list may cover several volumes. Most lists are in rough date order, but some are arranged by subject and others by place. At the front of each list there should be an Introductory Note, which gives more detail about the class than Part 2 of the *PRO Guide*, and often includes instructions on how to order documents.

The Introductory Note for ADM 73 gives a range of piece numbers for staff records, which saves searching through the descriptions of all 465 pieces in this class.

```
                              ADM 73

                    GREENWICH HOSPITAL REGISTERS

The majority of these registers is concerned with four distinct classes of
person; In-Pensioners, Out-Pensioners, staff and children.

Applications by former warrant officers, ratings and Marines for admission as
In-Pensioners, arranged alphabetically, are in pieces 1-35. They consist
chiefly of certificates of the applicants' services issued by the Navy Pay
Office. Though issued from 1790, these describe services which in some cases
go back at least forty years before. Pieces 36-69 are chiefly registers of
the In-Pensioners of the Hospital at various dates.

Pay books of out-pensions form pieces 95 to 131. They give only the name of the
Out-Pensioner and the amount of his pension. The signatures of those who drew
their pensions in cash appear as a receipt; the letter R against others stands
in this case for 'Remitted' (to those living at a distance from the Hospital).

Pieces 70 to 88 and 132 to 153 are lists and registers of the staff of the
Hospital.

The papers submitted on behalf of children applying for admission to the
Greenwich Hospital Schools are arranged alphabetically in pieces 134-389. In
almost every case they include certificates of the applicants' fathers'
services. Registers of the children admitted are in pieces 390-449.

October 1984
```

In the class list of ADM 73, pieces 83 to 88 look as though they might be useful in this search.

Reference ADM 73	ADMIRALTY – GREENWICH HOSPITAL REGISTERS, &c ADM 73
	Date **Description**
82	1865–1869 Muster Book of Servants
83	1704–1864 General Entry Book of Nurses
84	1766–1863 Entry Book of Nurses
85	1783–1863 Register of Nurses
86	1847–1865 Register of Nurses and Servants
87	1704–1772 Alphabetical List of Nurses
88	1772–1864 Ditto
89	1800–1801 Register of Children at Clarence House

The lettercode **ADM**, the class number **73**, and the piece number **83** are the items of information which will be needed for ordering the first of these documents via the computer.

1.11 New ways to search the records: using computerized catalogues

As well as the traditional methods described above, you will reasonably soon have the option of searching through the whole combined catalogue of *Guide* and lists on computer. This will eventually be accessible over the world wide web, and will contain record descriptions of all of our holdings. An interim version of the lists only is in use at the time of writing, with the current title of *Inventory List Database* (ILDB) – sometimes known as the Lists Online. This can be seen at Kew and at the FRC.

You may find that you need to operate the two systems of searching together until the online catalogue is completed. For example, a keyword search on *Greenwich* and *nurses* in the ILDB turned up (at the time of writing) an entirely different set of references than the traditional search, and did not bring up ADM 73 at all. It all depends if the keyword you are using for your search was included in the title, the header or the text of the original list – titles and headers are not picked up by the search.

Lettercode	Class	Piece	Item	Scope	Date	Details
ADM	6	329		Register of rating's widows applying for admission to **Greenwich** Hospital as **nurses**	1817–1831	→
ADM	6	331		Register of rating's widows applying for admission to **Greenwich** Hospital as **nurses**	1819–1842	→
ED	82	70		**Greenwich**, Dreadnought Training School for **Nurses**	1927	→

As you can see, the first two look excellent for our search. Clicking on the arrow gives the further detail, that the registers come from a class called ADM 6, Admiralty and Secretariat: Various Registers, Returns and Certificates. It does not give any details about the content of the record: to find out more, you will need to order the documents, using a different computer.

The ILDB is not designed to give details about individuals. It gives the overall description of each document, and not a list of its contents. It is at its best (and that is a very exciting best) when pulling together references to subjects or places, when it can do in seconds what would take months of ploughing through paper lists.

Some other computerized searches are also available. The most popular is the WO 97 database, of soldiers discharged to pension, 1760–1854. Databases of taxation returns and equity proceedings are also being constructed, but are not yet ready.

1.12 Using the PRO Library

The PRO Library has not been open to the public for very long, and it is still a rather under-used resource. It has excellent sets of periodicals and journals, for all kinds of history. Its holdings of local record society publications are a tremendous resource, and you may even find that the information you are looking for has been printed. (Ask at Library Enquiries Desk for Mullins, *Texts and Calendars*, which is a guide to what each local society has produced.)

The Library has long runs of annual publications, such as the *Army List*, *Crockford's Clerical Directory*, the *India List* and many more. It holds a very large collection of books relating to the myriad of subjects covered by the records in the PRO.

The Library has the indexes to *The Times* and the Parliamentary Papers (from 1801) on CD-ROM, as well as several other useful CD-ROMs. These can produce extraordinary amounts of information – the Parliamentary Papers in particular are full of details, and using the index on a key word search can turn up all kinds of published returns of people marginally involved in government, or giving evidence on subjects of social concern. Some of these have been noted in the text, but the field remains wide open for discoveries.

1.13 A starting place? Publications, indexes and pedigrees

You may have arrived at the PRO with a specific query, or with a planned programme of research. At some point, it may be worth taking a side-step, and looking in three or four places to see if any extra information can be picked up quickly.

There are three easy places to check for information in print about a particular person. The first is the *Dictionary of National Biography*, which is in the Library. This contains brief biographies of many thousands of people whose lives were thought to have some national significance. The second is the *British Biographical Archive*. This is a compilation of over 300 other English language biographical dictionaries published between 1601 and 1929, put together on microfiche in a single alphabetical order of surname. It is on open access in the Microfilm Reading Room. The third is a CD-ROM, available in the Library, called the *Biography Database 1680–1830*. The current issue contains over 100 directories (national, town and trade); over 1,500 book subscription lists; apprenticeship lists from the Stationers' Company 1701–1800; birth, marriage, death and bankruptcy notices from the *Gentleman's Magazine* from 1731–1750; and much more.

It contains roughly 900,000 records, and is searchable by name, title, office, occupation and address. It is updated regularly to include more sources.

Indexes to records are not only available at the PRO. Other record offices and libraries obviously have their own indexes, and very many people index records for their own purposes, which they are prepared to search for a fee. It may be that there is an index somewhere which will save you days of work, or suggest new lines of enquiry. To find out, look at Gibson and Hampson, *Specialist Indexes for Family Historians*, which should be available at every enquiry desk.

Another source which may be worth checking every so often, as you garner more names for your family tree, is the large number of pedigrees that have ended up in the public records, usually in support of some legal claim. Look at the indexes filed with the lists of J 67 and J 68 to start with. Others are in the Chancery Masters Exhibits in C 103–C 114, and some are scattered in all kinds of classes. You can look at the indexes to the *PRO Guide* to identify other classes, and then look at the lists, or you can search the ILDB using *pedigree* as a keyword. This will bring up lots of pedigree cattle, but maybe also an entry for a family you are interested in. Most of the pedigrees are listed or indexed only by the 'principal person' – the pivotal person in the legal proof of entitlement to whatever was being claimed. An early work by Wrottesley, *Pedigrees from the Plea Rolls, 1200–1500,* may be worth looking at.

1.14 New skills and knowledge: language and dates

As you move backwards from the twentieth century, you will find that you need to acquire new skills and knowledge to understand the documents properly. You will come across odd forms of writing, different methods of dating, archaic measurements, incomprehensible legal phrases and, of course, Latin (in general use for many legal records until 1733). This is all on top of the fact that in very many documents (particularly in registers where a few clerks were entering similar information, year in, year out), there are all kinds of abbreviations which meant something at the time – and which now might as well be in double Dutch.

For books to help with understanding the writing, and the Latin, see the bibliography to Chapter **5**. For understanding old weights and measurements, try Chapman, *How Heavy, How Much and How Long? Weights, Money and Other Measures Used by Our Ancestors.* For legal phrases, and procedures that you don't understand, there are several legal dictionaries in the Map Room. The multi-volume *Oxford English Dictionary* is in both the Map Room and the Library. This can be very helpful when you are satisfied that you have read a word correctly, but you still have no idea what it means.

Dates are an area where you have to learn about old dating practices, and then refer to a crib when needed, to help you date documents correctly. Munby's *Dates and Time* is a fascinating account of the subject, but you may still need access to the classic work, Cheney's *Handbook of Dates*.

For much of the documented past, people in England dated years not by the calendar year (e.g. 1780) but by the regnal year (how long the monarch had been on the throne). A new regnal year began on the anniversary of the monarch's accession to the throne. Thus, 1 Elizabeth I ran from the death of Mary on 17 November 1558 to 16 November 1559; 2 Elizabeth I ran from 17 November 1559 to 16 November 1560; and so on, until 45 Elizabeth I stopped at her death on 24 March 1603, and 1 James I began.

Another problem with years is that, although New Year's Day was celebrated on 1st January, the actual year number did not change until 25th March. This was the Annunciation or Lady Day, nine months to the day before Christmas. This practice did not change officially until 1752, but for some decades beforehand, dates from January to March 24th were expressed as being in 1641/2. You will find that most dates given in PRO lists and publications have been silently amended to the modern form of the year.

The third thing to look out for is Old Style and New Style – the difference between English dates and European dates, from 1582. Pope Gregory XIII reformed the calendar in 1582 by cutting out ten days to return the calendar to the solar year. Other countries followed this lead at different times: broadly speaking, Catholic states adopted the New Style in the 16th century, Protestant states in the 18th century, and Orthodox states in the 20th century. People corresponding between countries would date their letters with both dates, as 12/22 December 1635, for example. All kinds of oddities crop up: William of Orange, for example, left Holland on 11th November 1688, to arrive in England on 5th November. In the United Kingdom the change took place in 1752, when Wednesday the 2nd September was followed immediately by Thursday the 14th September. This was ignored by the accounting and hiring records, so that the old accounting day of Lady Day (25th March) slipped to 5th April ('Old Lady Day'), still the turn of the financial year in Britain.

In early modern documents you often find that instead of using the day and month, saint's days and religious feasts are used, so that you could find the phrase 'Tuesday after the Annunciation', or 'in the eve of St Martin'. To translate these, you need to know when the feast day was, and the calendar for that particular year. You can find both of these from the lists and tables in Cheney's *Handbook of Dates* (available at all the enquiry desks and in the Map Room).

The legal system had its own calendar, based around the old agricultural and religious cycles. The legal year began with the Michaelmas term (starting on 6th October), followed by the Hilary, Easter and Trinity terms. Between the terms were the vacations. In the Lent vacation (Hilary to Easter) and the Summer vacation (Trinity to Michaelmas), the judges from the central courts travelled round the country on the assize circuits. For details of the legal terms for each year, look at Bond's *Handy Book of Dates*, in the Library.

You may well find that the patterns of the religious, agricultural and legal calendars are reflected in the records you use: they were certainly reflected in your ancestors' experience of life.

1.15 Photographs

The public records contain numerous photographs, but there is no single comprehensive listing of photographic images or index to people who may appear in them. A partial index of places, names and subjects may be consulted in the Research Enquiries Room.

Very few series of personnel records on individuals contain photographs of them. One notable exception, available on microfiche only, is the series of index cards for certain merchant seamen, described in **25.5** and illustrated in Figure 12.

The record class COPY 1 contains a wealth of photographic images from the Victorian and Edwardian periods that were registered for copyright deposit purposes. When they portray ordinary people it is normally as bystanders or in anonymous group photographs, although there are exceptions (see Figure 2 showing Mr Joseph Pearce). However, if you are looking for prominent politicians, churchmen, actresses, sportsmen and the like, COPY 1 is a significant source. There is an index to such portraits among the COPY 1 photographs, compiled by the National Portrait Gallery, in the Research Enquiries Room.

The Public Record Office has a commercial image library which can supply photographic images to users able to cite the precise document references for the photographs they require. For further details, telephone 0181 392 5225.

1.16 The Friends of the PRO

The Friends of the PRO receive a newsletter (*Prophile*) and access to events. They also undertake voluntary work in cataloguing records and improving lists and indexes. They have completed work of enormous importance to family history, such as the WO 97 database and the indexes to wills and administrations, 1701–1749. At present, they are taking part (amongst other things) in the Equity Database Project, which will open up the records of the equity courts to family and other historians. This may sound rather dry, but these records are an incomparable source for the lives and concerns of people in the past, and are currently hidden by an impenetrable set of 'finding' aids (see **47.4**).

If you want to find out more about the Friends, write to the Secretary of the Friends, at the Public Record Office address.

1.17 Tracing living people

The Public Record Office is not the place to trace missing people. The hunt for living relatives should start with Rogers' very helpful book, *Tracing Missing Persons*. Under very special circumstances, the Salvation Army will undertake to trace living relatives, but this is usually only to mitigate suffering. The Association of Genealogists and Record Agents will supply the names of agents who will make a search for a fee. Tracing may also be carried out through the Department of Social Security. Details of this procedure are contained in leaflet PAS 6, available from the FRC (ONS).

1.18 Family history: an introductory bibliography

Many of the works mentioned in this and subsequent bibliographies can be seen in the PRO Library or reading rooms, or bought in the PRO shops at the FRC and Kew.

General guides to historical sources
M Abbott, *Family Ties: English Families 1540–1920* (London, 1993)
D Hey, *The Oxford Guide to Family History* (Oxford, 1993)
A Macfarlane, *A Guide to English Historical Records* (Cambridge, 1983)
C D Rogers and J H Smith, *Local Family History in England, 1538–1914* (Manchester, 1991)

Biographical dictionaries and specialist indexes
British Biographical Archive (London, 1984 continuing)
Dictionary of National Biography (London, 1909 continuing)

J S W Gibson and E Hampson, *Specialist Indexes for Family Historians* (FFHS, 1998)
G Wrottesley, *Pedigrees from the Plea Rolls, 1200–1500* (London, c.1906)

General guides to dates, etc.
J J Bond, *Handy-Book of Rules and Tables for Verifying Dates* (London, 1869)
C R Chapman, *How Heavy, How Much and How Long? Weights, Money and Other Measures Used by Our Ancestors* (Lochin Publishing, 1996)
C R Cheney, *Handbook of Dates for Students of English History* (London, 1991)
L H Munby, *Dates and Time: A Handbook for Local Historians* (British Association for Local History, 1997)

General guides to family history research
M J Burchall, *National Genealogical Directory* (annual)
Federation of Family History Societies, *British Isles Genealogical Register* (FFHS, 1997)
Federation of Family History Societies, *Register of One Name Studies* (FFHS, reissued regularly)
T V FitzHugh and S B Lumas, *A Dictionary of Genealogy* (4th edn, 1994)
J S W Gibson, *Unpublished Personal Name Indexes* (FFHS, 1987)
R Harvey, *Genealogy for Librarians* (London, 1992): useful for everyone interested in genealogy
M Herber, *Ancestral Trails: The Complete Guide to British Genealogy and Family History* (Sutton, 1997)
S Raymond and J S W Gibson, *English Genealogy: An Introductory Bibliography* (FFHS, 1991)
S Raymond, *British Genealogical Periodicals: A Bibliography of their Contents* (FFHS, 1991)
P Saul, *The Family Historian's Enquire Within* (1997)

Periodicals
Family History, Institute of Heraldic and Genealogical Studies
Family History Monthly
Family History News and Digest, Federation of Family History Societies
Family Tree Magazine
Practical Family History
Prophile, The Friends of the Public Record Office
The Genealogists' Magazine, The Society of Genealogists

General guides to the Public Record Office
British National Archives (Government Publications Sectional List 24, last published 1984)
S Colwell, *Dictionary of Genealogical Sources in the Public Record Office* (London, 1992)
J Cox, *The Nation's Memory, A Pictorial Guide to the Public Record Office* (London, 1988)
J Cox, *New to Kew?* (PRO, 1997)
J Cox and S Colwell, *Never Been Here Before? A Genealogist's Guide to the Family Records Centre* (PRO, 1998)
List and Index Society: exact copies of lists as on the PRO shelves at the time of publication
Public Record Office, *PRO Guide to the Contents of the Public Record Office* (microfiche edition, PRO 1996 – revised edition 1999)
Public Record Office, *Guide to the Contents of the Public Record Office* (London, 1963, 1968)

Directories of archive institutions
J Foster and J Sheppard, *British Archives: A Guide to Archive Resources in the United Kingdom* (London, 1995)
J S W Gibson and P Peskett, *Record Offices and How to Find Them* (FFHS, 1998)
Royal Commission on Historic Manuscripts, *Record Repositories in Great Britain* (PRO, 1997)

Missing persons
C D Rogers, *Tracing Missing Persons* (Manchester, 1986)

2 Censuses of population

2.1 Census returns: England, Wales, the Isle of Man and the Channel Islands, 1801–1911

From 1801 onwards, information about the population of the United Kingdom has been collected every ten years by means of a census. The census (enumeration) returns taken together form the most important and useful modern source for genealogical, local, demographic and other studies in the care of the PRO. The census returns are the nearest we can come to a ten-yearly snapshot of a family's development, and they can record children whose existence might otherwise have gone undetected.

The returns of 1841, 1851, 1861, 1871, 1881 and 1891 in theory should include all people in England, Wales, the Isle of Man and the Channel Islands on a specific night in those years. The census recorded everyone present at each specific address overnight on the chosen enumeration date (always a Sunday, and from 1851 in the spring), so an entire family unit, plus collateral relatives, lodgers, employees, servants and friends may be included. Not everyone was at home, of course, and not everyone had a home. There are many institutional entries for barracks, schools, ships, and even prisons and asylums (not all of which give names). However, most searches start and end with the family household. From 1851, the relationship of everyone to the head of the household is given.

Censuses started in 1801, but until 1841 censuses were simply headcounts, and did not name individuals. The information collected varied from census to census. As the information given to the census enumerator is treated as confidential for 100 years, the 1901 census will not be open to the public until 2002. However, for the 1901 returns only, direct descendants or next of kin (if the person has died childless) may apply for a search to be made for the age and place of birth of a named person, at a precise address. Application forms are available from the FRC, and a fee is charged. Information can only be extracted from the 1911 returns if it is clearly needed to establish a legal entitlement (for example, for an inheritance), and if the information is not available from any other source. Again, application forms are available at the FRC, and a fee is charged.

2.2 Where to read the census returns, 1841–1891

The central London office of the PRO, at the Family Records Centre, Myddelton Street, London EC1R 1UW, holds microfilm copies of the census returns for England, Wales, the Isle of Man and the Channel Islands for 1841, 1851, 1861, 1871, 1881 and 1891. A reader's ticket is not needed. The censuses are the only records held by the PRO that cannot be seen at Kew.

The FRC offers a limited paid search service for these records. For up-to-date details, and application forms, use the FRC address or contact numbers in **1.6**.

Many county record offices and local history libraries hold microfilm or microfiche copies of the census returns for their local area. For more information see Gibson and Hampson, *Census Returns 1841–1891 in Microform: a Directory of Local Holdings*. In the USA, copies of all available census returns are held by the Genealogical Society of Utah in Salt Lake City (address in **48**).

2.3 Finding the right entry: name indexes and general information

Before starting a search, you need to know where to look. There are some name indexes to the census, but there is no overall index except for 1881. However, much work has been done on census indexing by very many groups and individuals unconnected with the PRO, and it may be that an index exists for the locality you are interested in. The best way to find out is to check Gibson and Hampson, *Marriage, Census and Other Indexes for Family Historians*, which is arranged by county. Many of these indexes are held by individuals, who charge for a search to help cover their costs. The FRC has many additional finding aids such as street indexes to towns with a population over 40,000, and many other name indexes for specific places, produced by family history societies. Most of these name indexes relate to the 1851 census.

However, if you don't have an exact address but have some clues that far back, the 1881 census is the place to start, as it has an index including about 26,000,000 names. For this, thanks are due to the very many people involved in the 1881 Project, coordinated by the British Genealogical Record Users Committee. The 1881 index can be seen at the FRC (PRO), at the Family History Centres run by the LDS, at the Society of Genealogists, and at many other places as well.

However, apart from the 1881 index, most finding aids are to help you find a known address. You need to have at least an approximate home address, or an idea of where your ancestors might have been on the night of the census (e.g. on holiday, in an institution such as a prison or a workhouse, working away from home, or on board a ship in port or within territorial waters). Remember that many addresses will have changed over time, as streets lengthened and were renumbered in the expanding cities and towns of Victorian England. There are specialist works available at the FRC to help with this problem for London. The censuses are arranged by place, grouped in the registration districts used for the registration of births, marriages and deaths. Maps of these registration districts can be found in RG 18: facsimiles can be seen at the FRC. They are arranged by year, and can be useful in identifying the registration districts of the smaller places that do not appear in the indexes to the census.

This chapter provides basic information: for a guide to using the census, see *Making Use of the Census*, by Lumas, written from an unrivalled depth of knowledge of the make-up and genealogical use of these records. For the history, original use, structure and complexities of the census records, see *A Clearer Sense of the Census*, by Higgs, which explains the ideas behind the compilation of the censuses, and warns against accepting their contents as literal truth.

There are some pitfalls in using the censuses, and interpreting the evidence is not always as straightforward as it might appear. A good general rule is, the younger the person described, the more accurate the information on age and place of birth.

2.4 What was in the 1801–1831 censuses?

The censuses of 10 March 1801, 27 May 1811, 28 May 1821 and 29 May 1831 were confined to the compilation of numerical totals (by parish) of the following: houses habited and uninhabited; families; men and women; occupations (in broad categories); and various statistics of baptisms, marriages and burials. A partial enumeration of age was taken in 1821, and a more extensive investigation into occupations took place in 1831.

People's names were not recorded in the official returns for these years. However, in the course of carrying out the censuses, some local enumerators did compile unofficial listings of named individuals. Those which survive in local record offices are listed by Gibson and Medlycott in *Local Census Listings 1522–1930*, or in Chapman's *Pre-1841 Censuses and Population Listings*.

Most of the information in these records was published in Parliamentary Papers: an incomplete set can be seen at the Public Record Office, at Kew. A reader's ticket is needed to consult them. The original documents were destroyed in 1904, with the exception of the returns of numbers of baptisms, marriages and burials by parish, 1821–1830, which survive as HO 71: Home Office: 1831 Census: Clergymen's Return. These records are also held at Kew.

2.5 What is in the 1841 census?

The names of individuals were first officially included in the census taken on 6 June 1841. The 1841 census is written in pencil, which can make it difficult to read. The information collected for each person included full name; age; sex; and occupation. For those under 15, ages were given exactly (if known): for people over 15, ages were rounded down to the nearest five years. For example, someone of 64 would appear as 60, another of 29 as 25. Some information relating to the place of birth was also given, but was restricted to whether or not a person was born in the county of residence (Y for Yes, N for No), and, if not, whether in Scotland (S), Ireland (I), or foreign parts (F). The 1841 census also gives the same kind of information as earlier censuses on housing. It indicates which individuals lived in a particular house, and individual households within that house. The relationships between members of the same household are not recorded, but can often be inferred.

The surviving records of the 1841 census for England and Wales, the Channel Islands and the Isle of Man form part of the record class HO 107.

2.6 What is in the 1851–1891 censuses?

These censuses were taken on 30 March 1851, 7 April 1861, 2 April 1871, 3 April 1881 and 5 April 1891. From 1851, the information recorded becomes more precise, and also more legible, as the entries are written in ink. The full address was given. For each person was recorded: full name; exact age; marital status; relationship to head of household; sex; occupation; parish and county of birth; and various medical disabilities. The 1891 returns contain additional information on employment status, and, for Wales, on the language spoken. Individuals were recorded in the households and houses in which they lived.

The surviving records of the 1851 census for England and Wales, the Channel Islands and the Isle of Man form part of the record class HO 107: Census Returns. Those of 1861, 1871, 1881 and 1891 are in the record classes RG 9, RG 10, RG 11 and RG 12 respectively.

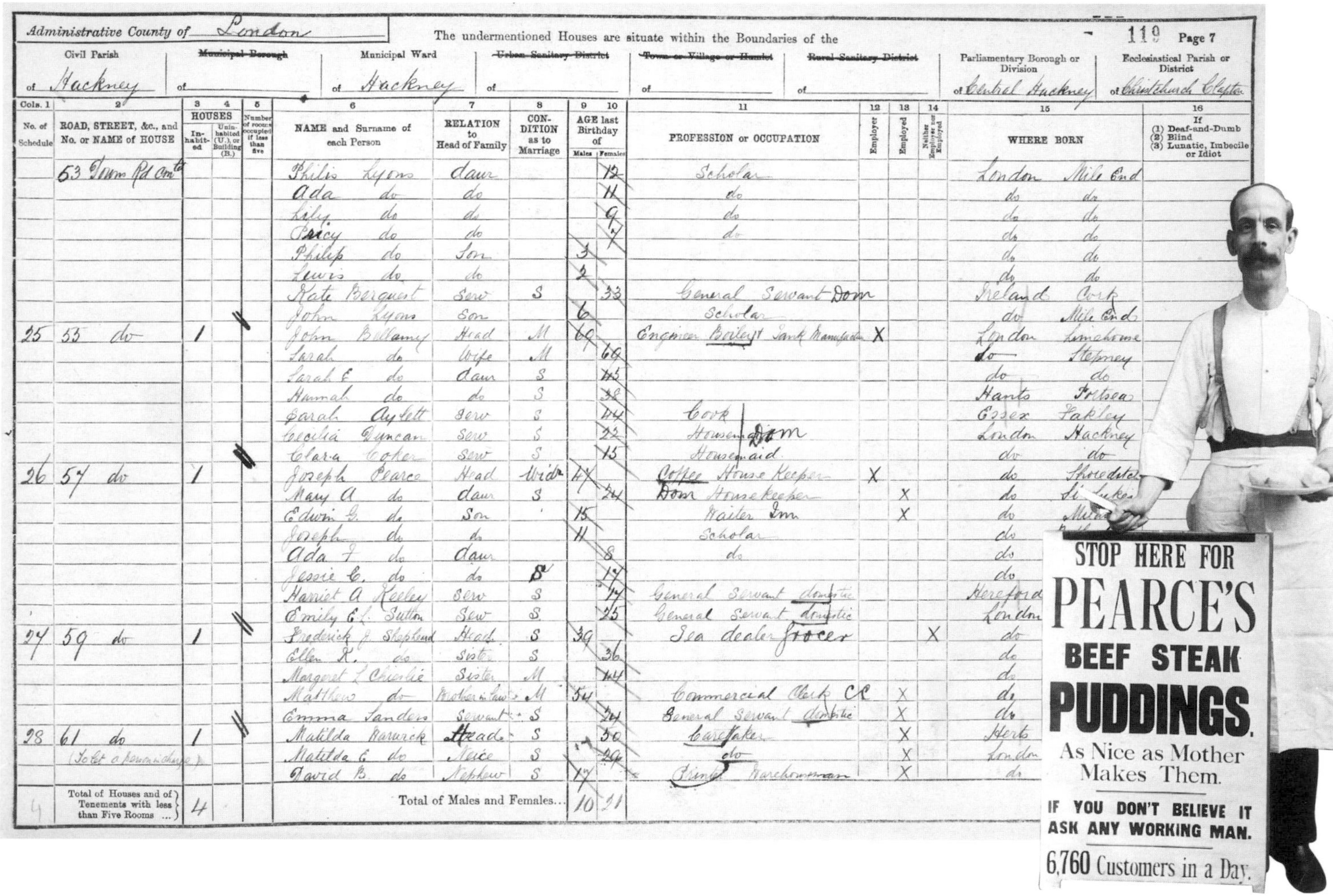

Figure 2 The 1891 census entry for the Pearce family of 57 Downs Road, Hackney (RG 12/197, fo. 119), and a photograph taken of Joseph Pearce to advertise his business (COPY 1/404).

Don't forget the 1881 index – 26,000,000 names! (see **2.3**). There are also many indexes for the 1851 census, which can be seen at the FRC or consulted elsewhere. Indexing of other censuses has been more sporadic. See Gibson and Hampson, *Marriage and Census Indexes for Family Historians.*

2.7 How are the census records arranged?

The census returns are arranged in small books covering enumeration districts of usually a few hundred houses. They are seen on microfilm. The 1891 census returns can also be seen on microfiche. Small towns, parishes and hamlets can readily be searched in their entirety. The returns for large towns and cities fill numerous books, so you have to know the address of an individual before beginning a search for them in the census (except for 1881). There are street indexes to help you find a particular street in a large town on the right film, available at the FRC and at Salt Lake City.

To help you once you are at the FRC, there are a series of leaflets giving specific instructions and up-to-date advice on how to use the various finding aids to each census.

2.8 Census returns: other places

Scottish census returns are held by the Registrar General for Scotland, New Register House, Edinburgh EH1 3YT. Those for 1841 to 1891 are open to public inspection. The indexes to the 1881 and 1891 Scottish censuses, and a transcript of the 1881 census, can be seen at the FRC, on the *Scottish Link*. There is a charge for using this, and a place has to booked in advance: for more information, contact the FRC (address and contact numbers in **1.6**). See also **8**.

Census returns for Ireland are held by the National Archives, Four Courts, Dublin 7, Republic of Ireland. Unfortunately, few 19th century Irish census returns have survived but the Irish returns for 1901 and 1911 are fairly complete, and are open to public inspection there. See **9** for more details.

Colonial census returns, if they survived, will be kept in the appropriate national archives. However, the PRO docs hold a few colonial censuses. The most well known of these are the censuses of convicts (and some free settlers) in New South Wales and Tasmania, 1788–1859 (HO 10: see **40.4** for further details). In addition, the PRO has a census of 1811 from Surinam, detailing slaves and free black and white inhabitants (CO 278/15–25); a 1715 census of the white population of Barbados (CO 28/16); and a census of the colony of Sierra Leone on 30 June 1831 (CO 267/111).

2.9 Censuses of population: bibliography

W A Armstrong, 'The Interpretation of the Census Enumerators' Books for Victorian Towns', in H J Dyos, ed. *The Study of Urban History* (London, 1968)

M W Beresford, 'The unprinted Census returns for 1841, 1851 and 1861 for England and Wales', *Amateur Historian*, vol. V, pp. 260–269

M E Briant Rosier, *Index to Census Registration Districts* (FFHS, 1995)

C Chapman, *Pre-1841 Census and Population Listings* (Dursley, 1994)

J S W Gibson and E Hampson, *Census Returns on Microform, A Directory to Local Holdings* (FFHS, 1997)

J S W Gibson and E Hampson, *Marriage, Census and Other Indexes for Family Historians* (FFHS, 7th edn, 1998)

J S W Gibson and M Medlycott, *Local Census Listings, 1522–1930, holdings in the British Isles* (FFHS, 1994)

E Higgs, *A Clearer Sense of the Census: the Manuscript Returns for England and Wales, 1801–1901* (London, 1996)

R Lawton, ed., *The Census and Social Structure, an Interpretative Guide to nineteenth century Censuses, for England and Wales* (London, 1978)

S Lumas, *Making Use of the Census* (London, 1997)

E McLaughlin, *The Censuses 1841–1881* (FFHS, 1995)

M Medlycott, 'Some Georgian 'Censuses': The Militia Lists and 'Defence' Lists', *Genealogists' Magazine*, vol. XXIII, pp. 55–59

D Mills and C Pearce, *People and Places in the Victorian Census: A Review and Bibliography, 1841–1911* (Historical Geography Research Group, 1989)

M Nissel, *People count: A history of the General Register Office* (London, 1987)

K Schurer and T Arkell, ed., *Surveying the People* (Oxford, 1992)

R Smith, 'Demography in the 19th Century', *Local Historian*, vol. IX (1970–71)

P M Tillot, 'The Analysis of the Census Returns', *Local Historian*, vol. VIII (1968–69)

E A Wrigley, ed., *An Introduction to English Historical Demography* (Cambridge, 1966)

E A Wrigley, ed., *The Study of Nineteenth Century Society* (Cambridge, 1972)

3 Birth, marriage, divorce and death in England and Wales

3.1 From 1837: the Family Records Centre (ONS)

The first place to look for records of birth, marriage or death in England and Wales, is the Family Records Centre in central London (address and other details in **1.6**). You need to go to the groundfloor searchroom run by the General Register Office of England and Wales (a division of the Office for National Statistics). This is referred to here as the FRC (ONS).

The FRC (ONS) holds indexes to all births, deaths and marriages registered in England and Wales since civil registration began on 1 July 1837. The indexes are arranged by date of registration, and then alphabetically. There are four sets for each year, covering each quarter, and labelled with the last month in each quarter – March, June, September and December. From 1983, the indexes cover the whole year. The indexes to the Adopted Children Register from 1927 are also here (see **3.14**). The FRC (ONS) also holds the main collection of records of birth, death and marriage of English and Welsh people at sea or abroad (see **4**), as well as similar records returned by the armed services. For registers and indexes of Scots and Irish births, marriages and deaths (at home, overseas and in the services), kept by the General Register Offices of Scotland, Ireland and Northern Ireland, see **8** and **9**.

The actual registers of birth, marriage and death are not kept at the FRC, but at the ONS's office at Southport. Applications to buy a certified copy of the register entry (identified from the indexes) are sent by the FRC (ONS) to Southport, and the certificate is then either posted to you, or returned to the FRC for collection. Several of the larger record offices and libraries have copies of the ONS indexes on microfiche: a list of where they are held can be obtained from the FRC (ONS). If you are able to identify the certificate you want, you can order a copy direct from Southport by post, phone or e-mail. The address of the ONS at Southport is given in **1.6**.

The FRC (ONS) produces its own guidance in a booklet called *General Register Office: Tracing Records of Births, Marriages and Deaths*. There is also the PRO specialist publication, by Cox and Colwell, *Never Been Here Before? A Genealogists' Guide to the Family Records Centre*. In addition, the subject is covered in all the general genealogical guides, and in several specific ones.

3.2 Can't find an entry in the indexes?

Failure to find a birth, marriage or death entry in the indexes may be for these reasons:

- The event took place in another year or quarter. It is worth searching a couple of years either side of the expected date.
- Before 1875 there was no penalty for non-registration and there may be omissions in the birth and death registers. A study by Hughes comparing Liverpool baptismal records with registered births has shown a shortfall of almost 33 per cent as late as 1874. You may need to look at parish and non-parochial registers until 1875.
- Before 1927 there was no formal adoption procedure and there is no record of the birth of the adopted child under the name by which he or she was known.
- There may have been a clerical error when the entry in the local registrar's register was transferred to the central register.
- Some people were known by a christian name which was not the first forename on their birth certificate.
- The child may not have been named by the date of registration. Entries under the sex of the infant are given at the end of each surname section.
- In the nineteenth century at least 10 per cent of marriages took place after the birth of the first child.
- A birth or marriage may have been registered by the Army: see **4.5** and **18.2**.
- Registers of births on Lundy Island, in the Bristol Channel, were treated as foreign registers, and are in the PRO, in RG 32–RG 35, indexed by the general indexes in RG 43. Some records from the Channel Islands were treated the same way.
- Did the event happen somewhere outside England and Wales? Try the registers of births, marriages and deaths at sea or overseas for people normally resident in England and Wales (see **4**).
- People normally resident in Scotland, Ireland and Northern Ireland will be found in the registers kept there (including registers of births, marriages and deaths at sea or overseas) (see **8** and **9**).

It may be worth checking the Registrar General's correspondence on births, marriages and deaths, from 1874, at Kew (RG 48). These papers include files on individual cases of difficulty, but some are closed for 50 or 75 years.

Announcements of many births, marriages and deaths may be found in local newspapers held in public libraries and in the British Library Newspaper Library collection at Colindale (address in **48**). For more details, see Gibson's *Local Newspapers 1750–1920*.

3.3 The *International Genealogical Index*

If you want to trace a baptismal or marriage record from before July 1837, start with the *International Genealogical Index*, known as the *IGI*. This is an index to births, baptisms and marriages world wide. The indexes to the British Isles cover the period from the beginning of parish registers to about 1885. (Religious registration was required in England and Wales from 1538, in Scotland from 1552, and in Ireland from 1634, but few of the earliest registers survive.) The indexes for England and Wales are mainly to Church of England parish registers and to nearly all the non-parochial registers in RG 4 in the PRO.

The *IGI* covers the British Isles in several separate sequences; one for each English and Scottish traditional county, one each for Ireland, the Channel Islands, and the Isle of Man, and two for Wales, to cover the Welsh system of naming. The *IGI* is available at both the FRC (PRO) and Kew (Kew has the old edition when the FRC gets a new one), but we cannot provide prints. However, these are available from the sets of the *IGI* kept at the Guildhall Library, the Society of Genealogists and the Genealogical Library of the Church of Jesus Christ of Latter Day Saints. Local libraries and record offices may well have the local county index: see Gibson's book on the *IGI*.

There are some drawbacks to the *IGI*. Its coverage is not complete, as some registers have not been included. There is no guarantee that the registers which have been covered are included in full. In addition, useful information which may appear in the register, such as age or father's occupation, is not given in the *IGI*. If you do find a likely ancestor in the *IGI*, you are strongly advised to check the source, or a transcript of it, yourself. If the entry looks as if it comes from a parish register, you can usually discover the present location of the register, and the existence and whereabouts of any transcripts, from *The Phillimore Atlas and Index of Parish Registers*, edited by Humphery-Smith. If the entry refers to a nonconformist chapel, then it is most probably in RG 4, and can be seen on microfilm at the FRC (PRO) or at Kew: some of the nonconformist registers contain a lot more information than is included in the *IGI*.

3.4 Parish registers before 1837, kept locally

The parish registers of the Church of England, the main source for baptisms, marriages and burials between 1538 and 1837, are kept locally, either still in the church or in a local, county or diocesan record office. Very few in fact survive from 1538: the average starting date for surviving registers is 1611 for England, and 1708 for Wales. To discover the present location of the registers of a particular parish, consult *The Phillimore Atlas and Index of Parish Registers*, edited by Humphery-Smith (at the FRC and Kew). *The National Index of Parish Registers* (a multi-volume work with general volumes covering the various types of sources available for Anglican, nonconformist, Catholic and Jewish genealogy, and county volumes listing the availability of parish and other registers) is well worth consulting at the FRC (PRO). You can also discover the existence of copies of parish registers from these works, which give their date range and whereabouts.

3.5 English and Welsh registers, before 1837, at the PRO and FRC (PRO)

The PRO and the FRC (PRO) have a major source for registered baptisms, marriages and burials in England and Wales – a very large collection of non-parochial religious registers, from outside the parish structure of the Church of England. Some of the registers date from after 1837, but they can still be useful as a complement to the civil registers, as failure to use the civil registration system was not penalised until 1875. The PRO also has some regimental registers of births and marriages for Army and Militia regiments in England and Wales (see **18.3**) and for the Royal Marines (see **20.8**).

3.6 Non-parochial registers: the background

The non-parochial registers in the PRO (RG 4–RG 8) are often referred to as 'nonconformist registers'. However, in addition to several thousand Protestant nonconformist registers, the collection also includes a number of Church of England registers from churches outside the usual parish structure, seventy-seven Catholic registers, and a few registers of foreign churches in England, as well as some cemetery records.

Before 1837, the parish register was the only official place to register baptisms, marriages and burials. Thousands of people refused to comply with the Church of England rites and wished to be baptised and buried by their own church, and to record these events in the registers of their own faith. However, from 1754 to 1837, marriages had to be performed by a beneficed Anglican clergyman in order to be acknowledged in law. An exception was made for Quakers and Jews, because of the detailed way they recorded marriages. Other nonconformists, in order to ensure the legitimacy of their children, and their ability to inherit, had to marry in the Anglican church, and have the event recorded in the parish register. Nonconformist registers between 1754 and 1837 therefore record details of births/baptisms and deaths/burials only. After 1837, they may include marriages as well.

When civil registration was set up in 1837, most nonconformist registers and some Anglican non-parochial registers were collected by parliamentary commissioners. They were deposited in the newly created General Register Office, where they were used to issue birth certificates which had the status of a legal record (these registers are now RG 4–RG 6). Another collection was made in 1857 (now part of RG 8; some were placed in RG 4). On both occasions the registers of most Catholic churches and Jewish synagogues were retained by their congregations. Not all nonconformist registers were surrendered to the General Register Office. Some remained with the congregations, or the minister or priest, and still do so; yet others are in county record offices, or with the archives of the colleges and societies of the various denominations. Look at the *National Index of Parish Registers* for guidance on their known whereabouts.

Both the 1837 and the 1857 collections were transferred to the PRO in 1961, and became widely available for the first time. Other registers were later deposited in RG 8 for safe keeping.

The three main collections, RG 4, RG 5 and RG 8, can be seen at the FRC (PRO) and Kew. The other class, RG 6, is still seen in the original and can therefore only be seen at Kew. Many, but not all, of the births and baptisms in the authenticated registers in RG 4 have been included in the *International Genealogical Index*.

3.7 Using nonconformist registers

The PRO has several thousand nonconformist registers and certificates from England and Wales (RG 4, RG 5, RG 6, RG 8). The main churches represented in the PRO's holdings are the Society of Friends, or Quakers (in RG 6), the Presbyterians, the Independents or Congregationalists, the Baptists, the Wesleyan and other Methodists, the Moravians, the Countess of Huntingdon's Connexion, the Bible Christians and the Swedenborgians, as well as various foreign churches. The English Independent congregation of St Petersburg, Russia, also deposited its registers of births, baptisms, and burials, 1818–1840 (RG 4/4605).

With the exception of the Quaker registers (see **3.9**), nonconformist registers are in RG 4 and RG 8, largely depending on whether they were collected by the 1837 or the 1857 commission. There are certificates from the two central registries of births in RG 5. Most of the registers are in RG 4, and have been indexed in the *IGI*; there are many fewer in RG 8, and these are not centrally indexed. However, they are exactly the same kind of registers as in RG 4, and should not be overlooked. The revised lists and the Introductory Notes of RG 4 and RG 8 were republished by the List and Index Society in 1996.

The registers in the PRO date from 1567 to 1970. The earliest registers belong to the foreign Protestant churches who were granted toleration in England well before any native dissent was made lawful. Registers of English dissenting congregations are very rare before active persecution stopped; the earliest English registers date from the 1640s. The last date, 1970, is something of an oddity, from the dissenting church of Cam, Gloucestershire: it is the last entry in a volume in almost constant use between 1776 and 1970 (RG 8/12C). Most of the registers come from the eighteenth and early nineteenth centuries. After 1754 they do not include marriages, although these do reoccur after 1837 in a few registers in RG 8.

Nonconformist registers often served a far wider area than the traditional Anglican parish, because of the way the various denominations were organised. Nonconformity was a very widespread movement in the eighteenth and nineteenth centuries: the 1851 ecclesiastical census showed that a quarter of the population were regular attenders of nonconformist chapels.

Indications that you should investigate the nonconformist registers, and the large amounts of biographical material kept by some of the denominations, might be a long family history of nonconformity; if a post-1837 marriage took place in a nonconformist chapel or in a register office; and if a parish register has a suspiciously high number of marriages and burials of one surname, in proportion to the number of baptisms. On the other hand, known nonconformist ancestors may need to be traced back to the parish registers, for pre-conversion events, occasional conformity, and the records of marriage and burial (if there was no local nonconformist burial ground).

Having discovered a nonconformist ancestor, it is worth digging a little deeper into his or her beliefs, and the organisation and discipline of the particular denomination. There is a specialised guide which gives more detailed advice than can be given here. This is Shorney's *Protestant Nonconformity and Roman Catholicism: A Guide to Sources in the Public Record Office*. Steel's *Sources for Nonconformist Genealogy and Family History* covers archive holdings in the PRO and elsewhere. Another useful guide is by Palgrave-Moore, *Understanding the History and Records of Nonconformity*. A general introduction to the beliefs and regional concentrations of the various nonconformist denominations is *The Geography of Religion in England*, by Gay.

Less extensive works can also be very useful; for Baptists, try *My Ancestors were Baptists*, by Breed; for Quakers, *My Ancestors were Quakers*, by Milligan and Thomas; for Methodists, *My*

Ancestors were Methodists, by Leary and Gandy. These also give indications as to the published works available in denominational libraries such as Dr Williams's Library.

3.8 Two nonconformist central registries of births, [1716]–1838

There were two nonconformist central registries, set up in an attempt to provide legally acceptable records of birth. Many thousands of births were recorded in these registries, whose records are now in the PRO. The registers and indexes they produced are now in RG 4, but the certificates from which the registers were compiled are in RG 5. All these sources can be seen at the FRC and Kew.

The Protestant Dissenters' Registry at Dr Williams's Library, then in Redcross Street, London, was founded in 1742; it served the congregations of Baptists, Independents and Presbyterians in London and within a twelve-mile radius of the capital. However, parents from most parts of the British Isles and even abroad (see Figure 3) also used the registry. Almost 50,000 births were registered in it. The Register was started in 1742, with retrospective entries going back to 1716, and continued to 1837 (RG 4/4658–4665, with indexes at RG 4/4666–4676). The certificates used to compile the registers also survive (RG 5/1–161, with the same index as the registers). Parents wishing to register a birth had to produce two parchment certificates signed by their minister and by the midwife and one or two other people present at the birth, giving the name and sex of the child, the name of the parents, the name of the mother's father and the date and place (street, parish and county) of birth. After 1828, paper certificates were required instead, which had to be signed by the parents as well; these signatures made them more acceptable as legal proof. On receipt of the two certificates, the registrar entered all the details, except the address of birth, in the register, filed one of the certificates (now in RG 5) and returned the other to the parents with his certificate of registration.

The Wesleyan Methodist Metropolitan Registry, founded in 1818 at 66 Paternoster Row, London, provided for the registration of births and baptisms of Wesleyan Methodists throughout England, Wales and elsewhere, independently of any congregational records. Over 10,000 children were registered here. The registers continued till 1838, with retrospective registration of births going back to 1773 (RG 4/4677–4679, with an index at RG 4/4680). One of two original certificates submitted by the parents was entered in the register and filed (RG 5/162–207, indexed by RG 4/4680), and the other was marked as entered and was returned to the parents. The certificates and the register entry have the name and sex of the child, the name and address of the father, the name of the mother and of both her parents, the date and place of birth, and the name of the Wesleyan circuit, with the signature (or name, in the register) of the parents, the witnesses to the birth, and the baptising minister.

For more information on these, look at the Introductory Notes filed before the class lists of RG 4 and RG 5.

3.9 Quaker registers

The records and registers of the Society of Friends, or Quakers, 1613–1841, are very full, and in excellent order. However, to understand and use them properly, you do need to understand the rather complicated administrative structure of the Society. This is explained in *My Ancestors were*

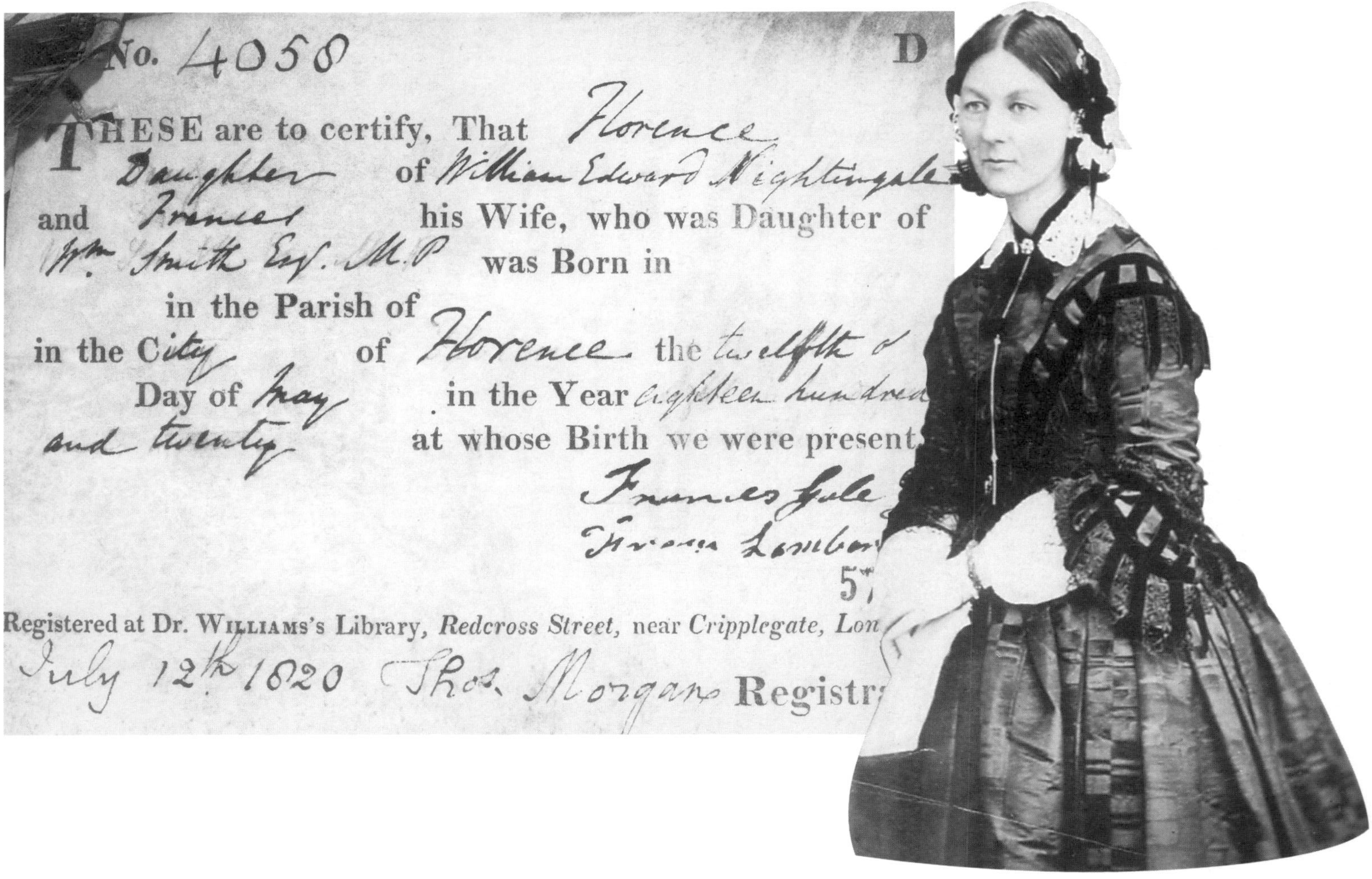

No. 4058 D

THESE are to certify, That Florence Daughter of William Edward Nightingale and Frances his Wife, who was Daughter of Wm. Smith Esq. M.P was Born in in the Parish of in the City of Florence the twelfth Day of May in the Year eighteen hundred and twenty at whose Birth we were present.

Frances Gale

Registered at Dr. Williams's Library, Redcross Street, near Cripplegate, Lon

July 12th 1820 Thos. Morgan Registr

Figure 3 Florence Nightingale was born in Florence in 1820. Her birth was registered two months later in the Protestant Dissenters' Registry (Dr Williams's Library) in London (RG 5/83, no. 4058). Her photograph comes from COPY 1/11, fo. 34.

Quakers by Milligan and Thomas, and also in Steel's *Sources for Nonconformist Genealogy and Family History*; the latter includes a full discussion of Quaker birth, marriage and death registers and practices. You also need to understand the distinctive Quaker dating practices (they used numbers for the names of months and days, as they would not use the common names derived from pagan gods). For an explanation of these, and how they changed significantly over time, see Munby, *Dates and Time*, Appendix 11.

These registers are now in the PRO at Kew, arranged by (county) Quarterly Meeting and by Monthly Meeting, together with original birth and burial notes, and original marriage certificates and copies, 1656–1834 (RG 6). There are also a few registers and other records, 1761–1840, at RG 8/81 and 87–89. Most local meetings were under the Quarterly Meeting of their own county, but several are to be found with the records of unexpected quarterly meetings. There is a 'Key to Cross-Border Locations' filed with the list, which shows (for example) that the records of the meeting of Ringshall, Buckinghamshire, are to be found in the Quarterly Meeting of Bedfordshire and Hertfordshire.

Quaker birth certificates were signed by witnesses at the birth, who also had to give their own residence. The marriage certificates were signed by a large number of witnesses, not all of whom were Quakers. Some of the witnesses were identified as relatives. Marriage between two Quakers, conducted according to the Quaker usage, was accepted as legal from 1661, and was exempted from Lord Hardwicke's Marriage Act in 1753.

Outside the PRO, there are indexes to (or rather alphabetical digests of) the registers, made in 1840–1842 and 1857, which are kept at Friends House Library (address in **48**): these can be consulted for a fee. Duplicate digests were also made, and sent to the county-based Quarterly Meetings in place of their registers. For more information on their present location, and on Quaker records in general, consult *My Ancestors were Quakers*. The Introductory Note to RG 6, filed with the class list, is well worth reading. Both the list and the Introductory Note have been published by the List and Index Society.

3.10 Catholic registers

For various reasons, only seventy-seven Catholic churches surrendered their registers to the commissioners in 1837; they are now in RG 4. Of these, 44 came from Yorkshire, 13 from Durham, 10 from Northumberland, 2 from Lincolnshire and 1 each from Cumberland, Dorset, Hampshire, Lancashire, Nottinghamshire, Oxfordshire, Warwickshire and Westmorland: however, some may have been personal to the priest, and thus cover events in other places as well. Most date from the mid or late eighteenth century, but there are two or three dating from the late seventeenth century.

For the location of other Catholic registers, see the county volumes of the *National Index of Parish Registers*, and *Sources for Roman Catholic and Jewish Genealogy and Family History*, by Steel and Samuel. The latter also discusses the information in the registers.

3.11 Registers of foreign churches in England

The registers of several foreign churches are in RG 4, listed separately except for those of the Scottish churches, which are included in the county lists; there are also a few in RG 8. Most are

Huguenot (French and Walloon Protestant) registers, from the several churches of London, 1599–1840, and from Bristol 1687–1807, Canterbury 1590–1837, Norwich 1595–1752, Plymouth 1692–1807, Southampton 1567–1779 and Thorpe-le-Soken 1684–1726 (in RG 4); Huguenot registers from Dover, 1646–1731, are in RG 8/14. The Huguenot Society has published most of these registers. The other foreign registers are all from London; they are those of the French Chapel Royal 1700–1754, the Dutch Chapel Royal 1689–1754, the German Lutheran Chapel Royal 1712–1836, the German Lutheran churches 1694–1853, and the Swiss church, 1762–1839, all in RG 4.

Two later French registers came from the French Episcopal Church of the Savoy, in Bloomsbury, London, 1843–1900 (RG 8/34), and from the Reformed French Church in Brighton, 1865–1879 (RG 8/94).

The registers and papers of the Russian Orthodox church in London, 1721–1927, which are mostly in Russian, are at RG 8/111–304; they include registers of births, marriages and deaths. For a register of marriages in the Greek Church in London, 1837–1865, see J 166.

3.12 Anglican registers in the PRO

The commissioners for non-parochial registers collected some Anglican registers as well as nonconformist registers, in both 1837 and 1857. Most of these Anglican registers came from the custody of the Consistory Court of London in 1837, and are either from abroad (see **4.4**), or relate to the so-called 'Fleet marriages' (see **3.15**).

Other Anglican registers came from Mercers' Hall, Cheapside, London (marriages, 1641–1754, and burials, 1640–1833, RG 4/4436) and from the chapels royal at St James's Palace, Whitehall and Windsor Castle, 1647–1709 (RG 8/110). Some of the later registers of the chapels royal, 1755–1880, were deposited directly in the PRO (PRO 30/19/1), but others remain in the custody of the Chapel Royal, St James's Palace: ask for more details. In addition, the PRO has marriage licences for marriages in the Chapel Royal, Whitehall (not royal marriages), 1687–1754 and 1807 (RG 8/76–78). There are also some odd registers elsewhere in the PRO's holdings. Among the PRO's own records are the registers of the Rolls Chapel, Chancery Lane, 1736–1892, with gaps (PRO 30/21/3/1). Another Anglican oddment is the long series of registers from the Dockyard Church of Sheerness, Kent, covering 1688–1960 (ADM 6/429–433 and 438).

However, the bulk of the reputable Anglican registers in the PRO came from the military, naval and charitable hospitals, as non-parochial registers. The birth, marriage and death registers of Greenwich Hospital (including the Royal Naval Asylum and the Royal Hospital Schools) cover 1705–1864 (RG 4/1669–1679 and RG 8/16–18): those of the Army's Chelsea Hospital cover 1691–1856 (RG 4/4330–4332, and 4387). Although Greenwich Hospital and Chelsea Hospital were Navy and Army institutions, these registers appear to include local inhabitants as well. For details of other Army registers, see **4.5**, **18.2** and **18.3**. For details of Royal Marine registers, see **20.5**.

One of the PRO's main hospital holdings is the series of records of the British Lying-In (i.e. maternity) Hospital, Holborn, London. This was set up in 1749, and catered for the distressed poor (married women only) with special attention to the wives of soldiers and sailors. Admission was by recommendation: many women appear to have been the wives of servants, recommended by their husbands' employers. The baptismal registers, 1749–1830 (RG 8/62–66) are simply a hospital-composed list of names, parents and dates of birth and baptism until 1814, when proper

Anglican baptismal registers appear, and give the parents' address. However, they are supplemented by a fascinating source, the hospital's own record of the admission of the mother and the birth, which gives the names of the parents, the occupation of the father, the age of the mother, place of settlement (place of marriage after 1849), the expected date of delivery, the date of admission, the date of delivery, the name of the child and date of baptism, the date of discharge or death, and the name of the person on whose recommendation the woman was admitted (RG 8/52–61). These hospital records cover 1749–1868, and give details of 42,008 admissions, and about 30,000 baptisms, by no means all of Londoners; one women at least came from the Cape of Good Hope, and others came from Yorkshire, Ireland, the Isle of Wight and Jersey.

Another register from a charitable institution is the marriage register of the chapel of God's House Hospital, Kingston-upon-Hull, 1695–1715 (RG 8/101).

From less charitable institutions, the prisons, there are a few records of births and burials. The Westminster Penitentiary has a register of baptisms, 1816–1871 (PCOM 2/139) and another of burials, 1817–1853 (PCOM 2/140). There is a register of deaths and inquests at the Millbank Penitentiary, 1848–1863 (PCOM 2/165): in this case, most burials were in the Victoria Park cemetery (see **3.17**). For other prison records, see **39**, and for other inquests, see **37**.

3.13 Foundlings, 1741 to present

For London foundlings (abandoned children), try the records of the Foundling Hospital, London, set up by Thomas Coram in 1741. These are split between the PRO, the ONS, and the London Metropolitan Archives (LMA) (address in **48**). At Kew are the registers of baptisms and of all too many burials, for 1741–1838 (RG 4/4396 and 4328). These registers continue from 1853–1948 in the keeping of the ONS (Corrections Branch). An index is available at the FRC (ONS) and short birth certificates may be bought in the usual way. However, details of parentage will be given only by the Thomas Coram Foundation (address in **48**). They also hold a very affecting collection of tokens, left by the mothers with their children. Similar tokens are among the records held by the LMA, which holds the majority of the other records, including petitions from parents for the admission of their child (the system in operation from 1760), apprenticeship registers, minutes, etc.

For registration of foundlings after 1 July 1837, look in the birth indexes, under 'Unknown' (which appears after Z), at the FRC (ONS). In 1977 the Abandoned Children Register was introduced: the children are indexed in the usual way under the name given to the child.

3.14 Adoption

Certificates of any adoption in England and Wales since 1 January 1927 may be obtained from the FRC (ONS). They show the date of the adoption, the name of the child adopted, and the full name and address of the adoptive parents. The FRC (ONS) has booklets available at their enquiry desk on *Access to Birth Records, The Adoption Contact Register* and *Information for Adopted People and their Relatives.*

Before 1927 there was no system of legal adoption and it is usually extremely difficult to trace private arrangements. Some charities, such as Barnardos, arranged adoptions, and may conduct searches for a fee. See Stafford, *Where to Find Adoption Records.*

3.15 Fleet marriage registers, and other marriage records

In 1753, Lord Hardwicke's Marriage Act (26 George II c.33) ruled that the only lawful marriage was one celebrated by a beneficed Anglican clergyman, in an Anglican church after banns or with a licence. An exception was made for Jews, and also for Quakers, who kept excellent records and who had an elaborate method of validating marriages, including signature of a marriage certificate by many witnesses: see **3.9**. As a result, nonconformists had to marry in the Anglican church.

However, Lord Hardwicke's Marriage Act was not aimed directly at preventing nonconformist marriages, but at preventing clandestine Anglican ones. Before it came into effect in 1754, unbeneficed and sometimes unscrupulous clergymen were able to make a living by performing marriages on request, in places exempt from ecclesiastical jurisdiction. One of the most popular of these was the Fleet Prison and its precincts in London; the registers kept by the presiding ministers are known as Fleet registers (RG 7). The report of the 1837 commissioners on non-parochial records on the Fleet marriages is worth quoting at length.

> The generality of them were celebrated by Clergymen of low character, some at the Chapel of the Fleet, others at various taverns and other places within the precincts of the Fleet and King's Bench Prisons, and the Mint in Southwark. These Registers were, in some instances, in the keeping of the Ministers who performed the ceremony, and they were also often kept by the proprietors of the houses or taverns in which the marriages happened to have taken place. After the door was closed against marriages of this description by the operation of the Marriage Act (in 1754), it appears, that a clerk of one of the Fleet Ministers collected a number of them together, and opened an office, where reference might be had to them. Another office for the deposit of these registers was opened in another part of the town; but in 1813 the great bulk of them came into the hands of a private individual, of the name of Cox, from whom the Government purchased them in 1821, and, by the direction of Lord Sidmouth, then Secretary of State for the Home Department, they were deposited in the Registry of the Consistorial Court of London. We apprehend that by far the greater number of the Registers of the Marriages celebrated within the precincts of these several places are comprised in this collection. There are, however, exceptions; for two of the Fleet Registers are known to be in the possession of a professional gentleman in Doctors' Commons, a third has found its way into the Bodleian Library at Oxford. [Now Rawlinson Ms.360.]

> The Chapel at May Fair was built about 1730, and Marriages took place there under the same circumstances with those in the places above referred to. Many of the Registers of this Chapel formed a part of the purchase made by the Government in 1821, the remainder are preserved in the church of St George, Hanover Square.

These registers from the Fleet and King's Bench Prisons, the Mint and the May Fair Chapel, 1694–1754, are now in the PRO (RG 7); in addition, there are two volumes covering 1726–1735 which were brought into court as evidence (PROB 18/50).

The information in the Fleet registers should be treated with extreme caution, as the dates given are unreliable (particularly before 1714), and names or indeed whole entries may be fictitious. The Fleet registers have entries from over the whole country, but with more from London and the home counties; about 200,000 marriages are thought to have been celebrated there. The Fleet was frequented for marriages and for some baptisms by craftsmen and sailors in general; professionals and the aristocracy went to the more salubrious May Fair Chapel instead. Such clandestine marriages could result in prosecution, and there are records of many such cases among the *ex officio* Act Books of the Commissary Court of London in the Guildhall Library, and in the records of the Consistory Court of London in the London Metropolitan Archives. For more information see 'The Rise and Fall of the Fleet Marriages' by Brown, or the chapter on clandestine marriages in Steel's *Sources of Births, Marriages and Deaths before 1837 (I)*. Herber has started producing a series of transcripts of the Fleet registers, called *Clandestine Marriages in the Chapel and Rules of the Fleet Prison 1680–1754*: so far transcripts of RG 7/162 (1736–1754) and RG 7/118 (1736–1748) have been published.

There is an index to Fleet marriages for Sussex, south-west Kent and south-east Surrey, arranged chronologically within parish of residence of bride and groom; an index cross-referring to the bride's surname is in preparation.

Other marriage indexes are to more regular unions. The Pallot Index, covering the years c.1780–1837, includes marriages from most established churches in London and extracts from nonconformist registers; it is held by the Institute of Heraldic and Genealogical Studies, who will search it for a fee (address in **48**). The Boyd Marriage Index, available at the Society of Genealogists and the Guildhall Library, has a 12 per cent coverage of English marriages between 1538 and 1837; the PRO has odd volumes of the Boyd Index at the FRC (PRO), covering grooms, 1538–1625 and 1726–1800, and brides, 1575–1600 (A–S only), 1601–1625, 1751–1775 (E–R only) and 1776–1800. See Gibson and Hampson, *Marriage and Census Indexes for Family Historians*, for information on these and other marriage indexes.

There are some marriage licences for the Chapel Royal, Whitehall, 1687–1754 and 1807 in RG 8/76–78, but in general the PRO is not the place to look for these documents. See Gibson's *Bishops' Transcripts and Marriage Licences.*

3.16 Divorce

Before 1858 (except in Scotland) true divorce was rare and expensive, and achieved by private bill in the House of Lords. There was only one divorce bill before 1670. The PRO has a very few of these private acts for divorce, in C 89 and C 204, but they should be available at the House of Lords Record Office.

The church courts could decree a legal separation, known as divorce *a mensa et thoro* (i.e. from board and bed), but the parties had to undertake not to remarry. (Some decrees in Chancery in disputes over property rights and settlements after a divorce *a mensa et thoro* have been found in C 78.) In order to remarry, the marriage had to be declared null from the beginning, on the grounds of want of ability to marry (e.g. a pre-contract to marry another, or want of consent to the marriage: for example, if the parties were under age and therefore incapable of consenting). This total dissolution of a marriage was described as a divorce *a vinculo matrimonii* (from the bond of matrimony). These uncommon procedures were abolished in 1754. Records of the proceedings in the church courts, which are deposited in diocesan record offices, are largely unindexed and can be extremely difficult to interpret.

Appeals from ecclesiastical courts in matrimonial cases went to the High Court of Delegates between 1532 and 1832, and to the Judicial Committee of the Privy Council from 1833 until 1858. Copies of the proceedings of the lower ecclesiastical courts for 1609–1834 are in DEL 1 (indexed in DEL 11/7), and for 1834–1858 in PCAP 1. The cases as presented to the appeal courts are in DEL 2, DEL 7 and PCAP 3: judgements are included. These records have been relatively little used, but they can be very informative.

After 1858, all divorce cases were heard by the new Court for Divorce and Matrimonial Causes, until 1873, when the Probate, Divorce and Admiralty Division of the Supreme Court took over. Divorce files, 1858–1943 are in J 77, with a 75 year closure: the indexes, 1858–1958 (J 78) have the usual 30 year closure. Permission to consult individual case papers in the files which are still closed under the 75 year closure may be obtained from the Principal Registry of the Family Division (address in **48**). The Principal Registry also has records of divorces since 1944, and will search them for a fee.

3.17 Burial grounds

Although the nonconformist registers do include details of deaths and burials, burials were usually in the parish churchyard, and noted in the parish register, until nonconformist burial grounds were established. Some of these were small and local, such as the Protestant Dissenters' Burial Ground at Great Dunmow, Essex, 1784–1856 (RG 4/597) or the Dissenters' Ground at Boston, Lincolnshire, 1789–1856 (RG 4/24–25). However, nonconformists also established large burial grounds or cemeteries for dissenters; this practice later spread to all denominations.

The main cemetery records in the PRO are those of the:

Bethnal Green Protestant Dissenters' Burying Ground, or Gibraltar Burying Ground, 1793–1837 (RG 8/305–314);

Bunhill Fields Burial Ground, City Road, London, 1713–1854 (RG 4/3974–4001, 4288–4291 and 4633, with indexes at RG 4/4652–4657): other records, including an alphabetical list of persons buried, 1827–1854, are kept in the Guildhall Library;

Bunhill Burial Ground or Golden Lane Cemetery, London, 1833–1853 (RG 8/35–38);

Victoria Park Cemetery, Hackney, London, 1853–1876 (RG 8/42–51; each volume is arranged in letter order);

South London Burial Ground, East Street, Walworth, London, 1819–1837 (RG 4/4362);

Southwark New Burial Ground, London, 1821–1854 (RG 8/73–74);

Necropolis Burial Ground in Everton, Liverpool, for all denominations, 1825–1837 (RG 4/3121).

For information on the location of other London burial records, see *Greater London Cemeteries and Crematoria,* by Wolfston.

Also worth consulting are the records of the removal of tombs and gravestones from churchyards, cemeteries and burial grounds of all denominations (including some Jewish ones), in order to develop the land for some other purpose (RG 37). These are modern records of the actual removals and reinterments, but the tombs and gravestones themselves date from 1601 to 1980, with most coming from the later eighteenth and the nineteenth centuries. The files usually include a list of names, where these were discoverable, and frequently contain transcripts of the monumental inscriptions. They also indicate the place of reinterment.

3.18 Birth, marriage, divorce and death in England and Wales: bibliography

T Benton, *Irregular marriage in London before 1754* (Society of Genealogists, 1993)

G R Breed, *My Ancestors were Baptists* (Society of Genealogists, 1995)

R L Brown, 'The Rise and Fall of the Fleet Marriage', in R B Outhwaite, ed. *Marriage and Society* (London, 1981)

D H Clifton, *My Ancestors were Congregationalists* (Society of Genealogists, 1997)

J Cox and S Colwell, *Never Been Here Before? A Genealogists' Guide to the Family Records Centre* (PRO, 1997)

Dr Williams's Trust, *Nonconformist Congregations in Great Britain: A list of histories and other material in Dr Williams's Library* (London, 1973)

Factsheet on Tracing the Natural Parents of Adopted Children (FFHS, 1987)

J D Gay, *The Geography of Religion in England* (London, 1971)

General Register Office, *Abstract of Arrangements respecting Registration of Births, Marriages and Deaths in the UK and other Countries of the British Commonwealth of Nations, and in the Irish Republic* (London, 1952)

General Register Office, *General Register Office: Tracing Records of Births, Marriages and Deaths* (ONS, 1997)

J S W Gibson, *Bishops' Transcripts and Marriage Licences* (FFHS, 1991)

J S W Gibson, *Local Newspapers 1750–1920* (FFHS, 1987)

J S W Gibson, 'Marriage Licences, Bonds and Allegations', *Family History*, vol. V, no. 25 NS, no. 1, pp. 7–32

J S W Gibson and E Hampson, *Marriage and Census Indexes for Family Historians* (FFHS, 7th edn, 1998)

J S W Gibson and M Walcot, *Where to Find the International Genealogical Index*, (FFHS, 1985)

M Herber, *Clandestine Marriages in the Chapel and Rules of the Fleet Prison 1680–1754* (London, 1998)

A Horstman, *Victorian Divorce* (London, 1985)

D Hughes, 'Liverpool infant mortality rates c.1865–1874: A city much maligned?', *Lancashire Local Historian*, No. 6, 1991, pp. 32–43

C R Humphery-Smith, *The Phillimore Atlas and Index of Parish Registers* (Chichester, 1984)

International Genealogical Index, compiled by the Church of Jesus Christ of Latter Day Saints

W Leary and M Gandy, *My Ancestors were Methodists* (Society of Genealogists, 1998)

List and Index Society, *Non-Parochial Registers of Births, Marriages and Deaths (RG 4, 8)*, vols. 265 and 266 (1996)

List and Index Society, *Society of Friends' Registers (RG 6)*, vol. 267 (1996)

O R McGregor, *Divorce in England* (London, 1957)

E McLaughlin, *The FRC (ONS)* (FFHS, 1998)

H Mellor, *London Cemeteries: Illustrated Guide and Gazetteer* (Godstone, 1985)

E H Milligan and M J Thomas, *My Ancestors were Quakers* (Society of Genealogists, 1983)

L H Munby, *Dates and Time: A Handbook for Local Historians* (British Association for Local History, 1997)

National Index of Parish Registers (Society of Genealogists, 1968 continuing). For individual volumes, see the works listed under D J Steel

M Nissel, *People Count, A History of the General Register Office* (London, 1987)

P Palgrave-Moore, *Understanding the history and records of Nonconformity* (2nd edn, Norwich, 1989)

Parliament, *Report of the commissioners appointed to inquire into the state, custody, and authenticity of registers or records of births or baptisms, deaths or burials and marriages, in England and Wales other than parochial registers* (London, 1838: parliamentary paper presented to both Houses)

Parliament, *Report of the commissioners appointed to inquire into the state, custody and authenticity of certain non-parochial registers or records of births or baptisms, deaths or burials, and marriages in England and Wales (1857)* (London, 1858: parliamentary paper presented to both Houses)

A Ruston, *My Ancestors were English Presbyterians/Unitarians* (Society of Genealogists, 1993)

D Shomey, *Protestant Nonconformity and Roman Catholicism: A Guide to Sources in the Public Record Office* (PRO, 1996)

G Stafford, *Where to Find Adoption Records* (British Agencies for Adoption and Fostering, 1993)

D J Steel, *Sources for Nonconformist Genealogy and Family History* (National Index of Parish Registers, vol. II, 1973)

D J Steel and E R Samuel, *Sources for Roman Catholic and Jewish Genealogy and Family History* (National Index of Parish Registers, vol. III, 1974)

D J Steel and others, *Sources of Births, Marriages and Deaths before 1837 (I)* (National Index of Parish Registers, vol. I, 1968)

M Walcot, 'English Marriage Indexes', *Genealogists' Magazine*, vol. XIV, pp. 204–208
E Welch, 'Nonconformist Registers', *Journal of the Society of Archivists*, vol. II, pp. 411–417
P S Wolfston, *Greater London Cemeteries and Crematoria* (Society of Genealogists, 1998)
T Wood, *An Introduction to Civil Registration* (FFHS, 1994)

4 Births, marriages and deaths overseas and at sea

4.1 General introduction

There are considerable numbers of sources available within Britain for births, marriages and deaths of Britons in other countries and at sea. Civil registration records were kept abroad by British consulates, or at sea by the masters of British merchant ships. From various dates in the nineteenth century, they were obliged to send on the information they had recorded to the separate General Register Offices of England and Wales, Scotland, Ireland (and Northern Ireland, from 1922), or to the Registrar General of Shipping and Seamen, who then forwarded the information to England, Scotland or Ireland. The army also kept their own registers, whether at home or abroad. Regimental registers before 1881 seem to have ended up with the General Register Office of England and Wales (although the PRO has a few – see **18.3**). Armed service registers for army, navy and (later) air force, from about 1881, and registers (or indexes) of war deaths may be found in the relevant General Register Office.

The various General Register Offices compiled their own registers and indexes from the information thus returned. These registers are the obvious place to start. See **8** and **9** for the Scottish and Irish registers kept by their General Register Offices. The registers kept by the General Register Office for England and Wales (GRO) at Southport are not open to public inspection. Certified copies have to be bought in the same way as home certificates (see **3.1**). The indexes to the various types of register can be consulted at the FRC (ONS) and also at Kew: they are listed in **4.14**. In the course of time, many of the original records from which these registers had been created came to the PRO. The consular records are in FO classes, and the marine records and registers are in BT classes: they are freely available for inspection subject to the normal closure rules.

In addition to the sources discussed above, there are records of religious registration, which date from much earlier. These tend to be split between the PRO and the Guildhall Library, which has a large deposit of the Bishop of London's records. The Bishop of London had a historic jurisdiction over Britons abroad (mostly in Europe), and registers were returned to him. Some also went to the General Register Office of England and Wales, and were later sent on the PRO (RG classes). For religious registration, you may well need to go to both the Guildhall and the PRO, and to consult Yeo, *The British Overseas* (a guide to the sources at the Guildhall) in tandem with **4.15**.

The PRO's overseas holdings as are currently known (but not marine or armed forces registers) are listed by country, in **4.15**.

The subject of overseas and marine registration is quite complicated. In this chapter, records for overseas registration are noted in **4.2–4.6** and **4.14–4.15** and marine registers are noted in **4.7–4.11** and **4.14**. For armed forces' registers, look at **18.2**.

4.2 Overseas registers for England and Wales: an introduction

Overviews of the records in the Guildhall and some other places, and in some of the Foreign Office records at Kew, are included in *The British Overseas*, by Yeo. This lists the sources country by country: but it does *not* include the overseas registers kept by the GRO at Southport, nor other records at Kew. This present chapter lists *only* the indexes of the GRO registers (**4.14**) and the holdings of the PRO (**4.15**). As a result, you need to consult both *The British Overseas* and this book in order to get full information on what is available for a particular country. A copy of *The British Overseas* can be seen at both Kew and the FRC.

One general point is that, in the case of British colonies, registration records were and are kept locally, and you will need to enquire in the country concerned. Look at Yeo, *The British Overseas*, to find the addresses for the official holdings. There are microfiche copies of the indexes to the Australian registers, 1790–c.1900, at the Society of Genealogists. After 1940 (births) and 1950 (marriages and deaths) you may find something in the registers kept by the United Kingdom High Commissions in colonies and ex-colonies. Indexes to these are kept at the FRC (ONS) (see **4.5** and **4.14**).

An exception to the rule of colonial records being held in those countries is provided by pre-independence India. Records of British and European baptisms, marriages and burials in the Indian sub-continent, including Burma and Aden (1698–1948, with a partial continuation to 1968), are at the India Office Library and Records (address in **48**). There are also some Indian records in the PRO and at the FRC (ONS). Some other exceptions are listed in **4.15**

There are sections of the *International Genealogical Index* that relate to records of births, baptisms and marriages in countries other than Britain. These can be seen at the Society of Genealogists and at the Genealogical Library of the Church of Jesus Christ of Latter Day Saints (see **3.3**).

4.3 Religious registers, from the 17th century onwards

Religious records of baptisms, marriages and burials in foreign countries are either still held locally (especially if there was a formal church organisation), or were returned to the Bishop of London. Most of these Bishop of London registers have since been deposited in the Guildhall Library, where there is a very extensive collection called the Bishop of London's International Memoranda (see *The British Overseas* for further details). However, some, originally sent to the Bishop for safe keeping, were later deposited in the General Register Office of England and Wales, and have now been passed on to the PRO (RG 32–RG 35).

4.4 Overseas civil registration from 1849

Statutory civil registration of English and Welsh citizens in foreign (*not* colonial) countries began in 1849, under the Consular Marriages Act, although on a voluntary basis. Civil registration of Scots abroad began in 1860, and of the Irish abroad in 1864. Since then, the Foreign Office has returned registers of births, marriages and deaths, compiled at its embassies and consulates, to the General Register Offices of England and Wales, Scotland, Ireland (1864–1921) and Northern Ireland (from 1922); the full addresses are given in **48**. There is a numerous collection of odd registers collected by the General Register Office of England and Wales, which may be accessed (though not seen) at the FRC (ONS): some from overseas and some (the regimental registers of births and marriages) partly from this country as well. The other General Register Offices of Scotland and Ireland were also supposed to receive similar information: see **8** and **9**.

The ONS searchroom at the Family Records Centre, and now the PRO at Kew (microfiche only), have indexes to the official sets of registers. These contain information returned to the General Register Office of England and Wales by British consuls, British High Commissions, the British armed forces, and the institutions responsible for the registration of births and deaths on ships, aircraft, hovercrafts and offshore installations. Public access is only to the index: you cannot see the register, which is kept at Southport, but have to purchase a copy of the particular certificate you want, in the usual way (see **3.1**). The indexes are listed in **4.14**.

4.5 Confusion and duplication: making the best use of the records at Kew

With so many statutory and non-statutory registers, returns and copies being sent to so many different places, it is not surprising that duplication and confusion exist. In theory, Kew may contain more information, as the data in the registers kept by British representatives was collected by them once, and then divided and sent to different destinations. In addition, the records at Kew are open for inspection.

Try using the ONS indexes (also available on microfiche at Kew) to the registers kept by the GRO at Southport to find the initial information you are looking for. Then check to see if the PRO has a consular or religious version for the right place and date (use **4.15**), or a marine register (see **4.14**). This way, you can browse in the whole register at the PRO, rather than buying a single copy certificate. If you are looking for someone who lived in a close-knit British community abroad, you may find all kinds of clues in the register as to the life they led and the people they knew. You should also find that the consular registers include information not in the ONS registers – that is, information sent to the General Register Offices of Scotland, Ireland and Northern Ireland.

4.6 Foreign registers in the PRO

The holdings of the PRO overlap the registers in the FRC (ONS) in many respects, although they are not as up-to-date. The PRO has duplicates of many of the consular returns (see **4.2**), and also has a number of regimental registers, and records of births, marriages and deaths at sea. There are some unique records as well.

The major unique source is the collection of miscellaneous non-statutory registers and records, 1627–1958, deposited by the General Register Office in the PRO in 1977 (RG 32–RG 36, with indexes in RG 43). They relate to the births, baptisms, marriages, deaths and burials abroad, and on British and foreign ships, of British subjects, nationals of the colonies, of the Commonwealth, or of countries under British jurisdiction. Some foreign nationals are also included. The indexes, in RG 43, are seen on microfilm. References, by country, are given in **4.15**; however, this includes only the most well represented countries in RG 32–RG 36, and there are many others besides (e.g. Uruguay and Gibraltar). You should check in the indexes in RG 43 even if the country you are interested in does not appear in **4.15**, or if it does with a wrong date-range.

The embassy and consular records of the Foreign Office at Kew often contain duplicates of the statutory registers sent in to the General Register Offices from 1849 onwards, and also contain earlier records. Although they do not cover the whole range of registers at the FRC (ONS), there are some Foreign Office registers that appear to be unique. Even when they duplicate the FRC (ONS) registers they have the considerable advantage that you can browse through them, if they are over 30 (in some cases 50) years old. For details of the various registers, listed by country, see **4.15**.

There is also a 46 volume series of consular correspondence with the Foreign Office on marriages abroad, covering 1814–1905. The series is split between FO 83 and FO 97, with a register and index for 1814–1893 at FO 802/239. It includes information on some individual marriages. Also in FO 83 are covering despatches to certificates of marriages abroad giving the names of the parties, 1846–1890; general correspondence and circulars on consular marriages; and acknowledgements of receipt of certificates by the Bishop of London's Registry.

References to similar correspondence can be traced in the Foreign Office card index for 1906–1919, and in the printed index for 1920–1957; both these indexes are in the Research Enquiries Room at Kew. However, many of the documents they refer to no longer exist.

As many of these records appear to partly duplicate the records in the Guildhall, it is worth checking *The British Overseas* to find out which place has the more complete collection. The list in **4.15** indicates whether *The British Overseas* gives references to other sources outside the PRO. Records at the Guildhall, as at the PRO, are produced directly to the public, sometimes on microfilm.

Other records of births, marriages and deaths abroad occur elsewhere among the public records; these are included in **4.15**. Two possible sources that are not listed in **4.15** are the Protestant Dissenters' Registry at Dr Williams's Library, and the Wesleyan Methodist Metropolitan Registry. Both of these registered births abroad as well as in the United Kingdom. For more details, see **3.8**.

4.7 Marine registers: an introduction

Records of births, marriages and deaths at sea from 1831–1958 are in RG 32, indexed by RG 43. An official registration system was in operation from 1851, and the registers it created are available in the records of the Registrar General of Shipping and Seamen, at Kew. These should cover all the events that were later transmitted to the various General Register Offices. Indexes to the GRO registers for England and Wales are available at both the FRC (ONS) and Kew: they start in 1837. Seamen and passengers were registered differently until 1891.

4.8 Deaths of seamen, 1851–1890

By the Seamen's Fund Winding-up Act 1851, the masters of British ships were required to hand over the wages and effects of any seamen who had died during a voyage. Registers (BT 153) were maintained until 1889–1890 (but 1882–1887 do not survive). They provide useful information: the name, Register Ticket number, date of engagement, and the place, date and cause of the man's death, with the name and port of his ship, the master's name, the date and place of payment of wages, the amount of wages owed and the date they were sent to the Board of Trade. The indexes to these registers (BT 154, BT 155) are by seamen and by ship, and give simple page references.

Associated with the registers are printed monthly lists of dead seamen (BT 156) giving name and age, rating, nationality or birth place, last address, and cause and place of death. There are also nine manuscript registers (BT 157), containing half yearly lists of deaths, classified by cause.

4.9 Births, deaths and marriages of passengers, 1854–1891

Following the Merchant Shipping Act of 1854, registers (now BT 158) were compiled from the official logs of births and deaths at sea. If a ship was lost with all hands, no log survived for a return to be made. From 1888, only deaths were recorded in these registers. Masters were further required by the Registration of Births and Deaths Act of 1874 to report births and deaths on board ships to the Registrar General of Shipping and Seamen, where they were entered in two separate registers (BT 159, BT 160). These contain more information than the marine registers held by the GRO at Southport (**4.14**), as they include the information sent to the General Register Offices of Scotland and Ireland, and information relating to other nationalities. Indexes are available.

See **4.10** for marriages at sea, 1854–1972.

4.10 Passengers and seamen: births and deaths, 1891–1964, and marriages, 1854–1972

From 1891 a new series of registers (BT 334) begins which combine records of passengers and seamen at sea.

Birth entries (available 1891–1964, indexed to 1960) record: name of ship, official number, port of registry, date of birth, name, sex, name of father, rank or profession or occupation of father, name of mother, maiden surname of mother, father's nationality/birthplace and last place of abode, mother's nationality/birthplace and last place of abode.

Death entries (available 1891–1964, indexed to 1960) record: name of ship, official number, port of registry, date of death, place of death, name of deceased, sex, age, rating (for seamen), rank or profession or occupation (for non-seamen), nationality and birthplace, last place of abode, cause of death, remarks.

The class also contains indexes to births and deaths; these are arranged both by ships' names and individuals' names. It should be noted that, although the Registrar General of Shipping and Seamen was required to report births and deaths to the appropriate Registrar General of Births, Deaths and Marriages, over 50 per cent of the entries in BT 334 are blank in the column headed 'Which RG has been informed', reflecting the international make-up of the shipping fleets.

One register of deaths and births at sea (1892–1918), first reported at Falmouth, has survived in CUST 67/74.

Marriages are entered in one odd register, covering 1854 to 1972, in BT 334/117. The records name of ship, official number, names of both parties, ages, whether single, widow or widower, profession or occupation, fathers' names, professions or occupations of fathers. A note at the front indicates that the General Register Office did not require returns of these marriages, as they were not conducted in an appointed place.

For records after 1964, use the GRO general indexes, available at the FRC (ONS) and Kew (see **4.14 no. 1**).

4.11 Other sources for deaths, etc., at sea

Details of some births and baptisms at sea (potentially from 1831 and 1931) are also included in RG 32/1–16 (indexed in RG 43/2). There are also registers of marriages aboard naval ships, 1842–1889 (RG 33/156, indexed in RG 43/7). These often appear to be the marriages of people living in places where other methods of obtaining a valid British marriage may have been difficult, such as the Cayman Islands. Deaths of British citizens on board French ships, 1836–1871, are in RG 35/16 (in French); deaths on board Dutch ships, 1839–1871, are in RG 35/17 (in Dutch): both are indexed by RG 43/4.

Registers of the deaths of emigrants at sea, 1847–1869, are in CO 386/169–172.

4.12 Commonwealth War Graves, and other burial grounds

The Commonwealth War Graves Commission has details of servicemen who died overseas and on ships in the two World Wars, and can often supply detailed information. Write to the Commonwealth War Graves Commission, Information Office (address is in **48**) or check their Debt of Honour Register on http://www.cwgc.org/ for more details.

The British Association for Cemeteries in South Asia (BACSA) is a voluntary organisation which deals with the preservation, conversion and registration of European cemeteries in South Asia (Persian Gulf to Hong Kong), and in particular those that were formerly administered by the East India Company, and the British government in India. It compiles records of both civilians and soldiers, and produces a twice-yearly magazine, *Chowkidar*. For more information, contact the BACSA Secretary: a stamped addressed envelope would be appreciated. The address is in **48**.

4.13 Births, marriages and deaths of Britons overseas and at sea: bibliography and sources

Published works
General Register Office, *Abstract of Arrangements Respecting Registration of Births, Marriages and Deaths in the United Kingdom and the Other Countries of the British Commonwealth of Nations, and in the Irish Republic* (London, 1952)
K Smith, C T Watts and M J Watts, *Records of Merchant Shipping and Seamen* (PRO, 1998)
J Wall, 'The British Association for Cemeteries in South Asia', *Genealogists' Magazine*, XXIV, pp. 1–4
G Yeo, *The British Overseas, A Guide to Records of Their Births, Baptisms, Marriages, Deaths and Burials Available in the United Kingdom* (Guildhall Library, London, 4th edn,. 1994)

Unpublished finding aids
RG 43: indexes to most of RG 32–RG 36, and to RG 4/4605, on microfilm. Some entries relate to registers held by the GRO at Southport

4.14 Indexes at the FRC (ONS), and also available at Kew, to the Overseas, Armed Services and Marine Registers kept by the General Register Office of England and Wales at Southport

General Indexes, from 1966		
1966-date	1	**Registers of Births Abroad; and Marriages Abroad; and Deaths Abroad [Civilian and Armed Forces]** These registers took over from the Air, Consular, Marine, Miscellaneous, and Services series, and apparently from the marriage and death sections of the United Kingdom High Commission series (all below). The birth indexes give name, mother's maiden name, place of registration and date or year of birth. The marriage indexes include the spouse's surname. The death indexes give age.
Colonial Indexes, 1940–1981		
1940–1981	2	**UKHC Registers of Births Abroad 1950-1965; and Marriages; and Deaths** These registers were kept in colonies and ex-colonies by the United Kingdom High Commissions. Although the birth registers start in 1950, they do include a few births from the 1940s.
Civilian Indexes, 1818–1965		
1849–1965	3	**Consular Registers of Births; and Marriages; and Deaths** Arranged alphabetically within a range of five or so years; no closer indication of date is given. The indexes include name and consul's registration district: from 1906, the spouse's name is given in the marriage index, and the age in the death index. These are the statutory consular registers, kept as a result of the 1849 Act. Among the Foreign Office embassy and consular records at Kew are the duplicates kept by the consulates. It may be worth using this index, and then looking at the duplicate registers at Kew: this would save the cost of buying the wrong certificate if the index is not sufficiently precise. However, the reference given in this index does not apply to the Kew registers. You will need to match up the place of registration with the right consulate, and then find that consulate's records from **4.15**.
1837–1965	4	**At sea: Marine Registers of Births; and Deaths** These give name and year of English and Welsh births and deaths at sea; after 1875, the name of the ship is given as well. The age is given for deaths. From 1837 to 1874 they relate to events occurring on British merchant and naval ships; from 1875, to other ships carrying passengers to or from the United Kingdom as well.
1947–1965	5	**Air Registers of Births; and Deaths** The index gives name, age (for deaths), place and year of births and deaths occurring in civil aircraft in flight.
1941–1965	6	**Protectorates of Africa and Asia: Registers of Births** The registers for 1895–1957, and the indexes up to 1940, are at Kew

1956–1965	7	**Miscellaneous Foreign Registers of Births, Marriages and Deaths** The index gives name, place and year. Most entries appear to be from the Gulf States, Singapore, etc.
1818–1864	8	**Index to Registers of Births, Marriages and Deaths in the Ionian Islands** The index is to a military register, a civil register, and a chaplain's register. It gives names only. See also **4.15**, under **Greece**.

Armed Forces Indexes, 1761–1965

1761–1924	9	**Regimental Registers of Births** These record the birth of childen of serving soldiers in the United Kingdom and abroad (from c.1790). The indexes are arranged alphabetically, giving name, place, year and regiment. There are also marriage registers, but these are not indexed and cannot be inspected: see **18.2** for more information.
1796–1880	10	**[Army] Chaplains' Returns of Births; and Marriages; and Deaths** These all relate to events abroad. The index gives name, place and a date range of 2–3 years.
1881–1955	11	**Army [and other services] Returns of Births; and Marriages; and Deaths** These all relate to events abroad. The indexes give name, station and date. They also include the Navy, despite the title. From 1920, entries relating to the Royal Air Force are included.
1956–1965	12	**Service Departments Registers of Births; and Marriages** These relate to Army, Navy and Air Force births and marriages abroad. The indexes give name, station and year.

Armed Forces: Indexes to War Deaths, 1899–1948

1899–1902	13	**Natal and South Africa Forces**
1914–1921	14	**Army Other Ranks' War Deaths**
1914–1921	15	**Army Officers' War Deaths**
1914–1921	16	**Naval War Deaths**
1914–1921	17	**Indian Services' War Deaths**
1939–1948	18	**Army Other Ranks' War Deaths**
1939–1948	19	**Army Officers' War Deaths**
1939–1948	20	**Naval Ratings' War Deaths**
1939–1948	21	**Naval Officers' War Deaths**
1939–1948	22	**RAF War Deaths**
1939–1948	23	**Indian Services' War Deaths**

4.15 Table of overseas birth, marriage and death records in the PRO

African Protectorates	births 1911–1946; marriages 1912–1935; deaths 1911–1946	RG 36 [2]
Algeria	deaths 1840–1958	RG 35/14–15, 20–24 [2]
Angola *Luanda*	births 1865–1906; marriages 1871–1928; deaths 1859–1906	FO 375/1–4
Argentina [1] *Buenos Aires*	marriages 1826–1900	FO 446/3–6, 28–30
Ascension Island [1]	baptisms/births from 1858–1861 and onwards deaths 1858–1920	RG 32 [2] RG 35 [2]
Austria [1] *Vienna*	deaths c.1831–1920 marriages 1846–1890 marriages 1883–1891 baptisms 1867–1886 and onwards	RG 35/20–44 [2] FO 83 [3] FO 120/697 RG 32 [2]
Belgium [1] (including *Belgian Congo*) Antwerp Brussels Ghent	deaths 1831–1871 deaths 1871–1920 military deaths in hospital, etc., 1914–1920 (In alphabetical order, but not indexed in RG 43. There are no certificates for surnames beginning with C, F, P, Q or X.) baptisms and burials 1817–1852; marriages 1820–1849 baptisms and burials 1831–1836, 1841–1842; marriages 1832–1838, 1841–1842 baptisms 1840 and onwards marriages and deaths: correspondence 1927–1951 marriages 1816–1890 marriages 1846–1890 marriages 1849–1850	RG 35/1–3 [2] RG 35/20–44 [2] RG 35/45–69 RG 33/1–2 [2] RG 33/155 [2] RG 32 [2] FO 744 RG 33/3–8 [2] FO 83 [3] RG 33/9 [2]
Bermuda [1]	naval dockyard baptisms, marriages and burials 1826–1946	ADM 6/434, 436, 439

1 You may also need to consult Yeo, *The British Overseas*.
2 Entries in RG 32–RG 36 are largely indexed by the various indexes in RG 43. See the RG 43 class list.
3 Indexed in FO 802/239.

Brazil [1]		
Bahia	marriages 1816–1820	RG 33/155 [2]
Maranhão	marriages 1844	RG 33/155 [2]
Parà	births and deaths 1840–1841	RG 33/155 [2]
Rio de Janeiro	marriages 1809–1818	RG 33/155 [2]
	births 1850–1859	FO 743/11
	baptisms 1850 and onwards	RG 32 [2]
	marriages c.1850 and onwards	RG 34 [2]
	burials 1850 and onwards	RG 35/20–44 [2]
	marriages 1870–1890	FO 83 [3]
São Paulo	births 1932; marriages 1933	FO 863/1–2
Brunei	births 1932–1950	RG 36 [2]
Bulgaria [1]		
Plovdiv	births 1880–1922; deaths 1884–1900	FO 868/1–2
Rustchuk	births 1867–1908; deaths 1867–1903	FO 888/1–2
Sofia	births 1934–1940	FO 864/1
Varna	births 1856–1939; deaths 1851–1929	FO 884/1–5
Burma		
Rangoon	marriages 1929–1942	RG 33/10 [2]
China [1]	births, marriages and deaths 1869–1876	FO 681/1
Amoy	births 1850–1950; marriages 1850–1949; deaths 1850 1948 (see also **China** FO 681/1)	FO 663/85–95
Canton	births 1864–1865, 1944–1950; marriages 1865, 1943–1949; deaths 1865, 1944–1950 (see also **China** FO 681/1) for a list of British subjects in Canton, 1844–1951, see FO 694	FO 681/2–9
Changsha	births 1905–1941; marriages 1906–1936; deaths 1906–1933	FO 681/10–12
Chefoo	births 1861–1943; marriages 1872–1940; deaths 1861–1942	FO 681/13–22
Chengtu	births 1902–1915; marriages 1904–1924; deaths 1904–1926	FO 664/3–5
Chinanfu (Tsinan)	births and marriages 1906–1935; deaths 1906–1931, 1937	FO 681/23–27
Chinkiang	births 1865–1866, 1899–1926; marriages 1865–1866, 1896–1959; deaths 1865–1866, 1889–1927 (see also **China** FO 681/1)	FO 387/4–5, 7–11
Chungking	births 1888–1951; marriages 1891–1949; deaths 1891–1950	FO 681/28–34
Darien	births and marriages 1907–1940; deaths 1910–1940	FO 681/35–88
Foochow	births 1858–1866,1905–1944; marriages 1909–1942; deaths 1858–1866, 1921–1945	FO 665/3–8

Formosa (Taiwan)	(see also **China** FO 681/1) births, marriages and deaths 1866 deaths 1873–1901	FO 681/57 FO 721/1
Hankow	(see also **China** FO 681/1) births 1863–1951; marriages 1869–1949; deaths 1861–1950	FO 666/2–22
Ichang	(see also **China** FO 681/1) births 1879–1938; marriages 1881–1937; deaths 1880–1941 (damaged by fire)	FO 667/2–6
Kuikiang	births 1866–1929; marriages 1872–1928; deaths 1863–1929 (see also **China** FO 681/1)	FO 681/39–45
Kunming	births 1949–1951; deaths 1950	FO 668/2–3
Kwelin	births 1942–1944; deaths 1943	FO 681/46–47
Mukden	births and deaths 1949 (date of registration); marriages 1947–1948	FO 681/48–49, 79–80
Nanking	births 1930–1948; marriages 1929–1949; deaths 1930–1947	FO 681/50–53
Newchang	births, marriages and deaths between 1869 and 1876	FO 681/1
Ningpo	births 1858; marriages and deaths 1856–1858	FO 670/2–4
Peking	(see also **China** FO 681/1) births 1911–1914; deaths 1911–1913 (date of registration)	FO 564/13–14
Shanghai	(see also **China** FO 681/1) births 1856–1864; marriages 1851; deaths 1851–1864	FO 672/1–3
	marriages 1852–1951	RG 33/12–20 [2]
Shanghai, Union Church	marriages 1869–1951	RG 33/21–32 [2]
Shantung Province	(see also **China** FO 681/1) marriages 1912–1914	RG 33/33 [2]

Swatow	births 1864–1865, 1947–1949
	  (date of registration); marriages 1865;
	  deaths 1864–65 (see also **China** FO 681/1)
		FO 681/54–56

Taku	births 1862–1875; deaths 1871–1875	FO 673/9–10
Tengyueh	births 1904–1941; marriages 1913–1941; deaths 1906–1941	FO 681/60–62
Tientsin	births 1864–1951; marriages 1862–1952; deaths 1863–1952	FO 674/297–327
Tsingtao	(see also **China** FO 681/1) births 1911–1950; marriages 1923–1949; deaths 1921–1951	FO 675/7–10
Wei-hai-wei	births 1899–1929; marriages 1905–1940; deaths 1899–1929, 1938–1941	FO 681/63–71
	births, marriages, deaths 1899–1930	RG 33/34 [2]
	births, marriages, deaths 1899–1930	RG 36 [2]
	index to births, marriages and deaths 1899–1930	RG 43/19 [2]
Whampoa	births and deaths 1865	FO 681/72–73
Yunanfu	(see also **China** FO 681/1) births 1903–1948; marriages 1904–1949; deaths 1903–1950	FO 681/74–78

1 You may also need to consult Yeo, *The British Overseas*.
2 Entries in RG 32–RG 36 are largely indexed by the various indexes in RG 43. See the RG 43 class list.
3 Indexed in FO 802/239.

Colombia [1] *Cartagena*	marriages 1824–1827 marriages 1846–1890 births 1853–1924; deaths 1858–1927	RG 33/155 [2] FO 83 [3] FO 736/2–3
Denmark [1] *Copenhagen* For Danish colonies, see **West Indies**	deaths 1842–1872 marriages 1846–1890 marriage affidavits 1853–1870 marriages 1853–1874 baptisms 1866–1870; marriages and burials 1869–1870 and onwards	RG 35/4–7 [2] FO 83 [3] FO 211/236 RG 33/35 [2] RG 32 [2]
Ecuador *Guayaquil*	births, marriages and deaths 1879–1896	FO 521/2
Estonia see **Russia**		
Falkland Islands [1]	births and baptisms [1853–1951] marriages [1854–1951] burials 1854–[1951]	RG 32 [2] RG 34 [2] RG 35/20–44 [2]
Finland [1] *Helsinki* *Kristinestad* *Raahe (Brahestad)* *Tampere* *Turku (Åbo)* *Vyborg*	births 1914–1924 deaths 1924 deaths 1928 deaths 1930 births 1906–1923; deaths 1909–1934 births 1928; deaths 1929 births 1924–1931; deaths 1929–1937	FO 753/19 FO 768/5 FO 756/1 FO 755/1 FO 769/1–2 FO 754/1–2 FO 751/1–3

France [1]
 	
 Boulogne
 	
 Brest
 Calais and St Omer
 	
 Dieppe
 Le Havre
 Le Tréport
 Nantes
 Paris
	deaths 1831–1871
	 deaths 1871–1920
	 military deaths in hospital, etc., 1914–1920
	    (In alphabetical order, but not indexed in
	    RG 43. There are no certificates for
	    surnames beginning with C, F, P, Q or X.)
	 baptisms and burials 1815–1896;
	    marriages 1829–1895
	    (index at RG 33/161)
	 births 1842
	 baptisms 1817–1878; marriages 1818–1872;
	    burials 1819–1878
	    (index at RG 33/49)
	 births 1872–1892; deaths 1871–1894
	 baptisms, marriages and burials 1817–1863
	 births 1917–1926; deaths 1899–1929
	 marriages 1851–1867
	 baptisms, marriages and burials 1784–1789,
	    1801–1809, 1815–1869; marriages 1869–1890
	 deaths 1846–1852
		RG 35/8–13 [2]
		 RG 35/20–44 [2]
		 RG 35/45–69
		
		 RG 33/37–48
		
		 RG 33/155 [2]
		 RG 33/50–55
		
		 FO 712/1–3
		 RG 33/56–57 [2]
		 FO 713/1–2
		 FO 384/1
		 RG 33/58–77 [2]
		
		 RG 35/11 [2]

Rouen *French colonies (Cochin* *China, Guadeloupe,* *Guyana, Haiti, India,* *Martinique, Mexico, New* *Caledonia, Réunion,* *Saigon, Shanghai,* *Senegal, Society Islands)* (See also **Algeria,** **Réunion, Madagascar,** **Tahiti** and **West Indies**)	marriages 1852–1890 marriages 1935–1937 baptisms 1843–1844 deaths 1836–1871	FO 83 [3] FO 630/1 RG 33/78 [2] RG 35/14–16 [2]

Germany [1]
Aachen
Bavaria
 	
Berlin
 	
Bremen
Bremerhaven
 	
Cologne
 	
Darmstadt
 	
Dresden
 	
Düsseldorf
 	
Essen
Frankfurt
 	
Hanover
 	
Karlsruhe
Konigsberg
Leipzig
Munich
Saxony
Stuttgart
(See also **Poland**)
	deaths c.1831–1920
	deaths 1925
	baptisms, marriages and deaths 1860–1861
	marriages 1860–1861
	marriages 1884–1897 (see also RG 32)
	marriages 1846–1890
	births 1944–1954; deaths 1944–1945
	births 1872–1914; marriages 1893–1933
	births 1872–1893
	marriages 1903–1914
	births and marriages 1850–1866;
	   deaths 1850–1866 and 1879–1881
	births 1880; marriages 1920–1934
	births 1869–1898; deaths 1871–1905
	marriages 1870–1890
	births, baptisms and burials 1817–1836
	marriages 1846–1890
	births and deaths 1859–1866
	births 1901–1907; marriages 1899–1900
	births 1873–1884; baptisms 1903–1907;
	   marriages 1873–1878, 1893–1898;
	   deaths 1876–1884
	births 1922–1927
	marriages 1836–1865
	marriages 1846–1869
	baptisms, marriages, deaths and
	   burials 1839–1859
	marriages 1846–1869
	births 1861–1866
	births 1860–1864; deaths 1859–1864
	marriages 1864–1885
	marriages 1850–1865; deaths 1850–1860
	marriages 1846–1890
	marriages 1850–1865; deaths 1850–1869
	marriages 1847–1890
		RG 35/20–44 [2]
		FO 604/7
		FO 151/3
		FO 149/99
		FO 601/2–6
		FO 83 [3]
		FO 601/2–6
		FO 585/1–5
		FO 585/1
		FO 586/1
		FO 155/5–11, 17
		
		FO 604/8–10
		FO 716/1–2
		FO 83 [3]
		RG 33/79 [2]
		FO 83 [3]
		RG 33/80 [2]
		FO 292/2, 4–5
		FO 604/1–6, 8
		
		FO 604/11
		FO 208/90
		FO 83 [3]
		RG 33/81 [2]
		
		FO 83 [3]
		FO 717/1
		FO 718/1–2
		FO 509/1
		FO 299/22
		FO 83 [3]
		FO 218/3
		FO 83 [3]

Greece [1]	marriages 1846–1890	FO 83 [3]

Ionian Islands, Zante	baptisms, marriages, deaths and burials 1849–1859 The registers for 1818–1848 are at Southport: see **4.1**. The index covers both sets, and can be seen at the FRC (ONS) and at Kew: see **4.14 no. 8**.	RG 33/82 [2]
Hawaii	births 1848–1893 marriages 1850–1853 registers of British subjects 1895–1944	FO 331/59 RG 33/155 [2] FO 331/60–61
Hong Kong	deaths from enemy action in the Far East 1941–1945, indexed in RG 43/14 (see also **Indonesia** RG 33/132)	RG 33/11
Hungary *Budapest*	marriages 1872–1899	FO 114/1–5
Indian States [1] *Bikaner, Eastern Rajputana, Gwalior Hyderabad, Jaipur, Madras States, Mysore, Punjab States, Travandrum and other states* *Jammu and Kashmir, Kolhapur and Deccan states, Udaipur* *Srinagar*	births and deaths 1894 1947 (most from 1930s and 1940s) (indexed in RG 43/15) births 1917–1947 (indexed in RG 43/15) deaths 1926–1947 (indexed in RG 43/15)	RG 33/90–113 RG 33/157–158, 160 RG 33/159
Indian Sub-continent [1] *French India*	deaths c.1831–1920 deaths 1836–1871	RG 35/20–44 [2] RG 35/16 [2]
Indonesia **(Dutch East Indies)** [1] *Borneo* *Borneo and Sarawak* *Java* *Oleh Leh* *Sumatra*	deaths 1839–1871 deaths 1871–1920 births 1907; deaths 1897–1907 deaths from enemy action 1941–1945 births 1869–1941; baptisms 1906; deaths 1874–1898 and 1912–1940 deaths 1839–1871 births and deaths 1883–1884 births and deaths 1883–1884	RG 35/17 [2] RG 35/20–44 [2] FO 221/2–3 RG 33/132 [2] FO 803/1–3 RG 35/20–44 [2] FO 220/12 FO 220/12
Iran (Persia) [1] *Bushire* *Isfahan* *Tabriz*	births 1903–1950; marriages 1895–1950; deaths 1899–1950 births, marriages and deaths 1849–1895 births 1829–1950; marriages 1893–1951; deaths 1892–1943 births 1851–1951; marriages 1850–1950; deaths 1882–1931	FO 923/1–25 FO 560 FO 799/34–37 FO 451/1–9

1 You may also need to consult Yeo, *The British Overseas*.
2 Entries in RG 32–RG 36 are largely indexed by the various indexes in RG 43. See the RG 43 class list.
3 Indexed in FO 802/239.

Iraq (Mesopotamia) [1]	births, marriages and deaths 1915–1931 (with marriage indexes in RG 33/138–139)	RG33/133–137 [2]
	births, marriages and deaths 1915–1931 (indexed in RG 43/16)	RG 36 [2]
Israel see **Palestine**		
Italy [1]	deaths 1871–1920	RG 35/20–44 [2]
Agrigento	births 1857–1904; deaths 1857–1885	FO 653/2–4
Catania	births 1878–1939; deaths 1878–1904, 1919–1940	Fo 653/5–7
Florence	marriages 1840–1855, 1865–1871	RG 33/114–115 [2]
	marriages 1856	FO 352/43
Gela	births 1904–1930	FO 653/8
Licata	births and deaths 1871–1900	FO 720/1
Livorno (Leghorn)	births, baptisms, marriages and burials 1797–1824	RG 33/116–117 [2]
Marsala	births 1847–1922; deaths 1847–1919	FO 653/9–11
Mazzara	births 1810–1911	FO 653/12–13
Messina	births and deaths 1854–1957	FO 653/14–17
Milazzo	deaths 1887–1903	FO 653/18
Naples	baptisms, marriages and burials 1817–1822	RG 33/118 [2]
	baptisms, marriages and burials 1835–1836	RG 33/155 [2]
Palermo	births 1837–1891, 1932–1940; deaths 1850–1919	FO 653/19–21
Porto Empedocle	births 1906	FO 653/22
Rome and Tuscany	baptisms and marriages 1816–1852	FO 170/6
Rome	marriages 1870–1890	FO 83 [3]
	marriages 1872–1889	RG 33/119 [2]
Sicily	births 1810–1957; deaths 1847–1957	FO 653/2–38 and FO 720/1
	baptisms 1838	RG 33/155 [2]
Syracuse	births 1909–1918; deaths 1912–1919, 1953–1957	FO 653/23–25
Taormina	deaths 1909–1922	FO 653/26
Trapani	births 1871–1906, 1924–1927	FO 653/27–28
Turin	marriages 1847–1869	FO 83 [3]
	marriages 1858–1864	RG 33/120 [2]
Venice	marriages 1874–1947	RG 33/121 [2]
Japan [1]	marriage declarations and certificates 1870–1887	FO 345
Kobe	baptisms and marriages 1874–1941; burials 1902–1941	RG 33/122–126 [2]
Nagasaki	births 1864–1940; marriages 1922–1940; deaths 1859–1944	FO 796/236–238
Osaka	marriages 1892–1904	RG 33/127–130 [2]
Shimonoseki	births 1903–1921; marriages 1906–1922; deaths 1903–1921	FO 797/48–50
Tokyo	marriages 1870–1890	FO 83 [3]
	marriages 1875–1887	FO 345/34
Yokohama	marriages 1870–1874	FO 345/34

Jordan *Amman*	births 1946; marriages 1927	RG 36 [2]
Kenya (East African Protectorate)	births 1904–1924 (partly indexed by RG 43/18)	RG 36 [2]
Latvia see **Russia**		
Lebanon *Beirut*	marriages c.1859–1939	FO 616/5
Libya *Tripoli*	marriages 1916, 1931–1940; deaths 1938–1939	FO 161/4–7
Lithuania see **Russia**		
Madagascar [1] *Diego Suarez* *Tamatave* *Tananarive (Antananarivo)*	births 1907–1921 deaths 1935–1940 births 1865–1868	FO 711/1 FO 714/1 FO 710/1
Malaysia [1] *Borneo* *Borneo and Sarawak* *Johore* *Sarawak*	births 1917–1949 births 1920–1948; deaths 1941–1945 births 1907; deaths 1897–1907 deaths from enemy action 1941–1945 births 1924–1931 births 1910–1948; marriages 1921–1935; deaths 1910–1948	RG 36 [2] RG 33/131–132 [2] FO 221/2–3 RG 33/132 [2] RG 36 [2] RG 36 [2]
Malta [1]	marriages 1904–1936	FO 161/7
Mauritius see **Reunion**		
Mexico *Mexico City* *Vera Cruz*	marriages 1850 and onwards deaths c.1850–1920 burials 1827–1926 marriages 1846–1869 births and deaths 1854–1867 births, deaths and burials 1858–1867	RG 34 [2] RG 35/16, 20–44 [2] FO 207/58 FO 83 [3] FO 723/1–2 RG 33/140 [2]

Netherlands [1]
The Hague
 	
The Hague
Rotterdam
For Dutch colonies, see
Indonesia, Surinam and
West Indies
	deaths 1839–1871 and 1871–1920
	baptisms 1627–1821; marriages 1627–1889;
	  births 1837–1839, 1859–1894;
	  deaths 1859–1907 (These also include
	  some church records; for others, see FO 259.)
	marriages 1846–1890
	baptisms and marriages 1708–1794
		RG 35/17 & 20 44 [2]
		RG 33/83–88 [2]
		
		FO 83 [3]
		RG 33/89 [2]

1 You may also need to consult Yeo, *The British Overseas*.
2 Entries in RG 32–RG 36 are largely indexed by the various indexes in RG 43. See the RG 43 class list.
3 Indexed in FO 802/239.

Norway	deaths 1831–1920	RG 35/20–44 [2]
Bodo	births 1888–1890; deaths 1895	FO 724/1–2
Drammen	deaths 1906	FO 532/2
Kragero	deaths 1895	FO 725/1
Lofoten Islands	births 1850–1932	FO 726/1
Oslo (Christiania)	births 1850–1932; marriages 1853–1936; deaths 1850–1930	FO 529/1–14
Porsgrund and Skien	births 1885–1891	FO 531/2
Palestine [1]	births and deaths 1920–1935 (indexed in RG 43/17)	RG 33/141 [2]
	births 1923–1948; deaths 1941–1945 (partly indexed in RG 43/18)	RG 36 [2]
Jaffa	births 1900–1914	FO 734/1
Jerusalem	births 1850–1921; deaths 1851–1914	FO 617/3–5
	military baptisms 1939–1947	WO 156/6
Sarafand	military baptisms 1940–1946; banns of marriage 1944–1947	WO 156/7–8
Paraguay	births 1863 and onwards	RG 32 [2]
	deaths 1831–1920	RG 35/20–44 [2]
Peru [1]	births and deaths 1837–1841; marriages 1827 and 1836	RG 33/155 [2]
Poland [1]		
Breslau (Wroclaw)	births 1929–1938; deaths 1932–1938	FO 715/1–2
Danzig (Gdansk)	births 1851–1910; deaths 1850–1914	FO 634/16–18
Lodz	births 1925–1939	FO 869/1
Stettin	births 1864–1939; deaths 1857–1933	FO 719/1–2
Portugal [1]	deaths 1831–1920	RG 35/20–44 [2]
Azores	births, baptisms, marriages, deaths and burials 1807–1866	FO 559/1
	baptisms, marriages and burials 1835–1837	RG 35/155 [2]
	baptisms 1850–1857	RG 32 [2]
	burials 1850–1857	RG 35/20 [2]
Cape Verde Islands	marriages 1894–1922	FO 767/6–7
Lisbon	marriages 1846–1890	FO 83 [3]
	marriages 1859–1876	FO 173/8
Luanda see **Angola**		
Oporto	baptisms, marriages and burials 1814–1874	RG 33/142 [2]
	baptisms, marriages and burials 1837	RG 33/155 [2]
	baptisms, 1835 onwards	RG 32 [2]
	marriages 1835 onwards	RG 34 [2]
	burials 1835–1844	RG 35/20 [2]
Réunion (Mauritius)	deaths 1836–1871	RG 35/16 [2]
	marriages 1864–1921	FO 322/1–2
Romania [1]		
Braila	births 1922–1930; deaths 1921–1929	FO 727/1–2

Bucharest	births 1851–1931; baptisms 1858–1948: deaths 1854–1929	FO 625/2–4, 6
	marriages 1870–1890	FO 83 [3]
Constanta (Kustendje)	births 1866–1873	FO 887/1
Galatz	marriages 1891–1939	FO 517/1–2
Lower Danube	baptisms 1869–1907	FO 625/5
	marriages 1868–1914	RG 33/143 [2]
	burials 1869–1870	FO 786/120
Sulina	births 1861–1932; deaths 1860–1931	FO 728/1–2 and FO 886/1–2
Russia [1]	births, baptisms, and deaths 1835–1870	RG 35/18–19 [2]
	births 1849–1909; marriages 1849–1861; deaths 1849–1915	FO 267/44–46
	deaths 1871–1920 [2]	RG 35/20–44
Archangel	births 1849–1909; marriages 1849–1861; deaths 1849–1915	FO 267/44–46
Batum	births 1884–1921; marriages 1891–1920; deaths 1884–1920	FO 397/1–6
Berdiansk (Osipenko)	marriages 1901	FO 399/1
Ekaterinburg (Sverdlovsk)	deaths 1918–1919	FO 399/5
Estonia, Pernau	births 1894–1930; deaths 1894–1930	FO 339/11–12
Estonia, Tallin (Reval)	births 1866–1940; marriages 1921–1939; deaths 1875–1940	FO 514/1–9
Konigsberg (Kaliningrad)	births 1869–1933; marriages 1864–1904; deaths 1857–1932	FO 509/1–4
Latvia, Libau	births 1883–1932; deaths 1871–1932	FO 440/10 and FO 661/4–5
Latvia, Riga	births 1850–1910; deaths 1850–1915	FO 377/3–4
	births 1921–1940; marriages 1920–1940; deaths 1921–1940	FO 516/1–9
Latvia, Windau	births 1906–909	FO 399/19
Lithuania, Kovno, Memel	births 1924–1940; deaths 1922–1940	FO 722/1–4
Moscow	births 1882–1918; marriages 1894–1924; deaths 1881–1918	FO 518/1–4
Nicolaiyev	births 1872–1917; deaths 1874–1915	FO 399/7–8
Novorossisk	births 1911–1920; deaths 1896–1920	FO 399/9–10
Odessa	births 1852–1919; baptisms 1893; marriages 1851–1916; deaths 1852–1919	FO 359/3–12
Poti	births 1871–1906; deaths 1871–1920	FO 399/13–14
Rostov	births 1891–1914; marriages 1904–1918; deaths 1906–1916	FO 398/1–9
St Petersburg (Petrograd, Leningrad)	baptisms 1818–1840; burials 1821–1840. independent denomination (indexed in RG 43)	RG 4/4605 [2]
	births, baptisms, marriages, deaths and burials 1840–1918 (with an index for 1886–1917 in RG 33/162)	RG 33/144–152 [2]
	births 1856–1938; marriages 1892–1917; deaths 1897–1927	FO 378/3–9
	marriages 1870–1890	FO 83 [3]

1 You may also need to consult Yeo, *The British Overseas*.

2 Entries in RG 32–RG 36 are largely indexed by the various indexes in RG 43. See the RG 43 class list.

3 Indexed in FO 802/239.

Sebastopol	births 1886–1898; marriages 1910; deaths 1893–1908	FO 393/3, 15–16
Theodosia (Feodosiya)	births 1904–1906; deaths 1907–1918	FO 339/17–18
Vladivostok	births 1911–1927; marriages 1916–1923; deaths 1908–1924	FO 510/1–10
Singapore	births 1922	RG 36[2]
Somaliland (Somalia)	births 1905–1920 (partly indexed by RG 43/18)	RG 36[2]
Spain[1]	deaths 1831–1920	RG 35/20–44[2]
Aguilas	births 1875–1911; deaths 1874–1911	FO 920/1–2
Balearic Islands	births, marriages, deaths (1815–1880)	FO 214/51–53
Bilbao	deaths 1855–1870	FO 729/1
Cartagena	births 1847–1887; marriages 1858–1904; deaths 1855–1871	FO 920/3–6
Garrucha	births 1876–1890; deaths 1883–1905	FO 920/7–8
Madrid	marriages 1846–1890	FO 83[3]
	registers of British subjects 1835–1895, 1906–1931	FO 445
Pormàn	births 1907; deaths 1911	FO 920/9–10
Seville	births, marriages and deaths 1948	FO 332/14–16
Sudan[1]	births 1916–1950; marriages 1907–1950; deaths 1917–1946 (partly indexed by RG 43/18)	RG 36[2]
Surinam (Dutch Guiana)		
Paramaribo	births 1897–1966; marriages 1922–1929; deaths 1889–1965	FO 907/1–32
Sweden[1]	deaths 1831–1920	RG 35/20–44[2]
Gothenburg	marriages 1845–1891	RG 33/153[2]
	baptisms 1881–1890	FO 818/15
Hudiksvall	deaths 1884	FO 730/1
Oskarshamn	deaths 1887	FO 731/1
Stockholm	marriages 1847–1890	FO 83[3]
	births, marriages and deaths 1920–1938	FO 748
Switzerland[1]	marriages 1816–1833	FO 194/1
	deaths 1831–1920	RG 35/20–44[2]
Geneva	births 1850–1934; marriages 1850–1933; deaths 1850–1923	FO 778/13–22
Lausanne	births 1886–1948; marriages 1887–1947; deaths 1887–1948	FO 910/1–20
Montreux	births 1902–1939; marriages 1927–1933; deaths 1903–1941	FO 911/1–3
Syria[1]		
Aleppo	baptisms and burials 1756–1800	SP 110/70
Damascus	births, marriages and deaths 1932–1938	FO 684/16–17

Tahiti		
Papeete	births 1818–1941; marriages 1845–1941; deaths 1845–1936	FO 687/22–23
Raiatea	births, marriages and deaths 1853–1890	FO 687/34, 36–38
Taiwan see **China**		
Formosa		
Tristan da Cunha	marriages 1871–1951; deaths 1892–1949 (Registers of births and baptisms, 1867–1955, were returned to Tristan da Cunha in 1982)	PRO 30/65
Tunisia		
Bizerta	deaths 1898–1931	FO 870/1
Djerba	deaths 1925	FO 871/1
Gabes	deaths 1925	FO 872/1
Goletta	births 1885–1888	FO 878/1–2
Monastir	deaths 1905 1908	FO 873/1
Sfax	deaths 1896–1931	FO 874/1
Susa (Sousse)	deaths 1894–1931	FO 875/1
Turkey [1]	deaths 1831–1920	RG 35/20–44 [2]
Adana	marriages 1913, 1942 and 1946	FO 609/1–3
Adrianople (Edirne)	births 1888–1912; marriages 1887–1914	FO 783/3–7
Ankara and Konieh	births 1895–1909	FO 732/1
Constantinople	marriages 1885–1958	RG 33/154 [2]
(Istanbul)	marriages 1895–1924	FO 441/1–35
Dardanelles	births 1900–1914	FO 733/1
Smyrna (Izmir)	baptisms, marriages and burials 1833–1849	RG 33/155 [2]
Trebizond	registers of British subjects 1836–1913	FO 526
Uganda [1]	marriages 1904–1910 (partly indexed by RG 43/18)	RG 36 [2]
USA [1]		
Florida, Pensacola	births 1880–1901; deaths 1879–1905	FO 885/1–2
Hawaii see **Hawaii**		
Louisiana, New Orleans	births 1850–1932; marriages 1850–1881; deaths 1850–1932	FO 581/15–19
Massachusetts, Boston	births 1871–1932; deaths 1902–1930	FO 706/1–3
Michigan, Detroit	births 1910–1969; marriages 1936–1937; deaths 1931–1945, 1949–1968	FO 700/44–53
Minnesota, St Paul	births 1943–1966; deaths 1944	FO 700/71–74
Missouri, Kansas City	births 1904–1922, 1944–1966; marriages 1958–1961; deaths 1920–1926, 1943–1949, 1952–1965	FO 700/54–60
Nebraska, Omaha	births 1906	FO 700/61
Ohio, Cincinnati	births 1929, 1943–1948, 1951–1958; deaths 1947, 1950–1955	FO 700/31–35
Ohio, Cleveland	births 1914–1930, 1944–1969; deaths 1948–69	FO 700/36–43
Oregon, Portland	births 1880–1926; deaths 1929	FO 707/1–2
Pennsylvania, Pittsburgh	births 1954–1956	FO 700/63

1 You may also need to consult Yeo, *The British Overseas*.
2 Entries in RG 32–RG 36 are largely indexed by the various indexes in RG 43. See the RG 43 class list.
3 Indexed in FO 802/239.

Rhode Island, Providence	births 1902–1930; deaths 1920 (date of registration)	FO 700/8–9
Texas, Dallas	births 1951–1954; deaths 1951	FO 700/24–25
Texas, El Paso	births 1916–1930; deaths 1914–1926	FO 700/26–27
Texas, Galveston	births 1838–1918; deaths 1850–1927	FO 701/23–24
Washington, Aberdeen	births 1916; deaths 1914	FO 700/22–23
Washington, Tacoma	births 1896–1921; deaths 1892–1907	FO 700/20–21
Venezuela[1]	marriages 1836–1838	RG 33/155[2]
West Indies		
Antigua	baptisms and burials 1733–1734, 1738–1745; marriages 1745	CO 152/21, 25
Barbados	baptisms and burials 1678–1679	CO 1/44
Cuba	baptisms 1847–1848; marriages 1842–1849	RG 33/155[2]
Curaçao	births 1897–1966; marriages 1922–1929; deaths 1889–1965	FO 907/1–32
Danish (US) Virgin Islands, i.e.		
St Croix	deaths 1849–1870	RG 35/ 4[2]
St John	deaths 1849–1872	RG 35/4[2]
St Thomas	deaths 1849–1870	RG 35/4–7[2]
Dominica		
Aux Caves	births 1870–1905	FO 376/1
	deaths 1870–1905	FO 376/2
Dominican Republic	births 1868–1932; marriages 1921–1928: burials 1849–1910; deaths 1874–1889	FO 683/2–6
Guadeloupe	deaths 1836–1871	RG 35/16[2]
Guiana (Dutch) see **Surinam**		
Guyana (French)	deaths 1836–1871	RG 35/16[2]
Haiti	births 1833–1850; marriages 1833–1893; deaths 1833–1850	FO 866/14, 21–22
	births 1870–1907	FO 376/1–2
	deaths 1836–1871	RG 35/16[2]
Martinique	deaths 1836–1871	RG 35/16[2]
Montserrat	baptisms and burials 1721–1729; marriages 1721–1729	CO 152/18, 25
Nevis	baptisms and burials 1726–1727, 1733–1734, 1740–1745	CO 152/16, 21, 25
St Kitts	baptisms and burials 1721–1730, 1733–1734, 1738–1745; marriages 1733–1734, 1738–1745	CO 152/18, 21, 25
Zanzibar	births 1916–1918; marriages 1917–1919; deaths 1916–1919	RG 36[2]

1 You may also need to consult Yeo, *The British Overseas*.
2 Entries in RG 32–RG 36 are largely indexed by the various indexes in RG 43. See the RG 43 class list.
3 Indexed in FO 802/239.

5 Medieval and early modern sources for family history

5.1 Problems

Before the parish registers started in 1538, births, marriages and deaths were not officially recorded, although notes may well have been kept by the priest. However, many series of records of use for family history start well before 1538, and continue long after. In general they contain information about the wealthier members of society, and most ordinary people were very sparsely documented. Information about such people's lives does exist, but it occurs in records created for quite other purposes, such as land transfer or trials.

Medieval records are generally much more difficult to use than those from the sixteenth century and later. They are usually in a highly abbreviated form of Latin. English starts to become more common in informal documents in the late fifteenth century, but Latin was used in formal records until 1733 (except during the Interregnum). The handwriting and letter-forms are very different from those of the present day alphabet. The use of surnames was general by about 1300, but there was no consistency in spelling. Surnames were not always used, nor always passed from parent to child. Different surnames could be used in different contexts. Even a fairly distinctive surname may be difficult to trace and may offer little guidance on family relationships.

Two invaluable books for tackling the problems presented by the language, palaeography (handwriting) and diplomatic (the form of documents) of medieval records are *Latin for Local History*, by Gooder and *Latin for Local and Family Historians: A Beginner's Guide*, by Stuart (see **5.5**). Two useful, but inexpensive, guides to working with these records are *Examples of Handwriting 1550–1650* by Buck and *Simple Latin for Family Historians*, by McLaughlin. A useful tip, if you have a Latin document that you cannot understand, is to look at a similar document from the 1650s, when they were all in English. As so much of a formal document is common form, you may be able to use the English version to identify the whereabouts on the parchment of the crucial unique pieces of the Latin text that you need to concentrate on.

One further obstacle exists. Many of the surviving records come from the Exchequer, Chancery and the law courts, or relate to land law: to fully understand them, you do need to be prepared to do some reading. Try *A Guide to English Historical Records*, by Macfarlane; and *English Local Administration in the Middle Ages*, by Jewell.

5.2 Possibilities

Many of the most important medieval records have been published, or have detailed lists and indexes, and it is best to start with these: it is possible to go a long way using published works. Most of these are available in the PRO. Records for a particular county, which have been published by a county records society, can be seen in the Library, whereas those which cover the whole country are in the Map and Large Document Room.

Because so many medieval documents are large, the Map and Large Document Room has become the best place to use if you are looking at early records. Ask at the desk if you need advice: there should be someone with medieval knowledge available to give you general guidance. They will not be able to translate for you, nor to read documents on your behalf, although they can help with the odd word or two. You would need to employ an independent researcher if you find you cannot cope with the original documents.

Possible sources for genealogical information fall into two kinds: those where information is arranged or has been indexed by name, and those where the arrangement is by place. Where you start depends on what you know already. You may have to look at all kinds of records, as there are none which are obviously genealogical.

5.3 Records searchable by name

Wills are one of the most useful of the sources accessible by name, often giving considerable family detail. The PRO has medieval and early modern wills proved in the Prerogative Court of Canterbury, from 1383. They are those of wealthy men, unmarried women and widows dying in the south of England or abroad. For more information, see **6**.

Inquisitions post mortem are another fruitful source for people of some social status, and give the name and age of the next heir on the death of a landowner. They continue up to the 1640s. Many have been published by local record societies, as well as in the *Calendars of Inquisitions Post Mortem*: see **41.7** and **41.11** for more detail.

Up until the late 1500s, it is easy to check documents issued from, or inspected in, the royal Chancery and recorded on parchment rolls, as most have been published and indexed. Although largely concerned with people of sufficient status to have direct dealings with central government, they do contain many references to other people as well. The most important are the Patent Rolls (C 66) which contain, for example, grants of land, licences to alienate property held by tenure in chief, and grants of wardship; the Close Rolls (C 54) which record, amongst other things, enrolments of private deeds and other useful information such as writs of livery and seisin; the Fine Rolls (C 60), which include grants of wardship and marriage and writs of livery of seisin; and the Charter Rolls (C 53) which contain grants of property in the presence of witnesses. Details of the calendars are given in **5.5**. The Patent and Close Rolls continue into the twentieth century, but after the late and early 1500s, respectively, have not been published.

The registers of the King's (Privy) Council (not all of which are in the PRO) have also been published and indexed. Because it is easy to do, it may be worth checking these if you have a person you wish to know more about. The medieval council registers have been published as *Privy Council Proceedings, 1386–1542*. The registers of the later Privy Council have been published as *Acts of the Privy Council of England, 1542–1631*. They continue after 1631, but have not been published. There is no guarantee that a person came to the attention of the council, but you may find something of interest.

Other possible sources that are easy to use, and may perhaps contain something of interest, start in the early sixteenth century and continue till the mid eighteenth century. From 1509, large numbers of letters and papers survive relating to the government of the country, known as the State Papers, Domestic. These have been published (in brief) as *Letters and Papers . . . of Henry VIII*, and the *Calendar of State Papers, Domestic, 1547–1704,* and are very well indexed. It may be worth checking the indexes on the off chance that someone you are researching is mentioned. There are similar series for Scotland, Ireland, and for colonial and foreign affairs: see **5.5**. You may also wish to look among the records of the economic life of the nation, in the various series of *Calendars of Treasury Books and Papers, 1557–1745*, which are also well indexed.

Apart from those deeds enrolled on the Close Rolls, the PRO has deeds which came into the crown's hands when it acquired property through purchase, forfeiture or other forms of escheat, or were produced as evidence in law suits. Some of the PRO's extensive holdings of medieval deeds have been calendared and indexed, but there is no cumulative index, and it can be a lengthy job to look through all the lists (see **41.4**).

Law suits can be very informative, particularly the proceedings by English bill in the Courts of Chancery, Exchequer, Requests and Star Chamber. These are written in English: there are a very few indexes, but you may have to look through lists *at length*. Things will get much easier when these finding-aids have been computerized. Some of the records of these courts are partly indexed by the Bernau Index, at the Society of Genealogists. Chancery, from c.1380, tends to cover disputes over wills, marriage settlements, landed estates and other matters. Exchequer, from c.1558, has a bias towards economic disputes – manorial customs, mills, weirs, common lands, etc. It seems also to have taken over disputes about land sold at the Dissolution of the Monasteries from the Court of Augmentations, which has its own set of fascinating cases. For 'poor men's causes', try the records of the Court of Requests, from c.1485–1642. These contain cases concerning the title and ownership of property, dower, and jointure and marriage contracts, allegedly of poor men against mighty suitors. The Court of Star Chamber, c.1485–1641, was concerned with the enforcement of law and order. There are many cases about the goods of suicides. For more information on using the records of these courts, and of the less informative common law courts, see **47**.

5.4 Records searchable by place

To use the other types of records, those arranged by place, you need to have some idea of where your ancestors lived. If you have this, then it is possible to trace fairly humble people through manorial records. These were the records kept by or on behalf of the lords of manors, who acted both as agrarian landlords and as local judicial and administrative authorities. Manor court rolls recorded, amongst other things, land transactions within the manor, minor lawsuits between tenants, and minor breaches of the peace. It is sometimes possible to trace the inheritance of a peasant back through several generations. Rentals and surveys also name the tenants of the manor and describe their individual holdings. Ministers' and receivers' accounts were the accounts rendered by officials responsible for the revenues of manors and other estates. Like rentals and surveys, they also include the names of tenants. The PRO holds a considerable number of manorial documents, mostly from those manors which formed part of the crown lands. For further details about these documents see **41.2**, **41.5** and **41.6**.

Many manorial documents are held in archives outside the PRO: to discover whether there are any surviving records for a particular manor, contact the National Register of Archives (address in **48**).

The feet of fines (CP 25/1–CP 25/2) are the records of fictitious law suits entered into to evade conveyancing restrictions, and they run from 1190 to 1833 (see **41.3**). A foot of fine was the bottom copy of a series of three or more copies of a final agreement between two parties. Until the fourteenth century, those made in the central common law court appear in the records of the Court of Common Pleas and Court of King's Bench. From then on, they were made in the Court of Common Pleas only.

Other fines can be found in the palatinate jurisdictions. The fines are arranged by county. Many have been published by local record societies.

Muster rolls can be a valuable source of information, recording the names of able-bodied men liable for service in the militia. They do not list all men, only those between the ages of 16 and 60 years of age. Their principal value lies in the fact that they can establish the parish of a named male. In some cases it is possible from the valuation made of a man's lands and goods, to gain an indication of the status of the family. Unfortunately, there is no separate list of muster rolls which can be found in many different classes in the PRO, as well as elsewhere. You will need to look at Gibson and Dell, *Tudor and Stuart Muster Rolls*.

Taxation records can also be useful in tracing rich and poor, although the very poor were usually exempt. The class of Subsidy Rolls (E 179) includes the surviving assessments and returns made for many different taxes from the twelfth to the seventeenth century. The best known are probably the hearth tax returns which cover the years 1662–1674, providing the name of the householder and number of hearths for which he was responsible. There are even exemption certificates for paupers. There are records of many other taxes which can also be extremely useful. The terms of each tax are given in Jurkowski, Smith and Crook, *Lay Taxes in England and Wales, 1188–1688*.

The 1332 subsidy, for example, was the first for which assessments survive on any scale, although its catchment was primarily confined to prosperous householders. The poll tax returns of 1378–1380, which theoretically covered all male adults except the itinerant and the very poor, often give occupations and the relationships between members of the household. The subsidies of 1532–1535, again covered extensively the householders of middling and higher status. The lists are arranged by county, and the description of each document indicates the area covered (often by hundred or wapentake rather than parish or manor) and whether or not the names of assessed individuals are given (see **43**).

There are many pedigrees on the Early Plea and Essoin Rolls (KB 26), the *Coram Rege* Rolls (KB 27) and the *De Banco* Rolls (CP 40): see Wrottesley, *Pedigrees from the Plea Rolls*. You may also find useful the copious extracts, mainly from the *De Banco* Rolls and similar legal records, made by General Plantagenet-Harrison in the late nineteenth century. There are several volumes, all handwritten with indexes, which are on the whole reliable (now PRO 66/3). His main interests were in Yorkshire, and in all pedigrees, but you should be cautious in trusting to the accuracy of the latter.

5.5 Medieval and early modern sources for family history: bibliography

Published works: records
Acts of the Privy Council of England, 1542–1631 (London, 1890–1964)
Calendar of Charter Rolls, 1226–1516 (London, 1903–1927)
Calendar of Close Rolls, 1227–1509 (London, 1892–1963)
Calendar of Fine Rolls, 1272–1509 (London, 1911–1963)
Calendar of Patent Rolls, 1216–1509, 1547–1582 (London, 1891–1986) (for 1509–1547, see *Letters and Papers . . . of Henry VIII*) [The series is being continued in typescript drafts by the List and Index Society.]
Calendar of Inquisitions Miscellaneous, Henry III to Henry VII (London, 1916–1968)
Calendar of Inquisitions Post Mortem, Henry III to Henry IV, and Henry VII (London, 1898–1989)
Calendar of State Papers, Colonial, 1513–1738 (London, 1860–1969)
Calendar of State Papers, Domestic, 1547–1704 (London, 1856–1998)
Calendar of State Papers, Foreign, 1558–1589 (London, 1858–1950)
Calendar of State Papers, Ireland, 1509–1670 (London, 1875–1910)
Calendar of State Papers relating to Scotland, 1547–1603 (London, 1898–1969)

Calendar of Treasury Books, 1660–1718 (London, 1904–1961)
Calendar of Treasury Papers, 1557–1728 (London, 1868–1889)
Calendar of Treasury Books and Papers, 1729–1745 (London, 1898–1903)
Descriptive Catalogue of Ancient Deeds preserved in the Public Record Office (London, 1890–1915)
Inquisitions Post Mortem, Henry V–Richard III (List and Index Society, vol. 268–269, 1998)
Journals of the Board of Trade and Plantations, 1704–1782 (London, 1920–1938)
Letters and Papers . . . of Henry VIII (London, 1864–1932)
Privy Council Proceedings, 1386–1542 (London, 1834–1837)

Published works: guides

W S B Buck, *Examples of Handwriting 1550–1650* (Society of Genealogists, 1996)
A J Camp, *My Ancestor came with the Conqueror* (Society of Genealogists, 1988)
M Ellis, *Using Manorial Records* (PRO, 1997)
P Franklin, *Some Medieval Records for Family Historians* (FFHS, 1994)
R E F Garrett, *Chancery and other Legal Proceedings* (Shalfleet Manor, 1968)
J Gibson and A Dell, *Tudor and Stuart Muster Rolls* (FFHS, 1991)
E A Gooder, *Latin for Local History* (London, 2nd edn, 1978)
J Guy, *The Court of Star Chamber and its Records to the reign of Elizabeth I* (PRO, 1985)
R W Hoyle, *Tudor Taxation Records: A Guide for Users* (PRO, 1994)
H M Jewell, *English Local Administration in the Middle Ages* (David & Charles, 1972)
M Jurkowski, C Smith and D Crook, *Lay Taxes in England and Wales, 1188–1688* (PRO, 1998)
A Macfarlane, *A Guide to English Historical Records* (Cambridge, 1983)
E McLaughlin, *Simple Latin for Family Historians* (FFHS, rev. edn, 1991)
J Morris, *A Latin Glossary for Family and Local Historians* (FFHS, 1989)
P B Park, *My Ancestors were Manorial Tenants* (Society of Genealogists, 1994)
J F Preston and L Yeandle, *English Handwriting 1400–1650* (Binghamton, USA, 1992)
D. Stuart, *Latin for Local and Family Historians: A Beginner's Guide* (London, 1995)
J Titford, 'Pre-Parish Register Genealogy: English Sources in the Public Record Office', in K A Johnson and M R Sainty, eds *Genealogical Research Directory 1998* (Sydney, 1998)
G Wrottesley, *Pedigrees from the Plea Rolls, 1200–1500* (London, c.1906)
M L Zell, 'Fifteenth and Sixteenth Century Wills as Historical Sources', *Archives*, vol. XIV (1979), pp. 75–80

6 Inheritance: death duties, wills, administrations and disputes

6.1 Starting point, 1796-1903: death duty registers

The first place to look for wills and administrations between 1796 and 1858 are the death duty registers and their indexes, in IR 26 and IR 27. These are not arranged by date of death, but by date of probate or issue of the grant of administration. The indexes in IR 27 will tell you where the will was proved (judged valid) or the administration issued (when there was no valid will). This is a very helpful short cut to finding the actual will or administration, as there were very many probate courts before 1858. However, not all wills and administrations appear in the indexes, as not all estates were subject to the death duties.

The registers (IR 26) between 1796 and 1903 are also very useful for family historians, because they include information not found elsewhere. There is no such information available after 1903, as the Inland Revenue switched from using registers to individual files, which were destroyed after 30 years.

All the indexes in IR 27 can be seen on microfilm at both the FRC and Kew, as can the main series of registers in IR 26, for 1796–1857. However, the registers from 1858–1903 are stored off site. They are seen at Kew, but only on three working days' notice, so you may need to telephone in advance with the references. Many of the registers for the 1890s were destroyed by fire.

From 1796, legacy, estate and succession duty (death duties) were payable on many estates over a certain value, which itself changed over time. As the scope of estate duty was extended throughout the nineteenth century, so more people were included. Before 1805, the registers cover about a quarter of all estates: by 1857, there should be an entry for all estates except those worth less than £20. However, unless the assets were valued at £1,500 or more, the taxes were often not collected, and so the register entry was not filled in with all the details. Tax was payable on bequests to people outside a closely defined family circle (whittled down from offspring, spouse, parents and grandparents in 1796, to spouse and parents in 1805, and to spouse only in 1815).

The registers give different information than the wills (and much better information than administrations). In particular they will show what actually happened to a person's estate after death (rather than what they hoped would happen), and what it was actually worth, excluding debts and expenses. They can also give the date of death, and information about the people who received bequests (beneficiaries), or who were the next of kin, such as exact relationship to the deceased. Because the registers could be annotated for up to fifty years after the first entry, they can include a wealth of additional information such as dates of death of spouse; dates of death or marriage of beneficiaries; births of posthumous children; change of address; references to law suits in Chancery delaying the settling of the estate, etc.

The register entries use a lot of abbreviations: a leaflet is available at Kew and the FRC which explains them. For more information see the Introductory Notes to IR 26 and IR 27. For the procedure involved, see *Ham's Inland Revenue Yearbook*, which gives contemporary instructions. The PRO Library has copies of this annual work (under slightly varying titles) from 1875 to 1930.

At the FRC there is a card index (to IR 26/287–IR 26/321), and a typescript index (to IR 26/322–344 and IR 26/398–399), covering wills proved and administrations granted in the consistory courts of Bangor, Bath and Wells, Bristol, Canterbury, Carlisle, Chester, Chichester, Durham, Ely, Exeter, and Oxford, and lesser courts within those dioceses, for 1796–1811.

Copy wills were also once among the death duty records: these have largely been destroyed. Those for Cornwall, Devon and Somerset (from the major local probate courts) were sent to the respective record offices, to try to fill some of the gap caused by the loss of local probate records from those counties by enemy action. Those for Somerset have been indexed by Hawkings: the indexes can be seen at the FRC.

6.2 Wills as sources for family history

Wills are among the best sources for family history, particularly before the civil registration of births, marriages and deaths started in 1837. Not everybody left a will. Poor people had very little to bequeath. Others may have been sufficiently well off, but not had the control of any property – for example, most wives during the life of their husbands, before 1882. The estates of the more prosperous of those who died intestate (not leaving a valid will) were subject to letters of administration, granted through the same court as would have proved a will: the general information discussed below is the same for wills or administrations. As a rough estimate, for every three searchers looking for a will, one will be looking for letters of administration.

There is no national union index to wills or administrations, which are to be found in many record offices. However, the quality of the information you can gain from a will is often so high that it is well worth the effort of searching. It has been estimated that every will names about ten other people. If you can, try to look for wills of friends or relatives as well. You may find references to your person, to help build up a rounded view of the circle of kinship, friendship and business contacts that made up your ancestor's social world.

When you find and look through a will, you may get the impression that you are reading, in your ancestor's own words, about his faith or his different levels of affection for different members of the family. This may be a false impression. Wills were often written in formulaic language by clerks or lawyers. Nevertheless, they did express the wishes of the testator (the person leaving the will). For example, any declaration of faith is likely to have been one acceptable to the testator, even if not in his own words.

The evidence found in a will needs to be interpreted with caution. Firstly, descriptions of family relationships may be misunderstood by us. Thus the terms *father*, *brother* and *son*, *mother*, *sister* and *daughter* may be used to refer to in-laws as well as blood relatives. The term *cousin* was used for all types of kin. Secondly, the will might make no mention of real estate. Certain types of real estate, depending upon the terms of tenure, could be left by will after 1540; from 1660 the only exception to this is land held by copyhold, which was not devisable by will until 1815. Nevertheless, if an eldest son was to inherit the real estate as his father's heir-at-law, his father's will did not need to mention him or his inheritance. Similarly, married daughters may not be mentioned if they had had property settled upon them at the time of their marriages. The failure to leave a bequest to a near relative does not necessarily mean bad feeling. On the other hand, it may be wrong to assume that all legatees would be still alive at the time probate was granted, or that the testator necessarily left sufficient means to cover all bequests.

Before the establishment of the national (English and Welsh) Court of Probate in 1858, wills were proved in church courts, and some other courts with probate jurisdiction, such as manor courts (see **6.22**). The surviving records are now deposited in many different record offices, but the Public Record Office holds the records of the most important, the Prerogative Court of Canterbury. Because wills can be found in so many places, this chapter cannot be a full guide to the subject. For the most recent overview, read Herber, *Ancestral Trails*, Chapter 12. This gives an excellent explanation of the varying laws, customs and legal practices governing inheritance, and thus how wills were not an expression of a free choice as to the disposal of property. It also gives guidance on how to find the will and understand what it says. As with all evidence from the past, the more you know about the context in which a document was made, the less likely you are to misunderstand it.

Once you get to the PRO, especially if you are looking at medieval or early modern wills, you are strongly advised to read the Introductory Note to the PROB 11 class list for a clear and brief explanation of the law of property, the restrictions on what could be devised by will, and how people invented different ways of getting round the letter of the law in order to protect their estates from the crown's feudal rights, or to provide for younger sons, etc. Doing this may give you a completely different understanding of a will. All the Introductory Notes to the other PROB classes will also repay reading, if you find yourself using those records.

6.3 Wills and administrations after 1858

Wills proved from 12 January 1858 to the present day were proved (judged to be an accurate representation of the deceased lawful intentions) before the Court of Probate. From 1875, this has been part of the Supreme Court, under various titles. Wills may be read (for a small fee) at the Probate Searchroom in central London (address in **48**) between 10.00 a.m. and 4.30 p.m., Monday to Friday. The same applies to letters of administration, which may be granted if no valid will was made or could be found. Copies of wills and probate and administration grants are obtainable either in person or by post, provided you know the date of death. Applications should be addressed to the Court Service, York Probate Sub-Registry, Duncombe Place, York YO1 2EA. A handling charge is payable in addition to the copying charge.

However, microfiche copies of the indexes to these wills, for 1858–1943, can also be seen at the PRO, the FRC (PRO), and the Guildhall. The Society of Genealogists has microfilm copies. These indexes can be very informative, and can provide the date of death.

If you want to know more about the actual procedure involved in getting a grant of probate or letters of administration, look at *Ham's Inland Revenue Yearbook*, which gives contemporary instructions. The PRO library has copies of this annual work (under slightly varying titles) from 1875–1930.

6.4 Wills and administrations before 1858: in many record offices

Before 1858, a will was usually proved by one of the many church courts, whose records are usually held locally. The PRO holds the records of only one of them, the Prerogative Court of Canterbury (which was actually located at Doctors' Commons, in London, for most of its history). It can be quite a problem to find out which was the relevant court. For 1796 onwards, the death duty indexes provide this information in many cases: see **6.1**.

If the deceased held property in one archdeaconry the will would be proved (or letters of administration granted, if there was no will) in the archdeacon's court; if in more than one archdeaconry but within one diocese, in the bishop's diocesan court. However, if the deceased held personal property worth over £5 in two distinct dioceses or jurisdictions, then the estate was subject to the archbishop's provincial court, known as the Prerogative Court of York (PCY) or the Prerogative Court of Canterbury (PCC). The province of York covered Yorkshire, Durham, Northumberland, Westmorland, Cumberland, Lancashire, Cheshire, Nottinghamshire and the Isle of Man: Canterbury covered the rest of England and Wales. If the deceased held property in both provinces, then the will was proved in both the PCY and the PCC.

Records of the Prerogative Court of York are held at the Borthwick Institute of Historical Research in York. The surviving records of other courts with probate jurisdictions are deposited in local record offices. To find out where they are, try Gibson, *A Simplified Guide to Probate Jurisdictions*. From 1796 to 1858, the name of the relevant court is often given in the indexes to the death duty registers: see **6.1**. It may be well worth checking the PRO Library to see if the wills, or indexes to the wills, of these more local courts have been published by one of the many record societies. A check in *Will indexes and other probate material in the Library of the Society of Genealogists*, by Newington-Irving, can also save valuable time.

With the English Civil War, the situation grew complicated, as there were two rival PCC's, one with the King at Oxford, and one in London. If you are looking for a will which fell in the PCC's jurisdiction in the 1640s, read the advice in the PROB 11 Introductory Note (filed before the class list at Kew and the FRC). Between 1653 and 1660 almost all probate jurisdiction for England and Wales was administered by a single Court for the Proving of Wills and Granting Administrations. Its records are in unbroken series with those of the Prerogative Court of Canterbury, at the PRO: they are very well indexed, by place and occupation as well as by name.

If someone (subject or foreign) died overseas leaving property in England and Wales (including Bank of England stock or stock in one of the great companies such as the East India Company), then all the usual rules were ignored, and the will was proved at the PCC.

6.5 PCC: whose wills or administrations?

Although the PCC records relate mainly to the testamentary affairs of the wealthier sections of society in the province of Canterbury, the great prestige of the court attracted business to it that strictly speaking belonged to lower courts. As time went on, the declining value of money meant that the £5 barrier became less of a restriction, and in the eighteenth and nineteenth centuries the property of more and more people's estates came within its jurisdiction. From 1810, the Bank of England would not accept probate from any court except the PCC, for holders of Bank of England stock.

The largest number of people affected by the 'dying overseas' rule were poor seamen. This brought into the PCC a large number of wills of seamen of slight value, until 1815, when the affairs of seamen dying with less than £20 wages owing were directed to local church courts. Many Americans continued to hold property in England, and have their wills proved in the PCC: see Coldham's *American Wills and Administrations in the Prerogative Court of Canterbury, 1610–1857.*

However, as in all courts of probate before the Married Women's Property Act of 1882, it is rare to find wills made by married women, as their property was until then deemed to belong to their husbands. Wills by widows and spinsters exist in quantity.

6.6 PCC wills and administrations at the FRC, and at Kew

The PRO holds the records created or collected by the Prerogative Court of Canterbury, 1383–1858, including the wills of the Court for the Proving of Wills and Granting Administrations, 1653–1660. Administrations issued by the PCC date from 1559 to 1858. Copies of the main classes (PROB 11, some of PROB 12, and PROB 6) can be seen, usually on microfilm, at the FRC (PRO) as well as at Kew: all the other classes mentioned below have to be seen at Kew. In some cases, if the registered copy of the will in PROB 11 does not give information about marital status, occupation, or place of residence, it may be found in the probate act books, in PROB 8, at Kew.

Scott's *Prerogative Court of Canterbury: Wills and Other Probate Records* is a practical introduction to the wealth of the PCC records, and contains fuller information than can be included here. It includes samples of documents, and specific guidance on using particular finding aids.

6.7 Finding a will in the PCC: indexes, etc., 1383–1858

All the wills in the PCC are covered by personal name indexes. However there is no single union index. Instead there is a wide variety of different personal name indexes. Because many of these indexes have been compiled from the sometimes faulty contemporary 'calendars' (in PROB 12, PROB 13 and PROB 15), there are not guaranteed to be 100 per cent accurate. Several have one or more supplementary indexes, to place names, occupations and conditions, names of persons other than testators such as executors, and ships' names. The majority of them were compiled before the will registers were transferred to the PRO, and therefore do not use PRO references.

To find a will, you need to check one of the many indexes, in different formats for different periods. More detailed practical instructions on using the indexes are available in the reading rooms at the FRC and Kew. In addition, the lists of PROB 11 and PROB 12 have scholarly Introductory Notes if you want to investigate them in more depth.

Some of the indexes shown below cover both wills and administrations.

Indexes to wills

1383–1700	published indexes, in several date sequences
1701–1749	index compiled by the Friends of the PRO
1750–1800	index compiled by the Society of Genealogists
1801–1852	annual 'calendars' in PROB 12
1853–1858	two alphabetised 'calendars' in PROB 12

Most of these indexes are published works, and may be available locally: see **6.23** for a table identifying the full titles against the date range and volumes covered.

6.8 Understanding and using the will indexes and will registers

Will registers in PROB 11 bear a name before 1841: the same name was also applied to those calendars now in the classes PROB 12, PROB 13, and PROB 15 which cover single years, and therefore correspond to specific will registers. The earliest will registers in PROB 11 generally cover several years and consist of only one volume. By the end of the sixteenth century the practice of confining each register to the wills and sentences registered in a single year had been established, and (with the growth in the Court's business) registers came to be made up of more than one volume. With the passage of time the number of volumes in a register increased, and by the mid nineteenth century a single register might consist of twenty volumes.

Many of the indexes at the PRO, and older published sources, give you a reference based on the old register name. For example, looking for John Small in the index for 1649 gives the reference 64 Fairfax. This is composed of the name of the register and an internal quire number. You can convert the register name to a PROB 11 reference by looking at the PROB 11 list. You then have to identify the quire while looking at the register on microfilm.

These will registers each use a traditional numbering system, by quire instead of by page or folio. A quire consists of eight folios (i.e. sixteen pages). The quire number is *written* in roman or arabic numbers on the top left hand corner of the first page of the quire, and can be seen on the microfilm quite easily. An index entry is to the quire, and so may be to any of 16 pages within that particular quire: you just have to look through, using the details in the margin, to find the right will. When you have found it, take a note of the *stamped* folio number on the top of each right hand page. You will need this when using the self-service copiers. You can use either the quire number or the folio number to cite the document, but the folio number is more precise. Looking for John Small's will meant turning Fairfax into PROB 11/208, and quire 64 into folio 53.

6.9 Proving a will in the PCC

When a will was proved before the PCC, a copy of the will was made. A probate act (a commission, in the name of the Archbishop of Canterbury) was issued, and attached by a seal to the copy will. These were then given to the executor as his authority to carry out the distribution of the estate, according to the terms of the will.

The issue of the probate act was recorded in the probate act book (now in PROB 8 and PROB 9). The original will was filed by the registry, and if it survives, is in PROB 10. If the executor paid a fee, a copy of the will would also be made in the Court's will registers, with a clause noting the granting of probate entered after the will (now PROB 11). The vast majority of wills proved before the Prerogative Court of Canterbury were registered.

Nuncupative wills (wills which were spoken before witnesses, not written down and signed) are in PROB 11, if registered. They usually start like this:

> Memorandum that Anne Marshall of Bisham in the Countye of Berks Spinster beinge of good and perfecte mynde and memorie made her last will and Testament nuncupative in theis wordes followinge or the like effect
>
> PROB 11/135, fo. 266v

Nuncupative wills are also identified as nuncupative in their probate clauses, and sometimes in the entries in the calendars of wills in PROB 12, PROB 13, and PROB 15.

The texts of almost all wills proved were copied into large parchment registers, now seen on microfilm (PROB 11). The vast majority are in English; by the sixteenth century wills written in Latin are rare. Wills written in other modern European languages (usually Dutch and French), have an authenticated English translation. However the probate clauses appended to the text of the wills, and the texts of sentences (judgements), are in Latin until 1733, with the exception of those in registers for 1651 to 1660 which are in English. They generally follow a standard form, so this example should help you to make sense of others.

Probate clause of the will of William Christie
(PROB 11/572, fo.212v)

Probatum fuit hujusmodi Testamentum apud London coram Venerabili viro Roberto Wood Legum Doctore Surrogato Venerabilis et Egregij viri Johannis Bettesworth Legum etiam Doctoris Curiae Praerogativae Cantuariensis Magistri Custodis sive Commissarij legitime constituti Vicesimo Secundo die Mensis Februarij Anno Domini Millesimo Septingentesimo Decimo nono Juramento Thomae Willisee Executoris unici in dicto Testamento nominati Cui commissa fuit Administratio omnium et Singulorum bonorum jurium et creditorum dicti defuncti De bene et fideliter administrando eadem ad Sancta Dei Evangelia Jurato. Examinatur.

English translation

This will was proved at London before the worshipful Robert Wood LL.D [Doctor of Laws] surrogate of the worshipful and wise John Bettesworth also LL.D Master Keeper or Commissary of the Prerogative Court of Canterbury lawfully constituted on the twenty-second day of the month of February 1719 [/20] by the oath of Thomas Willisee named sole executor in the said will to whom administration of all and singular the goods rights and credits of the said deceased was granted being sworn on the holy gospels to administer the same well and faithfully. Examined.

6.10 Complications with executors: grants of administration with will annexed

If the executor appointed in the will was unable or unwilling to prove the will, letters of administration with will annexed were issued instead. This is noted in the probate clause, after the text of the will in PROB 11.

If the executor died, or renounced the administration of the estate before its distribution had been completed, letters of administration with will annexed *de bonis non administratis* (of goods not administered) were issued. This is noted in the margin of the register, alongside the text of the will.

If more than one executor was appointed, and the executors sought probate at different dates, a subsequent grant of probate was made. This is also noted in the margin.

Such marginal annotations can be highly abbreviated; often they are not as informative as the corresponding entries in the probate act books (PROB 8, PROB 9). Probate acts, letters of administration with will annexed, and letters of administration with will annexed *de bonis non administratis* are described in the Introductory Note to the PROB 8 list.

Administration acts with will annexed are entered in the probate act books (PROB 8, PROB 9), and the wills are registered in the will registers (PROB 11). Administrators with will annexed were required to enter into bonds for their proper administration of the estate, and such bonds are in the administration bond classes (PROB 51, PROB 54, PROB 46).

6.11 PCC original and other wills

So-called original wills are in PROB 10, stored off site. They take three days to be produced to Kew, so you will need to order them in advance. Original wills survive in almost complete sequence from 1620; before that date an 'original will' may in fact be a facsimile copy made by the court. There is usually no advantage in looking at the original if there is a registered copy in PROB 11.

Wills of some famous people were extracted from the original wills now in PROB 10, and

<table>
<tr><td colspan="3">Grant of administratio de bonis non administratis
(grant of administration of goods unadministered)
PROB 6/96, f 97^v</td></tr>
</table>

| *Elizabetha Carleton* | *Decimo Sexto die Em<u>ana</u>vit Com<u>missi</u>o Johanni Heskew Marito l<u>egi</u>timo et Adm<u>ini</u>stratori bonor<u>um</u> &c [jurium et creditorum] Elizabethae Heskew dum vixit filiae n<u>atu</u>ralis et l<u>egi</u>timae Eliz<u>abe</u>thae Carleton nup<u>er</u> par<u>o</u>ch<u>ia</u>e Sanc<u>t</u>ae Mariae Magdalenae Bermondsey in Com<u>itatu</u> Surriae def<u>unc</u>tae h<u>a</u>bentis &c <u>[dum vixit et mortis suae tempore bona jura sive credita in diversis diocesibus sive peculiaribus jurisdictionibus sufficientia ad fundandum jurisdictionem Curiae Praerogativae Cantuariensis]</u> ad Adm<u>ini</u>strandum bona jura et credita d<u>i</u>c<u>t</u>ae def<u>unc</u>tae p<u>er</u> Eliz<u>abe</u>tham Heskew modo etiam demortuam inadm<u>ini</u>strata De bene &c <u>[et fideliter administrando eadem ad sancta Dei evangelia]</u> jurato* | *ul<u>timus</u> [dies] Nov<u>embris</u>*

 ul<u>timus</u> [dies] Maij 1721 |
| Elizabeth Carleton | On the seventeenth day a commission was issued to John Heskew lawful husband and administrator of the goods etc [rights and credits] of Elizabeth Heskew while she lived natural and legitimate daughter of Elizabeth Carleton formerly of the parish of St Mary Magdalen Bermondsey in the county of Surrey deceased having etc [while she lived and at the time of her death goods rights or credits in different dioceses or peculiar jurisdictions sufficient to found the jurisdiction of the Prerogative Court of Canterbury] to administer the goods rights and credits of the said deceased not administered by the said Elizabeth Heskew now also deceased having been sworn [on the holy gospels] to well and [faithfully administer the same] | last [day] of November

 last [day] of May 1721 |

- Letters omitted from the original texts on account of abbreviation have been supplied underlined. Words omitted from the original have been supplied underlined in square brackets.
- The first date in the right hand margin is the date by which the administrator was required to return an inventory of the intestate's personal estate. The second date is the date by which the administrator was required to return an account of his or her administration of the estate.

placed in PROB 1. Some supplementary series of wills, usually copies or rejected wills, may be found in PROB 20–PROB 23.

Not all wills were registered in PROB 11. Between 1383 and 1558 unregistered wills (now in PROB 10) are indicated in the index by the letter F. Genuine cases of unregistered wills, particularly after 1660, are very rare. If a calendar or an index compiled from a calendar does not supply a quire number alongside the name of a testator, it is sometimes assumed that the will was not registered and that therefore there is no copy of the will in PROB 11. However, in the majority of these cases, the registered text of the will can be found in the will register by searching in the quires where the wills of other testators whose surnames began with the same initial letter and whose wills were proved in the same months were registered. In many other cases where no quire number is supplied, the entire entry in the calendar will be found to be a clerical error.

Probate copies of wills, as handed over to the executors, often turn up as evidence in legal disputes. The exhibits classes of C 103–C 114 and J 90 are full of them. The easiest way to find them may be to use the ILDB, once all the lists have been input.

6.12 Abstracts and other finding aids to PCC wills

In addition to the indexes and finding aids discussed above, and listed in detail in **6.23**, a large number of other indexes, finding aids, abstracts and editions of Prerogative Court of Canterbury and other wills and sentences registered in PROB 11 have been compiled. Some of them have been published, others deposited in such places as the Society of Genealogists' library. They have been compiled on varying principles to different types of wills, including those proved in particular periods of time, those relating to holders of certain surnames, those relating to particular counties or other geographical areas, and those of certain professions and occupations. The last two categories can be most useful to local and social historians.

Mention should also be made of four publications, each covering a single year, which abstract and/or index (by personal names, and in some cases by place names and occupations) all the wills registered in four particular years: 1620, 1630, 1658 and 1750.

PROB 11/135–136	J H Lea, *Abstract of wills in the Prerogative Court of Canterbury: Register Soame 1620* (Boston, Mass., 1904). A copy can be seen at the FRC, but not at Kew.
PROB 11/157–158	J H Morrison, *Prerogative Court of Canterbury: Register Scroope (1630)* (London, 1934). A copy can be seen at the FRC, but not at Kew.
PROB 11/272–285	William Brigg, *Genealogical abstracts of wills proved in the Prerogative Court of Canterbury: Register Wootton 1658*, 7 volumes (Leeds, 1894–1914). A copy can be seen at the FRC, but not at Kew.
PROB 11/776–784	George Sherwood, *A list of persons named in the PCC wills proved in the year 1750: Register Greenly (4,382 wills naming 40,320 persons arranged in eight groups topographically).* (London, privately published, 1918). There is a copy in the library of the Society of Genealogists, but not at the FRC or Kew.

There is no published list of all the different indexes, finding aids, abstracts and editions that have been produced. However, many of them are listed in Camp, *Wills and their whereabouts*, and in Gibson's *A Simplified Guide to Probate jurisdictions: where to look for wills*.

6.13 Grants of administration: intestates' estates, 1559-1858

Intestacy is the state of dying without leaving a valid will. The PCC would grant letters of administration to persons with a claim on an intestate's estate, where the estate came within the jurisdiction of the Court. Probate courts were required to grant administration of the estate to the deceased's widow or next of kin. Administration of the estate of a married woman was granted to her husband. The estates of illegitimate intestates who died unmarried and without issue were granted to the crown.

Grants of administration were registered in the administration act books (PROB 6). These are divided into 'seats' reflecting the clerical organisation of the PCC. The system of seats is explained in **6.15**.

The act book ordinarily records only the marital status and place of residence of the intestate, the name of the administrator and his or her relationship to the intestate, and the date of the grant. From 1796, and in many cases before that date, a valuation of the deceased's personal estate is given in the margin. The court was required to grant administration to the deceased's next of kin, and the entry in the administration act book may therefore include the names of relatives who had ignored summonses to appear before the court, or who had renounced their claims to administer the estate. Be wary of assuming that a known relative (closer in blood than the person to whom administration was granted) had died by the time the grant was made, merely because the known relative is not mentioned in the administration act book.

The information that the administration act books usually supply is as follows: the date of the grant of administration, the name of the intestate, his or her parish of residence, the name of the administrator and his or her relationship to the intestate, and the dates by which an inventory and an account had to be returned. The administration act books may also give information about the marital status, occupations, and places of death of the intestates. Information about intestates' occupations and places of residence becomes fuller with the passage of time, and by the nineteenth century administration act books often supply such additional details as the names of regiments in which the intestates were serving, or the names of streets in which they were living at the times of their deaths.

6.14 Finding an administration grant

All the administrations in the PCC are covered by personal name indexes. However there is no single union index. Instead there is a wide variety of different personal name indexes. Because many of these indexes have been compiled from the sometimes faulty contemporary 'calendars' they are not guaranteed to be 100 per cent accurate. The majority of them do not use PRO references.

To find an administration, you will need to check one of the many indexes, in different formats for different periods. More detailed practical instructions on using the indexes are available in the reading rooms at the FRC and Kew. In addition, the list of PROB 6 has a scholarly Introductory Notes if you want to investigate the subject in more depth. Some of the indexes shown below cover both administrations and wills.

Indexes to administrations

1559–1660	published indexes, in several date sequences
1661–1662	annual 'calendars' in PROB 12
1663–1664	typescript indexes
1665–1700	annual 'calendars' in PROB 12
1701–1749	index compiled by the Friends of the PRO
1750–1852	annual 'calendars' in PROB 12
	A card index covering 1750–1800 is at the Society of Genealogists: this can be searched for you, for a fee
1853–1858	two alphabetised 'calendars' in PROB 12

Most of these indexes are published works, and may be available locally: see **6.23** for a table identifying the full titles against the date range and volumes covered.

The indexes to administration acts supply the calendar year of grant, the month of the grant, and the place of residence of the deceased. Use the calendar year of the grant to find the right book in the relevant class list for PROB 6, PROB 7, PROB 8, or PROB 9. The month of the grant and the place of residence is usually enough to locate the particular administration or probate act within the act book.

Some of the published indexes supply folio references to the act books: these relate to the handwritten numbers in the volumes, and not to the stamped numbers. If a folio number is not supplied for grants of administration made before 1719, you have to note the month of the grant from the index and then search through the relevant monthly section of the act book. For grants made after 1719, you need to understand the 'seat' system used by the PCC (see **6.15**).

From 1719 to 1743 the act books in PROB 6 and PROB 8 are divided into monthly sections. Each monthly section is sub-divided into a subsection by seat. The subsections are not arranged in a consistent order. From 1744 to 1858 these act books are divided into five sections corresponding to the five seats of the Court. The seat sections usually appear in the following order: registrar's seat, Surrey seat, Welsh seat, Middlesex seat, London seat. Each seat's section is sub-divided into twelve monthly subsections, and the acts generally appear in alphabetical order by the initial letters of the testators' and intestates' surnames.

6.15 The 'seat' system used in the PCC, 1719–1858

In 1719 the PCC began a new system for organising the issue of grants of probate and administration. This system lasted until the abolition of the Court in 1858. You need to understand the system in order to locate an administration act in PROB 6 or PROB 7, a probate act in PROB 8 or PROB 9, an administration bond in PROB 46, or a commission to swear executors in PROB 52, during the period 1719 to 1858.

The business of granting probate and administration was divided by the Court between five seats. Each seat had a distinct area of responsibility.

Registrar's seat	Testators or intestates dying overseas or at sea, except in cases where the grant was made to the widow, and she lived in an area within the jurisdiction of one of the other seats, in which case probate or administration passed at that seat.
	Testators or intestates living outside the province of Canterbury.
	Estates which were, might be, or had been subject to litigation within the PCC. (If, however, a subsequent grant of probate or administration was made it would be passed at the seat which would have been responsible had there been no litigation.)
Surrey seat	Cornwall, Devon, Dorset, Hampshire, Somerset, Surrey, Sussex, Wiltshire.
Welsh seat	Berkshire, Derbyshire, Gloucestershire, Herefordshire, Leicestershire, Northamptonshire, Oxfordshire, Rutland, Shropshire, Staffordshire, Warwickshire, Worcestershire, Wales.
Middlesex seat	Bedfordshire, Buckinghamshire, Cambridgeshire, Essex, Hertfordshire, Huntingdonshire, Kent, Lincolnshire, Middlesex (except those parishes listed below), Norfolk, Suffolk.
London seat	City of London Charterhouse; Furnivall's Inn; Glasshouse Yard; Gray's Inn; Holy Trinity Minories; Liberty of the Rolls; Liberty of the Tower of London; Lincoln's Inn; Old Artillery Ground; Precinct of Norton Folgate; Precinct of St Katherine by the Tower; Precinct of the Savoy; St Andrew Holborn; St Anne Soho; St Botolph Aldersgate; St Botolph without Aldgate; St George Bloomsbury; St George the Martyr Holborn (Queen Square); St Giles Cripplegate; St Giles in the Fields; St James Clerkenwell; St James Westminster; St John Clerkenwell; St John the Evangelist Westminster; St John Wapping; St Leonard Shoreditch; St Luke Old Street; St Margaret Westminster; St Mary le Strand; St Mary Matfelon Whitechapel; St Sepulchre.

6.16 Understanding the administration act books

The administration act books in PROB 6 do not ordinarily give the complete texts of individual letters of administration, rather they record the information unique to individual letters. The vast majority of the entries in the administration act books take the form of cursory formulaic summaries of the original grants. Except for the period 1651 to 1660 the act books are in Latin until 1733. From 1651 to 1660, and after 25 March 1733, the act books are in English, although certain technical phrases and abbreviations continued to be used in Latin.

<table>
<tr><td colspan="3" align="center">Ordinary grant of administration
PROB 6/96, f 97ᵛ</td></tr>
<tr>
<td>Johannes
Bayly</td>
<td>Tricesimo die Emanavit Commissio Elizabethae Bayly
viduae Relictae Johannis Bayly nuper parochiae
Sanctae Mariae Rotherhithe in Comitatu Surriae sed in
Nave Regia Le Dreadnought defuncti habentis &
c [dum vixit et mortis suae tempore bona jura sive credita
in diversis diocesibus sive peculiaribus jurisdictionibus
sufficientia ad fundandum jurisdictionem Curiae
Praerogativae Cantuariensis] ad Administrandum bona
jura et credita dicti defuncti De bene &c [et fideliter adm
inistrando eadem ad sancta Dei evangelia] juratae</td>
<td>ultimus [dies] Novembris

ultimus [dies] Maij 1721</td>
</tr>
<tr>
<td>John Bayly</td>
<td>On the thirtieth day a commission was issued to
Elizabeth Bayly widow relict of John Bayly formerly of
the parish of St Mary Rotherhithe in the county of Surrey
but in the royal ship The Dreadnought deceased having
etc [while he lived and at the time of his death goods
rights or credits in different dioceses or peculiar
jurisdictions sufficient to found the jurisdiction of the
Prerogative Court of Canterbury] to administer the goods
rights and credits of the said deceased having been sworn
[on the holy gospels] to well and [faithfully administer
the same]</td>
<td>last [day] of November

last [day] of May 1721</td>
</tr>
<tr>
<td colspan="3">● Letters omitted from the original texts on account of abbreviation have been supplied underlined. Words omitted from the original have been supplied underlined in square brackets.
● The first date in the right hand margin is the date by which the administrator was required to return an inventory of the intestate's personal estate. The second date is the date by which the administrator was required to return an account of his or her administration of the estate.</td>
</tr>
</table>

In some instances a grant was made limited to a particular part of the deceased's estate, or with special conditions attached. Limited grants of the estates of soldiers and sailors limited to their wages were commonly made to creditors of the soldiers and sailors who had advanced them money on the security of their wages. Grants limited to Bank of England and East India Company stock held both by foreign nationals whose property was otherwise held in their countries of residence, and by trustees of married women, become increasingly common in the eighteenth and nineteenth centuries. Such grants are indicated in the PROB 12 index, and entered in full in PROB 6 and PROB 7. They may give detailed information about the relationship of the administrator to the deceased, and so can be of great genealogical value. Before 1744 limited and special grants of administration are generally to be found at the front of the section for the month in which they were passed. From 1744 (PROB 6/120) they are entered either in one group at the beginning or end of the different seat sections of the administration act books, or at the beginning of the appropriate monthly subsections of the seat in question. Limited and special grants of administration made after 1809 are entered in PROB 7.

6.17 What did administrators do?

Administrators had first to enter into a bond with the court to ensure that they fulfilled their responsibilities. Bonds generally give the names, marital status, occupations and places of residence of the administrator and his or her sureties. Those for 1714–1857 have recently all been made available for the first time, in PROB 46. However, the rate of survival before 1714 is poor and at present only a few sixteenth century bonds (PROB 51) can be seen.

Administrators were required to collect the credits owed to the intestate, and to pay the debts of the intestate, and the expenses of the estate (such as medical fees, funeral bills, and fees for the maintenance of dependants). The distribution of the estate after the payment of expenses and debts was regulated by statute and custom. One third of the estate was to be distributed to the wife of the intestate, and the remaining part was to be distributed in equal portions among the children of the intestate. Distribution of the estate could not be made until one year after the grant of administration was made, and beneficiaries were required to enter into bonds committing them to refund their portions or parts of their portions should it be necessary for them to do so if the administrator needed to settle unanticipated debts of the estate. Husbands of intestates received the whole of their wives' personal estates.

Twelve months after the grant of administration was issued, a person with a claim to a share in an intestate's estate could seek a judicial distribution of the estate: that is to say he or she could seek an order from the court requiring the administrator to distribute the estate in accordance with the Statute of Distributions. Such causes can be traced in the litigation classes of the Prerogative Court of Canterbury and provide valuable evidence of the distribution of estates. Orders for the distribution of estates are in PROB 16.

The date of death of an intestate, or of a testator whose executors were sworn outside London, can often be found in the warrant for the grant of administration or commission to swear executors (PROB 14).

Among the papers of the Bona Vacantia division of the Treasury Solicitor's Office (TS 17) there are records relating to intestates' estates which escheated to the crown when there was no next of kin.

6.18 Disposing of the estate: inventories and accounts: Kew

The executors or administrators had to prove to the court that they had carried out their functions properly. To do this, they had to submit inventories of the deceased's moveable property (including debts), and accounts of their expenditure (sometimes including expenditure on children over several years). This kind of probate record is relatively poorly used by family historians, despite there being a series of indexes to the relevant classes.

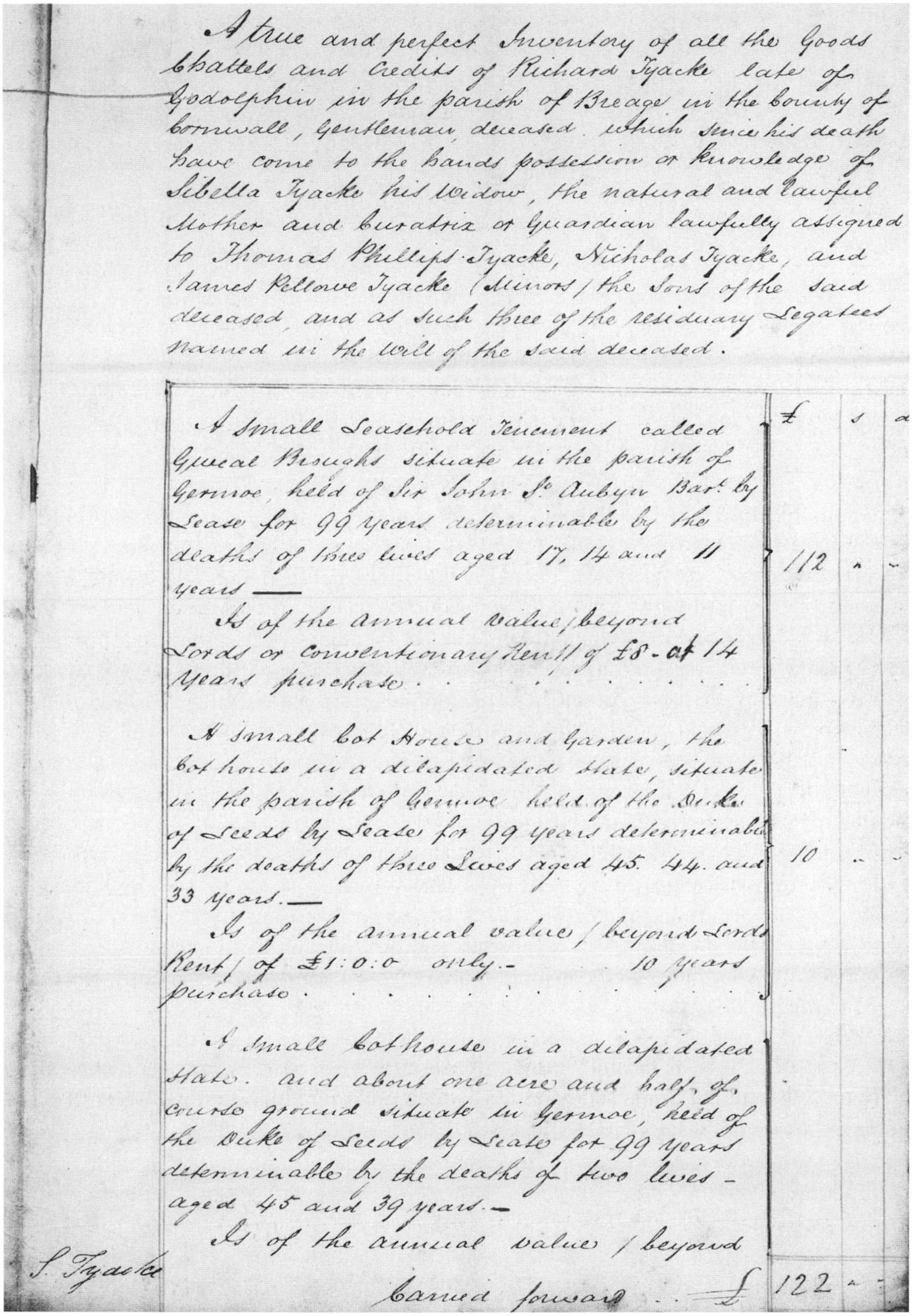

A true and perfect Inventory of all the Goods Chattels and Credits of Richard Tyacke late of Godolphin in the parish of Breage in the county of Cornwall, Gentleman, deceased. which since his death have come to the hands possession or knowledge of Sibella Tyacke his Widow, the natural and lawful Mother and Curatrix or Guardian lawfully assigned to Thomas Phillips Tyacke, Nicholas Tyacke, and James Pellowe Tyacke (Minors) the Sons of the said deceased, and as such three of the residuary Legatees named in the Will of the said deceased.

	£	s	d
A small Leasehold Tenement called Gweal Broughs situate in the parish of Germoe, held of Sir John St Aubyn Bart by Lease for 99 years determinable by the deaths of three lives aged 17, 14 and 11 years ——— Is of the annual value (beyond Lords or Conventionary Rent) of £8 - at 14 years purchase	112	.	-
A small Cot House and Garden, the Cot house in a dilapidated state, situate in the parish of Germoe held of the Duke of Leeds by Lease for 99 years determinable by the deaths of three Lives aged 45. 44. and 33 years.——— Is of the annual value (beyond Lords Rent) of £1:0:0 only.— 10 years purchase	10	-	-
A small Cothouse in a dilapidated State. and about one acre and half, of course ground situate in Germoe, held of the Duke of Leeds by Lease for 99 years determinable by the deaths of two lives - aged 45 and 39 years.— Is of the annual value (beyond			
S. Tyacke			
Carried forward . . £	122	.	-

Figure 4 Probate inventories, as well as giving information about family members, can provide a much wider social context. This one, for Richard Tyacke, which continues for several pages, reflects the Cornish society and economy of 1826: it comes from PROB 31/1235, no. 1030.

1417–1660	Inventories Series I	PROB 2	index with list
1642–1722	Cause Papers	PROB 28	index to causes, testators or intestates
1653–1721	Exhibits pre-1722	PROB 36	card indexes to causes, testators and intestates
1661–1720	Parchment Inventories	PROB 4	card indexes to names and places
1661–1732	Paper Inventories	PROB 5	index with list
1662–1720	Filed Exhibits with Inventories	PROB 32	index with list
1683–1858	Indexes to Exhibits	PROB 33	original indexes to exhibits in PROB 31 and PROB 37
1702, 1718–1782	Inventories Series II	PROB 3	index with list
1722–1858	Exhibits, Main Class	PROB 31	index of wills;card indexes of names and places to the inventories and other exhibits
1783–1858	Cause Papers, Later Series	PROB 37	indexes to testators and intestates

PROB 31 and PROB 37 are also indexed by place of residence, and include many people resident in the Americas and East Indies.

The rate of survival for these documents is very poor before 1666, and erratic for the later seventeenth century and early eighteenth century. After the mid eighteenth century, they were only exhibited if the estate was subject to litigation, if the administrator or executor renounced his or her responsibilities, or if the beneficiaries of the estate were children. As well as using the indexes to these classes, it is a good idea to look at the Introductory Note in front of the relevant class list, as it will give you information about what to expect.

Inventories, listing the deceased's personal property, and accounts, recording executors' and administrators' receipts and expenditure, may provide the most illuminating evidence about the deceased's social status, wealth and business activities. The inventories of the goods, chattels and credits of Richard Tyacke of Godolphin, Cornwall, submitted in 1826, account for a total value of over £25,000: they list leases for term of lives (one worthless as the person on whom the lease depended was on the point of death), shares in pilchard fishing (worthless), tin mines and merchant trade, debts owing, and the farm stock and furniture. With an inventory, remember that what is listed will probably not constitute the entire furnishings of a house, but only what belonged to the testator.

Sometimes you can get a declaration in place of an inventory, when the goods have already been disposed of. These can be quite informative, because they give the details of where the goods went. The one illustrated, from 1707, mentions the name of the nurse who looked after William Appletree in his fatal illness, his father and grandfather, four sisters and a brother, and a decree on his behalf in the court of Chancery in 1699 (somewhere else to look). The executor here is one Bowater Vernon, who may have served on HMS *Nottingham* with Appletree: it may be another clue worth following.

Accounts can be particularly valuable, as they may continue for some years and include all kinds of information – payments for the maintenance of dependants, details of funeral or nursing costs, etc.

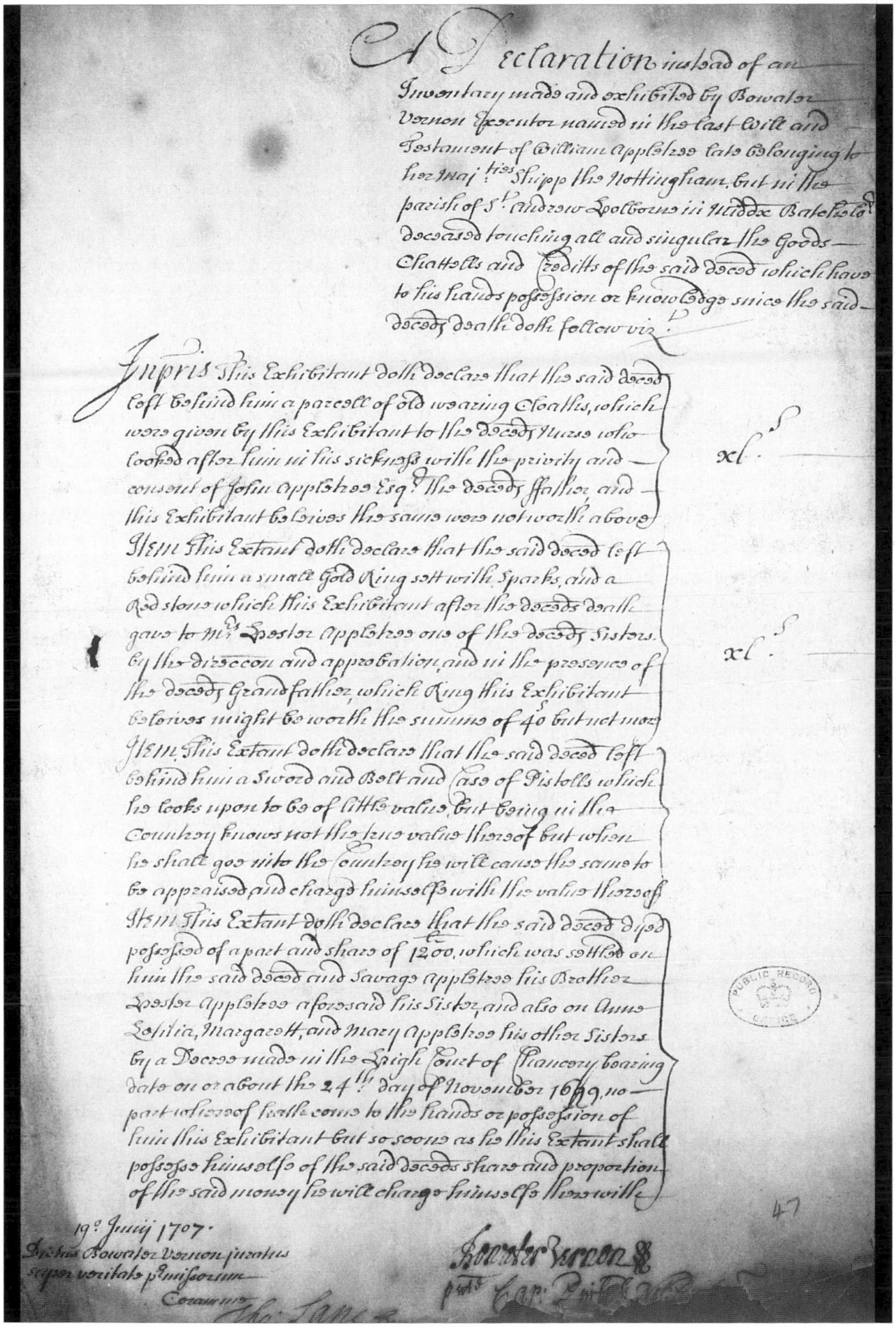

Figure 5 A declaration of what had happened to the goods of William Appletree, from 1707. This provides a lot of information to follow up – family details, service in the Navy, and a lawsuit in chancery (PROB 32/50).

6.19 Litigation before 1858: Kew

In many cases, a will was disputed in the PCC. Cox provides a fascinating history of testamentary disputes, in *Hatred Pursued Beyond the Grave*.

There are three main ways to discover if there was a dispute (a 'cause' in PCC language). Remember that before the mid 1700s, causes were known by the name of the plaintiff, and not by the name of the person whose estate was being disputed. The first clue may be from the will register in PROB 11, until about 1800: there may be a sentence (judgement) entered in the margin next to the will, if the victorious party had paid for this to be done. The second, and easiest, way is to check the card index to the initial proceedings (1661–1858) in PROB 18. This is arranged in two parts, by name of cause (e.g. Smith *contra* Jones) and by name of the deceased testator or intestate. Thirdly, if you go to the relevant act book (PROB 6–PROB 9) or the PROB 12 calendar, you may find a marginal note saying *by decree* or *by sentence* (sometimes abbreviated). This means that the estate was the subject of a law suit or cause.

The stages through which a cause passed are recorded in the acts of court (PROB 29, PROB 30). These records are concerned with procedure and you may find other classes of litigation records more fruitful. The main classes to check are allegations (the initial complaint, by the plaintiffs) in PROB 18, answers by the defendants in PROB 25, depositions in PROB 24 and PROB 26, cause papers in PROB 28 and PROB 37, and exhibits in PROB 31 and PROB 36. Scott, in *Wills and Other Probate Records*, gives a step by step account of finding records in two testamentary disputes. The basic procedure was very similar to that used by the equity courts.

Annotations of existence of a cause			
1559–1858	Act Books: Administrations	PROB 6	
1810–1858	Act Books: Limited Administrations	PROB 7	
1526–1828	Act Books: Probates	PROB 8	
1781–1858	Act Books: Limited Probates	PROB 9	
1384–1858	Registered Copy Wills	PROB 11	
1383–1858	Register Books	PROB 12	
Proceedings			
1661–1858	Allegations (i.e. the start of the cause)	PROB 18	card indexes to causes, testators and intestates
1664–1854	Answers	PROB 25	
1642–1722	Cause Papers	PROB 28	
1783–1858	Cause Papers, Later Series	PROB 37	index to testators and intestates. List and Index Society 184
Depositions			
1657–1809	Depositions	PROB 24	
1826–1858	Depositions Bound by Suit	PROB 26	indexes to causes, testators and intestates

Exhibits			
1653–1721	Exhibits pre-1722	PROB 36	card indexes to causes, testators and intestates
1662–1720	Filed Exhibits with Inventories	PROB 32	indexed by name. List and Index Society 204
1722–1858	Exhibits, Main Class	PROB 31	index of wills; card indexes of names and places to the inventories and other exhibits
Procedural records			
1536–1819	Acts of Court Book	PROB 29	
1740–1858	Acts of Court	PROB 30	indexes to causes, testators and intestates. List and Index Society 161

Sentences, the court's final judgement, were registered in PROB 11 if the successful party paid a fee for the registration, until the end of the eighteenth century. They are listed in the calendars in PROB 12 in a separate section which is to be found either adjacent to the section for surnames beginning with the letter *S*, or at the end of the volume. Sentences will give you the names of the deceased testator or intestate, the name of the parties to the cause, and the type of sentence.

Sentences were drafted by proctors for the opposing parties. The judge in the cause then promulgated the sentence that accorded with his verdict. The principal types of sentences were:

sententia pro concessione administrationis bonorum	sentence granting letters of administration
sententia pro confirmatione administrationis bonorum	sentence confirming the grant of letters of administration
sententia pro revocatione administrationis bonorum	sentence revoking letters of administration
sententia pro valore testamenti	sentence in favour of the validity of a will
sententia pro confirmatione testamenti	sentence confirming a grant of probate
sententia pro revocatione testamenti	sentence revoking a grant of probate

Other types of sentences related to the jurisdiction of the Prerogative Court of Canterbury, the production of inventories and accounts, and the validity of codicils.

The PCC was only concerned with the validity of wills presented for probate or the claims of persons seeking letters of administration. Cases concerned with the inheritance and devisal of real estate and with trusts were heard in Chancery (see **47.3**). A single will may have led to law suits in both the PCC and in Chancery at the same time.

6.20 Appeals before 1858: wills from other courts in the PRO

If probate was not granted by the PCC, it may be worth investigating to see if an appeal took place. Appeals from the Prerogative Court of Canterbury, and other church courts, in testamentary causes, went to the Court of Arches (whose surviving records are at Lambeth Palace Library) and to the High Court of Delegates. If either of these two courts granted probate, then the will may be found in their records, as well as in the PCC or the relevant lower court. Proceedings called before the Delegates can be seen at Kew (DEL 1 and DEL 2, both indexed by DEL 11/7; DEL 7, indexed by IND 1/10323; and DEL 8). Wills and affidavits brought into court, 1636–1857, are in DEL 10. The muniment books (DEL 9) contain transcripts of documents and exhibits in testamentary appeals, 1652–1859. Both are indexed in DEL 11/6 and DEL 11/7. After 1834, appeals lay to the Judicial Committee of the Privy Council until 1858: try PCAP 1 and PCAP 3.

6.21 Litigation after 1858: at Kew

After 1858, testamentary causes were no longer heard by ecclesiastical courts, but by the new Court of Probate (later part of the Probate, Divorce and Admiralty Division of the High Court), with appeal to the House of Lords. A 7 per cent sample of case files and papers relating to contentious probates of wills, from 1858 onwards, is in J 121.

6.22 Other probate records at Kew

Other wills are found throughout the public records: a useful book, *A List of Wills, Administrations, Etc, in the Public Record Office, London, England: 12th–19th century,* lists many of them. A copy can be seen in the Map Room. Because some of them are individually described in the lists, it may be worth trying a keyword search in the on-line catalogue. There are many wills in Chancery Masters' Exhibits, C103–C115, and there is a card index to them. There is also a list of wills and related records in E 211.

Some manor court rolls include enrolled wills. An exceptionally good example is the manor of Newcastle-under-Lyme, part of the Duchy of Lancaster. This has a series of enrolment books of deeds and wills, 1810–1934, in DL 30/510/1–510/63, with indexes in DL 30/511/1–511/4. Other Duchy manors, such as Knaresborough, also enrolled wills. It may be worth checking in the PRO's holdings of court rolls if you think that the person you are seeking was a tenant of a crown manor: see **41.2**.

The Paymaster General kept records of probates and letters of administration granted for Army and Navy personnel (it is not clear if they are for officers only) and their widows, between 1836 and 1915. The registers can give clues to relationships, and the later ones give the address of the deceased (PMG 50). Wills were deposited in the Navy Pay Office by naval ratings, Royal Marine other ranks and some warrant officers: see **19.25**. The PRO at Kew has registers of the wills, 1786–1909, in ADM 142, which act as an index to the wills, 1786–1882, in ADM 48. There is also a very incomplete card index available. There are also some Royal Marine wills in ADM 96. Wills of some army officers, 1755–1881, may be found in WO 42, and there is an index available at Kew. Wills and copies of wills may be found, very occasionally, among deceased soldiers' effects in the casualty returns, 1809–1910 (WO 25/1359–2410 and 3251–3471).

The probate records of the British Consular Court at Smyrna, Turkey, 1820–1929, and of the Shanghai Supreme Court, 1857–1941, are in FO 626 and FO 917 respectively. Other wills of some Britons in China, 1837–1951, are in FO 678/2729–2931.

6.23 Wills and administrations: indexes

Will indexes			
1	1383–1558	PROB 11/1–41	*Index of wills proved in the Prerogative Court of Canterbury*, [vol. I A–J, vol. II K–Z], eds J Challenor and C Smith, Index Library, X–XI (London, British Records Society, 1893–1895).
2	1558–1583	PROB 11/42A–66	*Index of wills proved in the Prerogative Court of Canterbury*, vol. III, eds S A Smith and L L Duncan, Index Library, XVIII (London, British Records Society, 1898).
3	1584–1604	PROB 11/66–104	*Index of wills proved in the Prerogative Court of Canterbury*, vol. IV, eds S A Smith and E A Fry, Index Library, XXV (London, British Records Society, 1901).
4	1605–1619	PROB 11/105–134	*Index of wills proved in the Prerogative Court of Canterbury*, vol. V, ed. E Stokes, Index Library, XLIII (London, British Records Society, 1912).
5	1620	PROB 11/135–136	J H Lea, *Abstract of wills in the Prerogative Court of Canterbury: Register Soame 1620* (Boston, Mass., 1904). Abstracts of all wills registered. A copy can be seen at the FRC, but not at Kew.
6	1620–1629	PROB 11/135–156	*Index of wills proved in the Prerogative Court of Canterbury*, vol. VI, ed. R H E Hill, Index Library, XLIV (London, British Records Society, 1912). See also 7 below.
7	1620–1624	PROB 11/135–144	*Year book of probates: Abstracts of probates and sentences in the Prerogative Court of Canterbury*, eds J Matthews and G F Matthews (London, 1914). This index contains some references not in 6 above. The abbreviations it uses are explained in 9.1 below, page 5. It does not have a place name index, but there is one in 6.
8	1630	PROB 11/157–158	J H Morrison, *Prerogative Court of Canterbury: Register Scroope (1630)* (London, 1934). Abstracts of all wills registered. A copy can be seen at the FRC, but not at Kew.
9			*Year books of probates (from 1630): Abstracts of probate acts in the Prerogative Court of Canterbury*, eds J Matthews and G F Matthews (London, 1902–1927)
9.1	1630–1634	PROB 11/157–166	vol. I (1902).
9.2	1635–1639	PROB 11/167–181	vol. II (1903).

9.3	1630–1639	PROB 11/157–181	*Sentences and complete index nominum (probates and sentences)* extra volume (1907). This volume indexes sentences 1630–1639, and all surnames in it and in 9.1–2
9.4	1640–1644	PROB 11/182–192	vol. III (1905). See also 13 below.
9.5	1645–1649	PROB 11/192–210	vol. IV (1906). See also 13 below.
			Tracing probate acts and wills 1643–1646 is subject to particular difficulties. Further information is supplied in the appendix to the PROB 10 introductory note.
9.6	1650–1651	PROB 11/211–219	vol. V (1909). See also 10 and 13 below.
9.7	1652–1653	PROB 11/220–232	vol. VI (1911). See also 10 and 13 below.
9.8	1654	PROB 11/233–242	vol. VII (1914). See also 10 and 13 below.
9.9	1655	PROB 11/243–251	vol. VIII (1927) [surnames A–Musgrave only]. See also 10 and 13 below. 9.8–9.9 do not have place name indexes, but there is one in 10 which covers the same period.
10	1653–1656	PROB 11/225–260	*Index of wills proved in the Prerogative Court of Canterbury*, vol. VII, eds T M Blagg and J Skeate Moir, Index Library, LIV (London, British Records Society, 1925). See also 13 below.
11	1657–1660	PROB 11/261–302	*Index of wills proved in the Prerogative Court of Canterbury*, vol. VIII, ed. T M Blagg, Index Library, LXI (London, British Records Society, 1936). See also 13 below.
12	1658	PROB 11/272–285	*W Brigg, Genealogical abstracts of wills proved in the Prerogative Court of Canterbury: Register Wootton 1658*, 7 volumes (Leeds, 1894–1914). Abstracts of all wills registered. A copy can be seen at the FRC, but not at Kew.
13	1640–1660	PROB 11/182–302	Sentences registered in PROB 11/182–302 are indexed in *Index to administrations in the Prerogative Court of Canterbury*, vol. VI, ed. M Fitch, Index Library, C (London, British Records Society, 1986).
14	1661–1670	PROB 11/303–334	*Prerogative Court of Canterbury: Wills, sentences and probate acts*, ed. J H Morrison (London, 1935).
15	1671–1675	PROB 11/335–349	*Index of wills proved in the Prerogative Court of Canterbury*, vol. IX, ed. J Ainsworth, Index Library, LXVII (London, British Records Society, 1942).
16	1676–1685	PROB 11/350–381	*Index of wills proved in the Prerogative Court of Canterbury*, vol. X, ed. C H Ridge, Index Library, LXXI (London, British Records Society, 1948).
17	1686–1693	PROB 11/382–417	*Index of wills proved in the Prerogative Court of Canterbury*, vol. XI, ed. C Ridge, Index Library, LXXVII (London, British Records Society, 1958).
18	1694–1700	PROB 11/418–458	*Index of wills proved in the Prerogative Court of Canterbury*, vol. XII, ed. M Fitch, Index Library, LXXX (London, British Records Society, 1960).

19	1701–1749	PROB 11/459–775	Friends of the Public Record Office, *Index to PCC wills and administrations* (London, 1998. Microfiche). The index has been compiled from PROB 12/71–119. Where entries in PROB 12/71–119 appear to be defective they have been checked against the administration act books (PROB 6), the probate act books (PROB 8), and the registered wills (PROB 11).
20	1750	PROB 11/776–784	G Sherwood, *A list of persons named in the PCC wills proved in the year 1750: Register Greenly* (4,382 wills naming 40,320 persons arranged in eight groups topographically) (London, privately published, 1918). There is a copy in the library of the Society of Genealogists, but not at the FRC or Kew.
21	1750–1800	PROB 11/776–1351	*An index to wills proved in the Prerogative Court of Canterbury 1750–1800*, ed. A J Camp, 6 vols (London, Society of Genealogists, 1976–1992). Compiled from PROB 13/186–242, checked (not systematically) against PROB 12/120–176.
22	1801–1852	PROB 11/1352–2164	PROB 12/177–271
23	1853–1858	PROB 11/2165–2263	PROB 12/272–288: *Calendar of the grants of probate and letters of administration made in the Prerogative Court of Canterbury, 1853–1857, 1858*, 16 vols (London, nd). (Locations of copies of this index outside the PRO are listed in Gibson, *Probate jurisdictions: where to look for wills*. The index has also been published in microfiche by Hampshire Record Office, together with the calendars of grants of probate and administration for the period 1858 to 1935.)

Wills of American testators

24	1610–1857	PROB 11/115–2262	P W Coldham, *American wills proved in London, 1611–1775* (Baltimore, 1992). It can be used to advantage in conjunction with his *American wills and administrations in the Prerogative Court of Canterbury, 1610–1857* (Baltimore, 1989). This work supersedes Coldham's earlier works on the same subject.

Administration indexes

25	1559 1571	PROB 6/1	*Administrations in the Prerogative Court of Canterbury*, [vol. I], ed. R M Glencross (Exeter, 1912).
26	1572–1580	PROB 6/2	*Administrations in the Prerogative Court of Canterbury*, vol. II (Exeter, 1917).
27	1559–1580	PROB 6/1–2	B Lloyd, Preliminary addenda and corrigenda to Mr R M Glencross's letters of administration granted by the Prerogative Court of Canterbury, 1559–1580 (typescript, 1979).
28	1581–1595	PROB 6/3–5	*Index to administrations in the Prerogative Court of Canterbury*, vol. III, ed. C H Ridge, Index Library, LXXVI (London, BRS, 1954).

29	1596–1608	PROB 6/5–7	*Index to administrations in the Prerogative Court of Canterbury*, vol. IV, ed. M Fitch, Index Library, LXXXI (London, BRS, 1964).
30	1609–1619	PROB 6/7–10	*Index to administrations in the Prerogative Court of Canterbury*, vol. V, ed. M Fitch, Index Library, LXXXIII (London, BRS, 1968).
31	1620–1630	PROB 6/10–13	*Prerogative Court of Canterbury: Letters of administration*, ed. J H Morrison (London, 1935).
32	1631–1648	PROB 6/14A–23	*Index to administrations in the Prerogative Court of Canterbury*, vol. VI, ed. M Fitch, Index Library, C (London, BRS, 1986). (This index also includes sentences registered from 1640 to 1660 in PROB 11/182–302).
33	1643–1644	PROB 6/234	Grants made by the Prerogative Court of Canterbury at Oxford, were omitted from 32 above. PROB 6/234 contains a contemporary index which has been reproduced and is available on the open shelves. (This reproduction was formerly PROB 12/23B.)
34	1649–1654	PROB 6/24–30	*Index to administrations in the Prerogative Court of Canterbury*, vol. 1, ed. J Ainsworth, Index Library, LXVIII (London, BRS, 1944). For further information on tracing administration acts 1653–1654 see the PROB 6 Introductory Note, appendix 2.
35	1655–1660	PROB 6/31–36	*Index to administrations in the Prerogative Court of Canterbury*, vol. II, ed. C H Ridge, 3 vols, Index Library, LXXII (A–F), LXXIV (G–Q), LXXV (R–Z) (London, BRS, 1949–1953).
36	1661	PROB 6/37	Surnames A–Sweetinge: typescript index.
37	1661	PROB 6/37	Surnames other than those in the sequence A–Sweetinge: PROB 12/38.
38	1662	-	The administration act book is not extant for 1662. Use PROB 12/39 (see also PROB 13/96–97, PROB 15/72).
39	1663–1664	PROB 6/38–39	Typescript index.
40	1665–1700	PROB 6/40–76	PROB 12/41–69.
41	1701–1749	PROB 6/77–125	Friends of the Public Record Office, *Index to PCC wills and administrations*, (London, 1998. Microfiche). The index has been compiled from PROB 12/71–119. Where entries in PROB 12/71–119 appear to be defective they have been checked against the administration act books (PROB 6), the probate act books (PROB 8), and the registered wills (PROB 11).
42	1750–1800	PROB 12/126–176	There is a card index to these administrations acts, largely compiled from PROB 13/186–236, at the Society of Genealogists, which the Society will search for a fee.
43	1801–1852	PROB 6/177–228	PROB 12/177–271.

44	1853–1858	PROB 6/229–233	PROB 12/272–288: *Calendar of the grants of probate and letters of administration made in the Prerogative Court of Canterbury, 1853–1857, 1858*, 16 vols (London, nd). (Locations of copies of this index outside the PRO are listed in Gibson, *Probate jurisdictions: where to look for wills*, 12. The index has also been published in microfiche by Hampshire Record Office, together with the calendars of grants of probate and administration for the period 1858 to 1935).
Administration acts relating to estates of American intestates			
45	1610–1857	PROB 6/7–233	P W Coldham, *American wills and administrations in the Prerogative Court of Canterbury, 1610–1857* (Baltimore, 1989). This work supersedes Coldham's earlier works on the same subject.

6.24 Wills and other probate records: bibliography

A J Camp, 'The Genealogist's Use of Probate Records', in G H Martin and P Spufford, eds *Records of the Nation* (British Record Society, 1990), pp. 287–298

A J Camp, *Wills and their whereabouts* (London, 4th edn, 1974)

E J Carlson, 'The historical value of Ely consistory probate records' in E Leedham-Green and R Rodd, eds *Index of the probate records of the Consistory Court of Ely 1449–1858, part 1: A–E*, Index Library CIII (London, British Record Society, 1994), xvii–lix. Of value for all church courts with probate jurisdiction

P W Coldham, *American Wills and Administrations in the Prerogative Court of Canterbury, 1610–1857* (Baltimore, 1989)

J Cox, *Affection Defying the Power of Death: Wills, Probate and Death Duty Records* (FFHS, 1993)

J Cox, *Hatred pursued beyond the grave* (HMSO, 1993)

A L Erickson, 'An Introduction to Probate Accounts', in G H Martin and P Spufford, eds *Records of the Nation* (British Record Society, 1990), pp. 273–286

J S W Gibson, *Probate Jurisdictions: Where to look for wills* (FFHS, 1994)

Ham's Inland Revenue Yearbook (annual: PRO library has 1875–1930)

D Hawkings, *Index of Somerset Estate Duty Office Wills and Letters of Administration 1805–1811* (1995)

D Hawkings, *Index of Somerset Estate Duty Office Wills 1812–1857* (2 vols, 1995)

M D Herber, *Ancestral Trails* (Sutton, 1997)

A List of Wills, Administrations, Etc, in the Public Record Office, London, England: 12th–19th century (1932)

C Marshall, 'In the Name of God? Will Making and Faith in Early Modern England', in G H Martin and P Spufford, eds *Records of the Nation* (British Record Society, 1990), pp. 215–249

E McLaughlin, *Wills before 1858* (FFHS, 1994)

E McLaughlin, *Wills from 1858* (FFHS, 1995)

R Milward, *A Glossary of Household, Farming and Trade Terms From Probate Inventories* (Derbyshire Record Society, *Occasional Paper No. 1*, 3rd edn, 1993)

N Newington-Irving, *Will indexes and other probate material in the Library of the Society of Genealogists* (Society of Genealogists, 1996)

M Overton, *A Bibliography of British Probate Inventories* (Newcastle, 1983)

PCC Sentences: a rough list transcribed from the original calendars for the period 1643–1652

M Scott, *Prerogative Court of Canterbury: Wills and Other Probate Records* (PRO, 1997)

'Wills and Administrations in the Court of Delegates', *The Genealogist*, new series 11 [1903], pp. 165–171, 224–227; 12 [1903], pp. 97–101 (Probate records in DEL 9)

7 Welsh genealogy

7.1 Welsh genealogy: records elsewhere

A major difficulty faced by family historians in Wales is caused by the late adoption of fixed surnames, and the relatively small stock of names that evolved from the previous naming practices – Jones, Davies, Pritchard, Price, Williams, Parry, Bevan or Evans, Thomas, etc. For advice on understanding the patronymic system used until the seventeenth or eighteenth century, look at Rowlands and Rowlands, *The Surnames of Wales,* or Morgan and Morgan, *Welsh Surnames.*

Parish Registers of Wales, by Williams and Watts-Williams, is a useful guide to the whereabouts of original parish registers and copies in Welsh record offices and libraries and in the library of the Society of Genealogists. The National Library also holds many parish registers and transcripts as well as wills, tithe records, title deeds and personal and estate records. These are described in the *Guide to the Manuscripts and Records, the National Library of Wales*. Wills proved in Welsh consistory courts before 1858 have been indexed by the LDS in *Abstracts and Indexes of Wills*. Most of the Welsh record offices produce their own genealogical leaflets, as does the Welsh Tourist Board. For a very useful directory of what is available where and when, see *Researching Family History in Wales*, by Istance and Cann. A good survey of the available literature, and of where finding aids to records in Wales can be seen in England, is given by Herber, in *Ancestral Trails*, pp. 556–559.

The records of Welsh courts before 1830, formerly held in the PRO in the WALE classes, have been transferred to the National Library of Wales. Relatively little survives before the introduction of the Courts of Great Sessions (similar to the English assizes) in 1540, but a lot thereafter. For details, see Parry, *A Guide to the Records of Great Sessions in Wales.* Monmouthshire was not included in the Great Sessions circuits, but was added to the English Western assize circuit in 1543.

One famous source which used to be in the PRO, the Golden Grove Book of Pedigrees (an early eighteenth century genealogical collection) is now in the care of the Carmarthenshire Archives Service (address in **48**).

7.2 Welsh genealogy: records in the PRO and FRC

Most of the records discussed in this book should be as helpful in tracing the history of Welsh families as they are for English families. There are some specific records which, because they relate solely to Wales, or because they are arranged by place, may be particularly helpful. Tax records in E 179 are the most obvious genealogical source, with the hearth taxes of the late 17th century being the most useful (see **43**).

For births, marriages and deaths from 1837, go to the FRC (ONS) (see **3.1**). Because of the strong nonconformist tradition in Wales, the nonconformist registers of births, marriages and deaths in RG 4 and RG 8 (for 1700–1858) are a very fruitful source. The list is arranged by county, with a further list available by denomination: see **3.6–3.8**. Census returns are also arranged by place (see **2**). The 1891 census notes whether people were Welsh speakers.

The University of Wales, Board of Celtic Studies, has published in its History and Law series several volumes giving brief details of sixteenth and seventeenth century disputes relating to Wales and Monmouthshire in the records of the courts of Star Chamber, Chancery, Augmentations and Exchequer: they are well indexed, and provide an easy way into these records (details given in the bibliography, where the relevant works are marked thus *). They can be seen in the Library at Kew, where there are also many works on Welsh history. The Exchequer equity depositions in E 134 continue to be searchable by county until 1760: they continue listed by date until 1841. For later indexes, use the Bernau Index at the Society of Genealogists (**47.3**).

The assize records for the Chester and North Wales circuit and the South Wales circuit, c.1831 onwards (ASSI 57–ASSI 67, ASSI 71–ASSI 77), effectively continue the records of the courts of Great Sessions, now in the National Library of Wales. The records of the Palatinate of Chester (CHES 1–CHES 38) also cover Flintshire, and other parts of North Wales.

The records of the Army are reasonably easy to search for Welshmen, because of the territorial basis of so many regiments and militia regiments (see **18**). There are registers of ex-soldiers and sailors living in Wales who were in receipt of a Chelsea or Greenwich out-pension, 1842–1862 (WO 22/114–117). Some of the entries relate to widows and children. Try also the WO 97 database of soldiers discharged to pension between 1760 and 1854, as it can be searched by county of birth as well as by name.

7.3 Early Welsh records in the PRO

Among the earlier records that stayed in the PRO are the records of some of the marcher lordships and of the principality. Because of the history of its conquest by the Normans and Plantagenets, medieval Wales was composed of the principality (basically Anglesey, Caernarvon, Merioneth, Cardigan and Carmarthen), run by the crown, and several quasi-independent marcher lordships, some of which had fallen into the crown's possession. In the 1530s and 1540s Wales was divided into shires and given a form of local government based on the English model. The marcher lordships were not actually abolished, and some of them continued to provide local courts. For more details, see the *PRO Guide*, part 1, sections 352–355.

The PRO has an unsurpassed collection of records from the marcher lordship of Ruthin or Dyffryn Clwyd, stretching from the thirteenth to the nineteenth centuries, including court rolls with lists of tenants, views of frankpledge, lists of freeholders and inhabitants, and proceedings in the lordship court, which handled debt cases until the 1820s. The court rolls are in SC 2; the other records are well listed in WALE 15.

There are also records from some other marcher lordships; most of these records are court rolls and surveys, and they are not as extensive as those of Ruthin. Records of marcher lordships held by the Duchy of Lancaster (Kidwelly, Ogmore, Monmouth, Brecon, Caldicot, Iscennen, etc.) are in DL 28–DL 30, DL 41–DL 42 and SC 2). Records of marcher lordships which had fallen into crown hands are in SC 2, SC 6, SC 11, SC 12, LR 2, LR 9, LR 11 and LR 13.

7.4 Welsh genealogy: bibliography

An * shows that this work is in the University of Wales, Board of Celtic Studies, *History and Law* series.

I Edwards, *A Catalogue of Star Chamber Proceedings Relating to Wales* (Cardiff, 1929) *

G Hamilton Edwards, *In search of Welsh Ancestry* (Chichester, 1986)

M Herber, *Ancestral Trails* (Sutton, 1997)

J Istance and E E Cann, *Researching Family History in Wales* (FFHS, 1996)

E G Jones, *Exchequer Proceedings (Equity) Concerning Wales. Henry VIII–Elizabeth* (Cardiff, 1939) *

T I Jeffreys Jones, *Exchequer Proceedings Concerning Wales in Tempore James I* (Cardiff, 1955) *

E A Lewis, *An Inventory of the Early Chancery Proceedings Concerning Wales* (Cardiff, 1937) *

E A Lewis and J Conway Davies, *Records of the Court of Augmentations relating to Wales and Monmouthshire* (Cardiff, 1954) *

S Lewis, *Topographical Dictionary of Wales* (London, 1840)

G Morgan, 'Welsh Names in Welsh Wills', *Journal of the Society of Archivists*, vol. XXV (1995), pp. 178–185

T J Morgan and P Morgan, *Welsh Surnames* (Cardiff, 1985)

National Library of Wales, *Guide to Genealogical Sources at the National Library of Wales* (National Library of Wales leaflet)

National Library of Wales, *Guide to the Manuscripts and Records, the National Library of Wales* (National Library of Wales, 1994)

G Parry, *A Guide to the Records of Great Sessions in Wales* (Aberystwyth, 1995)

B Rawlins, *The Parish Churches and Nonconformist Chapels of Wales: their records and where to find them* (Salt Lake City, 1987)

J Rowlands, *Welsh Family History; A Guide to Research* (Association of Family History Societies for Wales, 1993)

J Rowlands and S Rowlands, *The Surnames of Wales* (FFHS, 1996)

C J Williams and J Watts-Williams, *Cofrestri Plwyf Cymru, Parish Registers of Wales* (National Library of Wales and Welsh County Archivists Group, 1986)

8 Scottish genealogy

8.1 Scottish genealogy: records in Scotland, and access at the FRC

Civil registration of births, marriages and deaths began in Scotland on 1 January 1855. The records, along with many parish registers (c.1700–1855), minor foreign registers from 1855, and the decennial census returns for 1841–1891, are held by the Registrar General in Edinburgh at New Register House, Edinburgh EH1 3YT, where they can be searched for a fee. The indexes can be searched on computer (the *Scottish Link*) at the FRC (ONS) for an hourly fee, but certificates have to be ordered from Edinburgh. It is also available on the web at http://www.origins.net but a charge is payable. *Scottish Link* gives access to on-line indexes to the birth, marriage and death registers from 1 January 1855, including adoptions from 1930 and divorces from May 1984. It also accesses the computerized indexes of all the names in the Scottish Church Registers of births, baptisms, and marriages, 1555–1854 (excluding those church registers held by the Scottish Record Office); and the similar indexes to the Scottish census returns of 1881 and 1891 (about 3 million entries for each year). Note that deaths and burials are not covered before 1855.

New Register House also holds various series of registers of births, deaths and marriages which took place outside Scotland, but which relate to Scots or people normally resident in Scotland. These are similar to the registers for the English and Welsh abroad (see **4.1**). They include births and deaths at sea (from 1855); returns from foreign countries (from 1860); armed services registers (from 1881), war registers (from 1899); and consular returns (from 1914).

Wills, judicial records, deeds, etc., are in the Scottish Record Office: see Sinclair's *Tracing Your Scottish Ancestry*, and the *Guide to the National Archives of Scotland* (SRO). The Scottish Genealogy Society, the Scots Ancestry Research Society and the Association of Scottish Genealogists and Record Agents are available to undertake paid research. For information about clans, contact the Scottish Tartan Society. Addresses are in **48**.

8.2 Scottish genealogy: material elsewhere

The Society of Genealogists has a very extensive collection of Scottish materials. To find out what they have, look at Moore's *Sources for Scottish Genealogy in the Library of the Society of Genealogists*.

8.3 Scottish genealogy: records in the PRO

The PRO has the wills of Scots possessed of property in the form of goods, money and investments in England (see **6**), and also the records of Scottish churches in England (see **3**). The Apprenticeship Books include details of Scottish apprentices (see **27**) and the Scots are well represented in the records of the Merchant Navy (see **25**), the Metropolitan Police (see **23.3–23.5**), and of course, the armed forces.

The records of the Army are particularly fruitful, because of the territorial base of so many regiments and militia regiments (see **18**). Try the WO 97 database of soldiers discharged to pension between 1760 and 1854, as it can be searched by county of birth as well as by name. For ex-soldiers and ex-sailors living in Scotland and in receipt of a Chelsea or Greenwich pension, there are registers arranged by district pay office (e.g. Ayr, Paisley) for 1842–1862 (WO22/118–140). Some of the entries relate to widows and children.

For Scottish emigrants to North America see **14.6**.

Of course, the Secretaries of State, based in London, conducted a stream of correspondence with Scotland after the union of the two kingdoms. Much of this is included in the *Calendars of State Papers Domestic*, and in the (indexed) descriptive list of the State Papers, Scotland, 1688–1782 (SP 54), published by the List and Index Society. Many individuals are referred to in these papers. For the period before 1603, there are the separate *Calendar of Letters and Papers Relating to the Affairs of the Borders of England and Scotland* and *Calendar of State Papers Relating to Scotland and Mary, Queen of Scots, 1547–1603*.

8.4 Scottish genealogy: bibliography

Calendar of Letters and Papers Relating to the Affairs of the Borders of England and Scotland (London, 1894–1896)
Calendar of State Papers, Domestic, 1603–1704 (London, 1857–1972)
Calendar of State Papers Relating to Scotland and Mary, Queen of Scots, 1547–1603 (London, 1898–1969)
K B Cory, *Tracing Your Scottish Ancestry* (Edinburgh, 1996)
J P S Ferguson, *Scottish Family Histories* (Edinburgh, 1986)
G Hamilton Edwards, *In search of Scottish Ancestry* (Chichester, 1986)

M D Herber, *Ancestral Trails* (Sutton, 1997)

S Lewis, *Topographical Dictionary of Scotland* (London, 1846)

List and Index Society, *State Papers Scotland, Series Two (1688–1782)* (List and Index Society, vols 262–264, 1996)

D Moody, *Scottish Family History* (London, 1988)

M Moore, *Sources for Scottish Genealogy in the Library of the Society of Genealogists* (Society of Genealogists, 1996)

Scotland, A Genealogical Research Guide (Salt Lake City, 1987)

Scottish Record Office, *A Guide to the National Archives of Scotland* (Edinburgh, 1996)

C Sinclair, *Tracing Your Scottish Ancestry: A Guide to Ancestry Research in the Scottish Record Office* (London, 1997)

D J Steel, ed., *Sources for Scottish Genealogy and Family History* (London, 1970)

9 Irish genealogy

9.1 Irish genealogy: records in Ireland

So many Irish records have been lost or destroyed (notably in the burning of the Irish Public Record Office in 1922) that it is well worth making a preliminary approach to the Irish Genealogical Research Society for help. For a detailed recent overview of the surviving records and the availability of finding aids, and for general advice, see Herber, *Ancestral Trails*, pp. 559–568. Two indispensable works put out by the respective archives of Ireland and Northern Ireland are Grenham, *Tracing Your Irish Ancestors,* and Maxwell, *Tracing Your Ancestors in Northern Ireland*. For addresses, see **48**.

A population census was taken in Ireland every ten years between 1821 and 1911, and those that survive are in the National Archives in Dublin The records from 1861–1891 were deliberately destroyed by the government, and only a few of the 1821–1851 censuses survived the fire of 1922. For a list of survivals, and of transcripts or abstracts from lost censuses, see Gibson and Medlycott, *Local Census Listings, 1522–1930, holdings in the British Isles*. Unlike the early English censuses, these Irish censuses include names. Returns for 1901 and 1911 are fairly complete and are open. A census was also taken in the republic in 1926, which is now open to public inspection. Records of applications for old age pensions between 1908 and 1922 may have used census data as a proof of age, for these applicants were born before the introduction of civil registration in 1864. These applications survive at the National Archives in Dublin, and at the Public Record Office of Northern Ireland (PRONI), in Belfast. They have been indexed by name, and a copy of the index can be seen at the Society of Genealogists.

The civil registration of all births, marriages and deaths in Ireland began on 1 January 1864, although the civil registration of marriages other than Roman Catholic had started in 1845. The records for the whole of Ireland until 1921, for the republic of Ireland from 1921 to date, and of non-Roman Catholic marriages from 1 April 1845 are in the General Register Office of Ireland in Dublin. The records of births, marriages and deaths in Northern Ireland since 1 January 1922 are in the General Register Office of Northern Ireland in Belfast.

The two General Register Offices also hold various series of registers of births, deaths and marriages which took place outside Ireland, but which relate to people normally resident there. These are similar to the registers for the English and Welsh abroad (see **4.1**). Those at Dublin include births and deaths at sea (from 1864), consular returns (from 1864), armed services registers (from 1883), and indexes to war registers (from 1899). After partition, the General Register Office of Northern Ireland kept similar series, with marine registers and consular returns from 1922 , and armed service registers from 1927.

Irish parish registers have also suffered much destruction. The *International Genealogical Index* includes about 2,000,000 entries To find out what survives, and where it can be seen, use Mitchell's *A guide to Irish Parish Registers*. Anglican Church of Ireland parish registers started in 1634, but few survive before the late 1700s. They were used by only a minority of the population. About half had been deposited in the Irish Public Record Office for safe keeping, and were thus destroyed in 1922. Roman Catholic parish registers rarely date from before 1830. Mitchell's guide lists what survives for each parish, and includes Presbyterian and nonconformist registers. It also includes references to the copies held by the Society of Genealogists. For maps of Roman Catholic parishes (which were usually bigger than Anglican parishes), see Grenham, *Tracing Your Irish Ancestors*. For Presbyterian registers, look also at Falley, *Irish and Scottish-Irish Ancestral Research*. Many Presbyterian registers are still with the congregations, while others are held by the Presbyterian Historical Society in Belfast, which specialises in the history of Presbyterianism and its ministers.

Virtually all Irish probate records prior to 1904 were destroyed in 1922: Vicars's *Index* to them is now the main clue to what was once there. However, the Society of Genealogists has 18 volumes of abstracts from Irish wills, 1569–1909, and Herber gives details of abstracts of wills surviving in many locations. Calendars of all wills proved and administrations granted since 1858 may be seen at the National Archives and PRONI. PRONI has copies and extracts of many Ulster wills, and for a fee, the Ulster Historical Foundation (at the same address), will undertake genealogical searches. The Ulster Genealogical and Historical Guild publishes a newsletter and a regular list of research in progress.

For records of land holding from 1708, try the Registry of Deeds in Dublin. These can include copies of wills that were used to prove entitlement.

Most of the historic archive was destroyed in 1922: fortunately, some volumes of calendars had been published beforehand (and can be seen in the PRO library). Particularly useful are the published versions of the *Patent and Close Rolls of Chancery in Ireland, Henry VIII, Edward VI, Mary and Elizabeth, and for the 1st to 8th year of Charles I.* For other such publications, ask in the PRO Library to see HMSO, *Sectional List 24: British National Archives* to get the full titles.

9.2 Irish genealogy: records in the PRO

For records in the PRO relating to Irish history, and only incidentally to Irish genealogy, see Prochaska's book, *Irish History from 1700: A Guide to Sources in the Public Record Office.*

The State Papers, Ireland (SP 60–SP 67) contain despatches from the crown's representative in Ireland – the Lord Deputy or Lord Lieutenant, his council and other officials to the Secretaries of State. They sometimes contain copies of letters and petitions sent to them by soldiers, officials, Irish chiefs and private individuals; drafts and minutes of answers made to such despatches; accounts of expenditure or requests for funds; instructions sent out to officials; projects for English colonization or establishing new trades and industries; reports on the state of Ireland, etc. They are full of references to individuals, and are relatively easy to use as they have been published in précis and indexed from 1509–1670 in the *Calendar of State Papers, Ireland*. From 1670 to 1704, they have been included in the *Calendar of State Papers, Domestic*. In fact, the State

Papers, Ireland continue up to 1782: for the later period there are brief lists in the PRO and much fuller lists in the Public Record Office of Northern Ireland. The same type of letters and papers continue in various Home Office and Colonial Office classes after 1782, but they are not fully listed, nor indexed, and so are not easy to use. If you want to investigate these, try Prochaska and the *PRO Guide.*

Some of the records discussed more fully elsewhere in this book may be helpful in tracing Irish family history. The wills of Irish people who died with goods in England may have been proved by the Prerogative Court of Canterbury before 1858 (see **6**). The records of the Irish Tontines of 1773, 1775 and 1777 (see **44**) cover 1773–1871, and list many people, with addresses. The records of the Royal Irish Constabulary, 1836–1922, are full and informative: see **23.6**. For Irish Revenue Police, 1830–1857, who tried to prevent illicit distilling, try CUST 111: see also **24.8**. For Customs officers in Ireland, 1682–1826, see CUST 20. After this, try *Ham's Customs Year Book* and *Ham's Inland Revenue Year Book* which the PRO library has in an incomplete run from 1875–1930. These list Customs and Inland Revenue officials (up to 1923 for Ireland), and include a name index. For a general Irish directory to officials and people of status, see *Thom's Irish Almanac and Official Directory,* which the PRO Library has from 1844–1928, with an odd volume for 1944.

Of course, many Irishmen served in the Army and the Navy, and their records should be explored as described in **18** and **19**: see, for example, the muster rolls of the Irish militia, 1793–1876, in WO 13. Before the Union with the United Kingdom in 1801, Ireland had a separate Army with its own organisation and establishment (although the British Army drew heavily on Irish recruits). From 1801, Ireland remained a separate command, and the Irish regiments retained their Irish identity, but the Army was merged with the British Army. Records relating to the Army in Ireland, 1775–1923, are in WO 35.

The Royal Kilmainham Hospital, founded in 1679, acted as a permanent hospital for disabled soldiers (in-pensioners) and also distributed money to out-pensioners: there are registers of in- and out-pensioners in the admission books, 1704–1922 (WO 118), and discharge documents, 1783–1822 (WO 119). Other Irish soldiers and sailors had their pensions paid by the Royal Chelsea Hospital or by Greenwich Hospital. Records of these pensions, 1842–1862 and 1882–1883, are in WO 22/141–205 and 209–225, arranged by district: they are useful for tracing changes of residence and dates of death.

The only separate naval records for Irishmen are of nominations to serve in the Irish Coastguard, 1821–1849 (ADM 175/99–100).

The records of the Irish Reproductive Loan Fund, in T 91, may be helpful if you are looking for a family in Munster or Connaught in the mid 1800s. The fund provided loans at interest to the industrious poor, who had to provide some form of security for the loan. Records of the local associations which administered the loans survive for counties Cork, Clare, Galway, Limerick, Mayo, Roscommon, Sligo and Tipperary. In addition to the notes of security (signed by the debtor and two guarantors), there are loan ledgers, repayment books and defaulters books. They do not give much detail other than place of abode and occupation.

The Irish Sailors' and Soldiers' Land Trust was set up to provide cottages in Ireland, with or without gardens, for ex-servicemen (including airmen) after the First World War. In the 1920s and 1930s over 4,000 cottages were provided. Because of rent strikes in the republic, no further cottages were built there after 1932, but cottages continued to be built by the Trust in Northern Ireland until 1952. Provisions were later made to sell the cottages to the tenants or their widows. You will need to know the location of the cottage to use the records, as there are no name indexes. The tenancy files in AP 7 are the place to start. They are closed for 75 years, but privileged access can be given provided you sign a written undertaking not to publish or reveal the names or other particulars of people named in the tenancy files. Ask in the Research Enquiries Room for a copy of the form to sign.

Maps of Ireland may be seen in the Map Room. The earliest date from the late 1500s (the Barony Maps in ZMAP 5). The Survey of 1655–1658 (ZOS 7) was the legal basis for the identification of Irish lands. The 1839 6-inch Ordnance Survey maps in ZOS 15 are the most detailed: they have a key sheet near the beginning of each county volume. The 1-inch Ordnance Survey maps in ZOS 14 date from 1851–1852. Lewis's *Topographical Dictionary of Ireland* is also useful in identifying places, and filling out their history.

9.3 Irish genealogy: bibliography

Irish Roots Quarterly

D Begley, *Handbook on Irish Genealogy* (Dublin, 1976)
D Begley, ed., *Irish Genealogy; a Record Finder* (Dublin, 1982)
B de Breffny, *Bibliography of Irish Family History and Genealogy* (Cork and Dublin, 1974)
Calendar of State Papers, Domestic, 1670–1704 (London, 1895–1972)
Calendar of State Papers, Ireland, 1509–1670 (London, 1860–1912)
A Camp, *Sources for Irish Genealogy in the Library of the Society of Genealogists* (Society of Genealogists, 1990)
B Davis, *An Introduction to Irish Research, Irish Ancestry; a beginner's guide* (FFIIS, 1994)
M Falley, *Irish and Scottish-Irish Ancestral Research: A Guide to the Genealogical Records, Methods and Sources in Ireland* (GPC, 1989: reprint of 1962 edition, 2 vols)
J Gibson and M Medlycott, *Local Census Listings, 1522–1930, holdings in the British Isles* (FFHS, 1994)
J Grenham, *Tracing Your Irish Ancestors* (Dublin, 1992)
S Helferty and R Refause, *Directory of Irish Archives* (Dublin, 1993)
M D Herber, *Ancestral Trails* (Sutton, 1997)
S Lewis, *Topographical Dictionary of Ireland* (London, 1846)
M Mac Conghail and P Gorry, *Tracing Irish Ancestors* (Glasgow, 1997)
E MacLysaght, *Bibliography of Irish Family History* (2nd edn, 1982)
I Maxwell, *Tracing Your Ancestors in Northern Ireland* (PRONI, 1997)
B Mitchell, *A guide to Irish Parish Registers* (GPC, 1988)
J Morrin, *Patent and Close Rolls of Chancery in Ireland, Henry VIII, Edward VI, Mary and Elizabeth, and for the 1st to 8th year of Charles I* (London, 1861–1864)
W Nolan, *Tracing the Past. Sources for Local Studies in the Republic of Ireland* (Dublin, 1982)
A Prochaska, *Irish History from 1700: A Guide to Sources in the Public Record Office* (British Records Association and Institute of Historical Research, 1986)
Thom's Irish Almanac and Official Directory (Dublin, 1844 onwards)
A Vicars, ed., *Index to the Prerogative Wills of Ireland, 1536–1810* (Dublin, 1897: reprinted, 1989)

10 Isle of Man genealogy

10.1 Manx genealogy: records on the Isle of Man

The Isle of Man, though subject to the English Crown, has its own Parliament, laws and courts. See Narasimham, *The Manx Family Tree: A Beginners' Guide to Records in the Isle of Man*, for details of all the following records, and their indexes. For addresses, see **48**.

The civil registration of births and marriages on the Isle of Man began on a voluntary basis in 1849. It became compulsory for births and deaths in 1878, and for marriages in 1884. The original registers can be seen at the Isle of Man General Registry. Microfilm copies of the indexes up to 1964 can be seen at the Society of Genealogists, as can copies of some 19th century registers.

Parish registers survive for some parishes from the early 1600s. The *International Genealogical Index* (see **3.3**) is complete for Manx marriages, and refers to many baptisms. Microfilm copies of all parish registers can be seen at the Manx Museum, with some available at the Society of Genealogists.

Wills were proved in church courts until 1884, and then in the Manx High Court of Justice. Wills proved since 1911 are at the General Registry. Wills from the early 1600s to 1910 are kept in the Manx Museum. Wills of some wealthy Manx inhabitants may be found in the Prerogative Courts of York and Canterbury, before 1858: see **6**.

The Manx Museum has other records of interest to family historians, such as the militia records of the Manx Fencibles.

10.2 Manx genealogy: records in the PRO and FRC

The censuses from 1841–1891 cover the Isle of Man, and can be seen at the FRC, with copies at the Manx Museum. The 1851, 1881 and 1891 censuses have been indexed.

Of course, islanders may well turn up in any of the services and other records as described in this book. Topographically arranged records, such as the payments of pensions to ex-soldiers and sailors on the Isle of Man, 1852–1862 in WO 22/207, are particularly useful. Details of soldiers born in the Isle of Man, and discharged to pension between 1760 and 1854, may be found by searching the WO 97 database using *Isle of Man* as the search criterion. If you want to search the lists on-line in the ILDB, use *Isle* and *Man* as separate key words. The records of the Customs include staff lists for 1671–1922 and superannuation registers for 1803–1922 in CUST 39. The latter can give widow's pensions and the dates of birth of any children.

The sovereignty of the Isle of Man was purchased by the Crown from the Duke and Duchess of Athol in 1764. For correspondence between the Isle and the Secretaries of State, 1761–1783, see SP 48. The Privy Council was involved in the administration of the Isle of Man: some of its papers are in SP 48, but most are in PC 1 and PC 8. The Home Office has entry books of correspondence with Man, in HO 99, from 1760–1921. There are lists of charitable bequests, by parish, in HO 99/22, dating from c.1680 to c.1825. An investigation into smuggling in 1791 produced numerous depositions from Manx office-holders and worthies: they are in HO 99/21.

The Crown held extensive estates in Man, so it may be well worth checking among the records in the CRES, LRRO and LR lettercodes: CRES 40/88–92 for example is a set of volumes containing a detailed valuation of the properties of the Duke of Athol on Man, to be bought by the Crown, and of other Crown properties on Man, made in 1826.

10.3 Manx genealogy: bibliography

J R Dickinson, *The Lordship of Man under the Stanleys: Government and Economy in the Isle of Man, 1580–1704* (Manchester, 1996)

M D Herber, *Ancestral Trails* (Sutton, 1997) p. 569

J Narasimham, *The Manx Family Tree: A Beginners' Guide to Records in the Isle of Man* (Isle of Man, 2nd edn, 1994)

11 Channel Islands genealogy

11.1 Jersey

Most records are in Jersey. Records of baptism, marriage and burial before 1842 are held by the parish clergy, who may issue extracts from the registers in their custody. The civil registration of births, marriages and deaths in Jersey began in 1842. Registers of births, non-Anglican marriages and deaths are held by the Registrars of the island's twelve parishes. The registers of marriages in the Anglican church are still in the custody of the parish priests. Duplicate registers of all births, marriages and deaths are held by the Superintendent Registrar and he, like the Parochial Registrars and the clergy, can undertake fee-paid searches and issue certified extracts from those registers in his custody. The registers are not open to the public. The Superintendent Registrar cannot undertake genealogical research of a general nature. Try contacting either the Société Jersiaise or the Channel Islands Family History Society, who both hold a microfiche index for 1842–1900: one of their members may be prepared to undertake paid research.

A few records of births, marriages and deaths in Jersey are in the PRO, among the foreign registers in RG 32, indexed by RG 43.

The censuses at the FRC also cover Jersey (see **2**) and are obviously a main source. For 1851 and 1891 there are published name indexes for the whole of Jersey, thanks to the Channel Islands Family History Society, which are an enormous help. There is also, of course, the 1881 name index at the FRC.

The Association Oath roll for Jersey (C 213/462) appears by its length to contain the signatures, or marks and names, of all the island's men in 1696. It has been published in facsimile, with full transcripts, by A Glendinning as *Did Your Ancestors Sign the Jersey Oath of Allegiance Roll of 1696?* There is also a petition of c.1847, to Queen Victoria, not to amend the island's constitution, which is signed by 5,567 inhabitants (PC 1/4564), but this is not in any discernible order.

Details of soldiers born in Jersey, and discharged to pension between 1760 and 1854, may be found by searching the WO 97 database using Jersey as the search criterion. Details of ex-soldiers and sailors in receipt of a Chelsea or Greenwich pension, or their widows and orphans, living in Jersey, 1842–1862, may be found in WO 22/205–206. Muster rolls of the Jersey militia, 1843–1852, are in WO 13/1055. Many of the other records described in this book will also include islanders.

11.2 Guernsey, Alderney and Sark

Pre-civil registration records are held by the rectors of the ten Guernsey parishes, and by the vicars of Alderney and Sark. Civil registration of births, deaths and non-Anglican marriages in Guernsey began in 1840; in Alderney in 1850; and in Sark, of deaths in 1915. From 1919 all marriages and from 1925 all births and deaths in Guernsey, Alderney and Sark have been registered centrally in Guernsey by Her Majesty's Greffier (as Registrar-General of Births, Deaths and Marriages): these are open to public inspection at the Greffe, Guernsey. In addition, copies of the 19th century civil registration records can be seen at the Priaulx Library in St Peter Port, and also at the Society of Genealogists, where there are also indexes up to 1966. Enquiries relating to Alderney should be addressed to the Clerk of the Court; and to Sark to the Registrar.

Deeds, judicial records and wills may be consulted by searchers in person at the Greffe, Guernsey; all are indexed. Permission to consult wills of personalty from 1664 should be obtained from the Registrar of the Ecclesiastical Court. Microfilm copies of the 1841–1881 census returns for Guernsey, Alderney and Sark are also held at the Greffe as well as at the FRC, where there is a name index for 1881 (see also **2**). Pedigrees of leading island families, and copies of are held at the Priaulx Library, St Peter Port, Guernsey. For other records relating to Sark, see the Axtons' *Calendar and Catalogue of Sark Seigneurie Archives, 1526–1927*.

Some records of births, marriages and deaths in Guernsey, Alderney and Sark are in the PRO, among the foreign registers in RG 32, indexed by RG 43. Details of soldiers born in Guernsey, and discharged to pension between 1760 and 1854, may be found by searching the WO 97 database using Guernsey as the search criterion. Details of ex-soldiers and sailors in receipt of a Chelsea or Greenwich pension, or their widows and orphans, living in the Channel Islands, 1842–1852, may be found in WO 22/205. Muster rolls of the Guernsey militia, 1843–1852, are in WO 13/887.

For an extraordinarily vivid account of a life in Guernsey from about 1890–1970, you may like to try the acclaimed work by Edwards, *The Book of Ebenezer Le Page*.

11.3 The Channel Islands: general historical sources

The Channel Islands are subject to the Crown of England, but they are not part of the United Kingdom. Many of the records created there are in French.

For medieval records held in the PRO relating to the Channel Islands, try the various accounts in E 101 and the Chancery miscellanea in C 47. For a survey of this material, an account of the medieval government of the islands, and a list of wardens and sub-wardens, see Le Patourel, *The Medieval Administration of the Channel Islands, 1199–1399*.

For later general papers relating to the administration and domestic affairs of the Channel Islands, see the record classes below. All these will give you a perspective on life in the Channel Islands in the past. For example, the correspondence and papers for Alderney in 1821 included the census return (no names given), explaining that the total decay in trade had caused much emigration to America, France and the other islands. (For Channel Island emigration to North America, see the book by Turk.) The papers do sometimes contain references to individuals, such as the lists of French Protestants living in Jersey in 1750 (in SP 47/4), but they are a historical rather than genealogical source. Many are in French. Those with a calendar reference have been published and indexed.

Correspondence and papers between the Channel Islands and the Secretaries of State		
1547–1625	SP 15	*Calendar of State Papers, Domestic, Addenda*
1625–1649	SP 16	*Calendar of State Papers, Domestic, Charles I*
1660–1670	SP 29	*Calendar of State Papers, Domestic, Charles II*

1670–1781	SP 47	1670–April 1704 *Calendar of State Papers, Domestic, Charles II–Anne*; May 1704–1760 not calendared – use the manuscript précis in SP 130/63–64 1760–1775 *Home Office Papers of the Reign of George III*; 1776–1781 not calendared The Introductory Note to SP 47 tells you how to translate any obsolete references you may find in these published works into modern references
1782–1849	HO 98	
1840–1979	HO 45	
Entry books of the above correspondence		
1748–1760	SP 111	
1760–1921	HO 99	Calendared 1760–1775 in *Home Office Papers of the Reign of George III*
Correspondence and papers between the Channel Islands and the Privy Council		
18th–19th c.	PC 1	
1860–1956	PC 8	

For details of French refugees in Jersey, 1793–1796, see FO 95/602–603 and HO 98 (for all the islands).

11.4 The Channel Islands in World War II

The PRO holds material on the occupation of the Channel Islands by the Germans in World War II. For example, WO 208/3741 includes accounts of life in occupied Jersey and Alderney, taken in October 1944. Ask at the Research Enquiries Desk to see the Press Packs 92D and 96F for further references.

11.5 Channel Islands genealogy: bibliography

M Axton and R Axton, *Calendar and Catalogue of Sark Seigneurie Archives, 1526–1927*, List and Index Society, Special Series, vol. 26, 1991

M L Backhurst, *Family History in Jersey* (Channel Islands Family History Society, 1991)

L R Burnes, 'Genealogical Research in the Channel Islands', *Genealogists' Magazine*, vol. XIX, pp. 169–172

Channel Islands Family History Society, *The 1851 Census of Jersey: An All-Island Index* (1996)

Channel Islands Family History Society, *The 1891 Census of Jersey: An All-Island Index* (1994)

J Conway Davies, 'The Records of the Royal Courts', La Société Guernesiaise, *Transactions*, vol. XVI, pp. 404–414

G B Edwards, *The Book of Ebenezer Le Page* (1981)

A Glendinning, *Did Your Ancestors Sign the Jersey Oath of Allegiance Roll of 1696?* (Channel Islands Family History Society, 1995)

M D Herber, *Ancestral Trails* (Sutton, 1997) pp. 570–571

J Le Patourel, J H Lenfestey and others, *List of Records in the Greffe, Guernsey* (List and Index Society, Special Series, Vols 2 and 11, 1969 and 1978). Additional lists may be consulted in typescript at the Greffe

J H Le Patourel, *The Medieval Administration of the Channel Islands, 1199–1399* (Oxford, 1937)

David W Le Poidevin, *How to Trace your Ancestors in Guernsey* (Taunton, 1978)

M G Turk, *The Quiet Adventurers in North America* (Maryland, 1993)

12 Immigrants to Britain

12.1 Introduction

Individual immigrants have been coming to Britain for centuries. Migrants from Ireland and the colonies, who were deemed to have a natural loyalty to the Crown, were treated differently from aliens. Aliens were people from foreign countries, who acknowledged another sovereignty: they were treated as a separate legal species, with fewer rights, because they were under no legal constraint of loyalty to the Crown. As a result, they are in fact better documented than the colonial immigrants.

The journal *Immigrants and Minorities* may well contain articles of interest on specific immigrant communities not mentioned here (e.g. Lithuanians in Lanarkshire), which may provide further PRO references. Once migrants had arrived and settled, you will find people in the normal ways, through registration of births, marriages and deaths, the census, etc.

12. 2 Colonial immigration

Remember that the Irish were not treated as immigrants, but as internal migrants, so you will not normally find any records of people moving from Ireland to England and Wales. Many people used to do this on a seasonal basis, coming over for the harvest, and then going back to Ireland.

The British black community has been established for a long time: in the late eighteenth century , there may already have been about 20,000 black people in London alone (see Fryer, *Staying Power*). There are particular difficulties in tracing black descent before civil registration of births, marriages and deaths, as parish records of black people may not have included surnames. Clues that you may be looking at an entry relating to a black person in an early parish register are mention of colour, a classical name such as Pompey or Scipio, and adult baptism, which was unusual in the Anglican church. Try the Black Genealogical Society for further advice (address in **48**). There is a useful introduction to the subject by Pearl in 'Britain's Black African Ancestors'.

Many West Indians (both men and women) who later migrated to the UK had served there in the armed forces, or in the munitions industry, in the First and Second World War: see Sherwood, *Many Struggles: West Indian Workers and Service Personnel in Britain (1939–45)*. For colonial immigration from the West Indies and the Indian sub-continent after the 1948 Nationality Act (which granted UK citizenship to citizens of British colonies and former colonies), there is little as yet in the PRO in the way of information on individuals. Try the Inward Passenger Lists, which stop in 1960 (see **12.3**). However, much has been written on this recently (particularly because of the celebrations of the fiftieth anniversary of the arrival in 1948 of the *Empire Windrush* from the West Indies), so it may be worth checking your library or local history collection for publications such as the Phillips' *Windrush: The Irresistible Rise of Multi-Racial Britain*.

There have been Indian and Chinese communities in the UK for almost as long: for an introduction to the subject, see Visram, *Ayahs, Lascars and Princes: Indians in Britain 1700–1947*.

You may find the *Black and Asian Studies Newsletter*, put out by the Institute of Commonwealth Studies (address in **48**) to be of great value.

12.3 Immigration by sea, 1878–1960

The Inward Passenger Lists (BT 26) can be a useful source of information for immigrants arriving by sea between 1878 and 1960, from places outside Europe and the Mediterranean area (but including passengers picked up at European ports, if the ship had stopped there on its inward voyage). They give name, age, occupation and address in the United Kingdom, and the date of entry. Unfortunately, there are no name indexes and, as BT 26 is a very large class, it is vital to know at least an approximate date of arrival, or the port of entry, or the name of the ship. It may be worth checking in *Lloyd's Register* for further clues. A copy is available at the PRO. After 1906 the Registers of Passenger Lists (BT 32) give, under each port, the names of the ships and their dates of arrival. The Passenger Lists after 1960 have not been preserved: there are none for arrivals by air.

12.4 Medieval and early modern aliens

Medieval aliens (foreigners) had to pay double taxes, and there are separate lists of contributors to the 'alien subsidies' or taxes in E 179 (see **43**). There are also three surveys of aliens living in London, taken in November 1571 (SP 12/82); December 1571 (SP 12/84) and [September] 1618 (SP 14/102). These have been published by the Huguenot Society. Many early refugees came to England to escape religious persecution of Protestants and Jews on the continent (see section **32.4** and **35**). Others came for political reasons. Many of the exiles from the Palatinate, shipped from Holland to England *en route* to the Americas in 1709, chose to stay in England instead: for more details see **14.7**. References may be traceable through the published *Calendars of State Papers Domestic*, as well as through the main classes of Chancery enrolments (see **5.3**).

12.5 Denization of aliens

Foreigners resident in England, wishing to regularize their position, could apply for denization (which granted them most of a free subject's rights and the protection of the king's laws) or naturalization (which granted them all, and made them a subject of the crown). However, most foreign settlers did not bother to go through these legal formalities, and so do not appear in these records.

An alien was made a denizen by letters patent from the crown: as a denizen, he could purchase land, but could not inherit it. Any children born after the parents' denization appear to have been subjects: those born before could only be denizens. Denizens had the additional burden of paying a higher rate of tax, and were ineligible for government posts. Letters patent of denization were enrolled on the Patent Rolls (C 66) and the Supplementary Patent Rolls (C 67).

Denizations before 1509 can be traced through the indexes to the *Calendar of Patent Rolls*: in the early volumes individual names are not given in the index, and it is necessary to look under 'Denizations' or *'Indigenae'*. For the period 1509 to 1800, indexes to denizations have been published by the Huguenot Society. A copy of these, together with a typescript index to denizations between 1801 and 1873, is attached to the list of HO 1. The indexes are not absolutely complete.

Denizations of Protestant refugees, 1678–1688, are entered in SP 44/67. Some draft bills for denization, 1830–1880, are in C 197/29.

12.6 Naturalization of aliens

Naturalization was more expensive than denization. It originally required a private act of Parliament, as well as the swearing of oaths of allegiance and supremacy, and taking Holy Communion according to the Anglican rite, effectively disbarring Jews and Roman Catholics. It made the foreigner into the king's subject, able to inherit land, and affected the children born before naturalization as well. Indexes to naturalization by private act of Parliament up to 1900 are attached to the HO 1 list. The acts themselves may be seen at the House of Lords Record Office. Between 1708 and 1711, all foreign Protestants who took the oaths of allegiance and supremacy in open court were deemed to have been naturalized (KB 24, E 169/86; see **15.1**). The information from these oath rolls has been published by the Huguenot Society. Between 1740 and 1773, foreign Protestants in the Americas were naturalized by the same process: see **14.7**. Many Spanish Jews in Jamaica were also granted naturalization, which was easier for a Jew to get in the West Indies than in England.

In 1844, naturalization procedure was simplified, and the Home Office began granting certificates of naturalization. Copies of naturalization certificates issued between 1844 and 1871 are available in HO 1 (they were also enrolled on the Close Rolls, C 54, until 1873): those issued between 1870 and 1965 are in HO 334. Related correspondence on individual naturalizations may exist in HO 1 for 1844 to 1871, in HO 45 for 1872 to 1878, and in HO 144 from 1879 to 1922. The Home Office will consider applications from descendants to see closed correspondence from 1923 to 1936. There is a joint index to these classes (HO 1, HO 45, HO 144 and HO 334), attached to the HO 1 list. This gives name, country of origin, date of the certificate, place of residence (e.g. Liverpool), and the reference to the copy of the certificate and to any related papers. This index goes up to 1936: between 1937 and 1962, annual returns of aliens were presented to Parliament, and were printed as parliamentary papers. These are available in the Research Enquiries Room.

Enquiries about recent naturalizations should be sent to the Home Office: see **48** for the address.

12.7 Alien registration, 1793–1869

A system of registration of aliens (i.e. foreigners) entering the country was first set up by the Aliens Act of 1793, and was modified by subsequent statutes. On entering England, aliens were required to register with a Justice of the Peace, and to give their name, rank, address and occupation; a certificate was sent into the Aliens Office (part of the Home Office from 1836). The Aliens Act, 1836, required aliens to sign certificates of arrival: these survive in HO 2 for aliens arriving in England and Scotland, 1836–1852. The earlier certificates, before 1836, appear to have been destroyed by the Home Office, but local registration records before Justices or Clerks of the Peace may have survived in local record offices. An index of certificates, 1826–1849 (including those since destroyed), survives in HO 5/25–32. The certificates give nationality, profession, date of arrival, last country visited and sometimes other information as well. HO 2 is arranged by year, under the ports of arrival, so between 1849 and 1852 you may have to search at length, unless the Metzner index (see below) helps.

Some passes issued to aliens between 1793 and 1836 are in HO 1, recording name, port of entry, nationality, religion, occupation, place of residence and intended destination. Aliens arriving in English ports, 1810–1811, may be traced in FO 83/21–22.

Some lists of alien passengers, 1836–1869, were sent in to the Home Office by the masters of ships (HO 3): they are bound up in date order, and there is no general index. However, an incomplete name index, by Metzner, of German, Polish and Prussian aliens in HO 2 and HO 3, for 1847–1852 only, can be seen in the Research Enquiries Room. For entry books of correspondence about aliens, 1794–1909, see HO 5.

12.8 Refugees, 1788–1919

The PRO has records of annuities and pensions paid to some refugees for services to the crown. These include, for example, pensions to American loyalists, 1788–1837 (AO 3/276), allowances to Polish refugees, 1828–1856 (PMG 53, and T 1/409) and 1861–1865 (AO 3/1418), and allowances to Spaniards, 1855–1909 (PMG 53, and T 1/4285). The influx of French émigrés between 1789 and 1814 produced much government documentation (HO 69, PC 1, FO 95 and WO 1). In particular, the records of the Treasury's French Refugee Relief Committee, 1792–1828, contain lists of names of those receiving pensions (T 50, T 93).

For Belgian refugees, 1914–1919, there is a considerable amount of material entered on the 'history cards' in MH 8/39–93. Each card relates to a whole family, unless the refugee was single with no known relatives. The details given are names, ages, relationships, wife's maiden name, allowances and the address for payment.

Some hostel lists of refugees in 1917 are in MH 8/10.

12.9 Twentieth century: registration of aliens

Registration of aliens became a concern of MI5 at the time of the First World War, when a rigid system of port control was introduced. Some lists and addresses of suspected aliens are in KV 1. Police registration records may have survived locally (for example, Bedfordshire Record Office holds 25,000 record cards, from 1919 until the 1980s). See HO 213 for policy files of the Home Office Aliens Department from 1914 onwards.

A large collection of aliens' personal files opened between 1934 and 1948, with some earlier papers attached, has been selected for permanent preservation, but it will take very many years to process and release them, and they may not be released in full for 100 years. Although it is a very large collection, it will not include everyone naturalized in that period.

During the First and Second World Wars enemy aliens were interned by the British authorities. In both wars internment camps were established within the United Kingdom.

12.10 First World War: internees

Very few records of individual internees survive for the First World War. Specimen lists of German subjects interned as prisoners of war in 1915 and 1916 can be found in WO 900/45 and WO 900/46 and a classified list of interned enemy aliens can be found in HO 144/11720/364868. Nominal rolls of male enemy aliens of the age of 45 and upwards, submitted to the Secretary of State by commandants of internment camps, are included among a census of aliens in the United Kingdom from 1915 to 1924 in HO 45/11522/287235. References to individual internees can also be found among the card index to the Foreign Office general correspondence in the Research Enquiries Room.

Home Office records dealing primarily with policy relating to internees and internment camps can be found among the Home Office General Correspondence (HO 45) and Home Office Supplementary Correspondence (HO 144). Both classes of records are arranged by subject matter, and papers relating to internment and internees may be found under the headings 'Aliens' and 'War'.

Other material on enemy internees is in MEPO 2/1796–1799 (1917–1920).

12.11 Refugees in the 1930s and 1940s

For Jewish refugees, see **35.5**.

Records of the Czechoslovak Refugee Trust are in HO 294: they relate not only to Czechoslovak refugees, but also to German and Austrian refugees. The class includes some specimen personal files on families: these are closed for 50 years (some for 75 years) from the last date on the file.

12.12 Second World War: alien internees

Internees primarily consisted of enemy aliens, but during the first two years of the Second World War other aliens were also interned, including refugees who had fled Nazi Germany to escape persecution. Fears of invasion led to a general feeling of hostility towards all enemy aliens. After the outbreak of war in September 1939, known Nazi sympathizers were rounded up. This was the start of a campaign which lasted to mid 1940 by which time 8,000 internees had been gathered into camps, to be deported to the dominions. This harsh policy was gradually relaxed after the sinking of the SS *Arandora Star* by a German U-boat in July 1940, with the loss of 800 internees. This disaster led to vigorous protests about the British internment policy, which was changed to internment of enemy aliens in camps in Britain only.

Most internees had been released by the end of 1942. Of those that remained, many were repatriated from 1943 onwards. It was not, however, until late 1945 that the last internees were finally released.

A very small sample of personal case files of internees survive for the Second World War. These records, in HO 214, are particularly useful in depicting the life of an internee. The files were created whenever the Home Office became involved in a personal case for whatever reason. The index cards of aliens for the period 1939–1947, in HO 396, provide a more general source. The class consists of and includes name indexes to internees and aliens (considered for internment) at liberty in the UK. Some pieces are closed for 85 years but many give family history details such as date of birth, address, occupation and details of employers.

References to individual internees and internment camps may be found in the printed indexes of the general correspondence of the Foreign Office, available in the Research Enquiries Room. Surviving papers referred to in these indexes may be found in FO 371 but, before ordering any documents, you need to convert the old Foreign Office reference recorded in the printed index to a modern PRO reference: guidance is available on how to do this.

Other Foreign Office records relating to enemy aliens interned by the British are in FO 916.

The class consists of general files relating to reports on internment camps and a number of lists of alien internees, arranged by location, name and number of camp.

12.13 Second World War: internment camps

Nominal lists of internees can be found in HO 215. These records are arranged by name of internment camp and the documents record the internee's name, date of birth and (if applicable) date of release. HO 215 also contains general files relating to internment during the Second World War including subjects such as conditions in camps, visits to camps, classification and segregation of internees, regulations and enactments and the movement of internees abroad. HO 213 also contains a selection of files relating to internment camps during the Second World War, as do the classes HO 45 and HO 144 under the subject headings 'Aliens' and 'War'. For further information on defence regulation 18B and the internment of fascists please ask for Source Sheet No. 25, 'Fascism and anti-Fascism in the United Kingdom', at the Research Enquiries Desk. There is a memorandum on Isle of Man Internment Camps during the Second World War; ask at the Research Enquiries Desk for this.

12.14 Deportations, from 1906

Register of deportees, 1906–1963, are in HO 372. These tend to give name, nationality, date of conviction, offence, whether and when the deportation order was revoked. Related files are in HO 382 and HO 384.

For the first two years of the Second World War, approximately 8,000 enemy aliens were temporarily interned in British camps prior to being deported to the colonies and the dominions. Passenger lists survive for merchant vessels leaving British ports for ports outside Europe and the Mediterranean Sea in the class of records BT 26. These records are arranged by date and port of departure and are not indexed by surname and in order to use them it is necessary to know the name of the ship and preferably port of departure in order to avoid a very time consuming and speculative search. Registers of passenger lists in BT 32 give, under the different ports, the names of ships and the month of departure. These records are available on open access in the Research Enquiries Room.

Many ships carrying internees were lost at sea by enemy torpedoes and these losses resulted in ending the policy of deporting internees. Survivors' reports of lost vessels can be found among the Admiralty war history cases and papers in ADM 1. A card index, arranged by name of vessel, is located in the Research Enquiries Room. Similarly, official inquiries into such losses may be found among the War Cabinet Memoranda series in CAB 66. Ask at the Research Enquiries desk for the memorandum on the loss of the SS *Arandora Star*.

12.15 Poles in and after the Second World War

For Poles who fought in Polish units attached to allied armies, try the records of the Polish Resettlement Corps, set up in 1946 to ease their transition to civilian life in Britain and abroad (WO 315). Other records relating to Polish resettlement are in AST 18, with some in AST 7, AST

11, and AST 1/23. Many of these records are in Polish, and some are closed for 75 years.

12.16 Immigrants to Britain: bibliography

Published works

Black and Asian Studies Newsletter (Institute of Commonwealth Studies). Unfortunately, this journal is not available in the PRO library.

Calendar of Close Rolls, 1227–1509 (London, 1892–1963)

Calendar of Patent Rolls, 1216–1509, 1547–1582 (London, 1894–1986)

Calendar of State Papers, Domestic Series, 1547–1704 (London, 1856–1972)

Calendar of Treasury Papers, 1557–1728 (London, 1868–1889)

P Fryer, *Black People in the British Empire: An Introduction* (London, 1989)

P Fryer, *Staying Power: The History of Black People in Britain* (London, 1984)

Home Office Certificates of Naturalisation, Index, 1844–1936 (London, 1908–1937)

Huguenot Society, *Registers of Churches, of Huguenots in London and elsewhere* (London, 1887–1956)

Huguenot Society, *Returns of Aliens Dwelling in the City and Suburbs of London* (Publications of the Huguenot Society, vol. X)

Immigrants and Minorities (Frank Cass, 1982 onwards). Each volume generally includes a bibliography of recent published and unpublished works. Unfortunately, this journal is not available in the PRO library.

R E G Kirk, *Returns of Aliens in London, 1523–1603* (Huguenot Society, vol. X, London, 1900–1908)

W Page, *Denization and Naturalisation of Aliens in England, 1509–1603* (Huguenot Society, vol. VIII, Lymington, 1893)

Pearl, 'Britain's Black African Ancestors', *Family Tree Magazine*, vol. 11 no. 12 pp. 11–12

M Phillips and T Phillips, *Windrush: The Irresistible Rise of Multi-Racial Britain* (London, 1998)

Rotuli Parliamentorum, Edward I to Henry VII (London, 1783, Index, London, 1832)

W A Shaw, *Letters of Denization and Acts of Naturalisation for Aliens in England, 1603–1800* (Huguenot Society, Lymington, 1911, Manchester, 1923 and London, 1932)

M A Sherwood, *Many Struggles: West Indian Workers and Service Personnel in Britain (1939–45)* (London, 1984)

Slavery and Abolition (Frank Cass, 1980 onwards). Each volume generally includes a bibliography of recent published and unpublished works.

R Visram, *Ayahs, Lascars and Princes: Indians in Britain 1700–1947* (London, 1986)

Unpublished finding aids

Index to Denizations, 1801–1873, and to Acts of Naturalisation, 1801–1935, attached to HO 1 list

Indexes to 'Foreign' Churches in RG 4

Index of Memorials for Denizations and Naturalisations, 1835–1844

B Lloyd, 'List and Registers of Dutch Chapel Royal, 1689–1825'

Metzner index to German, Polish and Prussian aliens, 1847–1852, in HO 2 and HO 3

13 British nationals abroad

13.1 Licences to pass beyond the seas

For the late sixteenth and early seventeenth century, there are registers of people applying for licences before going overseas, in E 157. The earliest dates from 1572–1578. There are lists of soldiers taking the oath of allegiance before going to the wars in the Low Countries, 1613–1624, and licences to go abroad, mostly to Holland, 1624–1632. The registers of passengers to New England, Barbados and other colonies, 1634–1639, and 1677, have been printed by Hotten. For passes to go abroad between March 1650 and February 1653, see SP 25/111.

13.2 Passports

Before the First World War, passports were not required, and it was rare for someone travelling abroad to apply for one: most holders of passports were merchants or diplomats. Records of passports are often disappointing, as they contain little information.

Entry books of passes issued by the Secretaries of State, 1697–1784, are in SP 44/386–411, with another entry book, 1748–1794, in FO 366/544. There is no index. There are registers of passports issued, 1795–1948, in FO 610: for March to May 1915, the register is in FO 613/2. The entries are chronological, and show merely the date, the number of the passport issued, and the name of the applicant. There are indexes for 1851–1862 and 1874–1916, but they give no more information (FO 611). A very miscellaneous collection of over 2,000 British and foreign passports, 1802–1961, is in FO 655; they are listed haphazardly, giving date and place of issue. A small selection of case papers, 1916–1983, is in FO 737.

For more detail, it may be worth checking in the correspondence of the Passport Office, 1815–1905 (FO 612/21–71). Records of British passports issued in foreign countries and British colonies may sometimes be found in consular and colonial records.

13.3 Foreign Office, consular and colonial records

For births, marriages and deaths of Britons abroad, see **4**. These records, taken as a historical source, can establish the existence of an ex-patriate community: the large number of burials in Oporto, for example, may lead you on to finding out more about the British community there.

For the early modern period, you will need to explore the State Papers Foreign and Colonial: look, for example, at the *Calendar of State Papers, Colonial 1574–1738*. After 1782, the embassy and consular archives of the Foreign Office should be fruitful terrain to explore: there are very many classes involved, so see Atherton's guide for advice on finding your way round the enormous quantity of information accumulated by the Foreign Office. The Foreign Office Index in the Research Enquiries Room is well worth checking. Similarly, for the colonies and dominions, you may need to explore the records of the Colonial and Dominions Office. See the guides to these records by Pugh and Thurston. The many classes of foreign and colonial Original Correspondence are well worth exploring. There are leaflets available at the PRO to help you use the various indexes to these records. You may not find a direct reference to your ancestors, but you will find much about the institutions and events of where they were living.

13.4 Government gazettes from the colonies and dominions

The government of each British colony or dominion published its own newspapers, known as government gazettes (or official or royal gazettes), for most of the nineteenth and twentieth centuries. They can provide valuable information for family historians, because the PRO does not (with a few minor exceptions) hold the internal records of colonial governments. Government gazettes usually have an index at the beginning of each volume.

Gazettes frequently list or refer to named individuals. Some of the more common entries in which individuals appear in gazettes are lists of immigrants and emigrants, voters rolls, and notifications of appointments to positions in official bodies and the police and military services. Other items about individuals include notices concerning deaths and estates of the deceased, divorce, insolvency, and legal disputes and criminal cases. Frequently, the gazette will give valuable information about the person in question, including his or her address.

The majority of people named in the gazettes were settlers. However, members of colonized populations do appear in the records. This is especially true in countries where local people, at certain points, played a role in the workings of government – as policemen or clerks, for instance. Where people were legally property they might also appear in the records. Gazettes from the Caribbean, for example, carry advertisements for the return of slaves who had escaped. Some gazettes – depending on time and place – contain lists of Indian indentured labourers or of people applying for British citizenship. The records are also more likely to name male rather than female ancestors, but, since women did, for instance, own property, get divorced, leave wills and vote, their names do appear from time to time.

To find a particular person in the gazettes, you will need to know the colony and the period you are looking for. It will also help to have an idea of the kind of transaction the person may have been involved in. The names of individuals often appear in the annual indexes of the gazettes, but usually they are listed in subsections. For instance, those appointed to positions in the colony will probably be listed in the 'appointments' category of the index.

If you are looking for individuals working for colonial governments, you *may* also find them listed in the Blue Books. These were books in which (mainly statistical) information on each colony was reported. They are usually arranged in the CO and DO 'miscellanea' classes, but occasionally they can be found in the supplements to the gazettes. In addition, there are classes entitled 'public service lists' for Australia, Canada, Iraq, New Zealand and Nigeria.

To find all these records, consult the CO and DO indexes, filed with the class lists to these lettercodes.

13.5 Newspapers from the colonies and dominions

The PRO also holds a small selection of newspapers published in the colonies, mostly covering the period c.1830–c.1860, although there are a few eighteenth century examples. These are listed in the 'newspapers' section of the CO index, which also provides references for a few government gazettes. However, the British Library Newspaper Library has much more extensive holdings of colonial newspapers (address in **48**).

13.6 Other places to look

For nearly 9,000 Army pensioners in India, Canada and South Africa between 1772 and 1899, taken from WO 120/35, 69 and 70, see Crowder, *British Army Pensioners Abroad, 1772–1899*.

For wills proved in British probate courts in Turkey and China, see **6.22**. For the repatriation of mentally-ill Britons from China, 1908–1932, see C 211/70–75.

13.7 The British in India

The PRO is not the place to trace Britons in India. Most of the records of the British in India, including the registration of baptisms, marriages and burials, 1698–1948, and also wills, 1618–1948, are preserved among the India Office records at the British Library. Their biographical index contains 295,000 entries and is still growing. See also *Sources for Anglo-Indian Genealogy in the Library of the Society of Genealogists*. The National Army Museum also has useful material (see **18.27**). The British Association for Cemeteries in South Asia is also worth contacting, and you may be interested in the British in India Museum. The addresses are given in **48**.

However, the PRO Library holds a run of the annual *East India Register*, continued by the *India List* (under various titles) from 1791–1947, as well as the separate *Indian Army List*. These are all very informative and well worth a look.

13.8 British subjects interned by enemies, First and Second World Wars

For records relating to British subjects interned in enemy countries, look in FO 371, using the indexes. For World War II, look in FO 916 as well. This class consists of general files relating to reports on internment camps and a number of lists of British internees, arranged by location, name and number of camp. For civilian (including British) internees in enemy and enemy occupied colonies look in CO 980. See **36** for prisoners of war.

13.9 British nationals abroad: bibliography

L Atherton, *'Never Complain, Never Explain' Records of the Foreign Office and State Paper Office, 1500–c.1960* (PRO, 1994)

I A Baxter, *Brief Guide to Biographical Sources in the India Office Library* (London, 1979)

British Library, *India Office Records, Sources for Family History Research* (London, 1988)

J A Bryden, 'Genealogical Research in Gibraltar', *Genealogists' Magazine*, vol. XXIV, pp. 289–293

Calendar of State Papers, Colonial 1574–1738 (London, 1860–1970)

N K Crowder, *British Army Pensioners Abroad, 1772–1899* (Baltimore, 1995)

East India Register (various titles)

I V Fitzhugh, 'East India Company Ancestry', *Genealogists' Magazine*, vol. XXI, pp. 150–154

G Grannum, *Tracing Your West Indian Ancestors* (PRO, 1995)

India [Office and Burma Office] List, 1791–1947

Indian Army List, 1901–1939

M Moir, *A General Guide to the India Office Records* (London, 1988)

R B Pugh, *The Records of the Colonial and Dominions Office* (London, 1964)

Public Record Office, *The Records of the Foreign Office 1782–1939* (London, 1969)

Society of Genealogists, *Sources for Anglo-Indian Genealogy in the Library of the Society of Genealogists* (Society of Genealogists, 1990)

A Thurston, *Records of the Colonial Office, Dominions Office, Commonwealth Relations Office and Commonwealth Office* (London, 1995)

14 Voluntary emigrants

14.1 Emigrants: general points

The PRO has many records relating to emigration but, because of the nature and limited scope of many of them, there can be no certainty of finding information on any particular individual. Involuntary emigrants are easier to trace: see **40**, on the transportation of convicts. For records of births, marriages and deaths of Britons abroad, see **4**.

If you are trying to trace ancestors back *into* the United Kingdom, there is little likelihood of finding a family before the central registration of births, marriages and deaths (1837 in England and Wales, 1855 in Scotland) *unless* their place of origin is known. It is essential to do some preliminary research among published means of reference and in the archives of the emigrant's place of destination before starting the search in the Public Record Office. Much of the more easily accessible information about emigrants to America and Australia has been published over the years: the most useful items are listed in the bibliographies at **14.11** and **40.5**.

British colonies were established in North America from the late sixteenth century, and correspondence relating to settlement there may be found in CO 1, described and indexed in the *Calendar of State Papers Colonial, 1514–1739*. Large scale emigration also took place to Australia, New Zealand and Africa.

14.2 Emigrants: general sources, 1817–1894

The records of the Colonial Office include much material relating to emigrants. Emigration Original Correspondence, 1817–1896 (CO 384) contains many letters from settlers or people intending to settle in British North America, Australia, the West Indies and other places: there are separate registers for British North America for 1850–1863 (CO 327) and 1864–1868 (CO 328).

The Land and Emigration Commission was established in 1833 to promote emigration by providing free passage and land grants: ask at the Research Enquiries Desk for the memorandum on it, if you want more information. The Emigration Entry Books, 1814–1871 (CO 385) and the Land and Emigration Commission Papers, 1833–1894 (CO 386) give names of emigrants.

Many poor emigrants were provided with assistance for the passage by their parish, under the provisions of the 1834 Poor Law Amendment Act. The records of the administration of this assistance (MH 12) can include lists of emigrants, giving their occupation and destination: however, they are arranged by county and Poor Law Union, not by name, and can be very difficult to find (see **30**). Other records relating to parish-organized emigration will be found locally: see the article by Burchall, listed in the bibliography under North America and West Indies.

14.3 Emigrants: Outwards Passenger Lists, 1890–1960

Outwards Passenger Lists, 1890–1960 (BT 27) are lists of passengers leaving the United Kingdom by sea for destinations outside Europe and the Mediterranean area. They give the name, age, occupation and some sort of address of the passengers, but they are arranged by year and port of departure, and there are no name indexes. The Registers of Passenger Lists, 1906–1951

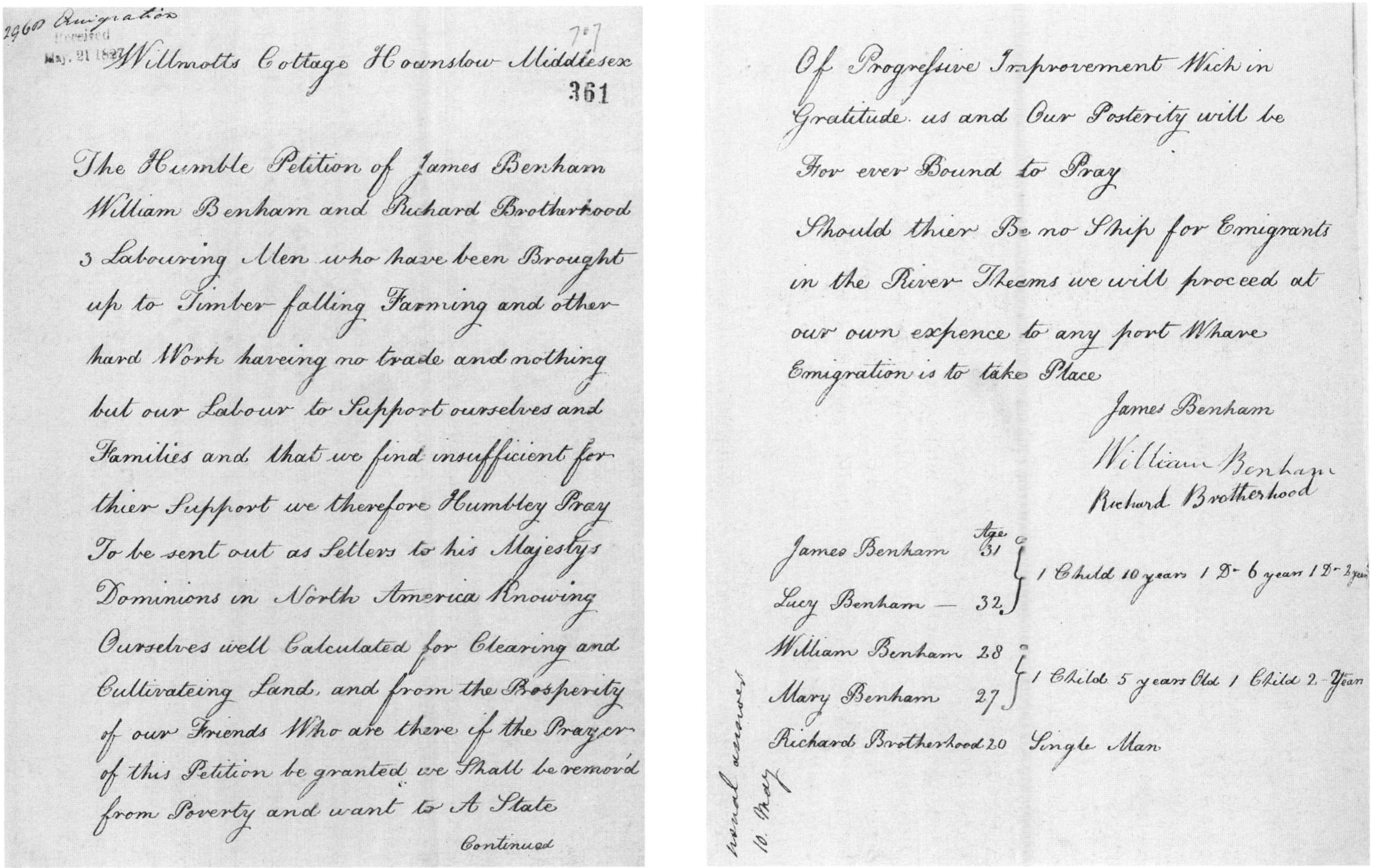

2960 Emigration
May 21 1827 Wilmotts Cottage Hounslow Middlesex
361

The Humble Petition of James Benham
William Benham and Richard Brotherhood
3 Labouring Men who have been Brought
up to Timber falling Farming and other
hard Work having no trade and nothing
but our Labour to Support ourselves and
Families and that we find insufficient for
their Support we therefore Humbley Pray
To be sent out as Settlers to his Majestys
Dominions in North America Knowing
Ourselves well Calculated for Clearing and
Cultivateing Land, and from the Prosperity
of our Friends Who are there of the Prayer
of this Petition be granted we Shall be removed
from Poverty and want to A State
Continued

Of Progressive Improvement Which in
Gratitude us and Our Posterity will be
For ever Bound to Pray

Should thier Be no Ship for Emigrants
on the River Thames we will proceed at
our own expence to any Port Where
Emigration is to take Place

James Benham
William Benham
Richard Brotherhood

James Benham   Age a
51   } 1 Child 10 years 1 Do 6 years 1 Do 1½ years
Lucy Benham — 32 }

William Benham 28 } 1 Child 5 years Old 1 Child 2 years
Mary Benham 27 }

Richard Brotherhood 20 Single Man

to Pray

Figure 6 A petition of three Middlesex labourers, from 1827, to be sent as settlers to North America. Many such petitions exist but they can be time-consuming to find. This one comes from CO 334/15, fo. 361.

(BT 32) list the ships leaving each port, which can be a useful way of finding the right record in BT 27. For Dominions Office correspondence on post-war assisted passages to Australia and other dominions, see DO 35/3366–3443.

14.4 Emigrants: possible sources for ex-soldiers and sailors, 1817–1903

Many ex-soldiers settled in the colonies. The awards of pensions to soldiers in British regiments stationed abroad, and in native or colonial regiments, 1817–1903, may be traced in WO 23/147–160. These registers are arranged by the date of the board which granted admission to pension, but entries relating to a particular place (e.g. Canada, West Indies, the Cape) are fairly easy to find. These registers can provide a birthplace and details of service. Many of the entries relate to British soldiers who left the army while their regiment was abroad, and who appear to have settled there.

Another potentially useful source for tracing people in receipt of a pension payable by the War Office (usually ex-soldiers and sailors, but also members of the East India Services) may be the registers of pension payments, 1842–1883, in WO 22, which are arranged by place of payment. There are separate registers for places like Canada, New South Wales and New Zealand, but also composite registers for miscellaneous colonies and for 'consuls' – who presumably had the responsibility for administering payments in foreign countries rather than colonies. The pensions were sometimes to widows or dependent children. See also **14.8**.

A long search in the following sample of records may be successful. The Admiralty records include, for instance, medical journals from emigrant ships (ADM 101), and registers of troops (ADM 108, MT 23) shipped to various parts of the world. The Audit Office accounts have references to pensions paid to colonists (AO 1–AO 3), and the Patent Rolls (C 66) contain entries relating to grants of offices and lands in America and elsewhere.

14.5 Emigrants to North America and the West Indies: material elsewhere

If you are tracing an ancestor back into Britain from North America, try to do some research locally before coming to the Public Record Office. In particular, try to get some idea of the port and date of entry into the new country, and the county or smaller area in the United Kingdom that your ancestor came from.

Records of immigration to the USA are held in the National Archives in Washington, along with service records, land records and census returns. Proper censuses began in the USA in 1790, and are available on microfilm. Registers of births, marriages and deaths are held by the individual state archives. The Public Archives of Canada has census returns on microfilm going back to the earliest French-Canadian census of 1666 and 1667. The French-Canadian records at Quebec are particularly full.

Photocopies, microfilms and transcripts of much of the PRO's North American material can be consulted at the Library of Congress, some state libraries, and the Public Archives of Canada. The Genealogical Society of Utah has microfilm copies of the 1841–1881 census returns for England and Wales, and a huge index containing a great deal of information from British sources.

There are several genealogical societies in North America, which it may prove useful to contact. The main national ones are the National Genealogical Society, for the USA, and the

Family History Association of Canada. There is also the International Society for British Genealogy and Family History, based in North America. See also *Genealogical sources in the United States of America*, by MacSorley (see **14.11**), which is intended for those wishing to undertake research from the UK.

14.6 Emigrants to North America and the West Indies: British emigrants

The PRO has a lot of material relating to early emigration to the West Indian and American colonies. Much of this has been printed in some form. Most of it is administrative in character, but it can include useful genealogical material. Main published sources include the records of the Privy Council (PC 1, PC 2 and PC 5), printed as *Acts of the Privy Council of England, Colonial Series*. Various useful classes of Treasury papers have been described and indexed in the *Calendar of Treasury Papers, 1557–1728* and the *Calendar of Treasury Books and Papers, 1729–1745*. The major early collection of papers relating to the West Indies and the American colonies (CO 1) has been described and indexed in the *Calendar of State Papers, Colonial, America and West Indies 1547–1738*, which includes references to the many other succeeding classes as well. Records relating to the West Indies are described in Grannum's *Tracing Your West Indian Ancestors*.

For unfree emigrants, see **40**.

Registers of passengers bound for New England, Barbados, Maryland, Virginia and other colonies survive for 1634–1639, and for 1677 (E 157): the information in them, together with similar information (from CO 1), has been printed in Hotten (see **14.11**). Port books (E 190) *may* list the names of passengers who were transporting dutiable goods, but you would need to have some idea of the port of departure or else be prepared for a very lengthy search. This has already been done for 1618–1688 for passengers to America, and there is an anonymous typescript index available.

There is a considerable amount of information on the inhabitants of Barbados, 1678–1680, including lists of property owners, their wives, children, servants and slaves, some parish registers, and lists of the militia (CO 1/44 no. 47 i–xxxvii, CO 29/9 pp. 1–3): there is a descriptive list of the various records (with no names) in the *Calendar of State Papers, Colonial America and West Indies, 1677–1680*, no. 1236, i–xxxvii, which should be consulted first. The white inhabitants of Barbados were listed in a census in 1715 (CO 28/16).

A useful, though unfortunately short-lived, register (T 47/9–12) was kept of emigrants going from England, Wales, and Scotland to the New World between 1773 and 1776. The information for England and Wales has been summarized in a card index, available at Kew, which gives name, age, occupation, reason for leaving the country, last place of residence, date of departure, and destination. For 1815 only, there are details of 757 settlers enrolling for emigration to Canada, at Edinburgh. Most came from Scotland, but some were from Ireland and England (AO 3/144).

Some information on colonists is contained in the correspondence and papers of the Colonial Office, which cover the West Indies as well as the continent of America, and start in 1574: see the printed calendars listed in **14.11**. The Chancery Town Depositions (C 24) contain interesting information about life in early colonial America, including much genealogical data, but they are not well listed: see the article by Currer-Briggs for reference to an index.

Details on tracts of land in West and East New Jersey, Pennsylvania, New England and elsewhere are in the records of the West New Jersey Society (TS 12), a company formed in 1691 for the division of the land. There are many names in the correspondence, minute books, share transfers, deeds and claims. For the settlement of East Florida in 1763, and compensation for its handing back to Spain in 1783, see the records in T 77, and the article by Foot. For employees and settlers of the Hudsons' Bay Company, see BH 1, and the article by Douglas.

In 1696, the mayor, recorder and commonalty of New York City swore the oath of association in support of William III: the resulting oath roll contains the signatures and marks of much of the male population of the city (C 213/470: see **15.1**).

Records relating to slave owners in the West Indies, 1812–1846, are among Treasury, Audit Office and National Debt Office papers (T 71, AO 14, NDO 4). The surveys in T 71 may give the names of owners, plantations and even sometimes the slaves. Among the Chancery Masters' Exhibits, in C 103–C 114, are many private papers from West Indies plantations.

During and after the American War of Independence, many people suffered losses on account of their loyalty to the British crown, and many subsequently migrated to Canada (British North America). They were entitled to claim compensation under the Treaty of Peace in 1783 and a new Treaty of Amity between Great Britain and the United States of America in 1794. The Treasury records contain the reports of commissioners investigating individual claims, and some compensation and pension lists, 1780–1835 (T 50, T 79). Commissioners were also appointed in 1802, and their papers contain lists of claimants of pensions, and papers supporting their claims (AO 12, AO 13). The Declared Accounts of the Audit Office (AO 1) contain the accounts of payments and pensions made. Similar claims for compensation to loyalists were made when East Florida was ceded to Spain in 1783, and they are now among the Treasury records (T 77).

Musters of Canadian militia and volunteers, 1837–1850, are in WO 13/3673–3717.

Americans who died with goods in England and Wales had their wills proved and inventories presented in the Prerogative Court of Canterbury (see **6**). These wills and administrations, 1600–1858, have been indexed by Coldham. For the inventories, see **6.18**.

For nineteenth century and later emigrants, see **14.2** and **14.3**.

The muster rolls for Canadian militia and volunteers, 1837–1843, may be worth checking (WO 13/3673–3717): earlier records are in Canada. For ex-soldiers and sailors (or their widows and orphans) in receipt of a Chelsea or Greenwich pension, who had settled in Canada, the registers of payment of the pension may be useful. There are separate volumes for Canada, 1845–1862 (WO 22/239–242) and for Nova Scotia, 1858–1880 (WO 22/294–296). The composite volumes for several colonies, 1845–1875, may also be useful (WO 22/248–257).

14.7 Emigrants to North America and the West Indies: foreign emigrants

Emigrants from other countries to the American colonies can sometimes be traced through records in the PRO. Lists of the names of Palatine subjects, who emigrated to America by way of Holland and England in 1709, occur in several classes: the easiest way to discover them is to use the published works by Knittle, MacWethy and the *New York Genealogical and Biographical Review*. (See also **12.4**).

Between 1740 and 1772, foreign Protestants living in the Americas could become naturalized British citizens by the act 13 George II, c.7: this required seven years' residence, the swearing of oaths of allegiance (making an affirmation for Quakers), and taking the sacrament according to the Anglican rite (the last requirement was waived for Quakers and Jews). Every year lists of those naturalized (now in CO 5) had to be sent to the Commissioners for Trade and Plantations in London, where they were copied into entry books (CO 324/55–56). These provisions covered the

West Indies as well as the American continent, but in fact only Jamaica (1740–1750), Maryland (1743–1753), Massachusetts (1743), New York (1740–1770), Pennsylvania (1740–1772), South Carolina (1741–1748), and Virginia (1743–1746) returned the lists to London. Over 7,000 foreign Protestants took advantage of this act: their names have been printed by Giuseppi in the Huguenot Society, volume XXIV.

Another method of naturalization, used by hundreds rather than thousands, was by the expensive process of obtaining an act of the colonial assembly (CO 5). To trace one of these naturalizations it will usually be necessary to have a good idea of the date and also the colony of residence.

14.8 Emigrants to Australia and New Zealand

European settlement of Australia began with the penal colony of New South Wales in 1788. In the PRO, there are few records relating to voluntary emigrants to Australia and New Zealand until the Passenger Lists (BT 27) begin in 1890: see **14.3**. In Australia, however, there is material relating to British settlers who received assisted passages there. In the PRO, there is far more extensive documentation of the transportation of convicts to Australia (see **40**). However, to some extent the records of convict transportation also cover free emigrants, as, in some cases, a convict's family would accompany him as voluntary emigrants, and can be traced through some of the same records.

Censuses of convicts were conducted at intervals between 1788 and 1859 in New South Wales and Tasmania (HO 10): although primarily concerned with the unfree population, they do contain the names of those members of the convicts' families who 'came free' or who were 'born in the colony'. The fullest is that of 1828: see the edition by Sainty and Johnson, *New South Wales: Census . . . November 1828*.

New South Wales Original Correspondence (CO 201) starts in 1784, and contains lists of settlers (and convicts), 1801–1821. The correspondence of 1823 to 1833 has also been indexed. The papers of the Land and Emigration Commission (CO 386) also contain correspondence and entry books of the South Australian Commission.

New Zealand was not used as a penal colony. Details of emigrants may be found in the New Zealand Company records, which contain registers of cabin passengers emigrating, 1839–1850, applications for free passage, 1839–1850, lists of German emigrants, and lists of maintained emigrants (CO 208).

Between 1846 and 1851, Army pensioners were encouraged to settle in New South Wales and New Zealand, although many of them failed as settlers. References to the settlement of ex-soldiers in Australia and New Zealand will be found in the PRO's *Alphabetical Guide to Certain War Office and Other Military Records*, under *Australia and New Zealand*, and there are lists of ex-soldier emigrants, 1830–1848, to Australia (WO 43/542) and New Zealand (WO 43/543).

Pensions from the Army and Navy were payable at district offices: records survive for offices in New South Wales, 1849–1880 (WO 22/272–275); in South Australia, Queensland, Tasmania and Victoria, 1876–1880 (WO 22/227, 297, 298 and 300); and in New Zealand, 1845–1854 and 1875–1880 (WO 22/276–293). For deserters, see Fitzmaurice or Hughes.

Microfilms of many PRO documents are available in Australia at the National Library in Canberra, and at the Mitchell Library in Sydney.

14.9 Emigrants to South Africa

Registers of payments to Army and Navy pensioners (including some widows and orphans) at the Cape of Good Hope and elsewhere in South Africa, 1849–1858 and 1876–1880, are in WO 22/243–244. The muster rolls of the Cape Levies, 1851–1853, may prove useful (WO 13/3718–3725).

Military records as a whole may be worth exploring for troops in South Africa (see **18**). For example, there are records of claims by civilians for compensation for property requisitioned during the Boer War, which are indexed (WO 148).

The Genealogical Society of South Africa will give advice: see also Lombard's article.

14.10 Children's emigration

Schemes to promote the emigration of poor children and orphans date back to the early seventeenth century. In the nineteenth century, it was encouraged by poor law legislation, and by the activities of charities such as Dr Barnardos. Most of the surviving papers at the PRO on child emigration in the late 19th and the 20th centuries are policy papers. Ask for the source sheet on child emigration, which gives an overview of the surviving papers. For a useful overview of the subject, read Bean and Melville's *Lost Children of the Empire*.

14.11 Emigrants: bibliography

General
Acts of the Privy Council of England, Colonial Series, 1613–1783 (London, 1908–1912)
L Atherton, *'Never Complain, Never Explain': Records of the Foreign Office and State Paper Office, 1500–c.1960* (PRO, 1994)
P Bean and J Melville, *Lost Children of the Empire* (1989)
Calendar of State Papers, Colonial, America and West Indies, 1574–1738 (London, 1860–1969)
Calendar of Treasury Books, 1660–1718 (London, 1904–1962)
Calendar of Treasury Papers, 1557–1728 (London, 1868–1889)
Calendar of Treasury Books and Papers, 1729–1745 (London, 1898–1903)
J S W Gibson, 'Assisted Pauper Emigration, 1834–1837', *Genealogists' Magazine*, vol. XX, pp. 374–375
Journals of the Board of Trade and Plantations, 1704–1782 (London, 1920–1938)
Public Record Office, *Alphabetical Guide to Certain War Office and other Military Records preserved in the Public Record Office*, Lists and Indexes, vol. LIII (London, 1931)
Public Record Office, *List of Colonial Office Records*, Lists and Indexes, vol. XXXVI (London, 1911)
Public Record Office, *List of Records of the Treasury, Paymaster General's Office, Exchequer and Audit Department and Board of Trade, prior to 1837*, Lists and Indexes, vol. XLVI (London, 1922)
Public Record Office, *List of State Papers, Domestic, 1547–1792, and Home Office Records, 1782–1837*, Lists and Indexes, vol. XLIII (London, 1914)
R B Pugh, *The Records of the Colonial and Dominions Office* (London, 1964)
A Thurston, *Records of the Colonial Office, Dominions Office, Commonwealth Relations Office and Commonwealth Office* (London, 1995)

North America and West Indies
C M Andrews, *Guide to the Materials for American History to 1783 in the Public Record Office of Great Britain* (Washington, 1912 and 1914)
Anon. 'Ships, Merchants and Passengers to the American Colonies 1618–1688' (unpublished MS, dated

Purley 1982). [Taken from the Port Books in E 190.]

C E Banks and E E Brownell, *Topographical Dictionary of 2885 English Emigrants to New England, 1620–1650* (New York, 1963, 1976)

C Boyer ed., *Ships' Passenger Lists: The South* (1538–1825); *National and New England* (1600–1825); *New York and New Jersey* (1600–1825); *Pennsylvania and Delaware* (1641–1825) (4 vols, Newhall, California, 1980)

M J Burchall, 'Parish-Organised Emigration to America', *Genealogists' Magazine*, vol. XVIII, pp. 336–342

P W Coldham, *American Loyalist Claims* (Washington, 1980) (Indexes AO 13/1–35, 37, which contain claims for compensation from American loyalists who escaped to Canada, 1774–1793.)

P W Coldham, *Bonded Passengers to America, 1615–1775* (Baltimore, 1983)

P W Coldham, *The Bristol Registers of Servants Sent to Foreign Plantations 1654–1686* (Baltimore, 1988)

P W Coldham, *The Complete Book of Emigrants, 1607–1776* (4 vols, Baltimore, 1987–1993)

P W Coldham, *Emigrants from England to the American Colonies, 1773–1776* (Baltimore, 1988)

P W Coldham, *English Adventurers and Emigrants, 1609–1660 Abstracts of Examinations in the High Court of Admiralty, with Reference to Colonial America* (Baltimore, 1984)

P W Coldham, *English Estates of American Colonists: American Wills and Administrations in the Prerogative Court of Canterbury, 1610–1699 and 1700–1799* (Baltimore, 1980)

P W Coldham, *English Estates of American Settlers: American Wills and Administrations in the Prerogative Court of Canterbury, 1800–1858* (Baltimore, 1981)

P W Coldham, *Lord Mayor's Court of London, Depositions relating to America, 1641–1736*, National Genealogical Society (Washington, 1980)

N Currer-Briggs, 'American Colonial Gleanings from Town Depositions', *Genealogists' Magazine*, vol. XVIII, pp. 288–294

D Dobson, *The Original Scots Colonists of Early America 1612–1783* (Baltimore, 1989)

D Dobson, *Scottish Emigration to Colonial America 1607–1785* (Georgia, 1994)

A Douglas, 'Genealogical Research in Canada', *Genealogists' Magazine*, vol. XXIII, pp. 217–221

A Douglas, 'Gentlemen Adventurers and Remittance Men' [Hudson's Bay Company], *Genealogists' Magazine*, vol. XXIV, pp. 55–59

R H Ellis, 'Records of the American Loyalists' Claims in the Public Record Office', *Genealogists' Magazine*, vol. XII, pp. 375–378, 407–410, 433–435

P W Filby, *American and British Genealogy and Heraldry* (Chicago, 2nd edn, 1975)

P W Filby, ed., *Passenger and Immigration Lists Bibliography 1538–1900* (Michigan, 1981)

P W Filby and M K Meyer, eds, *Passenger and Immigration Lists Index*, 13 vols (Michigan, 1981–1995) (Lists c.2,410,000 names of immigrants to USA and Canada, from the 16th to mid 20th centuries.)

W Foot, '"That most precious Jewel" – East Florida 1763–83', *Genealogists' Magazine*, vol. XXIV, pp. 144–148

G Fothergill, *A List of Emigrant Ministers to Australia 1690–1811* (London, 1904)

M S Giuseppi, *Naturalizations of Foreign Protestants in the American and West Indian colonies*, Huguenot Society, vol. XXIV, 1921

I A Glazier and M Tepper, *The Famine Immigrants: Lists of Irish Immigrants Arriving at the Port of New York, 1846–1851* (Baltimore, 1983)

G Grannum, *Tracing Your West Indian Ancestors* (PRO, 1995)

A C Hollis Hallett, *Early Bermuda Records 1619–1826* (Bermuda, 1991)

J C Hotten, *Original Lists of Persons emigrating to America, 1600–1700* (London, 1874)

C B Jewson, *Transcript of Three Registers of Passengers from Great Yarmouth to Holland and New England, 1637–1639*, Norfolk Record Society, vol. XXV (1954)

J and M Kaminkow, *A list of Emigrants from England to America, 1718–1759* (Baltimore, 1964)

W A Knittle, *Early Eighteenth Century Palatine Emigration* (Philadelphia, 1937)

A H Lancour, *A Bibliography of Ships' Passenger Lists, 1538–1825* (New York, 1963)

M E MacSorley, *Genealogical sources in the United States of America* (Basingstoke, 1995)

L D MacWethy, *The Book of Names especially relating to the Early Palatines and the First Settlers in the Mohawk Valley* (New York, 1932)

G E McCracken, 'State and Federal Sources for American Genealogy', *Genealogists' Magazine*, vol. XIX, pp. 138–140

B Merriman, 'Genealogy in Canada', *Genealogists' Magazine*, vol. XIX, pp. 306–311
National Archives and Record Service, *A Guide to Genealogical Research in the National Archives* (Washington, 1982)
New York Genealogical and Biographical Records, vols XL and LXI (New York, 1909 and 1910) (for Palatine emigrants)
G Sherwood, *American Colonists in English Records* (2 vols, London, 1932, 1933) (Lists passengers not mentioned in Hotten.)
C J Stanford, 'Genealogical Sources in Barbados', *Genealogists' Magazine*, vol. XVII, pp. 489–498
M Tepper, ed., *New World Immigrants* (Baltimore, 1980) (a consolidation of passenger lists)
M Tepper, *Passengers to America: A Consolidation of Ship Passenger Lists from the New England Genealogical Register* (Baltimore, 1988)
M Tepper, *American Passengers Arrival Records* (Baltimore, 1993)
D Whyte, *A Dictionary of Scottish Emigrants to the USA* (Baltimore, 1972)

Australia and New Zealand

C J Baxter, *Musters and Lists New South Wales and Norfolk Island, 1800–1802* (Sydney, 1988)
C J Baxter, *Musters New South Wales, Norfolk Island and Van Diemen's Land, 1811* (Sydney, 1987)
C J Baxter, *General Muster and Land and Stock Muster of New South Wales, 1822* (Sydney, 1988)
A Bromell, *Tracing Family History in New Zealand* (Wellington, 1991)
P Burns and H Richardson, *Fatal Success: A History of the New Zealand Company* (Auckland, 1989)
Y Fitzmaurice, *Army Deserters from HM Service* (Forest Hill, Victoria, 1988 continuing)
M Flynn, *The Second Fleet* (1993)
M Gillen, *The Founders of Australia, A Biographical Dictionary of the First Fleet* (Sydney, 1989)
D T Hawkings, *Bound for Australia* (Guildford, 1987)
H and L Hughes, *Discharged in New Zealand – Soldiers of the Imperial Foot Regiments who took their discharge in New Zealand 1840–1870* (Auckland, 1988)
L Marshall and V Mossong, 'Genealogical Research in New Zealand', *Genealogists' Magazine*, vol. XX, pp. 45–49.
J Melton, *Ship's Deserters 1852–1900* (Sydney, 1986)
A G Peake, *Bibliography of Australian Family History* (Dulwich, South Australia, 1988)
A G Peake, *National Register of Shipping Arrivals: Australia and New Zealand* (Sydney, 1992)
M R Sainty and K A Johnson, ed., *New South Wales: Census . . . November 1828 . . .* (Sydney, 1980)
N Vine Hall, *Tracing your Family History in Australia – A Guide to Sources* (London, 1985)
H Woolcock, *Rights of Passage: Emigration to Australia in the 19th Century* (London, 1986)

South Africa

E Bull, *Aided Immigration to South Africa, 1857–1867* (Pretoria, 1991)
R J Lombard, 'Genealogical Research in South Africa', *Genealogists' Magazine*, vol. XIX, pp. 274–276
E Mosse Jones, *Rolls of the British Settlers in South Africa* (Capetown, 1971)
P Philip, *British Residents at the Cape 1795–1819* (Capetown, 1981)

15 Oaths of allegiance

15.1 Oath rolls

Between the sixteenth and nineteenth centuries, people were required on various occasions to swear oaths in support of the crown and the Anglican church. Some of these oaths were sworn by those taking up or holding official positions and by lawyers on being admitted to the courts, others were sworn by aliens in the process of becoming naturalized British subjects, and others still were taken by people to signify their loyalty to the crown in times of political upheaval. Not all such oaths are recorded in the Oath Rolls held by the PRO. The most notable exception is an oath in support of Crown, Parliament and the Protestant Religion, intended to be taken by all men over the age of 18 in 1641. These Protestation returns were sent into Parliament, and are now in the House of Lords Record Office (address in **48**): they are listed by Gibson and Dell.

Anyone taking up any civil or military office was required by the Corporations Act of 1661 and the Test Act of 1672 to take the oaths of allegiance and supremacy, and to deliver a certificate into court stating that they had received the sacrament of the Lord's Supper according to the rites of the Church of England. These acts were not repealed until 1828. The Sacrament Certificates, signed by the minister and churchwardens of the parish, survive from 1672 to 1828, but are not always easy to use (C 224, CHES 4, E 196, KB 22).

The oath rolls are found in different places, depending on the occupation and place of residence of the person taking the oath. Oaths could be sworn before Justices of the Peace at Quarter Sessions or, if one resided within thirty miles of Westminster, at one of the central courts of law in Westminster Hall. As a result, oath rolls may be found either in local record offices or in the Public Record Office. Oath rolls, including classes devoted to the oaths of lawyers (see **28**), survive in the records of Chancery (C 193/9, C 184, C 214, C 215), Common Pleas (CP 10), Exchequer (E 169, E 200, E 3), and King's Bench (KB 24, KB 113). Oath rolls of attorneys in the courts of Chester and Durham also exist (CHES 36/3, DURH 3/217). Oaths of clergy (1789–1836) and of Roman Catholics after the conditions were relaxed (1778–1829) are in CP 37.

Between 1708 and 1711, all foreign Protestants who took the oaths of allegiance and supremacy in court, and who produced a sacrament certificate, were deemed to have been naturalized (KB 24, E 169/86: see **12.6**). The rolls in the PRO have been indexed by the Huguenot Society, in their volumes XXVII and XXV: other rolls, of oaths taken before the quarter sessions, may survive in county record offices. See **14.7** for oaths of allegiance on naturalization, in North America and the West Indies.

The Association Oath Rolls (C 213 and C 214: partly indexed by Bernau: see **47.4**) contain the signatures or marks and names of people subscribing to the 'Solemn Association' of 1696, in support of William III after an attempt had been made, by Jacobites, to assassinate him. The oath of association was taken by everyone in a position of any authority – all members of Parliament, all military, naval and civil office-holders of the crown, the clergy and the gentry, freemen of the city companies, and others besides. In some places, such as Jersey, Westminster and Suffolk, almost every adult male appears to have subscribed, and the returns approximate to a census of adult men: the Jersey roll has been published in full by Glendinning. Transcripts are also appearing for other counties, such as Surrey and Wiltshire. C 213 also includes rolls from certain colonies and overseas settlements, such as Holland, Malaga, Geneva, Jamestown and New York.

15.2 Oaths of allegiance: bibliography

J Gibson, *The Hearth Tax, Other Later Stuart Tax Lists, and the Association Oath Rolls* (FFHS, 1996)

J Gibson and A Dell, *The Protestation Returns 1641–42 and other contemporary listings: collection in aid of distressed Protestants in Ireland, subsidies, poll tax, assessments or grants, vow and covenant, solemn league and covenant* (FFHS, 1995)

A Glendinning, *Did Your Ancestor Sign the Jersey Oath of Allegiance Roll of 1696?* (Channel Islands Family History Society, 1995)

W A Shaw, ed., *Letters of Denization and Acts of Naturalisation for Aliens in England and Ireland 1701–1800* (Huguenot Society, vol. XXVII, Manchester, 1923)

A Supplement to Dr W Shaw's Letters of Denization and Acts of Naturalisation (Huguenot Society, vol. XXXV, Frome, 1932)

C R Webb, 'The Association Oath Rolls of 1695', *Genealogists' Magazine*, vol. XXI, pp. 120–123.

16 Electoral registration

16.1 Poll books and electoral registers

Poll books are locally compiled lists of men who were entitled to vote, and sometimes of votes cast, dating from the seventeenth to the nineteenth century. There are large collections in the British Library, the Guildhall Library and the library of the Society of Genealogists. County record offices and local libraries have collections relating to their own areas. For a guide to their use and whereabouts, see Gibson and Rogers, *Poll Books c.1696–1872*, or Sims, *A Handlist of British Parliamentary poll books*. The PRO Library has a small collection of poll books.

After the 1832 Reform Act an annual register of persons (still mostly male property-holders) entitled to vote was kept. They were compiled every year (except for 1916–1917 and 1940–1944) and are now mostly in local record offices. For a guide to their use and whereabouts, see Gibson and Rogers, *Electoral Registers since 1832 and Burgers Rolls*. Those few registers that the PRO has are listed here, and may be seen in the Library at Kew. Most come from the early 1870s, but there are some for Norfolk from 1832–1833.

16.2 PRO holdings of electoral registers

England

Bedfordshire	1874
Berkshire	1874; Wallingford 1874
Bristol City	1874
Buckinghamshire	1874; Aylesbury 1874; Buckingham 1874
Cambridgeshire	1872; Isle of Ely 1874
Cheshire	East 1874; Mid 1874; West 1874
Cumberland	East 1874; West 1874; Carlisle City 1875; Cockermouth 1874; Whitehaven 1875
Cornwall	1872–75; East 1874; West 1874; Bodmin 1874; Helston 1874; Launceston 1874; Liskeard 1872, 1873; St Ives 1875
Derbyshire	East 1868–69, 1870; North 1870; South 1870
Devon	1875; East 1874; North 1874; South 1874; Barnstaple 1874
Dorset	1874; Poole 1870; Shaftesbury 1872; Wareham 1871
Durham	North 1874; South 1874; Hartlepool 1874; Stockton 1875
Essex	East 1875; South 1875; West 1875; Colchester 1874
Gloucestershire	1872, 1874; Cirencester 1872; Stroud 1873; Tewkesbury 1874
Hampshire	1874; North 1874; South 1874; Andover 1874; Petersfield 1874
Herefordshire	1874
Hertfordshire	1875
Huntingdonshire	1874; Huntingdon 1874
Kent East	1874; Mid 1874; West 1874; Canterbury 1873
Lancashire	North 1874; North East 1874; South East 1874; South West 1874; Oldham 1873
Leicestershire	South 1874
Lincolnshire	Mid Lincs, Kesteven 1874; Mid Lincs, Lindsey 1874; North Lincs,

	Lindsey 1874; South Lincs, Kesteven 1874; Grantham 1874
Middlesex	1874
Monmouthshire	1874
Norfolk	East 1832–33; North 1874; South 1874; West 1832–33, 1874
Northamptonshire	North 1874; South 1874; Peterborough 1874
Northumberland	North 1874; South 1874; Berwick-upon-Tweed 1875
Nottinghamshire	North 1874; South 1874; East Retford 1872, 1874; Newark 1873
Oxfordshire	1874; New Woodstock 1873–74
Rutland	1874
Shropshire	North 1874; South 1874; Shrewsbury 1874; Wenlock 1874
Somerset	East 1874
Staffordshire	East 1874; North 1874; West 1874; Newcastle-under-Lyme 1873; Stafford 1874; Stoke-on-Trent 1871–72; Tamworth 1871–72; Walsall 1874; Wednesbury 1874; Wolverhampton 1874
Suffolk	East 1873, 1874, 1875; West 1874; Eye 1875
Surrey	East 1872; Mid 1872; West 1872; Guildford 1873
Sussex	1871, 1873; East 1874; West 1874; Chichester 1874; Horsham 1872; Midhurst 1871; New Shoreham 1871; Rye 1874
Warwickshire	North 1873, 1875; South 1874; Coventry City 1874
Westmorland	1872
Wiltshire	1872, 1874, 1875; South 1874; Calne 1874; Chippenham 1871; Cricklade 1873; Malmesbury 1871; Westbury 1874; Wilton 1874
Worcestershire	East 1874; West 1874
Yorkshire	East Riding 1874; North Riding 1874; West Riding, North 1874; West Riding, South 1874; Dewsbury 1874; Huddersfield 1875; Leeds 1874; Wakefield 1874; York City 1873

Wales

Anglesey	1873, 1874, 1875; Beaumaris 1870, 1874
Brecon	1871
Cardigan	1871–72, 1874; Aberystwyth, Cardigan and Lampeter 1871; Adpar 1871; Lampeter-Pontstephen 1871
Carmarthen	1872; Carmarthen Borough 1871
Caernarvon	1873, 1874, 1875; Caernarvon Borough 1873
Denbigh	1874, 1875
Flint	1874; Flint Borough 1875
Glamorgan	1873, 1874, 1875; Loughor and Neath 1874
Merioneth	1874
Montgomery	1872, 1874; Montgomery Borough 1874
Pembroke	1871–72; Pembroke Borough 1875
Radnor	1875; New Radnor 1873

16.3 Electoral registration: bibliography

J S W Gibson and C Rogers, *Electoral Registers since 1832 and Burgers Rolls* (FFHS, 1990)
J S W Gibson and C Rogers, *Poll Books c.1696–1872* (FFHS, 1994)
J Sims, *A Handlist of British Parliamentary poll books* (Leicester, 1984)

N Newington Irving, *Dictionaries and Poll Books, inluding almanacs and electoral rolls, in the Library of the Society of Genealogists* (Society of Genealogist, 1995)

17 Changes of name

17.1 Change of name by deed poll, 1851 onwards

A deed poll is the technical term for a deed involving only one party (poll meaning the parchment was smooth-cut, whereas an indenture or indented deed between two or more parties was cut in a zigzag way so each could be matched up with the other parts).

However, for most people deeds poll now have one meaning – change of name. Changes of name by deed poll were (and are) made before a solicitor who could enrol them, for safe keeping, in the Close Rolls of Chancery or the later Enrolment Books of the Supreme Court of Judicature. In fact, very few changes of name were enrolled, as it was not a legal obligation and extra fees were payable. Most people who come to the PRO looking for an enrolled change of name are disappointed.

The original deed poll will have been given to the person who changed their name. Although the solicitor who prepared the deed poll may have kept a copy on file, it is unlikely to be a certified copy, nor is the file likely to have been kept for more than five years. In fact, there may never have been a deed poll: a perfectly legal alternative such as a statutory declaration before a JP or Commissioner for Oaths (which could not be enrolled), or an advertisement in the newspapers, may have been used instead. (It may be possible to check local newspapers at the British Library Newspaper Library: address in **48**.) In fact, it is perfectly legal to simply change one's name without drawing any attention to the change, unless there is an intention to defraud. Many people who changed their name did not wish to draw attention to the fact. For example, in an age of difficult divorce, some people took their new partner's name to allow them the appearance of marriage, and any children the appearance of legitimacy.

From 1851 the indexes to the Close Rolls (C 54) include references to changes of name by deed poll which had been enrolled. In 1903, this function was taken over by the Supreme Court of Judicature Enrolment Books (J 18), with indexes also in J 18. The indexes vary from time to time: until 1903 only the former name is given, but since then both are present, either as a note or a cross-reference. These records and indexes are seen in the Map Room. For a change of name in the last five years, apply to the Royal Courts of Justice, Room 81 (address in **48**).

17.2 The *London Gazette*

From 1914, all deeds poll enrolled in the Supreme Court had first to be advertised in the *London Gazette* – but again, this does not mean all changes of name. However, for the duration of the Second World War, British subjects could only change their name if 21 days before doing so they had published in the *London Gazette*, the *Edinburgh Gazette* or the *Belfast Gazette* a notice giving details of the proposed change.

A supplementary index to both old and new names exists in the quarterly indexes to the *London Gazette* for 1938–1964: copies of the relevant pages are shelved by the J 18 indexes in the Map Room. The *London Gazette* itself may be seen in the PRO under ZJ 1.

17.3 Changes of name by foreigners in the UK, 1916–1971

Enemy aliens resident in Britain had been forbidden to change their names in 1916: the ban was extended to all foreigners in Britain in 1919. The only exceptions made were when a new name was assumed by royal licence; or by special permission of the Home Secretary; or when a woman took her husband's name on marriage. In the first two of these case, the change had to be advertised in the *Gazettes* (see above). These restrictions were removed in 1971, and anyone can now change their name.

17.4 Royal licences and private acts of Parliament: c.1700 onwards

Royal licences to change a name appear very infrequently among the records from the late seventeenth century. The change is usually in response to a bequest conditional upon adopting the deceased's name, or a marriage settlement requiring the husband to adopt the wife's name, or when a change to the coat of arms was also required. Warrants for such changes of name were entered into the current series of entry books; before 1782 in SP 44; from 1782 to February 1868 in HO 38; and from February 1868 in HO 142. These usually have internal indexes in each volume. Records of such changes of name were often advertised in the *London Gazette*. It may be worth also checking the records of the College of Arms (address in **48**).

Private acts of Parliament were also used in the same kinds of instance (although only once since the 1880s): the originals are in the House of Lords Record Office (address in **48**).

17.5 The Phillimore *Index to Change of Name, 1760–1901*

This is a composite index from several sources, and does not claim to be an index to all changes of name. Its full details are *An Index to Change of Name Under Authority of Act of Parliament or Royal Licence and including Irregular Changes from 1 George III to 64 Victoria, 1760 to 1901*. A copy is shelved with the C 54 finding aids in the Map Room.

The sources covered are: private acts of Parliament; royal licences published in the *London* and *Dublin Gazettes*; notices of changes of name published in *The Times* after 1861; with a few notices from other newspapers; the registers of the Lord Lyon, where Scottish changes of name were commonly recorded; records in the office of the Ulster King at Arms; and some private information.

It thus omits changes by royal licence not advertised in the *London Gazette*, and changes by deed poll enrolled in the Close Rolls but not advertised in *The Times*.

17.6 Changes of name: bibliography

J F Josling, *Change of Name, Oyez Practice Notes I* (London, 1980)
W P W Phillimore and E A Fry, *An Index to Change of Names, 1760–1901* (London, 1905)

18 The Army

18.1 Army records: introduction

Many of the service records of British Army soldiers discharged before 1920 are in the PRO: service records for soldiers discharged after 1920 have not yet been transferred to the PRO (see **18.30**).

There is very little before1660, and, for other ranks, not much more before about 1730. However, from the mid eighteenth century onwards, a considerable amount can be discovered about Army ancestors. This book can only indicate the most generally useful records: for more information on general sources see *Army Records for Family Historians*, by Fowler and Spencer.

For an introduction to the full range of War Office records, including those not discussed here (i.e. those that relate to warfare and Army administration) see Roper, *The Records of the War Office and related departments, 1660–1964*. These records too can be of great interest in discovering more about a soldier's life. If you do wish to trace records relating to a particular campaign or action, or to do with the general administration of the Army, you will find the *Alphabetical Guide to certain War Office and other Military Records preserved in the Public Record Office* to be a very useful descriptive index. The range of Army activity and interests, up to the Boer War, disclosed by this book is quite remarkable. Most entries are to subjects or places (e.g. *Lunatic Soldiers:- Asylums for, at Chatham and Yarmouth, cessation of, and suggestions for future treatment, 1841–1854*; or *Bermuda:- As health resort for soldiers, 1790*). Some relate to particularly eminent soldiers (e.g *Moore, Sir John, Lieutenant-General:- Monument to, at Coruna, its neglected state, etc., 1809–1816*). In addition, it contains a similar index for regiments (including colonial, foreign and militia regiments, and volunteer corps), which likewise includes entries of interest for family and social history (e.g. *Lancashire, The East, Regiment:- Sergeant T Hurford's legacy for clothing poor children of Regt., 1840*).

The PRO Library has an extensive collection of books and periodicals on military history, including many regimental histories.

There are many other places to look for information about soldier ancestors, outside the official War Office records in the PRO. The most obvious are the Imperial War Museum, the National Army Museum and the various regimental museums: these specialise in the life of the Army, and you should be able to discover some general idea of how your ancestor lived as a soldier. Most regiments have their own museums, some of which have archival collections. The Royal Military Police became a separate organisation from the middle of the nineteenth century, and enquiries about military policemen should be sent direct to them. The National Army Museum and the Army Museum Ogilby Trust also have collections. See *A Guide to Military Museums* by Wise, available at Kew. If private papers exist, they may be traceable through the National Register of Archives. Addresses are given in **48**.

18.2 Army registers of births, marriages and deaths, in the General Register Offices

These army registers in the General Register Offices are not as well known as they deserve to be. A few Army registers or records of births, marriages and deaths are in the PRO (see **18.3**); others may still be in the custody of the regiment.

The General Register Office of England and Wales (now the ONS) has various registers of Army births and marriages from 1761 to 1965, and of deaths from 1796 to 1965, kept at Southport. The contents of the registers can be accessed from indexes at the FRC (ONS) and at Kew (on microfiche). Certified copies can be bought: see **1.6** and **4.14** for more details.

There are several series of registers, some of them overlapping, with an uncertain amount of duplication and omission. The regimental registers of births/baptisms and marriages run from 1761 to 1924, covering events in Britain (from 1761) and abroad (from c.1790). There is an index to the births (giving name, place, year and regiment), but not to the marriages. To find out details of a marriage, you have to know the husband's regiment and a rough date. At the FRC is a list of the marriage registers, arranged by regiment: if your regiment is there, with entries for the right period, ask at the enquiry desk in the FRC to be put in touch with the Overseas Section, which may conduct a search for you.

Overlapping with the regimental registers are the Army chaplains' returns of births, baptisms, marriages, deaths and burials, 1796–1880. These all relate to events abroad, and they are indexed. Unfortunately, the indexes do not give the regiment, simply name, place and date range. From 1881 they appear to be continued by the Army [and Navy] returns, 1881–1955, of births, marriages and deaths overseas. From 1920, entries relating to the Royal Air Force are included. From 1956–1965, there are indexes to combined service department registers of births and marriages overseas: after 1965, service registers were abandoned, and entries were made in the general series of overseas registers.

Records for the military while on the Ionian Islands appear to have been kept separately. At the FRC there are registers, 1818–1864, of births, marriages and deaths: the index is to a military register, a civil register, and a chaplain's register. It gives names only, and can also be seen at Kew. See also **4.14** and **4.15**.

18.3 Army registers of births, marriages and burials at the PRO

The Public Record Office has a small number of regimental registers of births, baptisms, marriages and burials, of the kind kept by the FRC (ONS). Some of these are annotated with information on discharge: others have the baptismal entries of the children entered on the same page as the marriage certificate of the parents.

The PRO has baptism and marriage registers for:

	Former militia name		
3rd King's Own Yorkshire Light Infantry	1st West Yorkshire Militia	1865–1904	WO 68/499
Rifle Brigade, 6th battalion	114th Westmeath Militia	1834–1904	WO 68/439
Royal Horse Artillery		1817–1827, 1859–1883 (most are 1860–1877)	WO 69/63–73, WO 69/551–582
Somerset Light Infantry, 3rd and 4th battalions	Somerset Militia:	1836–1887,	WO 68/441
West Norfolk Regiment		1863–1908	WO 68/497
West Yorkshire Rifles, 3rd battalion	2nd West Yorkshire Militia	1832–1877	WO 68/499

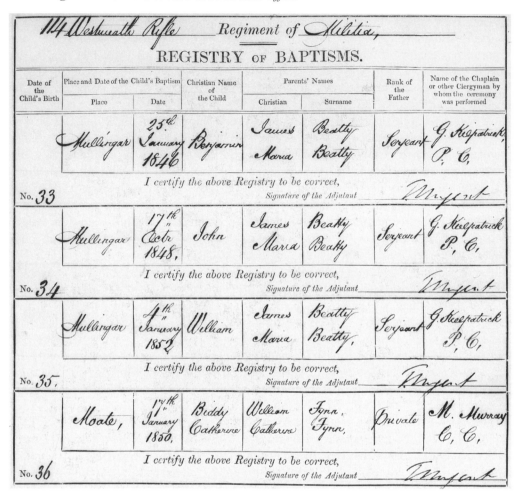

Figure 7 The Regimental Registers often bring together entries for a particular family. Similar registers are kept by the ONS, where individual copy certificates have to be ordered for each family member. Other registers may still be kept by the regiment. (WO 68/439)

In addition, there are Army registers of baptisms for Dover castle, 1865–1916 and 1929–1940; Shorncliffe and Hythe, 1878–1939; Buttervant, 1917–1922; and Fermoy, 1920–1921 (WO 156). This class also includes burial registers for the Canterbury garrison, 1808–1811, 1859–1884 and 1957–1958, and baptisms and banns of marriage for Army personnel in Palestine, 1939–1947.

The baptism, marriage and burial registers of the Royal Chelsea Hospital, for 1691–1856, are in RG 4/4330–4332, and 4387.

See **18.14** and **18.24** for other references to families.

18.4 Army war dead

Each regiment made regular returns of its casualties, where the usual round of one or two deaths from sickness is suddenly broken by long lists of men killed in action: see **18.19**, for more details.

Nominal rolls of the dead were kept for many of the campaigns fought during the second half of the nineteenth century:

China	1857–1858	WO 32/8221, 8224, 8227
	1860	WO 32/8230, 8233, 8234
New Zealand	1860	WO 32/825
	1863–1864	WO 32/8263–8268, 8271, 8276–8280
South Africa	1878–1881	WO 25/3474, 7770, 7706–7708, 7727, 7819
Egypt	1882,1884	WO 25/3473
Sudan	1884–1885	WO 25/3473, 6123, 6125–6126, 8382
Burma	1888	WO 25/3473
Sierra Leone	1898	WO 32/7630–7631
South Africa	1899–1902	WO 108/89–91, 338
China	1915	WO 32/4996B

Some of these have been published: Cook and Cook's *The Casualty Roll for the Crimea*, and the *South Africa Field Force Casualty List, 1899–1902*, are available at Kew, as are microfilm copies of *Soldiers died in the Great War*, arranged by regiment, and a copy of *Officers died in the Great War* (the First World War) (Imperial War Museum).

For indexes to the death registers for the Army war dead for the Boer War, 1899–1902, the First World War, 1914–1921, and the Second World War, 1939–1948, see **4.14**. At the PRO, there are French and Belgian certificates of the deaths for British soldiers who died in hospitals or elsewhere outside the immediate war zone, 1914–1920, arranged by first letter of surname (RG 35/45–69): certificates for surnames beginning C, F, P, Q and X are missing. For the Second World War, there are retrospective registers of deaths from enemy action in the Far East 1941–1945 (RG 33/11 and 132, indexed in RG 43/14). The Army Roll of Honour for the Second World War is in WO 304.

18.5 Soldiering before the Restoration

Before the Civil War (1642–1649) there was no regular standing army in Britain. From medieval times, able-bodied men aged between 16 and 60 were liable to perform military service within their counties, and occasionally outside them, in times of need. From the 1540s, the records of musters of this militia were returned to the secretaries of state, and many of these, with some earlier ones from 1522 onwards, are scattered among various classes in the PRO. Some muster books, however, were retained by the deputy lieutenants of the counties, and these are now in private collections or county record offices. See Gibson and Dell's *Tudor and Stuart Muster Rolls* for a county-organised analysis and directory of surviving muster rolls.

From the sixteenth century, regiments were raised to meet special requirements and were usually known by the names of colonels who commanded them: there was no central administration. Such few references as there are to individual soldiers should be sought among the State Papers Domestic, State Papers Foreign, and the Exchequer and Audit Office Accounts (AO 1–AO 3): the regimental index in the *Alphabetical Guide* (see **18.1**) is a good place to start. Other places to look are Exchequer Issues (E 403) and Exchequer Accounts (E 101) for the payment of military wages; the *Calendars of State Papers, Domestic* for widows' pensions; the licences to pass beyond the seas (E 157) for oaths of allegiance taken by soldiers going to the Low Countries, 1613–1624; and the Commonwealth Exchequer Papers for the Army during the Interregnum (SP 28). See SP 41/1 and 2 respectively for the establishment of the army in 1640, and muster rolls of the Scots Army in England in 1646. All officers serving on both sides in 1642 are listed in Peacock's book *The Army List of Roundheads and Cavaliers*. Warrants for commissions of the seventeenth century can be found in the State Paper Entry Books (SP 44).

Individual parliamentary soldiers who were owed arrears of pay after 1649 might be given certificates known as debentures which certified what they were owed and these debentures, secured on property confiscated by Parliament, could be used to purchase such properties which could then, in turn, be sold to pay off their debts. The class E 121, Certificates for the Sale of Crown Lands, contains thousands of names of officers and men who had served in the parliamentary forces, but it is arranged by the county in which the confiscated crown lands were situated and is not indexed, either by name or regiment; moreover, a particular regiment might be assigned several properties, in more than one county. It only covers England and Wales.

Similar debentures were issued to parliamentary soldiers who had served in Ireland where confiscated lands were to be divided by lot. Under 12,000 were subsequently returned for certificates of possession. Most soldiers did not settle but probably sold them on to their officers. About 7,500 grants were confirmed after 1660. Unfortunately, these debentures, which were held in Dublin, have not survived. Calendars of some grants that were confirmed after 1660, indexed by personal name, are in the *Fifteenth Report* of the Irish Record Commission (1825). The Books of Survey and Distribution, held by the National Archives in Dublin (some counties in print) record the final land settlement. References to troops serving in Ireland (mainly to officers) can also be found in the *Calendars of State Papers, Ireland*.

Records of the Committee for Indemnity (SP 24) which was set up to indemnify parliamentary soldiers and officials from legal liability for acts committed during the Civil War, contain many references to individual soldiers. Cases are arranged alphabetically.

Muster rolls for the Scots Army in England in January 1646, unindexed but arranged by regiment and company, are in SP 41/2.

18.6 The Army after 1660: organization

After the Civil War, a standing army became a permanent feature of government. Its administration was the responsibility of the secretary-at-war, with the help of an established bureaucracy which developed into the War Office. As a result, the records of the Army after 1660 are much fuller.

Some understanding of the organisation of the Army is needed if you are to make the best use of military records. The basic unit of the Army was the regiment, under the command of a colonel. The regiments were of various types; cavalry, infantry, artillery and engineers. A regiment usually consisted of two (or, later, more) battalions, each with about ten companies (troops in the cavalry) of about a hundred men each. One of these battalions would be based at the regimental depot, to recruit and train soldiers for the active battalions. Whenever a new regiment was needed a colonel was given a 'beating order' to enlist, and recruitment headquarters were established, usually in local inns. Garrisons were established for the quartering of troops throughout the country, and in times of war when the garrison troops were needed elsewhere, special battalions of veterans would be raised to take their place.

The Army was manned by commissioned officers (from the wealthier classes: commissions were generally bought), and other ranks (often drawn from the poorest classes, including criminals and paupers). From 1780 to 1914 there was voluntary enlistment, normally for life. Few stayed the course for life: some bought themselves out; some were wounded, incapacitated and discharged; many were discharged at the end of the various wars. Boys, in law if not in practice, had to be eighteen before they could enlist: younger boys often enlisted as drummers.

18.7 Militia regiments, volunteers and the Territorial Army

The eighteenth and nineteenth century militia was a county-based part-time force, additional to the standing army: it was not the same as the earlier militia (see **18.5**). Most militia records will be found in local record offices, although the PRO does have some major sources.

By the 1757 Militia Act, militia regiments were re-established in all counties of England and Wales, after a period of dormancy. A form of conscription was used: each year, the parish was supposed to draw up lists of adult males, and to hold a ballot to choose those who had to serve in the militia. The militia lists (of all men) and the militia enrolment lists (of men chosen to serve) should in theory provide complete and annual censuses of all men aged between 18 and 45 from 1758 to 1831. The surviving lists, held locally, can be very informative, giving details about individual men and their family circumstances. However, the coverage of the country, for various reasons, is not complete. For more information see Medlycott, 'Some Georgian 'Censuses': the Militia Lists and 'Defence' Lists', or Gibson and Medlycott, *Militia Lists and Musters, 1757–1876*. Records of the militia once formed are also usually in county record offices. Other locally-held sources are the poor law records, which can include orders for the maintenance of the children of militia men.

There are some major records relating to the militia in the PRO. Muster rolls of regiments of militia, 1780–1876, supplementary militia, 1798–1816, and local militia, 1808–1816, are in WO 13, together with those of other volunteer forces such as the fencibles, the yeomanry and the volunteers. In most cases, these muster rolls do not indicate place of origin.

More useful for family history are the Militia Attestation Papers, 1806–1915 (WO 96), which were filled in at recruitment, and, in most cases, were annotated to the date of discharge to form a record of service. They include the date and place of birth. Most date from the mid nineteenth century. Despite the covering dates, attestation papers are arranged in the order of precedence of the regular army unit to which the militia regiments were attached after the reorganisation of the Army in 1881. The class list of WO 96 gives the name of the regular unit as at 1881, not the earlier militia unit. The way round this problem is to consult the *Army List* of 1882 or after, and to find out from there which militia regiments were attached to which regiment. Some early Militia Attestation Papers for the period 1796–1815 can be found in WO 97. A computerized name index for these early papers can be found in the Microfilm Reading Room.

The Militia Records, 1759–1925 (WO 68), include records of some militia regiments in Great Britain and Ireland, and consist of enrolment books, description books, pay lists, returns of officers' services, casualty books, regimental histories, etc., and also registers of marriages, births and baptisms (see **18.3**). The Military Correspondence, 1782–1840 (HO 50), and the Military Entry books, 1758–1855 (HO 51) contain much material on the militia.

A few militia soldiers qualified for pensions as a result of service in the French Revolutionary and Napoleonic wars, and their discharge certificates among the ordinary Soldiers' Documents (WO 97) give their place of birth and age on enlistment: see **18.18**. Other details of militia pensioners, admitted to pension between 1821 and 1829, may be found in a peculiar register drawn up in 1858, and arranged first by year of admission, and then by age on admission (WO 23/25). There are also lists of militia men, wives and children who were eligible for bounties among the Subsidiary Documents to the Receivers' Accounts (E 182), but there are no indexes.

In 1908 the militia was restyled the Special Reserve, and it retained this title until after the First World War, when it became the militia once again before disappearing. The volunteer units of infantry, yeomanry (cavalry) and artillery, etc., were formed into the Territorial Force in 1908, which was renamed the Territorial Army in 1920. Most of the records are held locally: the muster rolls of some London and Middlesex Volunteer and Territorial regiments (1860–1912) are in the PRO (WO 70).

For more information about the Militia and Volunteers, see Thomas and Spencer, *Militia and Volunteer Forces 1757–1945*.

18.8 Commissioned officers: *Army Lists* and printed sources

All the printed sources here may be seen at Kew: to find out where exactly they may be seen, check on MORIS. Brief biographies of eminent soldiers may be found in the *Dictionary of National Biography*, and the *British Biographical Archive* (see **1.13**).

Details of officers granted commissions before 1727 can most easily be traced in Dalton's *English Army Lists and Commission Registers, 1661–1714*, in his *Irish Army Lists, 1661–1685*, and in his *George I's Army, 1714–1727*, all available at Kew.

The *Royal Military Kalendar* has details of officers of field rank (major) upwards. It was compiled in 1820, of officers then alive, so that the service covered goes back well into the eighteenth century.

The broad outline of an officer's career should be fairly easy to discover, using the *Army Lists*. Manuscript lists of Army officers were kept from 1702–1752 (WO 64); there is an index in the Research Enquiries Room. The first official *Army List* was published in 1740; since 1754 they have been published regularly. There are complete record sets, with manuscript amendments, of the annual lists (1754–1879) and the quarterly lists (1879–1900) in WO 65 and WO 66: incomplete sets are on open access. Large reference libraries may also have a set.

The *Army List* was arranged by regiment, with a name index from 1766 (engineer and artillery officers were included in the index only from 1803). From 1879 it included a gradation list of officers – i.e. a list in order of seniority, giving dates of birth and promotions, and, from April 1881, details of service. For later *Army Lists*, see Fowler and Spencer, *Army Records for Family Historians*. The *Army List* did not include militia officers before the mid nineteenth century. For more information on other printed sources for militia officers, see Thomas and Spencer, *Militia and Volunteer Forces 1757–1945*.

Hart's Army List was an unofficial list, produced between 1839 and 1915; it is particularly useful because it contains details of war service from 1839, which the official lists did not do until 1881. An incomplete set covering 1840–1915 is available on open access: a full set, and Hart's own papers, which can include additional biographical information for 1838–1875, are in WO 211.

For Royal Artillery officers, check the *List of Officers of the Royal Regiment of Artillery, 1716–June 1914*: for Royal Engineer officers, consult the *Roll of Officers of the Corps of Royal Engineers from 1660 to 1898.*

18.9 Commissioned officers: commissions

There were four sorts of commissioned officer:

general officers	these co-ordinated the efforts of the whole army: field marshal, general, lieutenant-general, major-general.
regimental officers	colonel (in command of a regiment), lieutenant-colonel, major.
company officers	captain (in command of a company) and his subalterns, lieutenant, cornet (cavalry), ensign (infantry). In 1871 cornets and ensigns became second lieutenants.
others	paymaster, adjutant, quartermaster, surgeon and chaplain.

There were also many other ranks, such as brigadier-general, colonel-commandant, brigade-major, etc. Officers were graded by seniority, which ruled promotion within the regiment: if an officer was promoted out of sequence, he was given brevet rank, e.g., as a brevet-major. Some officers held two ranks at the same time, the regimental rank, which was higher, and was usually a special appointment, and the army rank, which was the actual rank of his commission.

Officers held their rank by virtue of a royal commission. There is a small collection of original commissions, 1780–1874, in WO 43/1059. Until 1871, entry commissions could be purchased: as they were expensive, entry was usually restricted to the well off. Promotion too could be bought, although it was also awarded for merit. Warrants for the issue of commissions for cavalry and infantry officers, 1679–1782, are in SP 44, continued after 1782 by HO 51. Commission books were kept by the War Office, 1660–1873 (WO 25/1–88) and others. Applications for, and resignations of, commissions between 1793 and 1870 contain some personal details such as birth certificates and statements of service (in WO 31). Correspondence about the purchase and sale of commissions, 1701–1858, is in WO 4/513–520 (with internal indexes).

Royal Artillery and Royal Engineer officers were the responsibility of the Board of Ordnance until 1855, when they were transferred to the War Office: before 1855, there are separate records for them. Their original warrants and patents of appointment, 1670–1855, are in WO 54/939–945: other commission records too are available.

18.10 Commissioned officers: regimental service records

Service records were kept by the regiments only, until the early nineteenth century, when the War Office began to taken an interest. There are two indexes covering both the early regimental and War Office series (WO 76 and WO 25), one an index to regiments, and the other to names.

Regimental records of officers' services start in 1755. Not all regiments are represented, and the records of some were lost. The information kept by the regiments varies a great deal, but it usually gives the ranks held, service details, and some personal particulars. There is an incomplete card index to regimental service records. Don't forget the many regimental publications of officers' services: it may be worth checking the PRO Library.

The records of the Gloucester Regiment, 1792-1866, are in WO 67/24–27, and those of the Royal Garrison Regiment, 1901–1905, are in WO 19. Artillery officers' services, 1727–1751, are in WO 54/684: for 1771–1870, they are in WO 76. Returns of engineer officers, 1786–1850, are in WO 54/248–259, with service records, 1796–1922, in WO 25/3913–3919.

Not all officers were regimental officers. For staff officers, there is a staff pay index, 1792–1830 (WO 25/695–699), lists of staff at various dates between 1802 and 1870, some with addresses (WO 25/700–702) and general returns of staff in British and foreign stations, 1782–1854 (WO 25/703–743). There are general returns of the service of commissariat officers, who were not military officers, for 1798–1842 (WO 61/1–2), followed by a register of Commissariat and Transport staff, 1843–1889 (WO 61/5–6). Senior staff of the War Office are included in the *Army Lists*.

18.11 Commissioned officers: War Office returns of service, [1809]–1872

War Office records of officers' service started with five returns of service made by the officers themselves. The first series, made in 1809–1810, is arranged alphabetically, and gives details of military service only (WO 25/744–748). The second, compiled from returns made in 1828 by officers retired or on half pay (and therefore referring to service completed some years before), also gives age at commission, date of marriage and date of children's birth: it is arranged alphabetically (WO 25/749–779). Similar information was collected from serving officers in 1829, but this third series is arranged by regiment (WO 25/780–805). The fourth series was a repeat of the second, but made in 1847 (WO 25/808–823). The fifth series, of returns made mainly between 1870 and 1872, is arranged by year of return and then by regiment; it also gives personal details (WO 25/824–870). There is an incomplete card index to these records.

1809–1810	1st series	arranged alphabetically; gives details of military service only	WO 25/744–748
1828	2nd series	arranged alphabetically; covers only officers retired or on half pay (and therefore refers to service completed some years before). Age at commission, date of marriage and date of children's birth	WO 25/749–779
1829	3rd series	arranged by regiment; covers only serving officers. Age at commission, date of marriage and date of children's birth. *Wives* indexed separately, by maiden name, giving date and place of birth, marriage, children's birth, and sometimes death (Miss Fairbrother's index)	WO 25/780–805
1847	4th series	a repeat of the second	WO 25/808–823
1870–1872	5th series	arranged by year of return and then by regiment; gives personal details	WO 25/824–870

18.12 Commissioned officers: records of service and correspondence files, 1870–1922

In 1871 the system of obtaining commissions by purchase was stopped. At the same time, a new system of keeping personal records on officers was begun by the Military Secretary's department of the War Office. From 1870, individual units would keep details on individual officers, on an Army Form B 194-1, and these would in turn be bound into Army Books 83. These records are in WO 76, with some oddments in WO 25, for those whose service ended before 1914. They do not survive for officers whose service ended after 1914, as they were destroyed by enemy bombing in the Second World War.

A confidential report on each officer's ability was completed each year by the Commanding Officer of the unit and these were kept by the Military Secretary. Very few confidential reports have been preserved.

Along with these two forms, there was a correspondence file, which, depending on length of service, could become very bulky. These did survive the bombing, and are now the main source for officers who fought in the First World War, and who left the service between 1914 and 1922. These correspondence files covering service of any officer between 1870 and 1922 are arranged in two separate record classes WO 339 and WO 374. These files can contain details of an officers' estate if he died in service, reports made by repatriated prisoners of war, details relating to pensions, medical records and in fact almost anything not necessarily about his ability.

WO 339 is arranged by War Office 'Long Number': the index to these numbers is in WO 338 (available on microfilm). WO 374 is arranged in alphabetical order. In total some 217,000 individual files can be found in these two classes. Unfortunately many files of officers who obtained their commissions before 1901 were weeded or destroyed in the 1930s. You may find a lot of information, or you may find very little.

For more detailed information, see Fowler, Spencer and Tamblin *Army Service Records of the First World War*.

Files of those officers who saw service after 1922 are still maintained by the Ministry of Defence (address in **48**).

18.13 Commissioned officers: pension records before 1914

Before 1871 there was no general entitlement to a retirement pension; an officer would either move off the active list onto half pay, or would sell that valuable piece of property, his commission. The system of half pay to officers still holding a commission, but not on active service, was set up in 1641 to provide a retainer for the officers of disbanded regiments. It eventually expanded to become almost a kind of retirement pay, albeit one that was open to a lot of abuses. Half pay officers are included in the *Army List*, but sometimes do not appear in the index. Records of half pay do not contain much genealogical information. The most useful are probably the ledgers of payment, 1737–1921, in PMG 4. These give dates of death or of sale of the commission (which ended entitlement to half pay): from 1837 they also give addresses. Later ledgers give date of birth as well. From 1737 to 1841, the ledgers are arranged by regiment and are unindexed: from 1841 they are in one alphabetical sequence of names.

When the system of purchasing commissions was finally abolished, the current holders of commissions were eligible for compensation on their retirement. Registers were drawn up of all

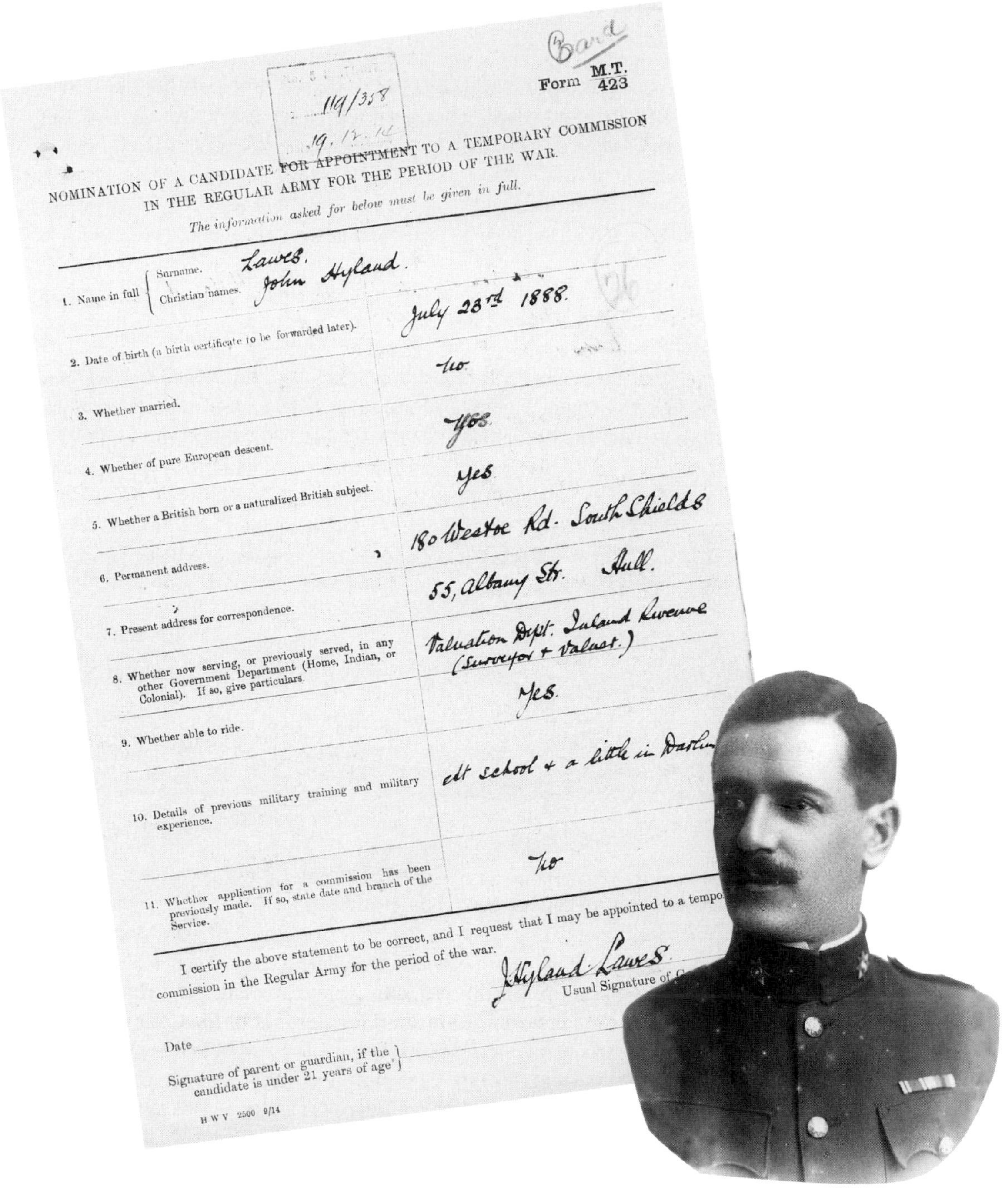

Bard

Form M.T. 423

[illegible]
119/358
19.12.14

NOMINATION OF A CANDIDATE FOR APPOINTMENT TO A TEMPORARY COMMISSION IN THE REGULAR ARMY FOR THE PERIOD OF THE WAR.

The information asked for below must be given in full.

1. Name in full { Surname. / Christian names.	Lawes. / John Hyland.
2. Date of birth (a birth certificate to be forwarded later).	July 23rd 1888.
3. Whether married.	no
4. Whether of pure European descent.	yes.
5. Whether a British born or a naturalized British subject.	yes.
6. Permanent address.	180 Westoe Rd. South Shields
7. Present address for correspondence.	55, Albany Str. Hull.
8. Whether now serving, or previously served, in any other Government Department (Home, Indian, or Colonial). If so, give particulars.	Valuation Dept. Inland Revenue (Surveyor + Valuer.)
9. Whether able to ride.	yes.
10. Details of previous military training and military experience.	At school + a little in Darlin
11. Whether application for a commission has been previously made. If so, state date and branch of the Service.	no

I certify the above statement to be correct, and I request that I may be appointed to a tempo commission in the Regular Army for the period of the war.

J Hyland Lawes.
Usual Signature of C

Date

Signature of parent or guardian, if the candidate is under 21 years of age

H W V 2500 9/14

Figure 8 John Hyland Lawes of the East Yorkshire Regiment (photo courtesy of A H Lawes) and his application for a commission in 1914 (WO 339/17910). These First World War officers' papers contain varying amounts of detail. Officers' records are far more likely to survive than those of other ranks, many of which were destroyed by bombing in 1940.

officers holding a commission on 1 November 1871, with the dates and estimated value of their commission, and with later annotations to show the date of retirement and the sum granted in compensation. These registers, which are in WO 74, do not give personal details.

Pensions were available for wounded officers from 1812. Registers of such pensioners, 1812–1892, are in WO 23/83–92; correspondence on such claims, 1812–1855, can be found in WO 4/469–493. Further correspondence, 1809–1857, can be found in WO 43: there is a card index to this. Actual records of payments are in PMG 9 (including First World War payments) and PMG 12.

For officers' pension records from the First World War, see **18.31**.

18.14 Commissioned officers: families

Provision of an authentic baptismal certificate was mandatory for those in government service: membership of the established church implied loyalty to the crown. As a result there are many baptismal certificates for Army officers in the War Office records. There are two main caches, for 1777–1868 in WO 32/8903–8920 (code 21A), which are mostly for militia officers, and for 1755–1908 in WO 42. The latter also contains certificates of marriage, birth of children, death and burial (see below). There are indexes to both.

Reports by officers of their marriage, 1830–1882, are in WO 25/3239–3245; some of the marriages date from the early years of the century.

1829	Serving officers: age, marriage and children. Index to officers. *Wives* indexed separately, by maiden name, giving date and place of birth, marriage, children's birth, and sometimes death (Miss Fairbrother's index)	WO 25/780 806
[1799]–1882	Reports of officers– marriages: indexed up to 1851 by maiden name of *wife*, giving place and date of birth and marriage, and witnesses (Miss Fairbrother's index)	WO 25/3239 3245

The various military registers of births, marriages and burials (see **18.2** and **18.3**) include references to officers' families, if they had followed the drum.

Other than this, more information is only likely to be found in military records if the officer died leaving his family in want. From 1708 there was provision for the payment of pensions to the widows of officers killed on active service; from 1720, pensions were also paid to the children and dependent relatives (usually indigent mothers over 50) in similar cases, out of the Compassionate Fund and the Royal Bounty. These pensions were not an automatic right, and applicants had to prove their need. Application papers for widows' pensions and dependents' allowances, 1755–1908, which can include proofs of birth, marriage, death, and wills, etc., are in WO 42: other such papers, of uncertain date (1760–1818?) are in WO 25/3089–3197, arranged alphabetically, with abstracts of applications, 1808–1825, in WO 25/3073–3089. There is an index in the Research Enquiries Room.

There are lists of widows receiving pensions, 1713–1829 (WO 24/804–883), and 1815–1892 (WO 23/88–92). Registers of payments, 1735–1811, are in WO 25/3020–3058, with indexes to pensions for 1748–1811 (WO 25/3120–3123). Similar registers for 1815–1895 are in WO 23/105–123. Ledgers of payments of widows' pensions, 1808–1920, are in PMG 11, but they give little information. Correspondence relating to widows' pensions, 1764–1816, is in WO 4/1023–1030: the volumes are internally indexed, and contain details on many widows. Selected correspondence on widows' pensions is also in WO 43: there is a card index in the Research Enquiries Room.

There are registers of compassionate allowances awarded to dependents, 1773–1812 (WO 25/3124–3125). Registers of those placed on the Compassionate List, 1858–1894 are in WO 23/114–119, with a summary for 1805–1895 in WO 23/120–123. There are also about 2,000 'compassionate papers' for 1812–1813 (WO 25/3110–3114), which are affidavits by the widows and children, in receipt of a compassionate pension, that they received no other government income. They are in rough alphabetical order, and give details of the officer, often the age of the children, and sometimes the name of the guardian, as well as some indication of county or country of residence (they were sworn before local justices). Correspondence relating to the Compassionate Fund, 1803–1860, is in WO 4/521–590. There are ledgers of payments, for 1779–1812 (WO 24/771–803), and for 1812–1915 (PMG 10), but they give little information. Ledgers of pension payments for the widows of foreign officers, 1822–1885, are in PMG 6 and PMG 7. For pensions and compassionate allowances to the widows and dependents of commissariat officers, 1814–1834, see WO 61/96–98.

Registers of pensions to the widows of Royal Artillery and Royal Engineer officers, 1833–1837, are in WO 54/195–196, with ledgers of payments, 1836–1875, in PMG 12. There is also a series of indexed registers of letters of attorney, 1699–1857, relating to Ordnance officers, civilian staff and creditors who expected to receive payments of any kind from the Ordnance Office (WO 54/494–510): many of these letters were made in favour of the wife or other close relative, or were letters granted by the probate courts to the widow as executrix.

Similar registers of powers of attorney for Army officers in general are in PMG 14 and PMG 51. There are entry books of powers of attorney apparently arranged by date, for 1759–1816 (PMG 14/104–125). For 1811–1814, there are alphabetical entry books (PMG 14/126–137). Registers of letters of attorney, 1756–1827, are in PMG 14/142–167: they include separate volumes of letters of attorney granted by widows, 1802–1821 (PMG 165–167). There is a single register of letters of attorney, 1755–1783, at WO 30/1. Later registers, 1836–1899, are in PMG 51.

18.15 Commissioned officers: chaplains

Until the end of the eighteenth century, chaplains were employed on a regimental basis, but after 1796 one chaplain served three or four regiments. The first Presbyterian chaplains were appointed in 1827; Catholic chaplains in 1836; Wesleyans in 1881, and Jewish chaplains in 1892. As chaplains were commissioned officers, they will be found in the *Army List* (see **18.8**). Certificates of service, 1817–1843, are in WO 25/256–258. Records of payment, 1805–1842, are in WO 25/233–251. The registers of retired pay, 1806–1837 (WO 25/252–253), give details of chaplains who saw service in the eighteenth century. Letters from chaplains, 1808–1836, are in the Chaplain General's Letter Books (in WO 7). See also **32.2**.

18.16 Other ranks: introduction

In the Army, the 'other ranks' were the privates (infantry) and troopers (cavalry), trumpeters and drummers, supervised by corporals and sergeants who were non-commissioned officers promoted from the ranks: specialist regiments and corps used different names. The basic information kept on each soldier reappears in different permutations in different types of document. This basic personal information comprises name, age, place of birth, trade on enlistment, place of enlistment, physical description and date of death or discharge. Some records contain information on wife, children or other next of kin.

Almost all service records were kept by the individual regiments, not by any central authority. As a result, if you are searching for an individual soldier, you really do need to know the regiment in which he served unless you are prepared for a lengthy and speculative search. This subject is discussed more fully in **18.18**. However, there are two series of Army-wide returns of service of non-commissioned officers and men. One contains statements of periods of service and of liability to serve abroad, as on 24 June 1806 (WO 25/871–1120). The other contains returns of the service of non-commissioned officers and men not known to be dead or totally disqualified for service, who had been discharged between 1783 and 1810 (WO 25/1121–1131). However, both series are still arranged by regiment, and only then alphabetically.

The main everyday service records of men in active service kept by the Army were the regimental muster book and the regimental pay list (see **18.21**). These provide a fairly complete guide to a soldier's Army career from enlistment, through movements with the regiment throughout the world, to discharge. However, because there are so many muster books and pay lists, and because they each cover such a short space of time, it can be a very lengthy task to search through them. It is worth investigating other records first, particularly the service records of soldiers retired to pension (see **18.17**), where the personal information is consolidated and is far more easily found, even if you are not sure that your ancestor received a pension. If you find that he was discharged without a pension before 1883, you may have to use the muster books and pay lists (but see **18.18** first). If your soldier died in service, you may find out quite a lot of information if you know the regiment, by using the casualty returns (see **18.19**): if these prove no use, try the muster books.

18.17 Other ranks: service records of soldiers discharged to pension before 1914

Service records, from 1760–1913, may be found in the Royal Hospital Chelsea Soldiers' Documents (WO 97). In general, before 1882 there was no record of the whole of the soldier's service unless he was one of the minority discharged to a pension. After 1883, records were kept even for men who only served for a short period of service. WO 97 is generally the first place to look in tracing a soldier ancestor, even though it covers a minority before 1883. The Soldiers' Documents give age, birthplace, trade or occupation on enlistment, a record of service including any decorations, the reason for discharge to pension, and, in some cases, place of residence after discharge and date of death. From 1883, they also contain details of next of kin, marriage and children.

If you know the county or country in which the ex-soldier was living between 1842 and 1862 for England and Scotland, or between 1842 and 1882 for Ireland and abroad, you may be able to find his regiment fairly easily, and perhaps some further clues. Between these dates there are records of payment of pensions, arranged by the district pay offices, which name the regiment served in (WO 22, and PMG 8 for payments in Hanover). For nearly 9,000 pensioners in India, Canada and South Africa between 1772 and 1899, taken from WO 120/35, 69 and 70, see Crowder, *British Army Pensioners Abroad, 1772–1899.*

Pension records, by their very nature, refer to service often begun many years before the date of the pension award. Do remember this when looking at the covering dates given below – they do not refer to the dates of service. A soldier may have been discharged to a pension for disability, or for long service of 21 years. After 1883, soldiers discharged after completing one of the new limited engagements, or who had bought their discharge, were also eligible for consideration for a pension.

The soldiers' documents are arranged by date of *discharge*, as follows:

1760–1854	by regiment:, but there is now a computer index: see below. *Does not include regiments on the Irish establishment before 1822*	WO 97/1–1271
1855–1872	by regiment, but an index exists in private hands: see below	WO 97/1272–1721
1873–1882	by cavalry, artillery, infantry or corps	WO 97/1722–2171
1843–1899	by name: papers which had been misfiled	WO 97/6355–6383
1883–1900	by name	WO 97/2172–4231
1900–1913	by name	WO 97/4232–6322
1900–1913	by name: papers which had been misfiled	WO 97/6323–6354

There is a computer database of records in WO 97 for soldiers discharged to pension between 1760 and 1854, courtesy of the Friends of the PRO: it is available in the Microfilm Reading Room. This is very helpful, and saves an enormous amount of time. You can search by name, birthplace, etc.

The Soldiers' Documents (WO 97) between 1854 and 1872 are arranged by regiment, but are not on the database. However, if you do not know the regiment, there is a privately-owned index, which you can pay to have consulted. For details ask at the Microfilm Reading Room desk for Gibson and Hampson, *Specialist Indexes for Family Historians.*

There are other, similar, records for Chelsea, which may be worth checking if there is nothing in WO 97. IF you think the man you are looking for was Irish (and very many in the Army were), then he may have been on the Irish Army Establishment, whose pensions were dealt with by the Royal Hospital Kilmainham. The Kilmainham Discharge Documents of Pensioners, 1783–1822, are in WO 119. These are arranged by discharge number, with indexes to these numbers in WO 118. After 1822, the Royal Hospital Chelsea handled all pensions. If the Kilmainham documents are not helpful, then there are some other sources to try.

The main class to check is WO 121, Discharge Documents of Pensioners. For the period 1787–1813 this class contains the documents which one would expect to find in WO 97. They are not duplicates of WO 97. In fact, they even include the papers of soldiers who were refused a pension. The records are arranged by date of the meetings of the admission board, and then by regimental seniority: they include approximately 20,000 certificates (WO 121/1–136).

Other possible sources are the Chelsea Regimental Registers, c.1715–1857 (WO 120): these are chronological lists of discharges to pension by each regiment (see **18.23**). There is a partial index for 1806–1838, available on request in the Microfilm Reading Room. Also worth checking are the records of deferred pensions, 1838–1896 (WO 131); and the Discharge Documents of Pensioners, Foreigners' Regiments, 1816–1817 (WO 122). See also **18.23**, for records relating to the actual payment of the pension to your soldier, which can provide information on his life after leaving the Army.

For more information on pensions and the Chelsea and Kilmainham Hospitals, see **18.23**.

For the service records of soldiers discharged between 1914 and 1920, see **18.30**.

18.18 Other ranks: how to find the regiment

Not all soldiers were discharged to pension, and thus easily found in WO 97. If you want to try to trace a soldier among the wealth of surviving records, you really do need to know which regiment he served in. Most records before 1873 are arranged by regiment. You may already have details of the regiment, from family knowledge or previous research. However, if you do not, there are still some possible ways to find out the regiment, other than through the identification of uniforms from old photographs (see the article by Barnes on this subject).

The regimental registers of births, 1761–1924, at the FRC (ONS) are indexed: the index gives the regiment and place of birth of children born to the wives of serving soldiers, if they were attached to the regiment. If you have some knowledge of offspring or areas of service, this can be an easy way to narrow the field. To actually identify the correct child, parent and regiment, you may have to buy more than one certificate (see **4.2** and **18.2**).

Another possibility, if the soldier died in service, would be to check the records of dead soldiers' effects, 1810–1822, 1830–1844 and 1862–1881, discussed in **18.19**. These are arranged by initial letter of surname and give the regiment, which opens up the regimental records to you. However, if the soldier died owing money to the Army, instead of *vice versa*, you are unlikely to find a reference to him here.

If you have any information on place of service, you may be able to identify the regiment from Kitzmiller's guide to locating British Army regiments, called *In Search of the 'Forlorn Hope'*. There is a similar guide by Laws for the various batteries of the Royal Artillery.

There are other possibilities as well, although using the following suggestions may be a lengthy process. Depending on the known information, an area of records to be searched can be limited. If a rough date of discharge is known, it may be possible to trace the regiment in which a soldier served by using various registers of discharges. These are not complete but, especially before the records in WO 97 are arranged purely alphabetically (see **18.17**), they are a useful potential source of information. A number of these pieces contain information on soldiers whose discharge document would not, in any case, be contained in WO 97. These discharges were:

1817–1829	by purchase	WO 25/3845–3847
1830–1838	by own request	WO 25/3848–3849
1830–1856	with modified pension	WO 25/3850
1838–1855	free or free deferred pension	WO 25/3851–3858
1856–1861	free permanent pension	WO 25/3859–3861
1861–1870	free permanent pension, modified/deferred pension, or purchase	WO 25/3863–3868

1852–1870	first period, incorrigible, ignominy, penal servitude, or 21 years with militia	WO 25/3869–3878
1856–1857	regiment under reduction	WO 25/3879–3882
1866–1870	Limited Service Act	WO 25/3883–3893
1863–1878	on return from India	WO 12/13077–13105
1871–1884	general register	WO 121/223–238
1882–1883	Gosport discharge depot musters	WO 16/2284
1883–1888	Gosport discharge depot musters Index available	WO 16/2888–2916
1884–1887	without pension (gives address to which discharged)	WO 121/239–257

18.19 Other ranks: casualty returns and registers of effects

If you know the regiment of your soldier, and have been unable to find his discharge documents, try the casualty returns, 1797–1910, which can provide quite a lot of personal information. Despite their title, the casualty returns refer to absences, desertions and discharges, not just to the dead and wounded. The information given is name, rank, place of birth, trade at enlistment, the date, place and nature of the casualty, any debts or credits, and the next of kin or legatee. Wills, inventories of effects, letters from relatives, and accounts are included very infrequently.

The main collection of monthly and quarterly regimental casualty returns covers 1809–c.1875, with a few entries and annotations in the indexes continuing up to 1910 (WO 25/1359–2410, 3251–3260, indexed in WO 25/2411–2755, 3261–3471). There is also a series of entry books of casualties, 1797–1817, from the Muster Master General's Office (WO 25/1196–1358).

If you do not know the regiment, try the records relating to payments to next of kin of dead soldiers: there are gaps in these records but they are arranged alphabetically and are easy to use. These are the registers of authorities to deal with the effects (possessions) of dead soldiers, 1810–1822 (WO 25/2966–2971). These are very informative: they give name, regiment, period of death, amount of effects and credits, date of order to agent, agent's name, person applying (usually next of kin) and his or her address

Less informative but still helpful, as they give the regiment, are: an index of effects, 1830 (WO 25/2974); a register of effects and credits, 1830–1844 (WO 25/2975); and record books of effects, 1862–1881 (WO 25/3476–3490, indexed by WO 25/3491–3501).

18.20 Other ranks: deserters

There is an incomplete card index to army deserters (1689–1830), compiled from bounty certificates of rewards paid out of locally-collected taxes to those who had turned the deserter in. The index covers only rewards paid out in London and Middlesex (from E 182/594–673) and in Bedfordshire, Berkshire, Buckinghamshire, Cambridgeshire and Cheshire (E 182/2–114). The main part of the index is of deserters, giving date and regiment, as well as a reference to E 182 by piece number and sub-number. There is also a sequence by county, as well as cross-references from entries like 'Dragoons', 'Fencibles' and 'Militia' to the main sequence. If you order one of these E 182 references, you will get one or more large boxes of tax documents, with no obvious clue as to where the bounty certificates will be. Look amongst the many unwrapped bundles of documents for a bundle wrapped up in linsen paper (a stiff brown paper).

Information on deserters was forwarded to the Army authorities by means of the casualty returns, 1809–1910 (see **18.19** for more details). There are registers of deserters, 1811–1852, in WO 25/2906–2934. Until 1827 they are kept in three series, for cavalry, infantry and militia (the latter up to 1820 only). After 1827 they are arranged by regiment. These registers give descriptions, dates and place of enlistment and desertion, and outcome. There are registers of captured deserters, 1813–1845, in WO 25/2935–2951, with indexes up to 1833 in WO 25/2952–2954. Deserters who surrendered themselves under proclamation, 1803–1815, are in WO 25/2955. On capture, some deserters were sentenced to imprisonment on the *Savoy* hulk: there are unindexed registers for the hulk, 1799–1823 (WO 25/2956–2961).

Local newspapers and (for 1828 to 1845) the police newspapers *Hue and Cry* and the *Police Gazette* carried details of deserters, giving name, parish and county of birth, regiment, date and place of desertion, a physical description and other relevant information. For deserters in Australia (HO 75), consult Fitzmaurice's book.

For First World War deserters, see Oram and Putkowski, *Death Sentences passed by the Military Courts of the British Army 1914–1924*.

18.21 Other ranks: muster books, pay lists, description books and numbers

The basic regimental service records were the muster books, pay lists and description books: these were used for the day-to-day administration of the regiment. The main series of muster books and pay lists is in WO 12, which covers 1732–1878. For 1877 to 1898, WO 10–WO 12 are continued by WO 16, but coverage is incomplete and the information given is very limited. Other series are of the artillery, 1710–1878 (WO 10), the engineers, 1816–1878 (WO 11), the militia and volunteers, 1780–1878 (WO 13), the troops at the Scutari depot involved in the Crimean War, 1854–1856 (WO 14), and the British, German and Swiss legions, 1854–1856 (WO 15).

In general, each muster book and pay list occupies one volume per year, and you may therefore have to search through several volumes. The first entry for the recruit in the muster generally gives his age, place of enlistment and trade, but does not give birthplace. If the soldier died in service, or was discharged, you should find an entry to that effect in one of the quarterly lists of men becoming non-effective: however, these lists are not always present. Where one does exist, it should give the birthplace of the man discharged or dead, his trade and his date of enlistment.

From about 1868 to about 1883, the musters also contain marriage rolls, which sometimes give information about children as well as wives, if they occupied married quarters.

There are two main series of description books. The regimental description and succession books are in WO 25/266–688: covering dates are 1778–1878, but not all the regiments' books start so early or go on so late, and only a small percentage of all soldiers are included. Some are arranged alphabetically, others by date of enlistment. The books give a description of each soldier, his age, place of birth and trade and successive service details. The depot description books, 1768–1908 in WO 67, give the same information, gathered as recruits were assembled at the regimental depot.

These description books in WO 25 are not books containing details of every man in the regiment who served between the covering dates. They began to be compiled in approximately 1825, or slightly earlier, after an investigation into the fraudulent claims of service. Regiments had to write down the services of every man in the regiment who was still serving at that time, and to list them in chronological order of enlistment (or alphabetically). Consequently, the further back one goes, the fewer the men from that period. Most books would appear to have between 1,000 and 1,500 names (some have a lot more), but considering that regimental strength was 1,000 and the regiments had been through twenty-two years of war and wastage, this is a small percentage of the total number. Depot rolls or description books (WO 67) are usually much fuller. Men were usually allotted a number, but this number does not appear on any forms until the 1830s. Depot rolls, however, do not list soldiers who enlisted where the regiment was stationed. Neither do they list soldiers who transferred from one regiment straight into another.

Incidentally, regimental numbering began as a direct result of this commission of enquiry. Each man, as he joined, was allotted a consecutive number. This would not be carried throughout his career: if he transferred into another regiment, he would be allotted a new number. It is possible to estimate when a soldier enlisted in a particular regiment if a point of reference is known, i.e. if a muster provides details of a man with a regimental number close to that of the ancestor. It is then possible to guess a year of discharge (add 21!). In 1917, the system changed and the first series of Army numbers came in. This was very short-lived and the second series (superseding the first) began in 1922. This allotted 'blocks' of numbers to particular regiments, and a man on first enlistment would be given a number in the relevant block which he would retain even on transfer to another regiment. This numbering system ran out in c.1941 and another began.

18.22 Other ranks: Artillery and Engineer (Sapper and Miner) service records

Because the Royal Artillery, the Royal Engineers, and the Royal Corps of Sappers and Miners were the responsibility of the Ordnance Office (and not of the War Office) until 1855, they have a different set of records. Until 1772, the Royal Engineers were officers only, using casual labour for the physical work: after this a Corps of Royal Military Artificers, composed of other ranks only, was raised. In 1811, it became the Royal Corps of Sappers and Miners, with both officers and other ranks. This was amalgamated with the Royal Engineers after the abolition of the Ordnance Office in 1856.

However, many documents relating to Sappers and Miners are described in the lists as relating to Royal Engineers. Entry books of discharges, casualties, and transfers of Artillery and Engineer (Sapper and Miner) soldiers, 1740–1859, are in WO 54/317–337. Service records of the Royal Artillery, 1791–1855, and for the Royal Horse Artillery, 1803–1863, are in WO 69. These include attestation papers, and show name, age, description, place of birth, trade, and dates of service, of promotion, of marriage, of discharge and of death. They are arranged under the unit in which the soldier last served: to find this, use the indexes and posting books (WO 69/779–782 and WO 69/801–839). This class also contains records of births and marriages (see **18.3**). Laws's guide to the location of Artillery batteries may be useful if you know only the area of service.

There is a miscellaneous collection of records of service for soldiers in the Artillery, Sappers and Miners, etc., and for civilian subordinates of the Board of Ordnance, arranged alphabetically in the Ordnance Office In-Letters (WO 44/695–700). There is an incomplete series of registers recording the deaths of soldiers in the Artillery, 1821–1873, in WO 69/583–597. Papers relating to Artillery and Engineer (Sapper and Miner) deaths and personal effects, 1824–1859, are in WO 25/2972–2973 and 2976–2978. Admission registers to pension for Royal Artillery disability and long service pensioners, 1833–1913, are in WO 116/125–185. Registers of Artillery and Sapper and Miner pensioners, compiled in 1834 but dating back to the Napoleonic wars, are in WO 23/141–145; they include descriptions.

Musters and pay lists for the Royal Artillery, 1708–1878, are in WO 10; for the Royal Sappers and Miners, and the Engineers, 1816–1878, they are in WO 11. Musters for both Artillery and Engineers, 1878–1898, are in WO 16.

18.23 Other ranks: pension records before 1914

The main system of Army pensions to other ranks was operated by the Royal Hospital Chelsea (London, founded 1681) and, for soldiers in the Irish establishment, the Royal Hospital, Kilmainham (near Dublin, founded 1679). Before (and after) the founding of these Royal Hospitals, disabled ex-soldiers were often granted places as almsmen in royal church foundations: petitions for such places, often giving details of service and wounds, for 1660 to 1751, are in SO 5/31.

Chelsea and Kilmainham supported both in-pensioners, who lived in the hospitals, and a much larger number of out-pensioners. Kilmainham operated a system of out-pensioners from 1698 to 1822, when its out-pensioners were transferred, as out-pensioners, to Chelsea. The last Kilmainham in-pensioners were transferred to Chelsea as in-pensioners, or to out-pension, in 1929. The service records of those soldiers who were discharged to pension have been described in **18.17**. However, both hospitals have other records which can be very useful, particularly for the period before the discharge documents start (i.e. 1756 for Chelsea and 1783 for Kilmainham), and for the ex-soldier's life after leaving the Army.

Admission registers for Kilmainham in- and out-pensions, 1704–1922, are in WO 118. Chelsea has two series, one for long service pensions, 1823–1920 (WO 116), and one for disability pensions, 1715–1913 (WO 118). These admission registers, which are arranged by date of discharge/admission to pension, generally give a brief description of the pensioner, age, place of birth, particulars of service and the reason of discharge. Royal Artillery disability and long service pensioners, 1833–1913, have separate admission registers (WO 116/125–185).

The Chelsea Regimental Registers (WO 120, seen on microfilm) give regimental lists of discharges to pension. They give a brief description, age, place of birth, particulars of service and reason of discharge, for the period c.1715–1843. For 1843 to 1857, they give only the date of award, rate of pension and the district pay office where the pension was paid. From about 1812 the dates of death have been added, the last dating from 1877. There is a partial index, covering 1806–1838.

For 1842 to 1883, out-pensions were paid through district pension offices, including many abroad. These records are arranged by place of the pension office, which can be very useful if you know only the area or country in which the man, or his dependents, resided, and not his regiment (WO 22, and PMG 8 for payments made in Hanover). There are separate registers of men admitted to pension from colonial regiments, 1817–1903, who did not have to appear in person. In many of these cases, details of service and birthplace are given (WO 23/147 160). Some of these entries relate to men from the British Army who retired while their regiment was overseas, and who were given permission to receive their pension there.

There are many other records from Chelsea Hospital, which can be very useful. In particular, the Chelsea registers, etc., 1702–1917 (WO 23), contain a vast amount of information, such as an alphabetical list of in-pensioners in 1837, muster rolls of the hospital, 1702–1789 and 1865; pension claims from soldiers in colonial regiments, 1836–1903; East India Company Army pensioners, 1814–1875; and the Chelsea registers, 1805–1895, of pensioners by regiment (as in WO 120), pensions for the Victoria Cross, wounds or other merit, and bounty.

Selected personal files on over 5,000 disabled soldiers and naval ratings, who served before 1914 and received disability pensions, are in PIN 71; the information contained includes medical records, accounts of how injuries were incurred, and the men's own account of the incident, and conduct sheets. These conduct sheets give place of birth, age, names of parents and siblings, religion, physical attributes, marital and parental status. The class is alphabetically arranged.

A sample of records (20,000) of soldiers medically discharged as a result of wounds or sickness received or contracted during the First World War are in PIN 26: see **18.31**.

18.24 Other ranks: families

Information on other ranks' families may be found in the regimental registers at the FRC (see **4.2** and **18.2**). There are sometimes references to next of kin in the casualty returns and registers of effects (**18.19**). From 1868–1883 marriage rolls, containing information of those wives and children who were on the regimental books, may be found with the muster books (**18.21**). PIN 71 contains over 1,000 personal files on the widows of Army other ranks and naval ratings whose service was before 1914. This is only a selection of such files, but it is alphabetically arranged, and the information contained is extensive.

18.25 Other ranks: schools for orphans and other children

The Royal Military Asylum was founded at Chelsea in 1801, as a boarding school for children of serving or dead soldiers. It was renamed the Duke of York's Military School in 1892, and was moved to Dover in 1909. Girls were admitted to the female branch until 1840: this was abolished in 1846.

At first, many of the children were not orphans, but most later entrants appear to have lost at least their father and quite frequently both parents. Children appear to have been admitted between the ages of 2 and 10, and were discharged in their mid-teens. Most of the girls not claimed by their parents were apprenticed, often as servants: the boys went into the Army, or were apprenticed if they were not fit for military service.

The admission and discharge registers, 1803–1923, are very informative: unfortunately they are arranged by date of admission (WO 143/17–26): one of the boys' registers, for 1804–1820, is in letter order. The information for the girls is the fuller: number, name, age, date of admission, from what regiment, rank of father (P, T, S etc., for private, trooper, sergeant), parents' names and if living, parochial settlement (on discharge?), when dismissed, and how disposed of (e.g. died, retained by parents while on pass, apprenticed). The boys' admission register gives the same information except that it does not give the parents' names. The discharge registers give more information on apprenticeship, regiment or other fate.

The Royal Hibernian Military School was founded in Dublin in 1769, for the children of soldiers on the Irish establishment: in 1924 it merged with the Duke of York's Military School. Unfortunately, most of its records were destroyed by enemy bombing in 1940: what survives is a boys' index book (WO 143/27), drawn up in 1863 with retrospective entries from c.1835, and with annotations up to c.1919. This gives name, class, references to petitions and registers now lost, corps, and remarks (e.g. volunteered 16th Foot 5 August 59).

18.26 Army medical services

The easiest way to start looking for officers is to consult *Commissioned Officers in the Medical Services of the British Army*, by Peterkin, Johnston and Drew.

There is a series of records of service of officers of the Medical Department, 1800–1840, in WO 25/3896–3912, which includes details of the professional education of surgeons. These records are indexed. There is a certain amount of information for 1811–1818 in WO 25/259–263: for 1809–1852, there are casualty returns of medical staff (WO 25/265, 2384–2385, and 2395–2407). For the period 1825–1867, there are registers of the qualifications of candidates for commissions in the Medical Department (WO 25/3923–3944). The Royal Army Medical Corps has a medal book, 1879–1896, which may be worth a look (WO 25/3992).

Testimonials of women wishing to nurse in the Crimea, c.1851–c.1856, may be found in WO 25/264. A few women nursed at Netley Hospital and on campaign after then. The much larger Army Nursing Service was established in 1884, and renamed Queen Alexandra's Imperial Military Nursing Service (QAIMNS) in 1902. Two reserve military nursing services were also established. In 1894 Princess Christian's Nursing Reserve was set up, to be renamed Queen Alexandra's Imperial Military Nursing Service Reserve in 1908. The Territorial Force Nursing Service, established in 1908, became in 1921 the Territorial Army Nursing Service.

The PRO has no service records for the Army Nursing Service as yet, although those for 1914–1918 should become available in the summer of 1999.

The records of professional qualifications and recommendations for appointment of staff nurses in QAIMNS, 1903–1926, are in WO 25/3956. There are some pension records, but few nurses served long enough to qualify for a pension. Pension records for nurses appointed before 1905 are in WO 23/93–95 and 181; pensions for QAIMNS nurses, 1909–1928, are in PMG 34/1–5; and First World War disability pensions for nurses are in PMG 42/1–12. There are some service records for National Aid Society Nursing Sisters, 1869–1891 (WO 25/3955).

The Royal Red Cross medal was instituted especially for military nurses in 1883 (WO 145). Nurses were also awarded medals for service in Egypt, 1882, and South Africa, 1899–1902 (WO 100) and the First World War (WO 329); the latter has a separate name index for nurses on microfiche. Details relating to some awards granted to members of the QAIMNS can be found in WO 162/65.

18.27 The Indian Army and the British Army in India

There was an army in India which was maintained by the East India Company until 1859. This army consisted of separate divisions of European and Indian troops, which were both officered by Europeans. After 1859 the Company's Indian troops became the Indian (Imperial) Army. The European Regiments became Regiments of the Line, and the Company's Artillery and Engineers became part of the Royal Artillery and Royal Engineers: these formed the British Army in India. See the *India Army List* in the PRO Library.

The service records of the British Army in India will be found with the other army records in the PRO: see **18.17**. There are musters of regiments in India from 1883 to 1889 (in WO 16), but there are none for the Artillery or the Engineers. When a soldier was discharged on his return home, this was recorded in the depot musters of his regiment (WO 67), in the musters of the Victoria Hospital, Netley, 1863–1878 (WO 12/13077–13105), or in the musters of the Discharge Depot, Gosport, 1875–1889 (in WO 16).

British officers after 1859 were trained at Sandhurst (cavalry and infantry) before beginning their careers in India. Their commission papers are thus at the PRO (see **18.8–18.9**), while their records of service are with the India Office records at the British Library. These can be consulted up to 1947.

The service records of European officers and soldiers of the Honourable East India Company's service, and of the Indian (Imperial) Army are mainly preserved with the India Office records, but there are some records in the PRO. Lists of officers of the European Regiments, 1796–1841, are in WO 25/3215–3219. Compensation for the sale of Indian Army commissions, 1758–1897, is recorded in WO 74. Alphabetical lists of East India Company Army pensioners (other ranks) for 1814–1866 are in WO 23/21–23, and there are more detailed registers for 1849–1868 in WO 23/17–20, and for 1824–1856 in WO 25/3137.

Indexes of the death of officers in all the Indian services for the First and Second World Wars can be seen at the FRC and Kew (see **4.14**). The National Army Museum has Hodson's Index, a very large secondary source card index of British officers in the Indian (Imperial) Army, the Bengal Army and the East India Company Army (but not the British Army in India): many of the entries go beyond bare facts to include colourful stories of life. Civilians and government staff are included if they had seen Army service. The cards from this index relating to the Bombay Marine, the East India Company's Navy, are to be passed to the National Maritime Museum: the main deposit of Bombay Marine records is in the India Office Library and Records.

18.28 American War of Independence, 1776–1783

The muster books and pay lists of many regiments involved in this war may be found (see **18.21**), but the certificates of men discharged in North America, which give the age and place of birth, can seldom be traced. It is unlikely that you will find anything but a man's name, rank and date of discharge in the musters. There are some pay lists and account books for Hessian troops, but they provide few personal details. Muster rolls of the Hessian troops in British pay in North America are held in Germany: there is an index available at the Research Enquiries Desk. Some Audit Office accounts (AO 3) may be useful for loyalist troops. The Loyalist Regiment Rolls for provincial troops are in the Public Archives of Canada.

18.29 South African (Boer) War, 1899–1902

The service documents of British regular soldiers who served in South Africa, and were discharged before 1913 are in WO 97 (see **18.17**): the service records of soldiers discharged after 1913 are discussed in **18.30**. The Medal Rolls (WO 100) sometimes contain a few personal details, such as the date of discharge or death, and the home address. For the British Auxiliary Forces, some records of the City Imperial Volunteers are at the Guildhall Library: the soldiers' documents of the Imperial Yeomanry, 1899–1902, are in the PRO (WO 128, indexed by WO 129). Other forces were raised locally in South Africa, and these records are in the PRO. Enrolment forms and nominal rolls of the local armed forces, 1899–1902, are in WO 126 and WO 127.

Further details about the records of the Imperial Yeomanry can be found in Thomas and Spencer, *Militia and Volunteer Forces 1757–1945*.

Indexes to the death registers of British soldiers who died in South Africa, 1899–1902, can be seen at the FRC and Kew: see **14.4**.

18.30 First World War, and soldiers discharged after 1913

Soldiers died in the Great War, seen on microfilm, lists all the men who died between 1914 and 1919, in regimental order. Officers are in volume 81. To find an individual, you must know his regiment, and in cases of common surnames, his service number. The information available from the microfilm includes some abbreviations:

(**B**) Place of Birth	(**D**) Died	(**K in A**) Killed in Action.
(**E**) Place of Enlistment	(**D of W**) Died of Wounds	

These details are followed by the (abbreviated) theatre of war where the soldier died, and the date of death. Any gallantry medals he may have won are also listed.

Surviving service records (like those in WO 97) for soldiers discharged after 1913 are in WO 363 and WO 364. Records of approximately 750,000 men who had been medically discharged as a result of sickness or wounds, contracted or received during the First World War, are in WO 364, available on 4,915 reels of microfilm in alphabetical order. These records are sometimes known as the 'unburnt documents'.

The surviving records of service of those men who completed service in the First World War either as regular soldiers or 'duration of the war servicemen only', are in WO 363, sometimes known as the 'burnt documents'. Here, if you are lucky, you can find the records of men who survived, men who were killed in action or who died of wounds, men who were prisoners of war, and even men executed for desertion. However, very many of these service records were destroyed by bombing in the Second World War, and you may find that you are unlucky. Also, not all of them are as yet available, as the process of microfilming them takes time. When the filming has been completed, there will be over 20,000 reels of microfilm, in alphabetical order, containing the records of approximately 2,000,000 men. This class is being filmed in blocks, by first letter of the surname. If you are making a special trip to check WO 363, it would be sensible to telephone or e-mail first, to see if the letters you are interested in have been released yet (details in **1.5**).

Also in the PRO are the registers of payments of pensions to disabled officers and men (PMG 9, PMG 42) and to the widows, children and dependants of officers killed or missing in action (PMG 11, PMG 44–PMG 47) during the First World War. For death certificates issued by the French and Belgian authorities for British and Commonwealth soldiers, see **18.4**. British death certificates for the First and Second World Wars can be obtained from the FRC (ONS) (see **4.2**). Information about burials abroad in both world wars can be obtained from the Commonwealth War Graves Commission: see **4.12**. For other suggestions, read Holding's books, *World War One Army Ancestry* and *More Sources of World War One Army Ancestry*.

For a fuller explanation of all the records relating to service in the army during the First World War, see Fowler, Spencer and Tamblin, *Army Service Records of the First World War*.

The records of service of soldiers discharged after 1920 are still maintained by the Ministry of Defence at CS (R) 2b. The records of men who served in the Home Guard are also maintained by the Ministry of Defence at the Army Medal Office. The addresses are given in **48**. Records of the Women's Army Auxiliary Corps (WAAC) from the First World War are in WO 398. For medals awarded, see WO 162/65.

18.31 First World War: disability and dependants' pensions

Pensions were granted for service in World War I, and widows were able to claim even if their husbands had died many years after 1918. This section covers all armed services: it is placed here because the Army had by far the most casualties.

Pensions to dependants of deceased officers, all services			
Pension etc	*Date*	*Reference*	*Information*
deaceased officers: pensions paid to relatives	1916 April– 1920 March	PMG 44/1–7	Name and address of the claimant, rank and name of officer, date of birth and date of payment. Some volumes indexed
missing officers: pensions to relatives	1915 March– 1920 March	PMG 47/1–3	Name and address of relative receiving pension, relationship to missing officer and name and rank of officer, dates of paymen
officers' children: allowances	1916–1920	PMG 46/1–4	Child/children's name; name, rank and regiment of father; record of payments and who collected the money
officers' widows' pensions	1917 September– 1919 July	PMG 45/1–6	Name and address of widow, officer's name, rank and date of birth, date of payments
officers' widows and dependants: special grants and supplementary allowances	1916–1920	PMG 43/2	Name and address of claimant, rank and name of officer, date of birth, and payment: indexed
all services, all ranks	1920–1989	PIN 26	See below

Pensions to disabled or invalid officers and men			
Pension etc	*Date*	*Reference*	*Information*
officers: half pay	up to 1921	PMG 4	
disabled officers and men		PMG 9, PMG 42	Registers of payments of pension
invalid officers: temporary retired pay and gratuities	1917 April – 1919 February	PMG 42/1–2	Rank, name, address, date of war rant, amount paid
all services, all ranks	1920–1989	PIN 26	See below

Pension case files are in PIN 26. This class contains 22,756 personal files on people awarded (or refused) pensions, from all services. Although large, this represents only 2 per cent of the pensions awarded. The class list is arranged by type of pensioner, and then alphabetically, so that it may be worth checking on the off chance. Unfortunately, it is not at all clear what all the various categories mean, so you may have to check in more than one sequence. The class is open, even if documents in it are not yet 30 years old. Earlier documents than 1920 exist in the files. The files can contain fascinating material, some medical, some social, and can cover many years, with claims being raised a good four decades or more after the end of the war.

Pension case files, all services	
PIN 26	*Type of pensioner*
1–203	All services, all ranks. Not in alphabetical order
204–16374	[Army: other ranks], disability
16375–16683	[Army: other ranks], disability (with some out of alphabetical order at the end)
16684–17178	Navy, disability
17179–19523	Widows (by name of husband) (See also PIN 82)
19524–19720	Alternative widows pensions (by name of husband) (See also PIN 82)
19721–19820	Mercantile Marine, death and disability
19821–19853	Dependants (by own name)
19854–19923	Men (DM series)
19924–19954	Officers (DO series)
19955–19984	Alternative disabled pensions
19985–20286, 22744	Nurses, disability
20287–21065	Overseas, death and disability
21066–22756	Officers, death and disability

An 8 per cent sample of widows' and dependants' pension case files, for all services, are in PIN 82. It is arranged in alphabetical order of serviceman's name, with his regiment or ship, and cause of death.

18.32 Military wills

If a soldier died abroad before 1858 and left assets over a certain amount (specified by statute), grants of probate or administration were issued in the Prerogative Court of Canterbury (see **6**). However, military wills of small estates did not have to be proved in court, so there is no record of these unless they have survived among pension applications and casualty returns in the War Office records: see **18.14** and **18.19** for more details. For registers of powers of attorney, see **18.14**.

18.33 Military medals

There are a considerable number of records relating to the creation and award of military medals, but they generally only give the barest details about the recipient. Because medal records contain little genealogical information, they are not discussed at length here. If you are interested in tracing the history of a medal's creation and design, consult the records of the Royal Mint, particularly MINT 16. This class also contains a little correspondence from a few recipients of medals.

There were three main types of military medal: for a particular campaign; for gallantry and meritorious service; and for long service and good conduct.

Campaign medals began with the Waterloo Medal. There was a medal for earlier service, mostly in the Peninsular War and America, 1793–1814, called the Military General Service Medal, but in fact this was not issued until 1847, and then only to men who had survived until that date: see the books by Kingsley-Foster and Challis (**18.34**).

The Waterloo Medal Book records the corps and regiments engaged in the battle, giving the name and rank of officers and men (MINT 16/112). Wellington's despatch of 29 June 1815, listing the officers killed and wounded, was printed as a supplement to the *London Gazette* of 1 July 1815: copies can be found in ZJ 1 and also in MINT 16/111. After Waterloo, medals were awarded for most major campaigns: examples are the Indian Mutiny Medal of 1857 and the Queen's South Africa Medal of 1899. Clasps were often awarded for particular battles within a campaign, such as a Sebastopol clasp for a Crimea Medal. The medal rolls for campaign medals, 1793–1913, are in WO 100 (seen on microfilm): they are arranged by regiment. Correspondence and papers relating to some of the actual medals are in MINT 16. The medal rolls for some campaigns which took place in India are held by the India Office Library and Records.

The campaign medals for the First World War are in WO 329. The name index to these medal rolls is available on microfiche in the Microfilm Reading Room. Original Army Medal Office references found on this index need to be converted to WO 329 references in order to order the individual medal roll.

Gallantry medals were first awarded during the Crimean War. All gallantry awards bestowed upon members of the British army were announced in the *London Gazette* (ZJ 1). The indexes of the *London Gazette* for the First and Second World Wars are available on the open shelves in the Microfilm Reading Room. Citations (the reason why) for all awards granted for gallantry during the First World War can be found in the *London Gazette*. Awards announced in the New Year or Birthday Honours (January and June) were not accompanied by citations.

Name indexes of recipients of the Distinguished Conduct Medal (DCM) and Military Medal (MM) awarded for gallant service in the First World War are available on microfiche. No citations were published for the Military Medal. A further register of the DCM can be found in WO 391.

A name index for the Military Cross (MC) awarded during the First World War can be found in WO 389. The register of Distinguished Service Order (DSO) can be found in WO 390.

Recommendations for awards for gallantry or meritorious service made during the Second World War are in the record class WO 373. This class, which is available on microfilm is arranged by operational theatre (where the award was won) and then in *London Gazette* date order. You have to know the type of award, the operational theatre and the date the award was announced, to consult this class. WO 373 also contains recommendation for most awards made to members of the army up to 1967, including Korea and Malaya.

Records of Long Service and Good Conduct Medals, for other ranks who had served 18 years, run from 1831 to 1953 (WO 102). The records of the Meritorious Service Medal, for non-commissioned officers, run from 1846 to 1919 (WO 101). The records include details of candidates for, as well as recipients of, these awards. A register of annuities paid to recipients of the meritorious or long service awards, 1846–1879, is in WO 23/84.

18.34 The Army: bibliography and sources

Published works
Army Lists, etc., of personnel
Army List (London, annually from 1754)
British Biographical Archive (London, 1984 continuing)
L S Challis, *Peninsula Roll Call* (London, 1948)
F Cook and A Cook, *The Casualty Roll for the Crimea* (London, 1976)
C Dalton, *English Army Lists and Commission Registers, 1661–1714* (London, 1892–1904)
C Dalton, *Irish Army Lists, 1661–1685* (London, 1907)
C Dalton, *George I's Army, 1714–1727* (London, 1910–1912)
C Dalton, *Waterloo Roll* (London, 2nd edn, 1904)
Dictionary of National Biography (London, 1909 continuing)
E Dwelly, *Waterloo Muster Rolls: Cavalry* (Fleet, 1934)
H G Hart, *Hart's Army List* (London, 1839–1915)
Imperial War Museum, *Officers died in the Great War* (London, 1921)
Imperial War Museum, *Soldiers died in the Great War* (London, 1921–1922)
K D N Kingsley-Foster, *Military General Service Medal, 1793–1814* (London, 1947)
List of Officers of the Royal Regiment of Artillery, 1716–June 1914 (London, 1914)
E Peacock, *The Army List of Roundheads and Cavaliers* (London, 2nd edn, 1874)
A Peterkin, W Johnston and R Drew, *Commissioned Officers in the Medical Services of the British Army* (London, 1968)
Roll of Officers of the Corps of Royal Engineers from 1660 to 1898 (London, 1898)
Royal Military Kalendar (London, 1820)
South Africa Field Force Casualty List, 1899–1902 (1972)

General works
D Ascoli, *A Companion to the British Army, 1660–1983* (London, 1983)
D J Barnes, 'Identification and Dating: Military Uniforms', in D J Steel and L Taylor, eds *Family History Focus*, (Guildford, 1984)
A P Bruce, *An Annotated Bibliography of the British Army, 1660–1714* (London, 1975)
Calendar of State Papers, Domestic (London, 1856–1972)
Calendars of State Papers, Ireland (London, 1860–1912)
N K Crowder, *British Army Pensioners Abroad, 1772–1899* (Baltimore, 1995)
P Dennis, *The Territorial Army 1907–1940* (Royal Historical Society, 1987)
C Firth and G Davis, *The Regimental History of Cromwell's Army* (Oxford, 1940)
Y Fitzmaurice, *Army Deserters from HM Service* (Forest Hill, Victoria, 1988)
S Fowler and W Spencer, *Army Records for Family Historians* (PRO, 1998)
S Fowler, W Spencer and S Tamblin, *Army Service Records of the First World War* (London, 1998)
J S W Gibson and A Dell, *Tudor and Stuart Muster Rolls* (FFHS, 1991)
J S W Gibson and E Hampson, *Specialist Indexes for Family Historians* (FFHS, 1998)
J S W Gibson and M Medlycott, *Militia Lists and Musters, 1757–1876* (FFHS, 1994)
G Hamilton Edwards, *In Search of Army Ancestry* (London, 1977)
N Holding, *The Location of British Army Records: a National Directory of World War One Sources* (FFHS, 2nd edn, 1987)
N Holding, *World War One Army Ancestry* (FFHS, 1982)
N Holding, *More Sources of World War One Army Ancestry* (FFHS, 1986)

Irish Record Commission, *Fifteenth Report* (1825)

J M Kitzmiller, *In Search of the 'Forlorn Hope': a Comprehensive Guide to Locating British Regiments and their Records* (Salt Lake City, 1988)

M E S Laws, *Battery Records of the Royal Artillery, 1716–1877* (Woolwich, 1952–1970)

W Lenz, *Manuscript Sources for the History of Germany since 1500 in Great Britain* (German Historical Institute in London, *Publications*, vol. 1). This has many references to German troops in British service in the eighteenth and nineteenth centuries.

M Medlycott, 'Some Georgian 'Censuses': the Militia Lists and 'Defence' Lists', *Genealogists' Magazine*, vol. XXIII, pp. 55–59

G Oram and J Putkowski, *Death Sentences passed by the Military Courts of the British Army, 1914–1924* (London, 1998)

Public Record Office, *Alphabetical Guide to certain War Office and other Military Records preserved in the Public Record Office* (Lists and Indexes, vol. LIII)

Public Record Office, *Lists of War Office Records* (Lists and Indexes, vol. XXVIII and Supplementary vol. VIII)

E E Rich, 'The Population of Elizabethan England', *Economic History Review*, 2nd series, vol. II, pp. 247–265. (Discusses the Elizabethan muster rolls.)

M Roper, *The Records of the War Office and related departments, 1660–1964* (PRO, 1998)

A Swinson, ed., *A Register of the Regiments and Corps of the British Army: the Ancestry of the Regiments and Corps of the Regular Establishments of the Army* (London, 1975)

W Spencer, *Records of the Militia and Volunteer Forces 1757–1945* (London 1997)

C T Watts and M J Watts, 'In Search of a Soldier Ancestor', *Genealogists' Magazine*, vol. XIX, pp. 125–128

C T Watts and M J Watts, *My Ancestor was in the British Army: How can I find out more about him?* (Society of Genealogists, 1995)

A S White, *A Bibliography of the Regiments and Corps of the British Army* (London, 1965)

T Wise, *A Guide to Military Museums* (Doncaster, 1986)

Unpublished finding aids

There are many indexes to Army records in the PRO, some of which have been mentioned in the text of this chapter; for more information, ask at the Research Enquiries Desk.

Hodson's Index: officers of the East India Company Army, Bengal Army and Indian (Imperial) Army is at the National Army Museum.

19 The Royal Navy

19.1 Naval records: introduction

There are no systematic records listing men serving in the Navy before the Restoration (1660). The various seventeenth-century State Paper classes can contain much information on the Navy, particularly during the Interregnum: these have been printed in brief in the *Calendar of State Papers, Domestic*, and are therefore fairly easy to use. In 1660, officers and men serving in the fleet took an oath of allegiance to Charles II (C 215/6): similarly, an oath of association to support William III was taken by the officers of the fleet in 1696 (C 213/385–389).

For the period 1660–c.1923, the relevant records are in the PRO at Kew, although tracing individuals is not particularly easy until the mid nineteenth century. The best archival guide to the possible sources is Rodger's handbook, *Naval Records for Genealogists*. This describes the various kinds of naval officers and ratings, the extensive range of service records (identifying 32 main types and giving descriptions and references), and provides lists of discrete series of records now split between several classes or submerged in one enormous class. As a result it is quite a complex book to use, but it has a comprehensive index. The information given here is only a small selection of the immense range of records that Rodger lists, and it concentrates on the period before the late nineteenth century. For information on the later records, you should consult Rodger. For a general history of the navy, see Rodger's *Safeguard of the Sea* and *The Wooden World*.

For a comprehensive guide, which tells you in detail what you can expect to find in each type of record, try Pappalardo's 'Royal Navy Genealogy'. This is available at the Research Enquiries Desk: it is the draft and fuller version of a forthcoming readers' guide, *Naval Records for Family Historians*.

This chapter on naval records is basically in two parts: sections **19.2–19.21** concentrate on service records while sections **19.22–19.25** discuss the wider range of personal information which can be discovered in pension records.

Of course, there are other places to discover more about life in the Navy, notably the National Maritime Museum at Greenwich, which has a huge collection of naval artefacts, records, etc., the Royal Naval Museum (see the article by Trotman), and the museum ships, HMS *Victory* and HMS *Belfast*; the addresses are given in **48**.

19.2 Commissioned officers: published sources

The fighting officers of the Royal Navy held office by virtue of a royal commission: they were, in descending order of rank, admiral of the fleet, admiral, vice-admiral, rear-admiral, commodore, captain, commander, lieutenant-commander, lieutenant and sub-lieutenant. The initial promotion to the commissioned rank of lieutenant was by examination: subsequent promotions were by merit and luck as far as captain, and by seniority above that. The names of the ranks changed their meanings somewhat over time, and in particular 'captain' was often used as the title for the officer in command of a vessel, whether he was a captain or a lieutenant.

The main printed source is Syrett and DiNardo's *The Commissioned Sea Officers of the Royal Navy 1660–1815*. From the end of the eighteenth century, it is fairly easy to trace the outlines of a commissioned officer's career in the Royal Navy. Start with the printed *Navy Lists*, which began as *Steel's Navy List* in 1782 and were updated quarterly from 1814. These contain seniority lists of officers, from lieutenant upwards, which are keyed to disposition lists of ships of the Navy with the officers appointed to them. *The Navy Lists* are available on open shelves in the Microfilm Reading Room, including the wartime confidential editions of 1914–1918 and 1939–1945 in ADM 177.

The *New Navy List*, compiled by Haultain, covers February 1841–February 1856. It contains similar information to the *Navy List*, but with the addition of details of war service, going back even to the 1780s. This too can be seen in the Microfilm Reading Room.

Other printed sources are also available. O'Byrne's *Naval Biographical Dictionary* gives the services of all commissioned officers alive in 1846. Admirals' and captains' services may be described in Charnock's *Biographia Navalis* (up to 1798), Campbell and Stevenson's *Lives of the British Admirals* (up to 1816), Marshall's *Royal Naval Biography* (up to 1835), and in the *Dictionary of National Biography*. See also the *British Biographical Archive* (**1.13**).

The PRO does not hold the officers' newspaper, the *Naval Chronicle*, which should be available at the British Library Newspaper Library. For a small part of its contents, see Hurst, *Naval Chronicle, 1799–1818: Index to Births, Marriages and Deaths*.

19.3 Commissioned officers: service records to c.1900

Before the mid nineteenth century, documents concerning commissioned officers do not include comprehensive records of service. The surveys, described in **19.9**, are the most convenient and complete records of officers' service, but they do not cover all officers and are not always to be trusted. After the mid nineteenth century, the first place to look is ADM 196 (see below).

There are various versions of an early list of all admirals, captains and commanders, with notes of their service, death or fate: the easiest to use are probably the alphabetical lists, 1660–1685 (ADM 10/15), 1660–1688 (ADM 10/10, which continues to 1746 arranged by seniority) and 1688–1737 (ADM 7/549). The first two also include lieutenants. For 1837, there is an address book for commissioned officers, mates, masters, surgeons, pursers and chaplains (PMG 73/2).

The Officers' Full Pay Registers, kept by the Navy Pay Office, were the authoritative record of an officer's service (ADM 24). They run from 1795 onwards, with a separate register for each commissioned rank (including surgeons and chaplains) until 1830, when a general register began; both series have indexes. The information included is not very full: name, rank and successive appointments. The Registers of Officers' Half Pay (a retainer for the services of unemployed officers, also used as a kind of pension for 'retired' officers) can provide addresses and other information over a much longer period, 1693–1836 (ADM 25/1–255; in seniority order). Earlier records of half pay, 1668–1689, are in Bill Books, entered in no particular order with many other entries as well (ADM 18/44–67); later ones, 1836–1920, are either indexed or in alphabetical order (PMG 15).These full and half pay registers were used for the issue of certificates of service, needed to establish entitlement to a pension, or as a passing qualification for a commission.

The passing certificates of master's mates and midshipmen qualifying as lieutenants often include certificates of service to date, and sometimes include baptismal certificates. Bound volumes of passing certificates and supporting documents, 1691–1832, are in ADM 107/1–63; later certificates, 1854–1867, are in ADM 13/88–101. There are indexes to ADM 107/12–50, and to the baptismal certificates found in ADM 107/7 and ADM 107/12–63. There is an incomplete collection of original passing certificates for 1744–1819, bound up in alphabetical order for each year (ADM 6/86–116). Certificates issued abroad, 1788–1818, are in ADM 6/117–118. There are also registers of the examination of prospective lieutenants, 1795–1832, which give name, age, qualifying service and remarks for each candidate (ADM 107/64–70). Registers of service of prospective candidates, 1802–1848, are in ADM 107/71–75. There are even records of young gentlemen failing to pass for lieutenant (sometimes with the reasons given) for 1801–1810 (ADM 30/31).

The earliest service registers were compiled by binding together certificates and annotating them. The first of these, covering admirals, captains, commanders and lieutenants, was compiled between c.1845–1875; the information contained predates this by many years (ADM 196/1–6, with an index in ADM 196/7). Later service registers are much fuller, containing dates of birth, marriage and death, names of parents and wives (but almost never of children), details of pay and pension, and assessments of character and ability. These registers were kept by several different departments, and an officer's career may be entered in three or four almost identical registers: this can be useful, as there are frequent gaps in the various series. These fuller service registers, dating from the mid nineteenth century onwards, but sometimes including information from before then, are mostly in ADM 196. There are indexes on open access (they do not refer to the whole class).

The records of officers commissioned after c.1900 will be released in 2000: see **19.15**.

19.4 Warrant officers: introduction

The senior warrant officers were the master, purser, boatswain, gunner, carpenter and surgeon (see **19.20** for surgeons): engineers were added later. However, masters became commissioned officers in 1808, as did pursers and surgeons in 1843, and engineers in 1847. Junior warrant officers (i.e. those who did not have to keep accounts) were the armourer, chaplain, cook, master at arms, sailmaker and schoolmaster. Rodger gives much more detail (particularly of the expansion of the warrant officers from three branches in 1867 to twenty-four in 1945, of which all but one could proceed to commissioned rank), and his book contains many references to scattered sources relating to the junior warrant officers, which are not given here. The records of service of warrant officers appointed after c. 1890 will be released in the year 2000: see **19.15**.

Chaplains can be traced through succession books (see **19.10**): there is also a published work, Kealy's *Chaplains of the Royal Navy, 1626–1903*. More recent records of chaplains are still held by the Chaplain of the Fleet.

As with commissioned officers, genuine service records do not start until the mid-nineteenth century. Before then, there are certificates of service, required either for promotion or pension purposes. There is a set of certificates of service for pension purposes for senior warrant officers, with compilation dates of 1802–1814, which includes service dating well back in the 1700s. The records relating to pensions, benefits to widows and orphans, and the Royal Greenwich Hospital and School are worth investigation: see **19.13** and **19.22–19.24**. There is also a black book of warrant officers not to be employed for future service, 1741–1814 (ADM 11/39). For 1837, there is an address book for commissioned officers, mates, masters, surgeons, pursers and chaplains (PMG 73/2).

See also **19.10** for a description of the succession books.

19.5 Warrant officers: masters' service records to c.1890

Masters' passing certificates for qualifications in seamanship date from c.1660–1830 (ADM 106/1908–2950); they may include certificates of baptism and service. One master may have had several certificates, as promotion to a different rate of ship required a different qualification. The certificates are arranged alphabetically.

There is an unusual series of service records for masters, compiled in the 1830s and 1840s, but covering the period 1800–1850 (ADM 6/135–268). Records were kept in individual files, containing passing certificates, certificates of service and a variety of other certificates and correspondence: the files are in alphabetical order of surname. Later registers of the more usual sort cover 1848–1882 (ADM 196/74–81).

19.6 Warrant officers: pursers' service records to c.1890

Pursers, later renamed paymasters, oversaw the supply and issue of the ship's stores, and also of the seamen's pay, when it became customary to pay them regularly. There are notes on candidates for promotion for 1803–1804 (ADM 6/121), and again for 1847–1854 (ADM 11/88). Passing certificates, giving service to date, are available for 1813–1820 (ADM 6/120), for 1851–1867 (ADM 13/79–82), and for 1868–1889 (ADM 13/247–8). The main series of service registers for pursers and paymasters covers 1852–1922 (ADM 196/11–12, 82 and 85 and ADM 6/443–444); for others, going back to 1843, see ADM 196/1 and 74–9.

19.7 Warrant officers: boatswains', gunners' and carpenters' service records to c.1890

Passing certificates, often giving previous service, for boatswains are available for 1810–1813 (ADM 6/122), 1851–1855 (ADM 13/83), 1856–1859 (ADM 13/85) and 1860–1887 (ADM 13/193–4). Certificates for gunners start earlier: they are available for 1731–1748, 1760–1797, and 1803–1812 (ADM 6/123–9). There are joint service registers for boatswains, gunners and carpenters, 1848–1855, in ADM 196/74–6; other registers, for 1855–1890, are in ADM 196/29–32, with an index in ADM 196/33. Boatswains and carpenters could and did transfer between sea service and dockyard work: records relating to dockyard employees are discussed in **19.16**.

19.8 Warrant officers: engineers' service records to c.1890

There are two series of service registers for engineers. One, including ratings and boys as well as officers, covers 1837–1879 (ADM 196/71 for 1837–1839, and ADM 29/105–11 for 1839–1879; with internal indexes). The other covers 1856–1886 (ADM 196/23–25, indexed by ADM 196/26–28). Both these series include the complete careers of engineers entering the service between these years; the latter also includes the complete careers of engineers actually in service in 1856.

19.9 Naval officers: surveys, 1817–1851

The end of the Napoleonic wars in 1815 meant that the Navy shrank in operational strength from 145,000 to 19,000 men. Because there was no means of retiring officers, there were ten times as many as were required. In order to discover which officers had the best claims to be employed, the Admiralty sent out circular letters to both commissioned and warrant officers, asking them to provide dates of birth or details of service: the replies were bound up and used for reference by the Admiralty. However, the coverage is by no means complete, as it depended on the officer receiving and replying to the letter: many replies were lost, and the accuracy of some of them is doubtful.

There are returns for surveys in 1816–1818 for boatswains, gunners and carpenters (ADM 11/35–37), and commissioned officers (ADM 9/2–17, indexed by ADM 10/2–5, and with strays at ADM 6/66). Another survey in 1822, repeated in 1831, asked for details of age from commissioned officers and masters (ADM 6/73–85; ADM 106/3517). Admirals were surveyed in 1828 (ADM 9/1, with an index at ADM 10/1, and strays at ADM 6/66). Between 1833 and 1835 masters and pursers were surveyed (ADM 11/2–3, masters; ADM 6/193–196, pursers). A survey of 1846 required commissioned officers to state age, address and previous service (ADM 9/18–61, with indexes at ADM 10/6–7): in 1851 masters were asked to provide the same information (ADM 11/7–8, indexed in ADM 10/6–7). Other surveys of masters were carried out in 1855 and 1861 (ADM 11/9), and pursers were surveyed again in 1852 and 1859 (ADM 11/42–4).

19.10 Naval officers: succession books

Succession books were a type of officers' service record arranged by ship, not by individual officer: however, most are indexed by name as well as ship, so they can provide a fairly easy way of tracing a commissioned or warrant officer from ship to ship.

In the usual form, a page was devoted to each ship, and the successive appointments to each position in the ship were listed. The earliest succession books cover commissioned and warrant officers, 1673 1688 (ADM 6/425 426), followed by admirals, captains and commanders only, 1688–1725 (ADM 7/655). There is a later series for captains, commanders and lieutenants, which covers the years 1780–1847 (ADM 11/65–72).

Masters, surgeons, surgeon's mates, sailmakers and some others appear in one series of succession books, 1733–1807, with a gap 1755–1770 (ADM 106/2896–2901). Another series is of pursers, gunners, boatswains and carpenters, as well as some dockyard officers, 1764–1831 (ADM 106/2898 and 2902–2906), with a further series of the same, 1800–1839 (ADM 76/192 and ADM 11/31–33).

Succession books, 1699–1824, of junior officers appointed by Admiralty warrant or order (i.e. midshipmen ordinary, volunteers per order, chaplains, masters at arms, schoolmasters and scholars of the Royal Naval Academy) are in ADM 6/427 and 185.

19.11 Naval officers: other sources

The ONS keeps Naval returns of births, marriages and deaths abroad from 1881 to date: see **4.14**. Indexes can be seen at the FRC and Kew.

There are many other possible sources of information in the PRO on an officer's career, such as records of candidates for promotion, black books of officers not to be employed again, confidential reports, and registers of officers unfit for service. These records are numerous and scattered: the easiest way to locate the ones relating to the particular rank that you are interested in is to consult Rodger's *Naval Records for Genealogists*.

In addition, there are, of course, the records of the ships in which the officer served. Logs kept by the captain (ADM 51, ADM 53, ADM 55), the master (ADM 52, ADM 54) and by lieutenants (at the National Maritime Museum) do not contain any personal information, but they do provide a professional record of the ship's voyages which can prove fascinating.

Surgeons, however, were required to keep a general journal on the health of all the ship's company and on possible circumstances affecting it, as the Navy had a keen interest in preserving the health of its men: as a result these logs are often the most approachable source for the history of a voyage (ADM 101, a selection only; and MT 32, from convict ships).

19.12 Naval ratings: musters and pay books

There was no centralized record of ratings' services until the introduction of continuous service in 1853. Before then, the main sources for tracing a seaman are the individual ship's muster book and pay book. To use these, you need to know the ships on which he served. If you are fortunate enough to have a seaman who was in receipt of a Chatham or Greenwich pension, for which there are indexed registers, you ought to be able to discover the ships he worked in quite easily (see **19.22–19.24**). Otherwise, you may need luck and hard work: a preliminary search in the certificates of service which were issued to some ratings (see **19.13**) might be well worth while.

Musters, or lists of the ship's company, are available from 1667 to 1878 (ADM 36–ADM 41, ADM 115 and ADM 117): there are a few medieval ones in E 101. The musters followed a standard format, described by Pappalardo, which gives the various abbreviations used. There were general musters, held annually, and eight-weekly monthly musters, which contain extra information on various deductions from pay, such as for treatment for venereal disease. Information on each member of the ship's company was entered into the following columns in both general and monthly musters: Number, Entry & Year, Appearance [i.e. arrival on board], Whence & Whether Prest or not, Age [added in 1764: it means age at entry to the ship, not at the time of the muster], Place & Country of Birth [added in 1764], No. and Letter of Ticket [for wages], Men's Names, Qualities, D DD or R [discharged, discharged dead or run; also DS, discharged to sick quarters], Time of Discharge & Year, Whither or for What Reason [e.g. DD – fell from aloft].

The pay books, 1691–1856 (ADM 31–ADM 35), which duplicate much of the information of the musters, have one big advantage; they contain 'alphabets' (indexes of surnames in alphabetical order of first letter only) from about 1765, some fifty years before the musters had them. It may be worth checking through the alphabets in the pay lists before going on to look at the musters, 1667–1878 (ADM 36–ADM 41). The pay books were copied from the musters, and may contain more errors: in some cases, they may also include information about next of kin to whom remitted wages were paid.

When tracing men from ship to ship, it may be useful to consult the hospital musters, particularly if the name was marked DS (discharged to sick quarters): see **19.21**.

19.13 Naval ratings: certificates of service

The standard way of tracing a naval seaman or rating, before the introduction of continuous service in 1853, is to use the muster books and pay books (see **19.12**). However, this can take so long and is so dependent on getting the right ship, that it is sensible to investigate easier sources: if you are lucky, you will save yourself considerable time.

Ratings needed to have a certificate of service to support a claim to receive a pension, a gratuity or a medal. Thus there are certificates of service issued by the Navy Pay Office, 1790–1865, among the papers of ratings and marines applying for entry to Greenwich Hospital as in-pensioners: although the certificates were issued from 1790, the services recorded go back at least forty years before then (ADM 73/1–35, arranged alphabetically).

Other such certificates issued between 1834 and 1894 are in ADM 29, for claims for pensions, medals, or admittance to Greenwich Hospital. This class also includes the entry books of certificates of service of warrant officers and ratings, 1836–1894, sent to Greenwich Hospital for the assessment of the claims of their children to be admitted to the Hospital Schools (ADM 29/17, 19, 25, 34, 43, 50, 59, 70 and 80–96: indexed by ADM 29/97–104). As orphans had priority, many of the certificates are of the service of men already dead, and, as always, the service predates the certificate by many years. The original certificates of service to which the entry books refer, together with supporting documentation such as baptismal and marriage certificates, are in ADM 73/154–389.

19.14 Naval ratings: continuous service records, 1853–c.1923

In 1853 began the first centralized registration of ratings, with the introduction of continuous service engagements. Each man had a continuous service number (ADM 139) and official number (ADM 188): the registers are arranged by these numbers, but there are alphabetical indexes. The first series covers ratings between 1853 and 1872 (ADM 139); the second (ADM 188) covers the careers of those who entered between 1873 and 1923. Both series give date and place of birth, physical characteristics on entry, and a summary of service. In the case of those who entered as boys, there is a form giving parental consent (only in ADM 139). The indexes for both classes are in the Microfilm Reading Room.

Naval returns of births, marriages and deaths abroad survive at the ONS from 1881–date: see **4.14**. Indexes can be seen at the FRC and Kew.

19.15 Naval officers and ratings: service records after 1891

The service records of ratings who entered the service between 1891 and 1923 are in the record class ADM 188. Between 1873 and 1894 the service numbers were issued to new entrants on a next man, next number basis. As the Royal navy became a more complex service, so it was decided to group service numbers together to identify the particular branch of the service an individual served in. Between 1894 and 1907 the service numbers were issued to the branches to be allocated as a new man joined that branch. It is therefore possible to find two men who joined the service on the same day, having wildly differing service numbers. Between 1873 and 1907 service numbers between 40,000 and 366,000 were issued.

In 1908 the service number was system changed again. Rather than have a plain numeric service number, alphabetical prefixes denoting the branch of the service were used; J for Seamen, K for Stokers; L for Domestics and M for Miscellaneous. Between 1908 when the system was started and 1923, the date of the last available record of service, the numbers available for each prefix are J 115433, K 63500, L 15101 and M 38000.

In 1903 the Royal Navy started a short service (SS) system whereby men could serve either 5 or 7 years in the service and the balance up to 12 years in the Royal Fleet Reserve. The SS papers are also in ADM 188. Those men with SS numbers 1–12000 served as seamen and those with numbers 100001–126000, served as stokers.

The formation of the Royal Naval Air Service (RNAS) in July 1914 created the need for a new service number prefix. The F prefix used by the RNAS was issued to 55,000 men between July 1914 and 31 March 1918. Men of the RNAS who became members of the RAF on formation had the F prefix removed and a 2 added to the front of their service numbers (see **21.2**).

The records of service of officers who received their commissions or warrants of appointment

LOST WITH HIS SHIP, THE CRUISER "NATAL," WHEN IT WAS BLOWN UP:
THE LATE CAPTAIN ERIC P. BACK, R.N.

The Admiralty announced on January 2: "His Majesty's ship 'Natal' (Captain Eric P. Back, R.N.
(Armoured-Cruiser) sank yesterday afternoon while in harbour as the result of an internal explosion.
About 400 survivors are reported." Captain Back, who was born in 1870, joined the Navy in 1884.
While Lieutenant of the "Monarch" he served with the Naval Brigade in South Africa, and was
twice mentioned in despatches, on one occasion "for ability and courage in taking the guns (two
12-pounders) across a plain exposed to rifle-fire." He was promoted Commander in 1902, and
Captain in 1908. In 1913 he was appointed Flag-Captain to the Commander-in-Chief at Plymouth.

Photograph by Russell, Southsea.

Figure 9 Eric Back and about 400 of his men died when the *Natal* exploded at anchor off Cromarty on 30 December 1915. His service record (in ADM 196/43, p. 142) was easy to find, and a search in the lists online produced several references to the *Natal* and the enquiry into her sinking. His photograph, and the information with it, comes from the *Illustrated London News*.

after 1900 are still maintained by the Ministry of Defence at CS(R)2a (address in **48**), and will not be transferred to the PRO until 2000.

There is a card index of naval officer casualties of the First World War (1914–1919) in the Research Enquiries Room at Kew: this names the person informed of the death. See also the indexes to the registers of naval war deaths, 1914–1921 and 1939–1948, available at the FRC (ONS) and Kew mentioned in **4.14**. Certificates have to be bought from Southport: see **1.6**. See also **4.14** for naval births, marriages and deaths abroad from 1881 to date.

19.16 Naval dockyard employees

Naval dockyards, situated all round the world, were run by civilian employees of the Navy Board, who were naval officers but not sea officers. However, there was considerable movement between the two branches of the service. The commissioners (in charge of the yards) and the masters attendant (in charge of ships afloat) were usually retired sea officers. Dockyard shipwrights, having served their apprenticeship, often became carpenters in the Navy, and might return to be master shipwrights, and in the same way the other master tradesmen and the boatswain were normally recruited from the sea service. The career of any skilled man may therefore have to be traced in the records of both services: naval pensioners often began a second career in the dockyards. A Naval Dockyards Society has recently been established (address for enquiries in **48**).

The main source for larger dockyards is the class of Yard Pay Books, 1660–1857 (ADM 42); for minor yards, treated as ships, try the pay books and musters in ADM 32, ADM 36, and ADM 37. In addition, ADM 106 contains some interesting sources, particularly the description books of artificers, 1748–1830; these include physical descriptions of the men in some yards.

There are other sources for dockyard employees given in the PRO leaflet, *Dockyard Employees*. This also gives a summary of records relating to individual yards, arranged by place. For information on the policing of the dockyards, see **23.2**.

For baptisms, marriages and burials, 1826–1946, in the naval dockyards in Bermuda, see ADM 6/434, 436 and 439. For registers of the Dockyard Church, Sheerness, 1688–1960, see ADM 6/429–433 and 438.

If you do find an ancestor who worked in one of the many naval dockyards, you may be interested in the photographs of work in dockyards, 1857–1961, in ADM 195.

19.17 Royal Navy apprentices

Information about dockyard and other naval apprentices may be found among the Admiralty and Secretariat Papers (ADM 1) and the Navy Board Records (ADM 106). In the Admiralty Digest (a subject index in ADM 12, relating to ADM 1 and other classes), it is worth checking under the heading 'Apprentices in Dockyards'. Examination results for dockyard and artificer apprentices, from 1876, are among the records of the Civil Service Commission (CSC 10).

There are apprenticeship registers for children from Greenwich Hospital School, 1808–1838, in ADM 73/421–448.

19.18 Sea Fencibles, Royal Naval Reserve, Royal Naval Volunteer Reserve and Royal Naval Air Service

The Sea Fencibles were a part-time organisation of fishermen and boatmen commanded by naval officers, formed for local defence, especially against invasion. Musters and pay lists, 1798–1810, are in ADM 28, together with the appointments of naval officers to the Sea Fencibles.

The Royal Naval Reserve was established in 1859; it was then a reserve force of merchant seamen, with a set limit of 30,000 men. By 1890, 20,000 had been enrolled. Service records of RNR officers, from 1862, are in ADM 240: RNR officers' records for the First World War should be released in 2000. A representative selection of service records of other ranks is in BT 164. Service records of RNR ratings for the First World War are not yet available. For other records of merchant seamen, see **25**.

Records of the Royal Naval Volunteer Reserve, 1914–1918, are in ADM 337. They are arranged by division in official number order, with some name indexes: you may have to use the naval medal rolls in ADM 171 to find the service number.

Records from 1919–1958 have not yet been transferred to the PRO: contact the Ministry of Defence, CS(R)2a (address in **48**).

Records of officers in the Royal Naval Air Service, 1914–1918, are in ADM 273. See also **21**.

19.19 Women's Royal Naval Service

The Women's Royal Naval Service was formed in late 1917. The personal records of some 450 WRNS officers' who served between 1917 and 1919 can be found in ADM 318. There is an alphabetical index of names of the files available at the beginning of the ADM 318 class list.

Two registers of appointments, promotions and resignations of WRNS officers' for the period 1917–1919 can be found in the record class ADM 321.

Records after 1919 have not yet been transferred to the PRO: contact the Ministry of Defence, CS(R)2a (address in **48**).

19.20 Naval medical services: surgeons and nurses

Surgeons and their mates were the only medical help available on individual ships, although nurses worked in naval hospitals and hospital ships from the seventeenth century.

Surgeons were warranted to ships by the Navy Board, having qualified by examination at the Barber-Surgeons' Company (until 1796). There is an incomplete collection of surgeons' passing certificates, c.1700–1800, issued by the Barber-Surgeons' Company in London, or by examining boards of surgeons at the outports or overseas (ADM 106/2592–2603, arranged alphabetically). There is an index to these in the Research Enquiries Room giving dates and texts of the certificates, but no references to the documents.

There are several series of service registers for surgeons: the longest covers 1774–1886 (ADM 104/12–29, indexed in ADM 104/11). One particularly interesting series of registers of service contains correspondence on the merits of individual officers, 1829–1873 (ADM 104/31–40). Another interesting series of reports on questions of pay, half pay and promotion of surgeons, 1817–1832, includes much personal information about named officers (ADM 105/1–9, with internal indexes). For other sources, consult Rodger's *Naval Records for Genealogists*. The Medical Journals, 1785–1880 (ADM 101) can provide an insight into the daily lives of some of these surgeons: although they are mostly concerned with treatment of patients, some entries provide interesting details of life on ship.

There are full pay books of surgeons and nurses at Haslar Hospital, 1769–1819 (ADM 102/375–397) and at Plymouth Hospital, 1777–1819 (ADM 102/683–700). Other volumes in ADM 102 include the pay lists, often bound up with the musters, of many hospitals and stationary hospital ships in Britain and many other parts of the world; the musters of sea-going hospital ships will be found with the other musters in ADM 36 and ADM 37.

Greenwich Hospital, in its original form, paid no widows' pensions, but it employed the widows of seamen in its infirmary. Service registers of such nurses exist between 1704 and 1876 (ADM 73/83–88). Other surviving records include applications for this employment made by the widows of ratings, 1819–1842 (ADM 6/331), and 1817–1831 (ADM 6/329).

During the nineteenth century the Navy ceased to employ women as nurses, until the establishment of the professional Naval Nursing Sisters in 1883, renamed Queen Alexandra's Royal Naval Nursing Service (QARNNS) in 1902. From 1884, Head Nursing Sisters were included in the *Navy List*: other nursing officers were included from 1890. There are service records for nurses, 1884–1918, in ADM 104. Succession books, listing nursing staff by hospital, are available for 1921–1939 (ADM 104/96).

19.21 Naval medical services: hospital records

There are extensive muster lists of patients in naval hospitals and stationary hospital ships at Antigua, Ascension Island, Bermuda, the Cape of Good Hope, Chatham, Deal, Gibraltar, Halifax in Nova Scotia, Haslar, Jamaica, Madras, Malta, Plymouth, Woolwich, Yarmouth and for many other hospitals and hospital ships as well, dating from 1740 to 1880 (ADM 102). There are also several musters of lunatics at Hoxton House, 1755–1818 (ADM 102/415–420) and at Haslar, 1818–1854 (ADM 102/356–373); Yarmouth too was a major hospital for naval lunatics. Reports on the treatment of naval lunatics, 1812–1832, are in ADM 105/28. The musters of sea-going hospital ships will be found with the other musters in ADM 36 and ADM 37.

19.22 Pensions to naval officers and ratings

Until well into the nineteenth century, provision of pensions within the Navy was haphazard. There was no general entitlement to a pension for long service (although half pay was used to provide a kind of pension for officers), but there was a limited number of pensions available for particularly deserving cases, and there is usually a certain amount of personal information recorded in support of claims to pensions.

The Chatham Chest, set up about 1590, and funded by a deduction from seamen's wages, paid pensions to the dependants of warrant officers (including midshipmen and surgeons), ratings and dockyard workers killed in action or on service. The earliest payments are in the account books, 1653–1657. There are registers of payments to pensioners, 1675–1799, with alphabetical lists of the pensioners at Lady Day in each year. The indexes of pensions, 1744–1797, give names, amount of pension, particulars as to wounds, names of ships in which they served, and other information. All these records are in ADM 82; there are also other records of the Chatham Chest in ADM 80.

Disabled seamen were often petitioners to the crown for places as almsmen in the royal church foundations: there is a register of such petitions, 1660–1751, in SO 5/31.

The Royal Greenwich Hospital was founded in 1694 as a home for infirm seamen and marines: in-pensioners lived there until 1869. There are entry books of these in-pensioners, 1704–1869, which give very full particulars, and are mostly indexed. Admission papers, although dating from 1790–1865, relate to service going back to at least 1750; they give descriptions, with details of service and the nature of disablement. Both entry books and admission papers are in ADM 73. Papers of candidates for admission, 1737–1859 are in ADM 6/223–266. The church registers of the hospital, 1705–1864 (RG 4/1669–1679 and RG 8/16–18) can be very interesting: most entries relating to in-pensioners are of deaths, and occasionally include some comment as to manner of death.

The hospital also supported many more out-pensioners, who lived elsewhere: they received the out-pension as a form of superannuation, but were often still in full employment elsewhere. There are registers of candidates for out-pensions, 1789–1859, in ADM 6/271–320. Pay books of out-pensions, 1781–1809, are in ADM 73/95–131. For 1814–1846 they are in ADM 22/254–443, arranged alphabetically. From 1842–1883 they were paid by the War Office, through district pension offices, including many abroad: these records are arranged by place (WO 22).

Other pensions were available for wounds, or for meritorious service, or for medals and honours. Records of these are in ADM 23 and PMG 16.

In 1853, ratings were given the prospect of receiving a pension after twenty years' continuous service: as many signed on at eighteen, naval pensioners were often much younger than the term suggests. Few records of superannuation to ratings survive.

A few officers also received Greenwich Hospital out-pensions: there are registers covering 1814 (ADM 22/254), 1815–1842 (ADM 22/47–9) and 1846–1921 (PMG 71). At various dates from 1836, officers became eligible for a retirement pension, or superannuation, either automatically on reaching a certain age, or upon application. Pension records for officers are extensive, and are fully listed by Rodger in *Naval Records for Genealogists*.

Warrant officers, and the civil establishment of the Navy, were paid pensions out of the Navy estimates; there are registers for 1694–1832 (ADM 7/809–822, indexed by ADM 7/823).

PIN 71 contains the personal files on over 5,000 disabled ratings and soldiers who served before 1914 and who received disablement pensions: the information contained includes medical records, accounts of how injuries were incurred, and the men's own account of the incident, and conduct sheets. These conduct sheets give place of birth, age, names of parents and siblings, religion, physical attributes, marital and parental status. The class is alphabetically arranged: unfortunately it is a selection only, and does not cover all disabled soldiers and sailors of that date.

For First World War pensions, see **18.31**.

19.23 Pensions and other benefits to widows and orphans

The Chatham Chest also paid pensions to the widows of warrant officers, ratings and dockyard workers killed in action or on service: the registers of payment were shared with the pensions to wounded men (ADM 82, described in **19.22**). Before the mid nineteenth century, Greenwich Hospital paid no widows' pensions as such, but employed seamen's widows in its infirmary. They may be traceable through the establishment books (ADM 73: see **19.20**, **1.10** and **1.11**).

Greenwich Hospital also provided a school for children of officers and men, to which orphans had priority of admission (see **19.24**).

The Charity for the Relief of Officers' Widows paid pensions to the poor widows of commissioned and warrant officers. Pay books, 1734–1835, are in ADM 22/56–237; for 1836–1929 they are in PMG 19/1–94. The papers submitted by widows applying for pensions between 1797 and 1829 include many marriage and death certificates (ADM 6/335–384): there is an index in the Research Enquiries Room. Similar papers for 1808–1830, referred for further consideration in doubtful cases, are in ADM 6/385–402.

The Compassionate Fund, voted by Parliament from 1809, was administered by the Admiralty: it dealt with pensions and grants to orphans and other dependents of officers killed in action or who had died in service, not otherwise eligible for assistance. The registers of applications for relief give the officer's rank, date of death, length of service and ship, date and place of marriage, the applicant's age, address and relationship to the dead officer, and other circumstances: they run from 1807 to 1836 (ADM 6/323–328). Pay books run from 1809 to 1921, giving the names and ages of recipients, and their relationship to the dead officer: from 1885 warrant officers' next of kin were eligible (1809–1836, ADM 22/239–250; 1837–1921, PMG 18).

The Admiralty's own pensions included pensions to the widows and orphans of commissioned officers, dating from 1673 (1673–1781, including widows of masters, ADM 18/53–118; 1694–1832, ADM 7/809–822, indexed by ADM 7/823; 1708–1818, ADM 181/1–27; later ones in ADM 22, ADM 23, PMG 16, PMG 19 and PMG 20). From 1830 warrant officers' widows were eligible for Admiralty pensions.

In addition to these pensions, a lump sum of one year's wages, known as the Royal Bounty, was payable to the widows, dependent children, or indigent mothers aged over 50, of officers and ratings killed in action. The papers submitted by dependants, in support of claims to the Bounty, consist mainly of marriage and death certificates, with other documents attesting the age, relationship or poverty of the applicants. There is a broken series of these running from 1672–1822 (ADM 16/3023–3025), with an index in the Reference Room, Kew. In addition, there are pay lists of the Bounty, 1739–1787, which give the name, address and relationship of the dependant, the name, quality and ship of the dead man, and the amount paid (ADM 106/3018–3020); these are not indexed.

These pension records are only the most important of those available: all are listed in detail in Rodger's book *Naval Records for Genealogists*. The exception is PIN 71, which contains over 1,000 personal files on the widows of naval ratings and Army other ranks whose service was before 1914. This is only a selection of such files, but it is alphabetically arranged, and very informative (see **19.22**). For First World War pensions, see **18.31**.

19.24 Royal Hospital School, Greenwich

The school, attached to the Royal Greenwich Hospital, was established for the sons of seamen shortly after the hospital was founded. In 1805 it was joined by a similar school for younger orphans (boys and girls), the Royal Naval Asylum. Orphans of officers and ratings killed in action or who had died in service had the prior claim for admittance, but entry was not restricted to them. The school admission papers, 1728–1870, include certificates of birth or baptisms for the children applying for entry, together with the marriage certificate of the parents, and details of the father's naval service (ADM 73/154–389: see also **19.13** for entry books). They are arranged by initial letter. The registers of applications, which are mostly indexed, include the same information, 1728–1883 (ADM 73/390–449). Registers of later claims are in ADM 161–ADM 163. The church registers, including many burials, for the Royal Hospital School and the Royal Naval Asylum are in RG 4/1669–1679, and RG 8/16–19.

19.25 Naval wills and powers of attorney

Copies or original wills made by officers and ratings are attached to many applications made after their deaths for their back pay: registers of these claims and wills can be used to find the names of next of kin.

There are two series of ratings' wills. Seamen's Wills (ADM 48) has wills, 1786–1882, alphabetically arranged: there are registers in ADM 142, which act as indexes, extending as far as 1909, plus a card index covering ADM 48/1–45. These registers give the date of death and, for the first 14 volumes, name, address and relationship of the executor. The second series, Seamen's Effect Papers (ADM 44), covers 1800–1860, and contains the claims by executors and next of kin for the back pay of ratings who died in service. Some of these include wills, birth and marriage certificates and other supporting documents. Indexes are provided by the registers in ADM 141, using an odd system of alphabetization.

Wills of commissioned and warrant officers, 1830–1860, may be found in similar claims for back pay by widows and next of kin in ADM 45: there is a card index to pieces 1–28 in the Research Enquiries Room.

Until 1815, seamen who died with over £20 of back wages owing to them (a frequent occurrence) had their wills proved in the Prerogative Court of Canterbury, whose records are in the PRO (see **6**). There is also a register of wills made at the naval hospital, Gibraltar 1809–1815 (ADM 105/40). Other wills of naval seamen, to c.1750, may be found in the records of the Commissary Court of London (London division) at the Guildhall Library.

Registers of powers of attorney, 1800–1899, often give details of next of kin, assigned to receive pay, or acting as executors (PMG 51). For c.1800–1839, they are arranged alphabetically (PMG 51/1–2). Probate registers for 1836–1915 are in PMG 50. ADM 154, registers of discharged dead cases, 1859–1878, may also be worth a look.

19.26 Naval medals

Medal rolls do not give detailed information about individuals: before 1914, they are arranged by ship, and there are no name indexes.

Campaign medal rolls for the Navy are in ADM 171. This class, which is seen on microfilm, includes the award of the following, and some other, campaign medals: the Naval General Service Medal (1793), the China Medal (1840, 1857 and 1900), the Crimea Medal (1854), the Indian Mutiny Medal (1857), the Ashanti Medal (1873), the Arctic Medal (1875–1876), the Queen's South Africa Medal (1899), the King's South Africa Medal (1901), the Africa General Service Medal (1902), the Delhi Durbar Medal (1911), the British War Medal (1914–1920), and the Victory Medal and Stars (1914–1920). Lists of recipients of the Naval General Service Medal, 1793–1840, are given in the book by Douglas-Morris.

Gallantry medals are discussed in detail by Pappalardo. They were first instituted during the Crimean War: others were added later, particularly during the First World War. Some surviving recommendations are in ADM 1 and ADM 116 (look under code 85 in both) Registers of gallantry awards to naval officers during the First World War are also in ADM 171; there is an index available, which gives the dates of entries in the *London Gazette*. Another index gives the dates of entries in the *London Gazette* for most awards to naval personnel from 1942 onwards. The PRO holds a complete set of the *London Gazette* in the class ZJ 1.

19.27 The Royal Navy: bibliography and indexes

Lists etc., of personnel
British Biographical Archive (London, 1984)
J Campbell and W Stevenson, *Lives of the British Admirals* (London, 1917)
J Charnock, *Biographia Navalis* (London, 1794–1798)
Dictionary of National Biography (London, 1909 continuing)
K Douglas-Morris, *The Naval General Service Medal, 1793–1840* (Margate, 1982)
N H G Hurst, *Naval Chronicle, 1799–1818: Index to Births, Marriages and Deaths* (Coulsdon, 1989)
A J Kealy, *Chaplains of the Royal Navy, 1626–1903* (Portsmouth, 1905)
J Marshall, *Royal Naval Biography* (London, 1823–1830)
National Maritime Museum, *Commissioned Sea Officers of the Royal Navy, 1660–1815* (London, 1954 and later)
Navy List (London, 1814 onwards)
W R O'Byrne, *Naval Biographical Dictionary* (London, 1849)
D Steele, *Steele's Navy List* (London, 1782–1817)
D Syrett and R L DiNardo, *The Commissioned Sea Officers of the Royal Navy 1660–1815* (Navy Records Society, 1994)

General works
Calendar of State Papers Domestic, Charles I (London, 1858–1897)
Calendar of State Papers Domestic, Charles II (London, 1860–1947)
Calendar of State Papers Domestic, Commonwealth (London, 1875–1886)
B Pappalardo, *Naval Records for Family Historians* (forthcoming: until publication, ask for the draft text 'Royal Navy Genealogy' at the Research Enquiries Desk)
N A M Rodger, *Naval Records for Genealogists* (PRO, 1998)
N A M Rodger, *The Safeguard of the Sea: A Naval History of Britain* (London, 1997 continuing)
N A M Roger, *The Wooden World: An Anatomy of the Georgian Navy* (London, 1988)
A Trotman, 'The Royal Naval Museum, Portsmouth: Genealogy at the King Alfred Library and Reading Room', *Genealogists' Magazine*, vol. XXIV, pp. 197–199

Indexes
ADM 1 Naval courts martial, 1680–1701: index
ADM 6 Widows' pensions: index
ADM 6 Naval chaplains: index
ADM 6/15–23: Commission and warrant books: index
ADM 6/193: Pursers: index
ADM 6/223–247: Registers of out-pensioners, candidates for admission to Greenwich Hospital: index
ADM 13 Officers' and warrant officers' marriage certificates: index
ADM 20 Treasurers' ledgers, 1660–1699: index
ADM 45/1–10: Officers and civilian effects papers: index
ADM 48 Naval wills: index
ADM 106 Naval surgeons: index
ADM 171/78–88: Royal Naval Medal roll, First World War: index
ADM 199 War history cases and papers: index
ADM 242 Naval officers casualties and ships losses, First World War. Index only: records to which these relate do not survive.

Awards of medals to foreign navy personnel, First World War: index.
Royal Navy Russian honours and orders, First World War: index.
Royal Navy service book index, applications and recommendations, First World War: index.
Ships convoys, Second World War: index.
Ships and submarines, Second World War: index.
Operations/Code Names, Second World War: index.

20 The Royal Marines

20.1 Introduction

There is a specialist guide by Thomas, *Records of the Royal Marines*. Soldiers formed part of the complements of ships of war from the earliest times, but the first British military unit to be raised specifically for sea service was the Lord Admiral's Regiment, formed in 1665. This subsequently became part of the Army establishment, and is the direct ancestor of the modern regiment, the Buffs. From 1690 additional Marine Regiments were raised in wartime for sea service, and disbanded at the end of the war, when the soldiers were discharged and the officers went on half pay. Oath rolls exist for the oath of association in support of William III taken by the First and Second Marine Regiments in 1696 (C 213/290–291).

Though intended for and usually employed in the sea service, these early Marine Regiments were part of the Army and were organized like other foot regiments. Parties serving at sea came under naval discipline and were borne on their ship's books (on a separate list) for wages and victuals (see **19.12**), but in other respects their administration and records did not differ from those of other foot regiments (see **18.21**). Marine Regiments sometimes served ashore as ordinary infantry, while other (non-Marine) infantry regiments contributed soldiers for sea service as necessary.

These Marine Regiments were disbanded for the last time in 1749. At the approach of war again in 1755, a new Corps of Marines was formed under Admiralty authority. This was not part of the Army, and it had no regimental structure, though it continued to use Army ranks and uniform. The fifty companies were divided for administrative and recruiting purposes between three divisions, with their depots at Portsmouth, Plymouth and Chatham. From 1805 to 1869, there was a fourth division, based at Woolwich. Both divisions and companies were purely administrative entities and not fighting formations; officers and other ranks were drafted for sea service without regard to them, and each ship's party of Marines commonly included men of several companies. The Marine depots maintained records similar to those of foot regiments, while Marine detachments at sea were borne on the ships' books as before. Marines sometimes served ashore, particularly as landing parties, when they would be organized into companies and battalions. If serving under military command in such circumstances they came under military discipline, but otherwise they were responsible solely to the Admiralty.

The duties of Marines afloat were, in action to lay down musketry on the enemy's decks; and otherwise to mount sentries and contribute to the unskilled labour of working the ship. From time to time they continued to be supplemented in these roles by infantrymen lent by the Army. Until the twentieth century the duties of the Royal Marines were almost entirely to provide detachments for ships. In 1914, however, a large force of Marines was landed to defend Antwerp, and some subsequently fought on the Western Front. In the 1930s the Marines developed a new role as part of the Mobile Naval Base Defence Organisation, and from 1942 they contributed units known as Commandos which operated under Combined Operations Headquarters, and specialized in raids on enemy coasts. After the war this became the principal duty of the corps.

Another category of troops serving afloat were the artillerymen who manned the mortars carried by bomb vessels. Disciplinary and other problems with them led the Admiralty in 1804 to form companies of marine artillery to man the bombs, which led to a formal division in 1859 between the Royal Marine Artillery (with barracks at Eastney, near Portsmouth) and the Royal Marine Light Infantry, which lasted until the two corps were amalgamated in 1923. They were known respectively as the Blue Marines and the Red Marines.

Correspondence and papers on policy matters, including the raising and deployment of marine companies, may be found in several classes of records. The In-Letters of the Admiralty include a special section for letters from marine officers 1787–1839 (ADM 1/3246–3357), and the Out-Letters also include a section for letters to, or concerning, marines for the period 1703–1845 (ADM 2/1147–1251).

The Royal Marines Museum, at Eastney, is worth a visit: the address is in **48**.

20.2 Royal Marines: commissioned officers

Commissions in the Royal Marines, unlike commissions in the Army, were not sold, but were free appointments. The scattered nature of Marine forces meant that a considerable number of junior officers was required, and that there was little chance for promotion within the Marines as the number of senior officers needed was so small. Some Marine officers went on to buy further promotion in the Army.

Commissions and appointments, 1703–1713, are recorded in ADM 6/405; for 1755–1814, they are in ADM 6/406. There is no index, and they contain no genealogical information. There are some lists of officers' services, 1690–1740, in ADM 96/1–2. There are two incomplete sets of *Lists of Marine Officers*, 1757–1850 and 1760–1886 (ADM 118/230–336 and ADM 192 respectively), which can be used to discover the outline of an officer's career: they are indexed from 1770. The *Navy List*, published annually from 1814, also includes Marine officers. There is a register of commissions issued between 1849 and 1858 (ADM 201/8).

There is a separate service register for officers of the Royal Marine Artillery, 1798–1855, in ADM 196/66. Marine officers' service records from 1837 to 1921, with some from 1793 onwards, will be found in ADM 196/58–65, 83 and 97–114. These records are indexed in ADM 313/110, copies of which are available in the Microfilm Reading Room, except for ADM 196/106–114, which have integral indexes. These dates are the dates of commission, and not of subsequent service; the last details available come from 1954. All enquiries concerning officers appointed after 1922 should be sent to the Royal Marines, Commandant General, at the address given in **48**.

There are some other sources which may be worth investigation. Pay records in ADM 96 can give some extra information. There are lists of half pay officers for 1789–1793 and 1824–1829 in ADM 6/410–413. The survey of officers conducted in 1822 (as for the Navy: see **19.9**) can provide details of age (ADM 6/409). For 1837, there is an address book for Marine officers on half pay (PMG 73/2). Confidential letters on officers' affairs, 1868–1889, are in ADM 63/27–30; they are indexed. The general administrative papers in ADM 193 and ADM 201 may provide more information on individuals.

20.3 Royal Marines: warrant officers

There are few separate records of warrant officers, many of whom went on to become commissioned officers. The only separate register relating to warrant officers' services covers 1904–1912 (ADM 196/67). For Woolwich division, 1812, there is an alphabetical list of warrant officers and ratings, entered for limited service (ADM 6/407). Further records of service for warrant officers can be found in ADM 196. There is a name index of Royal Marine warrant officers and references for their records in the ADM 196 class list.

20.4 Royal Marines: other ranks

Records relating to Royal Marines other ranks are abundant. Marines aboard ship (provided that their ship is known) can be found in the ship's muster books and pay lists: see **19.12**. There are three main series of records kept by the Royal Marines rather than the Navy which may be used in researching the service record of a marine (attestation forms, description books, and service registers) and each is arranged by Division. It will therefore cut down the length of your search if you can identify the Division in which your man served. A marine usually stayed in the same Division throughout his career. If you do not know the Division it may be possible to use one of the methods outlined below to find out in which Division a man served.

- Look in the card index to the attestation records in ADM 157
- If you know any of his medal entitlements, look at the campaign medal rolls in ADM 171.
- If you know the name of a ship he served on, and the date, use the *Navy List* (these are on the open shelves in the Microfilm Reading Room) or Ship's musters (ADM 36–39) to establish the ship's home port. Before 1947 marines who were to serve on board a ship were drawn from the same RM Division as the home port of the ship.
- If you know his Company number, and a date, consult the table in Appendix 1 of Thomas's *Records of the Royal Marines*. Or you can consult the tables of allocation of Company Numbers to Divisions as set out in the *Lists of Officers of the Royal Marines* in ADM 118/230–336 and ADM 192.
- If your man was a war casualty in the First World War consult ADM 242/7–10. These are documents similar to a war graves roll. For the Second World War see Good's *A Register of Royal Marine War Deaths, 1939–1945*, held in the Microfilm Reading Room.
- If you have an address where he lived, from a birth or marriage certificate, or from the census, you may assume with some certainty that he would have joined the nearest Division to that address. He would have belonged to that Division's 'catchment area'.

The attestation forms, 1790–1923 (ADM 157) were completed at the time of enlistment, but are now filed in order of discharge date (except for those of the Chatham division) up to 1883. They can include details of discharge or death. There is a card index, covering the first 659 pieces of the class ADM 157.

Each division also kept its own discharge books (ADM 81 and ADM 183–ADM 185). For the Woolwich division there is an alphabetical list of warrant officers and ratings who had entered for limited service, dated 1812 (ADM 6/407).

The description books, c.1750–1940 (ADM 158), consist of several different, though related, types of register, arranged by date of enlistment, and then by first letter of surname. They provide similar information to the Army's description books (see **18.21**); age on enlistment, parish of birth, and a brief physical description. They do not give details of service.

The service registers start in 1842: they are in ADM 159. In 1884, a system of divisional numbers was introduced, with each man having a unique number in his division. If you do not have the service number you should order the index for your man's surname in ADM 313. This should give you the service number. If you have not been able to identify his Division, you will have to order each piece within ADM 159 that contains his service number, regardless of Division. However, the information contained in these registers is useful: date and place of birth, trade, religion, date and place of enlistment, physical description, a full record of service, and comments on conduct, promotions, etc. The registers so far available cover men who enlisted up to 1923, some of whom served up to the Second World War.

For records of service of men enlisted after 1923, write to the Royal Marines, Drafting and Record Office, at the address given in **48**.

20.5 Royal Marines: records of families

Each division of the Royal Marines kept its own registers of births, marriages and deaths, of children and wives borne on the strength. These registers give the Marine's rank, and some information on posting from the division to a ship or station, under the heading 'disposal'.

Chatham	1830–1913	ADM 183/114–120
Portsmouth (marriages only)	1869–1881	ADM 185/69
Plymouth	1862–1920	ADM 184/43–54
Woolwich (marriages only)	1822–1869	ADM 81/23–25
Royal Marine Artillery	1810–1853	ADM 193
	1866–1921	ADM 6/437

Pensions to the widows of Marine officers will be found in ADM 96/523 (1712–1831), PMG 16 (1836–1870), PMG 20 (1870–1919), and PMG 72 (1921–1926). The last class, PMG 72, appears to relate to other ranks as well. For pensions to officers' children, 1837–1921, see PMG 18. More information on families may perhaps be found in the registers of powers of attorney, 1800–1899 (PMG 51).

For details of pensions and other help provided to families by the Royal Greenwich Hospital, which catered for the Marines as well as the Navy, see **19.23–19.24**.

20.6 Royal Marines: pension records

Pension records for the Royal Marines and their families are fairly extensive, but in general the records are the same as those for Naval pensions: the Royal Hospital Greenwich was founded to aid both the Navy and the Marines. For more details, see **19.22–19.24**. There are two alphabetical registers of Marine officers receiving Greenwich pensions, 1862–1908, which give considerable details (ADM 201/22–23).

20.7 Royal Marines: wills

There is a collection of Royal Marines wills and administrations, 1740–1764, in ADM 96/524. Wills were later deposited in the Navy Pay Office by Royal Marines other ranks, 1786–1909 (ADM 48, indexed by ADM 142). There is also a register of probates affecting the payment of pensions, 1836–1915, in PMG 50.

20.8 Royal Marines: medals

Medal records for the Royal Marines are the same as those for the Navy: see **19.26**. For correspondence on good conduct medals and gratuities, 1849–1884, which includes individual service records, see ADM 201/21.

20.9 The Royal Marines: bibliography

C Field, *Britain's Sea Soldiers* (Liverpool, 1924)
J A Good, *A Register of Royal Marine War Deaths, 1939–1945* (Southsea, 1987)
Public Record Office, *Royal Marine Records in the Public Record Office* (Information Leaflet)
Royal Marine Museum, *The Royal Marines: a Short Bibliography* (Southsea, [1978])
P C Smith, *Per Mare Per Terram: A History of the Royal Marines* (St Ives, 1974)
G Thomas, *Records of the Royal Marines (PRO, 1995)*

21 The Royal Air Force

21.1 Introduction

The Royal Air Force was formed on 1 April 1918, by the amalgamation of the Army's Royal Flying Corps (RFC) and the Navy's Royal Naval Air Service (RNAS), founded in 1912 and 1914 respectively. There is a specialist guide available, by Fowler and others, *RAF Records in the PRO.*

21.2 Records of service

Before the amalgamation, officers' service records will be found in either Army service records in WO 339 or WO 374 (see **18.12**) or Royal Naval Air Service registers of officers' service records in ADM 273. There is a name index for ADM 273.

Once the RAF was formed, it created its own records of service, rather than using those created by the Admiralty or War Office. These new records, which contain the records of those officers who served no later than the mid 1920s, are in AIR 76. AIR 76 is seen on microfilm and is arranged in alphabetical order.

Records of RFC airmen who were discharged before the formation of the RAF, may be found in WO 363 or WO 364 (see **18.20**). The records of RNAS other ranks can be found in ADM 188 (see **19.15**) and contain information relating to their service up to 31 March 1918 (the day before the RAF was formed).

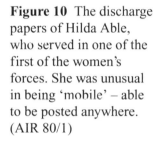

Figure 10 The discharge papers of Hilda Able, who served in one of the first of the women's forces. She was unusual in being 'mobile' – able to be posted anywhere. (AIR 80/1)

The records of service for RAF airmen with a service number of 329000 or lower, can be found in AIR 79. This class is arranged in service number order. An index to find the service number is in AIR 78, available on microfilm. The records of those men within this number range who went on to see service in the Second World War will not be found in AIR 79 as their records are still maintained by the Ministry of Defence. Details for these men, together with the records of men whose service number was 329001 or higher and officers who served after the mid 1920s can be obtained from RAF Innsworth (address in **48**).

Service records for the Women's Royal Air Force, 1914–1920, will be found in AIR 80.

Officers' careers can be traced in the *Air Force List*: a complete set is available at Kew. For 1939–1954 the *Confidential Air List* is kept separately (in AIR 10). Correspondence with officers, recommendations for awards and promotions, confidential reports and combat reports are found in AIR 1: indexes are available. For records of RAF prisoners of war, see AIR 20/2336, and **36.5**.

A muster of all other ranks serving in the RAF on formation can be found in AIR 1/819 and AIR 10/232–237. The muster can provide the rate of pay the individual received, his trade, the date of his last promotion and whether the individual was on an open engagement or was serving for the duration of the war only.

A brief biography of those RFC/RAF airmen whose service number was between 1 and 1400 (i.e. those men who joined the RFC before the First World War), can be found in *A Contemptible Little Flying Corps* by Webb and McInnes.

The FRC (ONS) has indexes to RAF war deaths, 1939–1948, and also to RAF births, marriages and deaths abroad, from 1920: these can also be seen at Kew. Copies of the actual certificates have to be bought from the ONS at Southport. See **4.14** and **1.6.**

21.3 Operational records

Operational records of the Royal Flying Corps during the First World War are available (AIR 1, AIR 23, AIR 25, AIR 27–AIR 29). Operational records of the RNAS can be found in ADM 1, ADM 116 and ADM 137. Medals awarded for First World War service are in WO 329 for the Royal Flying Corps and Royal Air Force, and in ADM 171 for the Royal Naval Air Service. Pensions to disabled airmen and gratuities for the First World War may be found in PMG 42.

Operations Record Books (AIR 24–AIR 29) are the diaries of the RAF and do not contain much personal detail, apart from promotions, transfers and awards. Crashes and casualties incurred during operations are recorded here. For those which happened on non-operational flights, apply to the Ministry of Defence, Air Historical Branch (address in **48**).

The RAF Museum at Hendon has photographs, air log books and a huge collection of privately-deposited officers' records, as well as planes. Its archive includes a card index of every aircraft that flew in the RAF. The Imperial War Museum at Duxford is another place to see early RAF planes. The addresses are given in **48**.

21.4 The Royal Air Force: bibliography

Air Force List (from 1918)
S Fowler, P Elliott, RC Nesbit, C Goulter, *RAF Records in the PRO* (London, 1994)
J V Webb and I McInnes, *A Contemptible Little Flying Corps* (London, 1989)

Figure 11 Members at 80 Squadron RAF, in Northern France, 1918 or 1919.
(AIR 1/1820/204/198/2)

22 The Coastguard and the preventive services

22.1 Introduction

The Coastguard was formed in 1822 by the amalgamation of three of the services for the prevention of smuggling. These were the Revenue Cruisers, the Riding Officers (both dating from 1698) and the Preventive Water Guard, set up in 1809. These three services were part of the Customs, although from 1816 the officers and men of the Revenue Cruisers were appointed by the Admiralty, and the Riding Officers were often appointed from the Army. The Riding Officers operated in Kent and Sussex: the Revenue Cruisers were largely confined to the Kent, Sussex and East Anglian coasts and the Thames estuary, until the end of the eighteenth century, when they covered the English and Welsh coasts. Scotland had its own fleet. In 1831 another preventive service, the Coastal Blockade (set up by the Admiralty in 1816), was also amalgamated into the Coastguard. These four preventive forces employed nearly 6,700 men at the time of amalgamation.

Confusingly, the Board of Excise had its own Revenue Cruisers and its own officers called Riding Officers: these covered the entire country, not just the coasts of Kent and Sussex, and were concerned with the collection (and preventing the evasion) of excise duty.

The Board of Customs had overall control of the Coastguard, despite the active role of the Admiralty, from 1822 until 1856, when the Admiralty was granted control by the Coastguard Service Act. After 1856, the duties of the Coastguard continued to be the defence of the coast, the provision of a reserve for the Navy, and the protection of the revenue against evasion by smuggling: over the next seventy years new responsibilities were added, stressing assistance to shipping. The Coastguard as run by the Admiralty consisted of three distinct bodies; the Shore Force, the Permanent Cruiser Force and the Guard Ships, naval ships which lay at major ports to act as headquarters of Coastguard districts.

22.2 The preventive forces: service records

For information relating to the (Customs) Riding Officers and the Preventive Water Guard, try the records of the Board of Customs (see **24.8**); for the (Excise) Riding Officers and (Excise) Revenue Cruisers, try the Excise records (see **24.8** again); for the Coastal Blockade, try the Admiralty records (see **19**); and for the Revenue Cruisers, try both the Admiralty and the Customs records.

A good place to start may be with the published reports made to Parliament about the operation of the various preventive services. There is a CD-ROM index to these in the PRO Library, and the reports can be seen on microfiche in the Microfilm Reading Room. These reports can include information such as name, age, place of birth, date of appointment, etc. Examples include officers and men appointed to the Preventive Boat Service (i.e. the Preventive Water Guard), November 1816–March 1819 (microfiche reference 1819. 20, 141–142), and Coastal Blockade men killed in conflicts with Kent and Sussex smugglers, 1821–1825 (microfiche reference 1825. 27, 154). Later reports on the Coastguard can give details of earlier service in the preventive services (see the CD-ROM index). Pension records for c.1818–1825 are in CUST 40/28.

Administration of the Revenue Cruisers was split between the Customs and the Admiralty, with the latter appointing the officers and men after 1816; this system continued when the Revenue Cruisers were merged into the Coastguard in 1822. Officers serving in Revenue Cruisers are given in the *Navy List* from 1814. Admiralty appointments to Revenue Cruisers of lieutenants, masters and boatswains for 1816–1831 are in ADM 6/56; for later appointments see *22.3*.

22.3 The Coastguard: service records

There are registers of Admiralty nominations of officers and ratings to the Coastguard in England, 1819–1866 (ADM 175/74–80, with indexes in ADM 175/97–98 for 1823–1866); in Ireland, 1820–1849 (ADM 175/74, 81, 99–100); and in Scotland, 1820–1824 (ADM 175/74). Nominations for England may also be found in ADM 6/199 (1831–1850), and in ADM 175/101 (1851–1856). Discharge records for 1858–1868 are in ADM 175/102. Many people from the Bombay Marine entered the Coastguard after 1856, when the East India Company gave up its navy (see also **18.27**). Between 1866 and 1886 there is an unexplained gap in the records. For Coastguard officers, 1886 to 1947, there are indexed Service Registers (ADM 175/103–107, 109–111). For Coastguard ratings, 1900–1923, there are service record cards (ADM 175/82A–84B, alphabetical, 1900–1923; ADM 175/85–89, with an index in ADM 175/108, 1919–1923; and ADM 175/90, 1919–1923). Discharge registers for 1919, when large numbers of Coastguards were paid off after the First World War, are in ADM 175/91–96.

Many men of the Coastguard had service in the Royal Navy prior to joining the Coastguard service, consequently a search in the RN ratings papers may be necessary (see **19.14** and **19.15**).

Officers serving in Revenue Cruisers (part of the Coastguard since 1822) are given in the *Navy List* from 1814. Admiralty appointments to Revenue Cruisers of lieutenants, masters and boatswains for 1816–1831 are in ADM 6/56; for 1822–1832 they are in ADM 2/1127. Quarterly musters of Revenue Cutters, 1824–1857, are in ADM 119. Men serving on the Revenue Cruisers can also be traced in the ship's Establishment and Record Books, 1816–1879 (ADM 175/24–73). For the establishment of the Revenue Cruisers between 1827 and 1829, try CUST 19/52–61.

Among the Customs records are some other items relating to the Coastguard. Coastguard minute books, 1833–1849, are in CUST 29/40–42; Coastguard statistics are in CUST 38/32–60; and CUST 39/173 contains the salaries and incidents of the Thames Coastguard, 1828–1832. Pension records, 1857–1935, are in PMG 23; other records of pensions, 1855–1935, are in ADM 23. Chief officers were also entitled to receive Greenwich pensions after 1866 (PMG 70).

During the First World War many men of the Coastguard qualified for medals, details of which can be found in ADM 171.

22.4 The Coastguard and the preventive services: bibliography

E Carson, *The Ancient and Rightful Customs* (London, 1972)
N A M Rodger, *Naval Records for Genealogists* (PRO, 1998)
G Smith, *Something to Declare! 1,000 Years of Customs and Excise* (London, 1980)
W Webb, *Coastguard: An Official History of HM Coastguard* (London, 1976)

23 Police forces

23.1 Introduction

Police forces in the sense that we now understand the term did not exist until the mid nineteenth century. Before then, the day-to-day work of policing was carried out by a number of local forces such as watchmen, constables, headboroughs and magistrates. The records they created are almost always held in local record offices. The first modern police force in the UK mainland was the Metropolitan Police Force. Although there were some earlier local experiments, provincial police forces did not begin until after the County Police Act of 1839, and no part of England and Wales could be compelled to provide a police force until the County and Borough Act of 1856. Storch's 'The policeman as domestic missionary' and Emsley's *The English Police* tell more about the social context within which the early police forces acted, and why there was so much opposition to them.

23.2 London

The Metropolitan Police Force was created in 1829. Its jurisdiction was initially defined as an area of about seven miles radius from Charing Cross (excluding the City of London) but this was extended in 1839 to a fifteen mile radius. In 1835 the Bow Street Horse Patrol was incorporated into the force, followed by the Bow Street Foot Patrol and the Thames Police Office in 1839. The Metropolitan Police also had responsibility for the police of the royal dockyards and military stations at Portsmouth, Chatham, Devonport, Pembroke, Rosyth and Woolwich, from 1860 to 1934. Some records of the Bow Street Horse Patrol are included in MEPO 2/25. An unindexed service register for the Bow Street Foot Patrol, 1821–1829 is in MEPO 4/508. This gives name, place of residence, age, place of birth, height, marital status, number of children, name of recommender, military service, and date of appointment together with date and reason for discharge.

The City of London Police is quite separate from the Metropolitan Police and its records are not held in the PRO. Surviving personnel records are good. They include a complete series of registers listing everyone who has ever served in the force, together with personal files on about 95 per cent of City of London police officers. For further information, write to the City of London Police Record Office (address in **48**).

23.3 The Metropolitan Police Force: service records

From the beginning, the Metropolitan Police Force attempted to recruit young men who were well built, physically fit, literate and of good character. Women were not recruited until 1919. Service records of policewomen do not survive.

Many recruits came from outside the metropolitan area, partly because poor living conditions meant that young Londoners often failed to meet the required standards of health but also because there was a prevalent belief that standards of moral fitness were higher in the provinces than in London. There was a high turnover of staff, especially in the very early years of the force.

Full certificate of service records survive only for the period from January 1889–November 1909 (MEPO 4/361–477). They are arranged by warrant number and give a description of the recruit, date of birth, trade, marital status, residence, number of children, name and place of last employer, previous public service, surgeon's certificate, postings to divisions, dates of promotion or demotion, and causes of removal. However there is a wealth of other material that can be used to reconstruct basic personal information about most Metropolitan Police officers, except that no records survive for the period between May 1857 and February 1869. In order to gain maximum information you may need to use more than one type of record.

The easiest source to use is the alphabetical register of joiners, covering September 1830–April 1857, and July 1878–1933 (MEPO 4/333–338). This normally gives name, rank, warrant number, division and dates of appointment and removal. The earliest volumes also supply the names and addresses of referees. The registers of leavers, March 1889–January 1947 (MEPO 4/339–351), are also relatively easy as each volume is indexed; they too will give name, rank, warrant number, division and dates of appointment and removal.

Other useful sources, each providing name, rank, warrant number, division and dates of appointment and removal, are:

- alphabetical register, 1829–1836 (HO 65/26), which also gives dates of promotion or demotion;
- numerical registers (arranged by warrant number), September 1829–March 1830 (MEPO 4/31–32), which also gives the officer's height and cause of removal from the force;
- attestation ledgers, February 1869–May 1958 (MEPO 4/352–360), which includes signatures of recruits and witnesses; there is a section at the back for police stationed at the royal dockyards and military stations; arranged by warrant number;
- returns of death whilst serving, 1829–1889 (MEPO 4/2), with an index (MEPO 4/448), which also gives cause of death.

Annual Police Orders (MEPO 7) can also be used to trace officers who were pensioned, promoted, dismissed and transferred, but they are subject to a 50 year closure.

Papers relating to the service of certain distinguished officers are held in the Special Series of correspondence and papers from the Commissioner's Office (MEPO 3/2883–2921): they are closed for at least 75 years.

Some name indexes are available in the Research Enquiries Room. The most extensive is a general alphabetical index of former serving officers, mainly based on information in police orders (MEPO 7), supplemented by the joiners ledgers, leavers ledgers, records of service ledgers and attestation ledgers (MEPO 4). There is also an index to officers who joined the Metropolitan Police, 1880–1889, and an index to pensioners who left the force between 1852 and 1889 (see below **23.4**).

23.4 The Metropolitan Police Force: pension records

Pension records are an excellent source of family history information. Before the Police Pensions Act was passed in 1890, pensions were awarded on a discretionary basis, but after that date they were granted as of right to officers who had served for 25 years and a modified pension/gratuity was paid to those who were discharged as medically unfit. Pensions and gratuities granted between 1829 and 1859 are mentioned in correspondence and papers (MEPO 5/1–90). Records of pensioners who retired or resigned between 1852 and 1932 are in MEPO 21.

The records in MEPO 21 contain detailed personal information, including physical description, date and place of birth, marital status, and dates of service. Until 1923 they also give details of promotions and postings, intended place of residence after retirement and names of parents and next of kin. After 1923, they include date and place of marriage, together with a physical description of the wife and her date and place of birth. The records are arranged by pension number (which approximates to a chronological order of resignation). Post-1932 pension records are still held by the Metropolitan Police.

A register of pensions to widows of officers killed on duty, 1840–1858 is in MEPO 4/33.

23.5 The Metropolitan Police Force: other records

Records relating to complaints and disciplinary actions against Metropolitan Police officers are held in MEPO 3 and HO 287.

There is an unindexed register of local constables sworn to act within the Metropolitan Police district, 1839–1876 (MEPO 4/3–5).

The Metropolitan Police District was divided into several divisions each under the charge of a superintendent: maps of the divisions and their changing boundaries can be found in MEPO 15. Divisional records have not been transferred to the PRO. Incomplete divisional records are held by the Metropolitan Police Museum, and those of the Thames division are held at the Wapping Police Station Museum. Neither of these is open to the public, but both will try to answer written enquiries: the addresses are given in **48**.

Other information on the early years of the Metropolitan Police can be found in *Hue and Cry* and the *Police Gazette*, 1828–1845 (HO 75). Records of investigations conducted by the Metropolitan Police are mainly to be found in MEPO 2, MEPO 3 and MEPO 4.

For information concerning gallantry awards to Metropolitan Police officers see below **23.11**.

23.6 Other police forces in England and Wales

The Metropolitan Police Force is the only British police force to be directly controlled by the central government (its chief officer, the Commissioner, reports directly to the Home Office). Its records are therefore held in the PRO. Other police forces in the UK are run by local government units. Their records are not public records and are not held in the PRO. In order to find out more about them you should try the appropriate local record office first. It may also be worth contacting the police force itself or the local police museum. A good, but now dated, guide to local police records is Bridgeman and Emsley (see bibliography, **23.12**)

The Royal Military Police keep their own records: write to the address given in **48**.

For railway police, see **26.2**.

23.7 Ireland

Until 1836, there were a number of local forces of constables in Ireland. Some information about the careers of superannuated constables can be found in *Parliamentary Papers: House of Commons Sessional Papers, 1831–1832, vol. XXVI, p. 465* (list of superannuations of local Irish forces). The list gives names, period of service, amount granted, and the nature of the injury which was the cause of the superannuation. Copies of *Parliamentary Papers* are readily available at the British Library and good local reference libraries; they are also available on microfiche at the PRO. In 1836, these local groups were united into a single force known as the Irish Constabulary, which was renamed the Royal Irish Constabulary in 1867. The RIC was responsible for the whole of Ireland with the exception of Dublin (policed by the Dublin Metropolitan Police, founded in 1786), and so was disbanded in August 1922, when the Irish Free State was established.

The service records of members of the Royal Irish Constabulary are held in HO 184. The registers are arranged by service number, but there are separate alphabetical indexes. They normally give name, age, height, religious affiliation, native county, trade, marital status, native county of wife (but not her name), date of appointment, counties in which the man served, length of service and date of retirement or death, but no information about parentage. The same record class (HO 184) also includes separate registers, with integral indexes, for officers and for members of the auxiliary forces (colloquially known as the Black and Tans) who helped suppress unrest in Ireland in the period immediately before independence. Further information about the activities of the Black and Tans is held in record class WO 35.

Pensions and allowances granted to officers, men and staff, and to their widows and children are recorded among the Paymaster General's records (PMG 48), and usually give the recipient's address. This class also includes registers of deceased pensioners (1877–1918) and of awards of pensions made on the disbandment of the force. Files on pension options at the time of disbandment, arranged by county, are held amongst the records of the Colonial Office (CO 904/175–6).

Records relating to appointments to the Irish Revenue Police, 1830–1857, are in CUST 111. This was a force initially under the control of the Board of Excise, but from 1849 controlled by the Board of Inland Revenue, formed to combat the making of malt and distillation of spirit in Ireland in contravention of the Irish (Illicit distillation (Ireland)) Act of 1831.

23.8 South Africa

The PRO has the original correspondence and registers of in- and out-letters of the Colonial Office, relating to the South African Constabulary, 1902–1908 (CO 526, CO 639 and CO 640). A large proportion of this correspondence relates to individuals: however, much of the correspondence that is noted in the registers has in fact been destroyed. The registers have name indexes, and can provide some information even if the correspondence noted has not survived.

Although there are no service records, information on individuals can be found. The general orders give appointments, postings, leave on medical grounds and resignations. There are some pension returns, supplying the name of the widow and place of payment (Britain or South Africa). There are also nominal rolls of various kinds: casualties, men taken on (sometimes supplying the name and address of next of kin), men placed on the married establishment, and men taken off the strength. In addition, individuals are sometimes mentioned in correspondence.

There appears to have been some confusion between the South African Constabulary and the various local armed forces: men who joined the Constabulary sometimes served with other forces (see **18.29**).

23.9 Palestine

As explained in **23.10**, personnel records of officers serving overseas do not normally survive amongst the records of the British government. The PRO does not hold any personnel records for the Palestine police. Some records relating to medal entitlement for members of the Palestine police are held by the Foreign and Commonwealth Office, Records and Historical Service Unit (address in **48**). These consist of a card index for awards of the Defence Medal, 1939–1945 and rolls for awards of the Defence and General Service medals. The card index entries always include the surname and initial of the first name of the recipient and whether the Defence or General Service Medal was awarded. The entries may also contain further information such as rank and number, full name and address together with file number and the date of issue of medals, but it is extremely unusual for all these details to be present on a single card. The medal rolls are not arranged in alphabetical order, but by rank and list number, so it can be difficult to identify individual entries. They are also fragile. The Records and Historical Services Unit is not open to the public but is prepared to answer written enquiries concerning the issue of medals. However, you should note that the cards cannot be used to prove whether someone was or was not a member of the police force at any time, and that they will not establish length of service of any individual nor whether there was any entitlement to a pension.

Colonial Office records held in the PRO sometimes contain information about the activities of the Palestine police. For the most part, however, they relate to political aspects of operations, major disturbances (involving large numbers of deaths, or extensive damage to property), and enquiries into corruption. They do not contain material on recruitment, promotion, resignations or routine administrative detail, nor information on day-to-day work. An excellent, although now dated, guide to records relating to Palestine is Jones's *Britain and Palestine*.

23.10 Other colonial forces

Generally, you are unlikely to find personnel records for individuals who served in colonial police forces or information about the day-to-day activities of colonial police forces in the PRO. Nor is it likely that such information is held by the Foreign and Commonwealth Office or any other government department for future transfer to the PRO. This is because such forces were administered by the government of the colony concerned rather than directly from the Colonial Office (later the Foreign and Commonwealth Office) in London, and any files created would have been in the possession of the relevant colonial government. They would have remained in that colony even after independence because they would have been essential to the day-to-day administration of policing in the newly independent country. However, as noted above for South Africa and Palestine, it is possible that some personal information is included in files that were created by the Colonial Office for other purposes. Such information is likely to be incidental to the main purpose of the file and is unlikely therefore either to be indexed or even indicated in the lists. Conducting a search of this kind would require considerable determination, a lot of time, and a willingness to accept that it may not be successful. If you wish to undertake such a search, you would be well advised to consult a good guide to colonial records such as the one by Thurston.

23.11 Honours and decorations

Although the PRO does hold Home Office files relating to recommendations for the award of the King's Police Medal from its introduction in 1909, all the information of substance in those files appears in Farmery's *Police Gallantry*. Farmery's book also uses information from the *Police Review*, and the *Police Chronicle* as well as other sources, and often includes a photograph of the individual concerned. It gives direct references to the Home Office files in HO 45. Awards were notified in the *London Gazette* but entries before 1960 do not include a citation. The PRO holds copies of the *London Gazette* in record class ZJ 1, and there is a copy of Farmery's book in the PRO library, but as both are published works, copies should also be available to you at a good local reference library or via the inter-library loan system.

Records relating to awards of the King's Police Medal to Metropolitan Police officers are:

- 1909–1951 register of Metropolitan Police Officers under consideration for the award, MEPO 22/2;
- 1909–1912 list of awards, MEPO 2/1300.

An indexed register of decorations, honours and awards to Metropolitan Police officers, 1945–1988, is in MEPO 22/1.

23.12 Police forces: bibliography

D Ascoli, *The Queen's Peace: the origins and development of the Metropolitan Police 1829–1979* (London, 1979)
I Bridgeman and C Emsley, *A guide to the archives of the police forces of England and Wales* (Police History Society, 1989)
C Emsley, *The English Police: a political and social history* (Hemel Hempstead, 1991)
J P Farmery, *Police Gallantry, The King's Police Medal, the King's Police and Fire Service Medal and the Queen's Police Medal for Gallantry 1909–1978* (Periter, Sydney, 1995)
P Jones, *Britain and Palestine* (Oxford, 1979)
S H Palmer, *Police and Protest in England and Ireland, 1780–1850* (Cambridge, 1988)
Police Historical Society, *Notes for Family Historians* (Police Historical Memo No. 1, 1987)
R D Storch, 'The policeman as domestic missionary: urban discipline and popular culture in northern England, 1850–1880', *Journal of Social History* (Summer, 1976)
A Thurston, *Records of the Colonial Office, Dominions Office, Commonwealth Relations Office and Commonwealth Office* (London, 1995)
R Whitmore, *Victorian and Edwardian Crime and Punishment from Old Photographs* (London, 1978)

24 Crown servants: office-holders and civil servants

24.1 The Royal Household before 1660

If you are looking for a member of the Royal Household before 1660, you may need specialist advice: a leaflet is available at Kew and on the PRO's web site. For a series of articles on the court, look at Starkey, *The English Court from the Wars of the Roses to the Civil War*.

Try the name indexes to SC 1, Ancient Correspondence, and SC 6, Ancient Petitions, and also to the printed *Calendars of Patent Rolls and Close Rolls*, for details of patronage. The Exchequer: Various Accounts in E 101 may contain information, but they are not indexed. Names of members of the Royal Household are separately listed for 1523–1696 in the E 179 taxation returns (see **43.1**). For the lower household answerable to the Lord Steward, there is an entry book for 1627–1641, LS 13/251. An index to the members of Charles I's household from LC 3/1 (1641) is filed with the list.

The Verge was the area stretching for twelve miles around wherever the household happened to be, and as the household was always on the move, the boundaries of the Verge were constantly changing The Marshal of the Household, who was in charge of discipline of the royal staff, had the right to try crimes which occurred within this area. See E 37 to 1623 and then PALA 6. For further details see Jones, 'The Court of the Verge'.

24.2 The Commonwealth

There is a break in the series of Royal Household records for this period, but some bills of the 1650s have been preserved in series of Bills and Vouchers LC 9/377–390 (1622–1843). There are also requests for arrears of payments dated in the 1660s. This series is mostly unsorted.

24.3 The Royal Household after 1660: general

There are published lists by Sainty and Burcholz of *Officials of the Royal Household, 1660–1837*, which you should consult first: they are available at Kew The Royal Archives hold a comprehensive card index of persons employed in the Lord Chamberlain's and Lord Steward's departments, 1660–1837, compiled from the records of the Lord Chamberlain and the Lord Steward, which are in the PRO, and from other sources elsewhere, and are prepared to answer postal enquiries. The address is in **48**.

The responsibilities of the two departments of the household could be broadly divided between above stairs (Lord Chamberlain's) and below stairs (Lord Steward's). In addition to the household records described below, there are many other sources for Royal Household servants, such as the accounts in E 101, E 351, LC 9, LS 1, LS 2, LS 3 and T 38.

24.4 The Lord Chamberlain's Department after 1660

The Lord Chamberlain was broadly responsible for 'upstairs': the chambers, the wardrobe, the office of robes, ceremonies, revels, musicians, chapels, housekeepers, messengers, yeomen of the guard, watermen, physicians, artists, craftsmen and other offices such as Librarian, Latin Secretary, Poet Laureate, Examiner of Plays, and Keeper of Lions at the Tower. A good place to start for 1660–1784 would be the Glencross Index, to many of the establishment records in LC 5 (filed with the LC 5 list). This includes the entry books of wills and letters of attorney of household servants, 1750–1784 (LC 5/104–106).

There are records of appointments, 1660–1851 (LC 3/61–71) and 1851–1901 (LC 5/237–241). LC 3/56–60 is a less complete series for various dates between 1685 and 1838. Established servants are named in LC 3/1–23, for various dates between 1641 and 1849. Records of payments, 1516–1782 are in LC 5/11–83.

Officers are not usually named in the Salary, Livery and Pension Books, LC 3/37–52 (1667–1857), except for pensioners, holders of offices about to be discontinued, and widows. LC 3/37 is a book of arrears for 1667–1685, where the names of both salaried and waged servants appear. Servants appointed to the Office of Robes appear in the Letter Books of that office, LC 13/1–5 (1830–1901).

Servants' names are given in respect of various payments and appointments in the Warrant Books of the Treasurer of the Chamber, LC 5/11–26 (1660–1800), the Comptroller, LC 5/27–30 (1754–1781), and the Wardrobe, LC 5/31–83 (1516–1782) LC 5/247 concerns officers and servants, 1864–97. Warrants of Several Sorts, LC 5/248–251 (1820–1866) include some appointments, among payments, general instructions and grants of grace and favour lodgings. Several of these are indexed by the Glencross Index, filed with the LC 5 list.

There is material relating to servants among the Correspondence Books in LC 1, while servants at various royal palaces appear in the Palaces Ledgers, LC 9/367–374 (1806–1846). Messengers' travelling expenses can be found in LC 10/1–9 (1784–1838).

Records about royal mourning may include lists of people receiving mourning clothes The servants of royal households other than those of the monarch and consort rarely appear, but the records of funerals in LC 2 may list the households of deceased royal persons. The household of the late Duke of York in 1827 is listed in LC 2/56. Housemaids are named in connection with mourning in the Bill Books for sundries, LC 11/144–5 (1846–1857).

24.5 The Lord Steward's Department after 1660

The Lord Steward was responsible for 'downstairs', until 1854, when his office was abolished, and its functions were taken over by the Master of the Royal Household, whose records are not public records, but are held by the Royal Archives. The Lord Steward, and later the Master, had responsibility for the kitchen offices (almonry, ewery, bakery, pastry, confectionery, buttery, spicery, poultry, larder, pantry, wine cellar, scullery), the counting house, the wood and coal yards, the gardens and stables, and a whole host of other offices such as keeper and repairer of the buckets. Warrants of appointments, 1660–1820, are in LS 13/246–267.

The names of servants, including purveyors, extraordinary staff and the higher officers of the stables appear in the Cheque Rolls, LS 13/6–13 (James I–George II). Certificate Books of Admission, LS 13/197–204 (1672–1820) include servants of the steward's department, stables, chapels, and the Secretaries of State. Special duties and leaves of absence are recorded in LS 13/205–208 (1766–1811).

In the middle ages household servants had been entitled to eat at the board as part of their remuneration. By the seventeenth century the entitlement had often been translated into money payments, or boardwages, the responsibility of the Lord Steward's Department, paid by the Board of Green Cloth. The Kitchen Ledgers, LS 9/60–77 (1660–1729) show these payments to the Steward's staff, staff of the Chamber and Wardrobe, including the Lord Chamberlain himself, the Secretaries of State and chapel staff. Other expenses are recorded, including travelling expenses, pheasant keeping and payments to widows and for burials. Receipt books for wages and allowances, LS 13/154–167 (1761–1816) contain the signatures of many servants for receipt of boardwages and other payments, including 'carpet and cushion money'. These chronological entries are not indexed.

The Creditors also record the payment of boardwages, LS 8 (1641–1854). The Creditors of two minor royal households survive in LS 8/315–316, Princess Charlotte, 1814–1815, and LS 8/317, Prince of Hesse-Homburg, 1818. The households of royal princesses and the Duke of Clarence are mentioned in LS 8/237 (1805). LS 13/321 records pensions for members of Princess Charlotte's household. Stable Creditors, LS 13/210–230 (1761–1781) show creditors and salary bills for the stables, Chamber and chapels. LS 13/295–299 (1815–1834) record allowances in kind, including 'pitchers and platters'. The names, and often the signatures of clerks, housemaids, footmen, laundresses, coachmen and postilions appear among those of servants of all household departments.

Records of the royal gardens, which provided produce for the table, appear in LS 10–12 (1796–1854), but staff, other than head gardeners, are rarely named. Garden labourers at Kew, Windsor and Hampton Court, 1834–1835, are named in LS 11/19–20. Gamekeepers are rarely named in the Royal Household records, although four gamekeepers at Richmond are named in LC 3/23 (1846–1849). There are detailed records relating to the employment of estate staff, such as gamekeepers, park and gatekeepers and fishermen, at Windsor Great Park in the records of the Crown Estate Office, in CRES 4 (1766–1958).

In 1854 the office of Lord Steward was abolished, and its functions were taken over by the Master of the Royal Household, whose records are not public records. Contact the Royal Archives (address in **48**) for more information.

24.6 Royal warrant holders

Today the issue of royal warrants to tradesmen is carefully controlled by the Royal Household. The grant of such a warrant entitles the holder to use the phrase 'By Appointment', and to display the royal coat of arms. From 1900, lists of royal warrant holders are published annually in the *London Gazette*. False claims to possession of royal warrants became a prosecutable offence under the Patents Act, 1883, and the Merchandise Marks Act, 1887. The issue of royal warrants to tradesmen was recorded systematically from the 1830s. Warrants to tradesmen supplying ceremonial items (e.g. peruke makers) and to those supplying more personal items (e.g. combs, perfumes and corset stays) to the office of robes, 1830–1901, are in LC 13/1–5. Warrants to tradesmen supplying such items as furnishings, linens and stationery for Queen Victoria are in LC 5/243–246. Each volume has an internal index. The original bills presented by tradesmen, whether warrant holders or not, are in LC 11.

Before the 1830s, the situation was not so well-regulated. Tradesmen's appointments, 1660–1837, appear with the appointment of household servants in LC 3/61–70. Unfortunately no appointments were recorded between 1767 and 1773 (LC 3/67, 1760–1793). LC 5/197–199 contain orders to tradesmen and for court mourning (1773–1827). Suppliers of all kinds of goods are named in the series of Warrant Books LC 5/132–163 (1628–1810). The Accounts (LC 9) and Bill Books (LC 10 and LC 11) may also reveal suppliers of goods to the household between 1600 and 1900. Office of Robes accounts can be found in LC 12 (1860–1901).

The Lord Steward's Department was responsible for the royal kitchens, cellars, stables and gardens. Suppliers to the department were appointed as purveyors. They were often appointed in the place of a previous purveyor, not to a salary or wage, but to enjoy 'rights, profits, privileges and advantages'. Some original warrants to purveyors survive in the series of Original Warrants, LS 13/246–250 (1761–1782). Other tradesmen also received this kind of warrant, e.g. cork cutter, wine chest maker, cake maker. Copies of these warrants were recorded in the Warrant Books, LS 13/251–267 (1627–1820). From 1674 they are divided into two series, Royal and Steward's. Warrants to purveyors appear in the Steward's series. Grocery, poultry, wines and wax candles are among the goods to be purveyed. Tradesmen's warrants do not appear to have been recorded in the Lord Steward's records after 1820, but there is a volume showing fees for warrants, which includes fees for purveyor's warrants, from 1838–1850 (LS 13/306).

The Kitchen Ledgers LS 9/60–77 (1660–1729) include the names of suppliers of such items as beer, glasses, bottles and toothpicks among other expenses. Suppliers are also named in the Mensils, LS 9/227–290 (1761–1814), monthly lists of the consumption of foodstuffs and wines, and also supplies of coals and brushes.

Orders to tradesmen are recorded in LS 13/134–153 (1763–1851).The tradesmen are not always named, especially in the earlier period, where often only the trade is given, e.g. the Brazier, the China and Glassman. There are orders for food, wine, beer, fuel, lights, china, cutlery, turnery, ironmongery, linen, floorcoverings and stationery. Tradesmen's bills appear in the Accounts Books in LS 2 (1761–1854). The Creditors in LS 8 show amounts owed to various suppliers. LS 8/1–98 (1641–1760) are a single series, while those for 1761–1815 are divided into three series (LS 8/100–270): Kitchen Creditors for foods; Household, for foods, fuel, lights and laundry; Incidental for stationery, hardware and cartage. There are also separate Creditors for Hampton Court Palace for 1795–1799. A new system, where quarterly accounts were arranged according to palaces, recorded the names of goods, suppliers and costs, LS 8/271–314 (1815–1854). Suppliers to the stables appear in the Stables Creditors, LS 13/210–230 (1761–1781).

24.7 Civil servants

Many senior civil servants are best sought, not in the records, but in such publications in the PRO library as the *Dictionary of National Biography*, or the *British Biographical Archive*. For 1883–1977, try the library's holdings of *Kelly's Handbook to the Titled, Landed and Official Classes*, which gives a potted biography. Sainty and others lists of *Office Holders in Modern Britain* cover the period 1660–1870, and include officials of the Admiralty, the Board of Trade, the Colonial Office, the Foreign Office, the Home Office, the Navy Board, the Royal Commissions of Inquiry, the Secretaries of State, the Treasury, and the Lord Chamberlain's and Lord Steward's Departments of the Royal Household. There are a number of official printed sources available at Kew on the postings of senior civil servants, but they do not provide personal information. The main one is *The British Imperial Calendar*, which runs from 1810 to 1972, when it became the *Civil Service Year Book*. From 1852 there is the *Foreign Office List*, and from 1862 the *Colonial Office List*.

There are few personal details about civil servants in the public records, and it is quite difficult to trace them. If you know the office or department, it is worth looking through its records to find establishment lists, etc., which may possibly be useful. If you want details of payments of wages and pensions, try looking in E 403 (a huge class with lots of little used material). Colwell's *Dictionary of Genealogical Sources in the PRO* has two pages of references to appointments and payments, which you may find helpful.

To discover where to find the establishment records of a particular office, including defunct offices, use the *PRO Guide*. As an example of what can be found, MAF 39 will give you staff lists for 1892–1947, with ranks and salaries; registers of service 1854–1929, and lists of those serving in the armed forces in the two world wars, for the Board of Agriculture (up to 1903), the Board of Agriculture and Fisheries (1903–1919), and the Ministry of Agriculture and Fisheries.

Another possibility, for nineteenth century departments, would be to explore the Parliamentary Papers, which contain annual reports from the various branches of the civil service, and also include many reports on aspects of its work. These may give you details of the work actually done, as well as establishment lists. There is a full set available on microfiche: from the indexes it is not clear if some of the returns are statistical, or if they contain personal information of some kind. If you do find useful lists as a result of exploring the Parliamentary Papers, please could you inform the staff at the Research Enquiries Desk, so that the information can be shared.

Other possible sources outside the particular department's own records may be among the records of the Treasury (e.g. the Departmental Accounts in T 38), the pension records of the Paymaster General (PMG 27 and PMG 28), and the records of the Civil Service Commission, although details given there are mostly to do with passing the qualifying examination (CSC 8 and CSC 10). One useful class of Civil Service Commission records, which used to be at the PRO but is now kept by the Society of Genealogists, is CSC 1, the evidences of age submitted by candidates for appointment between 1855 and 1880.

24.8 Customs officers and Excise men

In contrast to other civil servants, there is a fair amount of material for the employees of the two separate Boards of Customs and Excise. Customs officers were responsible for collecting duty on imports, and preventing smuggling, and excise men were responsible for collecting taxes levied on home products. For indexed directories of customs officers, excise men and other tax officials, 1875–1930, see *Ham's Customs Year Book* and *Ham's Inland Revenue Year Book*, in the PRO Library.

Warrants for the appointment of Customs officers, 1714–1797, are in C 208, indexed by C 202/267–269. The Customs Board minute books, in CUST 28, contain information on the first and later postings of Customs officers, with details of any praise or censure: they contain no family details, but they can be used to work out the details of a man's career. For Ireland, there are registers of officers' appointments, 1761–1823, in CUST 20/154–159.

For the Customs, there are pay lists and staff lists, arranged by place, in PRO 30/32/15–29 (1673–1689), CUST 18 (1675–1813), CUST 19 (1814–1829), CUST 39 (1671–1922) and T 42 (1716–1847). There is a separate series for Scotland, 1714–1829, in T 43. Similar records for Ireland (but also including some Excise men), 1684–1826, are in CUST 20. However, in general these give little personal detail, although very occasionally details of marriage might be given.

Some family details can be found in the pension records in CUST 39/145–151, which cover 1803 to 1922: these are closed for 75 years from the date of the record. For Ireland, there are pension records covering 1785–1851 in CUST 39/161. The most useful for family historians are, as always, the sections relating to widows' pensions, which give details of any children. Applications for pensions can be found in T 1, using the indexes in T 2 and T 108. Other family details can be found among the correspondence of the individual ports ('outports' in the Customs service) with the Customs Board.

Many of the sources for tracing Excise men are similar to the Customs records. There are pay lists for the English Excise, 1705–1835 (T 44) and the Scottish Excise, 1708–1832 (T 45). The Excise Board minute books, 1695–1867 (CUST 47), contain the same kinds of information as those of the Customs Board, as do the Excise pension records, 1856–1922 (CUST 39/157–159).

However, there are also the Excise Entry Papers, 1820–1870 (CUST 116). There is an alphabetical index to these. The Entry Papers usually consist of two letters, folded together. The first is a letter of recommendation, giving the name of the applicant, his age, place of birth, marital status (but no details of his wife), and a character reference. The second letter is from the Excise officer responsible for the applicant's training: this states whether he is proficient in writing, spelling and arithmetic.

Records relating to the Irish Excise men, 1824–1833, and the Irish Revenue Police, 1830–1857, are in CUST 110 and CUST 111. For later brief details, see *Ham's Customs Year Book* and *Ham's Inland Revenue Year Book*, in the PRO Library.

24.9 Crown servants: office-holders and civil servants: bibliography

The British Imperial Calendar (London, 1810–1972)
Colonial Office List (London, annually from 1862)
Court & City Register (London, 1742–1808)
Foreign Office List (London, annually from 1852)
E B Fryde, ed., *Handbook of British Chronology* (London, 3rd edn, 1986) (Lists monarchs, officers of
    state, archbishops and bishops, dukes, marquesses and earls, in chronological sequence)
C J Given-Wilson, *The Royal Household and the King's Affinity: Service, Politics and Finance in England,
    1360–1413* (New Haven, Conn., and London, 1986)
Ham's Customs Year Book (annual: PRO library has 1875–1930)
Ham's Inland Revenue Year Book (annual: PRO library has 1875–1930)
W R Jones, 'The Court of the Verge', *Journal of British Studies*, vol. X (1970)
Kelly's Handbook to the Titled, Landed and Official Classes (annual: PRO Library has 1883–197 *Royal
    Kalendar* (London, 1746–1849)
J C Sainty and others, *Office Holders in Modern Britain* (London, 1972–1998) This so far comprises:

I	*Treasury Officials 1660–1870*	J C Sainty	1972
II	*Officials of the Secretaries of State 1660–1782*	J C Sainty	1973
III	*Officials of the Boards of Trade 1660–1782*	J C Sainty	1974
IV	*Admiralty Officials 1660–1870*	J C Sainty	1975
V	*Home Office Officials 1782–1870*	J C Sainty	1975
VI	*Colonial Office Officials 1794–1870*	J C Sainty	1976
VII	*Navy Board Officials 1660–1832*	J M Collinge	1978
VIII	*Foreign Office Officials 1782–1870*	J M Collinge	1979
IX	*Officials of Royal Commissions of Enquiry 1815–1870*	J M Collinge	1984

X	*Officials of Royal Commissions of Enquiry 1870–1939*	E Harrison	1995
XI	*Officials of the Royal Household 1660– 1837: Department of the Lord Chamberlain and associated offices*	J C Sainty and R O Bucholz	1997
XII	*Officials of the Royal Household 1660– 1837: Department of the Lord Steward and the Master of the Horse*	J C Sainty and R O Bucholz	1998

G Smith, *Something to Declare! 1,000 years of Customs and Excise* (London, 1980)
D Starkey, ed., *The English Court from the Wars of the Roses to the Civil War* (London, 1987)

25 Merchant seamen

25.1 Introduction

The records relating to merchant seamen have been fully examined in a specialist guide, by Smith, Watts and Watts, *Records of Merchant Shipping and Seamen*: try this, if you find you want more detail. The Society of Genealogists has an extensive collection on merchant seamen, see Hailey, *Maritime Sources in the Library of the Society of Genealogists*. The collection includes copies of the petitions to Trinity House requesting charitable support, 1787–1854: the originals are at the Guildhall.

25.2 Looking for merchant seamen before 1835

For the period 1710–1811 there was a general tax on apprenticeship indentures (see **27**). The Apprenticeship Books (IR 1) and associated modern indexes, 1710–1774 (IR 17), do contain references to seamen both as apprentices and as masters. A register of apprentices from all over England, bound to fishermen in the south-east, survives for 1639–1664 (HCA 30/897). A list of children apprenticed to the sea from Christ's Hospital, 1766, survives in T 64/311. For the port of Colchester, there is a register of seamen's indentures covering 1704–1757, and 1804–1844 (BT 167/103).

Although some crew lists of merchant vessels do survive from as early as 1747, there are no systematic records of merchant seamen before 1835. Before then, you have to work out where the path of a seaman crosses with officialdom, which may incidentally provide some details of his activities. The records most likely to reveal such information relate to trade, taxation, legal disputes and the Royal Navy. Such material, by its very nature, will contain many more references to the masters of ships than to the ordinary seamen who sailed in them. The chances of finding information on a particular sailor are very slim. However before embarking on a search, you should consult the specialist guide on the topic, *Records of Merchant Shipping and Seamen* by Smith, Watts and Watts. For a general history, see Earle, *Sailors: English Merchant Seamen 1650–1775*.

The classes which may yield useful information include Port Books, 1565–1798 (E 190);

Board of Trade and Naval Officers' Shipping Returns, c.1678–1867; various CO classes, BT 6, HO 76, T 1 and T 64); records of the High Court of Admiralty, 1519–1943 (HCA 15–HCA 20, HCA 24, HCA 27 and HCA 30–HCA 31); records of the High Court of Delegates, 1536–1866 (DEL 1, DEL 2, DEL 7–DEL 11); Registers of Protection from being Pressed, 1702–1828 (in ADM 7); Letters of Marque, 1549–1834 (ADM 7/317–332, DEL 2, HCA 25, HCA 26 and PC 5); Registers of Passes, 1683–1845 (ADM 7/73–164) and the Receiver of Sixpences Accounts for the Thames, 1725–1830 (ADM 68/194–219) and the port of Exeter, 1800–1851 (BT 167/38–40).

25.3 Registration of seamen, 1835–1857

The Merchant Shipping Act 1835 ordered the registration of merchant seamen (with the aim of creating a reserve for manning the Royal Navy in time of war). Registers of seamen, and associated indexes, were created and information was entered in them from crew lists, the filing of which was also required by the same Act (see **25.7**). This form of registration of seamen lasted from 1835 to 1857.

There are three series of Registers of Seamen which were compiled directly from the crew lists. In addition there is a Register of Seamen's Tickets (1845–1854) which contains personal information, supplied by each seaman on applying for his register ticket, as well as that culled from the crew lists. All these registers give the seamen's age and place of birth and contain cross-references to the crew lists (see **25.7**).

The first (BT 120) consists of alphabetically arranged entries, 1835–1836. The second series (BT 112) covers 1835 to 1844: it is organized into two sections, one of which is roughly alphabetical, with the other being separately indexed (BT 119). In 1845 the ticket system, which lasted until October 1853, was introduced; these registers (BT 113) give date and place of birth as well as a physical description. Coastguards and Royal Navy, as well as merchant seamen, were often issued with a register ticket. The registers are arranged in order of ticket number to which there is a name index in BT 114. The last series (BT 116), which started in 1853 after the ticket system was abolished, lists seamen alphabetically. All these classes are seen on microfilm. See also **25.7**, on agreeemts and crew lists.

25.4 No registration of seamen, 1857–1913

Registration of seamen was abandoned in 1857 and, until its reintroduction in 1913, there is no easy way to discover the career of a merchant seaman, although crew lists do continue to be kept throughout this period. The Royal Naval Reserve, which was established in 1859, was officered and manned by merchant seamen, and there are some service records: see **19.18**. The Modern Records Centre at the University of Warwick has some National Union of Seamen material: the address is given at **48**.

25.5 Registration of seamen, after 1913

The Central Index Register (sometimes referred to as the Fourth Register of Seamen) was started in October 1913 and was maintained until 1941. It is believed that CR 1 and CR 2 index cards for

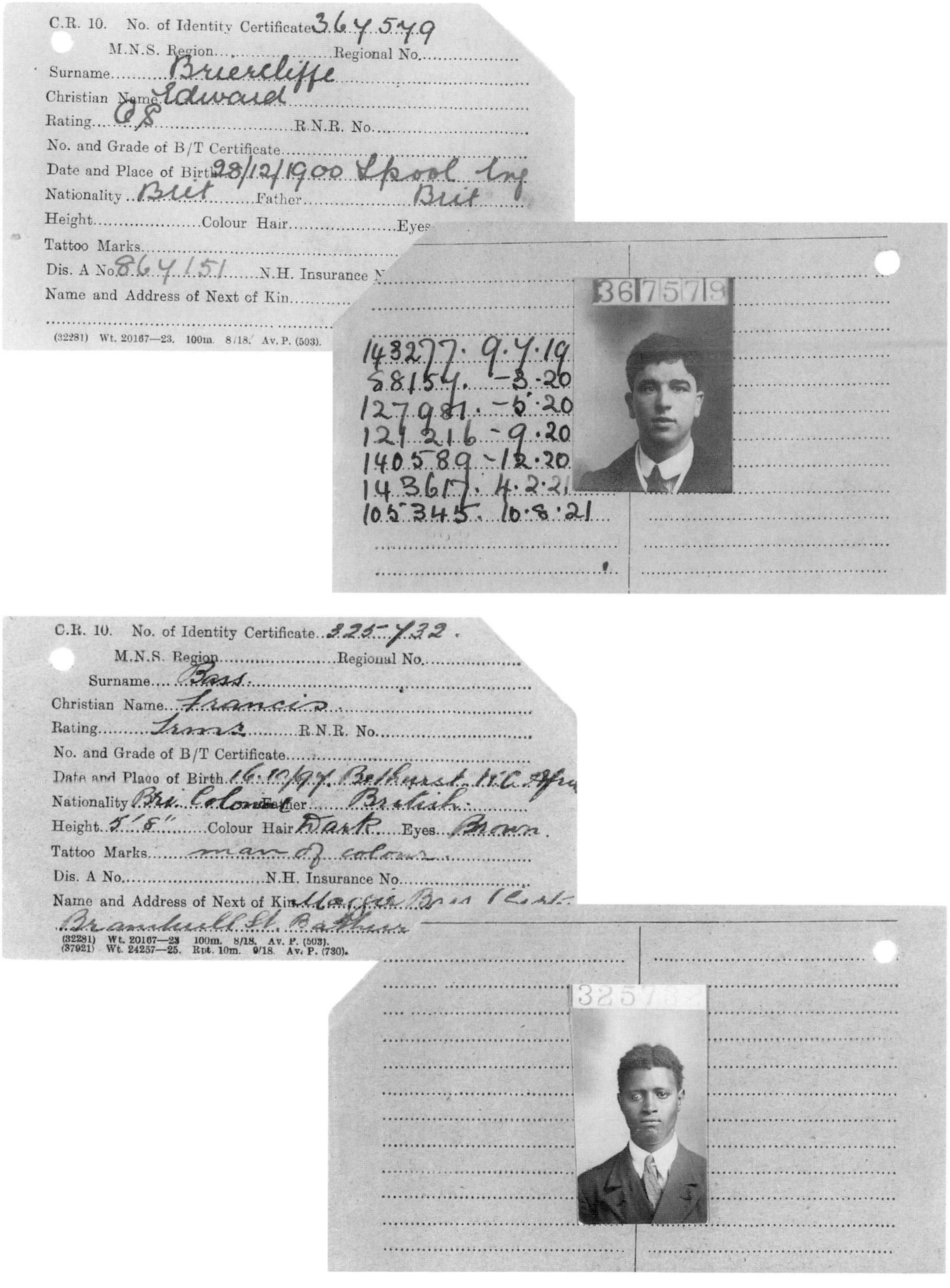
C.R. 10. No. of Identity Certificate 364579
M.N.S. Region.................Regional No.................
Surname Briercliffe
Christian Name Edward
Rating OS R.N.R. No.................
No. and Grade of B/T Certificate.................
Date and Place of Birth 28/12/1900 Lpool Eng
Nationality Brit Father Brit
Height.................Colour Hair.................Eyes
Tattoo Marks.................
Dis. A No. 864151 N.H. Insurance No.
Name and Address of Next of Kin.................
(32281) Wt. 20167—23. 100m. 8/18. Av. P. (503).

367579
143277. 9.7.19
58154. -3.20
127981. -5.20
121216 -9.20
140589 -12.20
143617. 4.2.21
105345. 10.8.21

C.R. 10. No. of Identity Certificate 325732
M.N.S. Region.................Regional No.................
Surname Bass
Christian Name Francis
Rating Trmr R.N.R. No.................
No. and Grade of B/T Certificate.................
Date and Place of Birth 16.10/97 Bathurst W.C. Afr
Nationality Bri. Colonial Father British
Height 5' 8" Colour Hair Dark Eyes Brown
Tattoo Marks man of colour
Dis. A No.................N.H. Insurance No.................
Name and Address of Next of Kin
(32281) Wt. 20167—23 100m. 8/18. Av. P. (503).
(37921) Wt. 24257—25. Rpt. 10m. 9/18. Av. P. (730).

Figure 12 Two merchant seaman's cards from the CR 10 series in BT 350. The amount of information given can vary quite considerably.

the period 1913 to 1920 were destroyed in 1969, although there is also a special index surviving covering the period 1913–1921 (CR 10 cards). About 1.25 million cards survive.

The Register consists of four large card indexes, seen on microfiche. The CR 1 cards, 1921–1941 (BT 349), provide the starting point for a search as they are arranged alphabetically by surname. They record place and date of birth, discharge number, rating, and a short description of the seaman; some of these cards also have a photograph of the seaman. The CR 2 cards, 1921–1941 (BT 348), are arranged numerically by discharge number and include a brief record of the ships on which the seaman served (by ship's number) and the dates of his signing on. The CR 10 cards, 1918–1921 (BT 350), form a special index (and, as well as including similar information to the CR 1 cards, bear a photograph of the seaman. This index, made by a 1918 Order under the Defence of the Realm Act, seems to have been intended to record the issue of seamen's identity certificates. The fourth index (BT 364) is believed to have been compiled, for reasons that are unclear, by extracting cards from the other three indexes. It is arranged numerically, with the CR 1 card leading, and there are usually three cards (CR 1, CR 2 and CR 10) for each seaman.

In 1941 the Essential Work (Merchant Navy) Order created a Merchant Navy Reserve Pool. All those who had served at sea during the previous five years were required to register and a new Central Register of Seamen (sometimes referred to as the Fifth Register of Seamen) was established. CR 1 and CR 2 cards of seamen who were still serving in 1941 were removed from the old Central Index Register, and placed in the new Central Register of Seamen which was maintained until 1972. This Fifth Register, and the current, Sixth Register, called the 'UK Register' and dating from 1973, is kept by the Registry of Shipping and Seamen, which offers a paid search service (address in **48**).

25.6 Musters, 1747–1835

From 1747, the masters or owners of merchant ships had to keep muster rolls for each voyage, containing the names of officers and seamen employed on the ship, their usual place of abode, dates of engagement and discharge, and the name of the ship in which they last sailed (BT 98): there are no indexes. The only surviving rolls from before 1800 came from Shields, Dartmouth, Liverpool and Plymouth. Some strays also survive for Plymouth, 1776–1780 (CUST 66/227) and Scarborough, 1747–1765 (CUST 91/111–112).

25.7 Using agreements and crew lists, 1835–1857

In 1835 a new system of crew lists and agreements was introduced, by the Merchant Shipping Act 1835: records are in BT 98. Masters of any ships belonging to UK subjects undertaking a foreign voyage, and masters of any British registered ships of 80 tons or more employed in the coastal trade or the fisheries, had to enter into a written agreement with every seaman on conditions of service. On return to the home port, the master of a foreign trade vessel had to deliver a list of the crew and the original agreements to the Registrar General of Shipping and Seamen. Documents for home trade vessels were delivered half-yearly at the end of June or December. Before 1857 these are arranged alphabetically by ships' names within port of registry; from 1857 they are arranged by the ship's official number. To find the official number, use *Lloyds Register of Shipping*, or the *Mercantile Navy List*; there are only incomplete sets of *Lloyds Register* and the

Mercantile Navy List at Kew, but there are full sets at the Guildhall Library (address in **48**).

The crew lists in BT 98 should provide name, age, place of birth, quality (i.e. rank), previous ship, date and place of joining, and time and date of death or leaving the ship. The crew lists are arranged by the year in which they were handed in. This should be the *end* of the voyage for foreign trade voyages and, for home trade voyages, at the end of June or December of the appropriate year.

If you want to trace an individual seaman in the crew lists, you must first refer to the appropriate seamen's register (see **25.3**) to get the ship's port of registration and name. Between 1835 and 1844, make a note of the number of the port and the name of the ship given in the register entry (ignore the port rotation number): there is a key to the port numbers in the class list for BT 98, and the crew lists are arranged by port of registry of the ship and then by ships' names.

Between 1845 and 1854, you will still need to start with the appropriate seamen's register, but the procedure is more complicated and differs for foreign and home trade. A full explanation is given in Smith, Watts and Watts, *Records of Merchant Shipping and Seamen*. The key feature is that, at this period, ships' names are not given, only the port number and a port rotation number, to which there is no key. Crew lists are organized annually (in BT 98) according to port of registry and ships' names, not port rotation numbers. Also, during this period, it is known that not all details of voyages were actually entered into the registers: those for 1849, 1850 and 1852–1854 appear never to have been entered at all even though the crew lists do survive.

From 1853 to 1857, details of voyages are to be found in the appropriate seamen's register, but now ships' names and port of registry are given, so the crew list should be readily located in BT 98 where they are arranged by year, port of registry and ship's name.

After 1857 you can no longer go through the seamen's registers to use the crew lists in BT 98, which thenceforth were arranged each year by ships' official numbers: these numbers can be found by consulting the *Mercantile Navy List* or *Lloyds Register of Shipping*. Since there is no longer an index of seamen indicating which ship they were on, it can take a great deal of hard work and good luck to trace individual seamen through the crew lists.

25.8 Logs, from 1850

The Mercantile Marine Act of 1850 required masters to keep a ship's Official Log recording illnesses, births and deaths on board, misconduct, desertion and punishment, and a description of each man's conduct. They were to be deposited after each foreign voyage, or half-yearly for home trade ships. They begin to appear amongst the records from 1852 onwards, though many have been destroyed; usually only those recording a birth or death have survived. Except for the period 1902–1919, where there is a separate class (BT 165), they are to be found with the agreements and crew lists in BT 98.

25.9 Current location of agreements, crew lists and log books, from 1861

From 1861 only a 10 per cent random sample of agreements, crew lists, and log books (which were generally filed together with the crew lists) are preserved at the PRO. Many have been preserved at other archives. The Registry of Shipping and Seamen (address in **48**) holds all crew lists 1939–1950, and from 1990 onwards. The PRO holds 10 per cent of all crew lists 1861–1938 and 1951–1980; these are to be found in BT 99, BT 100, BT 144 and BT 165. A 10 per cent sample of those for 1981–1989 is in the process of being transferred.

The National Maritime Museum (NMM; address in **48**) holds the remaining 90 per cent of crew lists for the years 1861, 1862 and all years ending in a 5 (except 1945). No handlist is available of these holdings. Those for 1975 and 1985 have not been arranged, and so access to them is restricted. Various county record offices, libraries and other repositories hold those crew lists not at the PRO or NMM, for the period 1863–1912. The Maritime History Archive (MHA), Memorial University of Newfoundland (address in **48**) took those crew lists not taken by any other institution for the years between 1863 and 1972, and offers a copying and research service, for a fee, in the material held by them. The MHA has published guides to their holdings and those of local repositories in the UK; copies of all these are available at Kew. After 1972 only the 10 per cent sample of agreements and crew lists held by the PRO have been preserved (with the exception of 90 per cent of those for 1975 and 1985 at the National Maritime Museum); the rest of these records, up to 1989, have been destroyed.

25.10 Certificates of competency and service: masters, mates and engineers

By an order of 1845, the Board of Trade authorized a system of voluntary examinations of competency for men intending to become masters or mates of foreign-going and home-trade British merchant ships (BT 143/1). Certificates for masters and mates gradually became compulsory and could be obtained by proving long service (service) or by examination (competency); details are to be found, up to 1921, in BT 122–BT 127. From 1862 there are also certificates for engineers (BT 139–BT 142), and from 1883 for skippers and mates of fishing boats (BT 129, BT 130, BT 138). Colonial certificates were entered separately (BT 128, BT 140). All series are well indexed. The certificate registers give name, place and year of birth, date and place of issue of the certificate, and rank examined or served in. Deaths, injuries and retirements have often been noted. The registers record details of the ships served in, and this may be followed up in the crew lists, in a similar way to that described above for ordinary seamen. Applications for certificates, for those issued in the UK up to number 103,000 are preserved at the National Maritime Museum; later applications are believed not to have survived.

From 1910, a combined index to masters, mates, engineers and skippers and mates of fishing boats was started to replace those formerly kept in registers (BT 127, BT 138 and BT 141). The term 'index' for this collection is a slight misnomer in that it is not an index to any other records; in effect it replaced the earlier registers and indexes and became a self-indexing register. It was kept in card form covering the period 1910 to 1930, covering home and foreign trade and each card gives: name, date and place of birth, certificate number, rating date of passing, port of examination. The index will become available, in due course, as class BT 352, but until it arrives at the PRO it is unavailable for consultation.

25.11 Merchant seamen: apprenticeships, 1824–1953

For apprenticeships before 1824, see **25.2**.

There are indexes of apprentices registered in the merchant fleet between 1824 and 1953 (BT 150). The earlier volumes give name, age, date and term of indenture and the name of the master:

entries in later volumes include the port where the apprentice signed on and the ship's name. In addition, specimens of copy indentures, taken at five-yearly intervals, are preserved in the Apprentices' Indentures, 1845–1950 (BT 151) and the Apprentices' Indentures for Fishing, 1895–1935 (BT 152).

Some later registers may survive amongst the Customs records, e.g. that for Scarborough (1884–1894) is in CUST 91/121 and it is possible that others may also be found.

25.12 Merchant seamen: births, marriages and deaths at sea, and wills

For births, marriages and deaths at sea, see **4.7–4.11** and **4.14**.

There are many wills of merchant seamen from the late seventeenth century to 1857 among the records of the Commissary Court of London (London Division) at the Guildhall Library (address in **48**).

25.13 Medals for gallantry at sea

Records of medals awarded for saving lives at sea, 1839–1882, are in FO 83/769. The Albert Medal was awarded for gallantry at sea: the medal register, 1866–1913 (BT 97), also includes awards to sailors in the Royal Navy until 1891. Records of other awards for gallantry at sea, 1856–1981, are in BT 261.

25.14 Merchant seamen: bibliography

N G Cox, 'The Records of the Registrar General of Shipping and Seamen', *Maritime History*, vol. II, pp. 168–188

P Earle, *Sailors: English Merchant Seamen 1650–1725* (London, 1998)

Guide to the Agreements and Crew Lists: Series II (BT 99), 1863–1912 (in three volumes) at the Memorial University of Newfoundland

Guide to the Agreements and Crew Lists: Series II (BT 99), 1913–1938 at the Memorial University of Newfoundland

A Guide to the Crew Agreements and Official Logbooks, 1863–1913, held at the County Record Offices of the British Isles, published by the Maritime History Archive, Memorial University of Newfoundland

J Hailey, *Maritime Sources in the Library of the Society of Genealogists* (Society of Genealogists, 1997)

Index to Crew Lists, Agreements and Official Logs at the Memorial University of Newfoundland, microfiche

Lloyds Register of Shipping (London, annually from 1764)

K Matthews, 'Crew Lists, Agreements and Official Logs of the British Empire 1863–1913, now in possession of the Maritime History Group, Memorial University', *Business History*, vol. XVI, pp. 78–80

Mercantile Navy List (London, annually from 1857)

K Smith, C T Watts and M J Watts, *Records of Merchant Shipping and Seamen* (PRO, 1998)

C T Watts and M J Watts, 'Unravelling Merchant Seamen's Records', *Genealogists' Magazine*, vol. XIX, pp. 313–321

C T Watts and M J Watts, *My Ancestor was a Merchant Seaman* (Society of Genealogists, 1986)

26 Railway workers

26.1 Railway staff records

The records of the nationalized railway companies, together with those of the canal, dock and shipping companies owned by them, were collected by the British Transport Historical Commission, and were formerly housed in London, York and Edinburgh. The Edinburgh collection has now gone to the Scottish Record Office, and the York and London collections have come to the PRO. However, some York records are at York, and some Scottish ones are at the PRO.

The core of the PRO collection is formed by the extensive records of the Great Western Railway, but the records of several hundred railway, canal and dock companies have also ended up at Kew. Other railway company records may be in local record offices. Read *Railway Ancestors*, by Hawkings, for detailed advice, and for lists (for each company) of the surviving records which may be useful for family historians, and their current location.

Comprehensive staff records have survived from relatively few railway companies, and there are no union indexes to the names of employees. You need to know the name of the railway company for which your man worked. Staff records of a kind exist, and those companies whose staff records are in the PRO are listed in **26.3**. Some staff records give only names, wages and positions, others may give a full record of service. For examples, see Hawkings, *Railway Ancestors*. For details of staff involved in law cases and arbitration, 1845–1947, see RAIL 1027/1–530.

Before ordering some of these staff records, you may have to sign an undertaking to respect the confidentiality of any personally sensitive information.

The covering dates given in **26.3** and in the lists themselves can be very misleading. For example, the dates given in the list for RAIL 426/14 are 1923–1937: in fact, the documents are history sheets for clerical staff retiring between 1923 and 1937, so the information in them actually goes back into the nineteenth century.

Another possible source of information on individuals may be the large collection of railway periodicals and staff magazines, kept under the lettercode ZPER. The company magazine may include articles on retiring employees.

Railway staff were sometimes sent abroad to undertake construction work on railways where there was a British interest (usually financial). Records relating to these railwaymen are scarce. The best place to look would be among the records of the Foreign Office or Colonial Office (see **13.3–13.4**).

26.2 Railway police

Some records for the railway police of the various railway companies are amongst the railway staff records in the PRO. For a detailed list, on a company by company basis, ask at the Research Enquiries Desk for Source Sheet 13. Information about the numbers and organization of the railway police c.1900 can be found in RAIL 527/1036. The occasional reference to 'Police Department' in the railway staff records often relates to other staff such as signalmen, etc.

26.3 Staff records at the PRO, arranged by name of railway company

Barry Railway Company	1886–1922	RAIL 23/46–60, 64–65
Birkenhead Railway Company	1852–1925	RAIL 35/24/5, 33–35, 45–46, 48, 51
Bodmin and Wadebridge Railway Company	1863–1884	RAIL 57/19
Brecon and Merthyr Tydfil Junction Railway Company	1880–1922	RAIL 65/31–35
Cambrian Railways Company	1898–1944	RAIL 92/142–148
Cardiff Railway Company	1869–1923	RAIL 97/32–43
Carmarthen and Cardigan Railway Company	1865–1875	RAIL 99/57–60
Chester and Holyhead Railway Company	1862	RAIL 113/53
Cleator and Workington Junction Railway Company	1879–1923	RAIL 119/13
Cornwall Railway Company	1889	RAIL 134/149
Darlington and Barnard Castle Railway Company	1856	RAIL 149/27
East Lincolnshire Railway Company	1848–1850	RAIL 177/21
Furness Railway Company	1852–1922	RAIL 214/97–104
Great Central Railway Company	1857–1949	RAIL 226/192–235, 637
Great Eastern Railway Company	1855–1930	RAIL 227/445–490, 514–535, 540–553
Great Northern Railway Company	1848–1943	RAIL 236/727–745
Great Western and Midland Railway Companies Joint Committee	1865–1915	RAIL 241/28
Great Western Railway Collection	1740–1967	RAIL 1014/22–27, 33, 36–37, 48–49
Great Western Railway Company (Staff Records)	1835–1954	RAIL 264/1–470
Great Western Railway Company (Correspondence and Papers)	1849–1888	RAIL 257/6–8
Great Western Railway Company (Miscellaneous Books and Records)	1933	RAIL 253/454
Great Western Railway Company (Registers of Accidents and Related Records)	1842–1939	RAIL 270/1–30
Hull and Barnsley Railway Company	1885–1927	RAIL 312/77–81
Hull and Selby Railway Company	1845–1875	RAIL 315/30
Isle of Wight Central Railway Company	1860–1963	RAIL 328/16–18
Lancashire and Yorkshire and Great Northern Joint Stations Committee	[1907?]	RAIL 341/7
Lancashire and Yorkshire Railway Company	1853–1941	RAIL 343/725, 748, 750, 827–845
Lancashire, Derbyshire and East Coast Railway Company	1904–1906	RAIL 344/56
Leeds Northern Railway Company	1847–1858	RAIL 357/29, 33, 39–40

Liverpool and Manchester Railway Company	1845	RAIL 371/22–3
London and Birmingham Railway Company	1833–1847	RAIL 384/126, 284–291
London and North Eastern Railway Company (Staff Records)	1920–1963	RAIL 397/1–13
London and North Eastern Railway Company (Minutes and Reports)	1932–1947	RAIL 390/897, 992, 1107, 1177, 1201–1202, 1206, 1214, 1220, 1226, 1236–1238, 1243, 1247, 1262, 1264, 1280, 1289, 1294, 1577
London and North Eastern Railway Company (Miscellaneous Books and Records)	1897–1927	RAIL 393/225–226
London and North Western and Furness Railways Joint Committees	1899–1906	RAIL 403/7
London and North Western and Great Western Railway Companies Joint Committee	1871–1897	RAIL 404/177–180
London and North Western and Lancashire and Yorkshire Railways Joint Committee	1861–1913	RAIL 405/43–44
London and North Western and Midland Railway Companies Joint Committee	1861–1911	RAIL 406/16
London and North Western Railway Company	1831–1927	RAIL 410/1217–1219, 1797–1986, 1267–1268, 1270–1271, 1402, 2212–2222
London and South Western Railway Company	1838–1944	RAIL 411/483–537, 665–667, 673
London, Brighton and South Coast Railway Company	1837–1925	RAIL 414/600–611, 630, 636, 750–796, 863–873
London, Chatham and Dover Railway Company, formerly the East Kent Railway Company	c.1859–1910	RAIL 415/ 104, 108–111, 173
London, Midland and Scottish Railway Collection	1869, 1910	RAIL 1015/8
London Midland and Scottish Railway Company (Staff Records)	1923–1946	RAIL 426/1–15
London Midland and Scottish Railway Company (Miscellaneous Books and Records)	1923–1947	RAIL 421/13
London Midland and Scottish and London and North Eastern Railway Companies Joint Committee	1891–1938	RAIL 417/16
London, Tilbury and Southend Company	1871–1923	RAIL 437/44–57
Manchester, Sheffield and Lincolnshire Railway	1847–1926	RAIL 463/174, 176–177, 210–250, 305–315
Manchester South Junction and Altrincham Railway Company	1905–1908	RAIL 465/55–56
Maryport and Carlisle Railway Company	1861–1912	RAIL 472/51
Mersey Railway Company	1885–1907	RAIL 475/41
Midland and Great Northern Railways Joint Committee	1879–1893	RAIL 487/78–80, 115

Midland and South Western Junction Railway Company	1891–1921	RAIL 489/21
Midland Railway Company	1864–1924	RAIL 491/969–1081, 1259
Neath and Brecon Railway Company	1903–1921	RAIL 505/13
Newcastle upon Tyne and Carlisle Railway Company	1845–1848	RAIL 509/96
North and South Western Junction Railway	1883–1916	RAIL 521/19
North Eastern Railway Company	1843–1957	RAIL 527/974, 977, 1043–4, 1049, 1058, 1092, 1895–1965, 2272–2277
North London Railway Company	1854–1920	RAIL 529/130–138
North Staffordshire Railway Company	1847–1923	RAIL 532/58–67
North Sunderland Railway Company	1893–1948	RAIL 533/75–76
North Union Railway Company	1841–1856	RAIL 534/29
Otley and Ilkley Joint Line Committee (Midland and North Eastern Railway Companies)	1865–1901	RAIL 554/24–25
Port Talbot Railway and Docks Company	1883–1918	RAIL 574/13
Rhondda and Swansea Bay Railway Company	1882–1922	RAIL 581/36–37
Rhymney Railway Company	1860–1922	RAIL 583/41–65
Sheffield District Railway Company	1897–1916	RAIL 611/25–26
Shropshire Union Railways and Canal Company	1844–1897	RAIL 623/66–68
Somerset and Dorset Railway Company	1863–1877	RAIL 627/6
Somerset and Dorset Joint Line Committee	1877–1928	RAIL 626/44–53
South Eastern Railway Company	1845–1944	RAIL 635/196, 206, 302–310, 399
South Eastern and Chatham Railway Companies Managing Committee	1850–1944	RAIL 633/343–382, 440–450
South Wales Railway Company	1844–1864	RAIL 640/30, 45, 47, 52, 55–56
Southern Railway Collection	1824–1963	RAIL 1017/2
Southern Railway Company (Staff Records)	1923–1957	RAIL 651/1–10
Southern Railway Company (Locomotive and Rolling Stock Records	1930–1942	RAIL 649/59
Stockton and Darlington Railway Company	1835–1856	RAIL 667/1283–1291
Stratford upon Avon and Midland Junction Railway Company	1873–1923	RAIL 674/11
Taff Vale Railway Company	1890–1924	RAIL 684/94–120
Trent Valley Railway Company	1845–1946	RAIL 699/5
Wirral Railway Company	1884–1926	RAIL 756/10–11
York and North Midland Railway Company	1848, 1843–1850	RAIL 770/77–81
York, Newcastle and Berwick Railway Company	1845	RAIL 772/106

26.4 Railway workers: bibliography and sources

Published works

H V Borley, *Chronology of London Railways* (Railway & Canal Historical Society, 1982)
E Carter, *An Historical Geography of the Railways of the British Isles* (Cassell, 1959)
F Hardy, 'Railway Records for Family Historians', *Genealogists Magazine*, vol. XXIII, pp. 256–260
D Hawkings, *Railway Ancestors* (1995)
T Richards, *Was Your Grandfather a Railwayman?* (FFHS, 2nd edn, 1989)
ZPER, *British Transport Historical Collection Library*, at Kew. For railway periodicals with this lettercode, see the *PRO Guide*, Part 2 under ZPER.

Unpublished finding aids

Card index of subjects to British Transport Historical Commission Records

27 Apprentices

27.1 Civilian apprenticeships

Apprentices were traditionally bound by indentures to serve their master for the space of seven years: the master was equally bound to teach the apprentice his trade. In the early years of the system, it was policed by the guilds, to which the master had to belong. Later apprenticeships were not necessarily with guild members, but they were still established by means of the legally enforceable indentures. The training of working people was not usually a matter of public record and the actual indentures of apprenticeship were private documents. If they survive at all they will normally be in private hands. There is the Crisp collection of about 1,500 indentures, from the seventeenth to nineteenth centuries, at the Society of Genealogists. Many records of apprenticeship survive with guild, London livery company (at the Guildhall Library) or parish records. Some local history societies have published apprenticeship registers.

Between 1710 and 1804, however, apprenticeship indentures were subject to tax and the records relating to this tax are in IR 1, with indexes in IR 17. The records continue until 1811, as the tax could be paid up to one year after the completion of the apprenticeship. As a general rule, you may need to search the records of several years' payments in order to find a particular entry, even when the date of the indenture is known. Duty was payable by the master at the rate of 6d for every £1 under £50 which he received for taking on the apprentice, and 1s for every £1 above that sum.

These Apprenticeship Books record the names, addresses and trades of the masters, the names of the apprentices and dates of their indentures. Until 1752 the names of apprentices' parents are given, but rarely after that year. There are indexes of masters' names from 1710 to 1762, and of apprentices' names from 1710 to 1774. These were made on behalf of the Society of Genealogists and copied from their originals in the Guildhall Library, London. Where the stamp duty was paid in London, entries will be found in the 'City' registers in this series; where it was paid elsewhere, entries will be found in the 'Country' registers.

Beware – masters did not have to pay stamp duty for apprentices taken on at the common or public charge of any township or parish, or by or out of any public charity (8 Anne, c.5, s.59). This means that very many apprentices were never subject to the duty, and are therefore not mentioned in the registers. In such cases, local or charity records, if they survive, are likely to be the only source of information on individuals – for example, the Foundling Hospital apprenticeship registers at the London Metropolitan Archives (address in **48**). The PRO has records of the apprenticeship of children from the Royal Naval Asylum, Greenwich, and the Duke of York's Military School, Chelsea: see **19.17** and **18.25** respectively. London livery companies often kept full records of membership, which give places of birth, previous residences and other details. For these, apply to the Guildhall Library. For Royal Navy and merchant seamen apprenticeships, see sections **19.17** and **25.11**. Among the War Office records there is a list of apprentices who enlisted in the Army but had to return to their masters until their indentures expired, 1806 to 1835 (WO 25/2962).

For apprenticeship lists from the Stationers' Company, 1701 to 1800, check the *Biography Database 1680–1830* in the PRO Library.

27.2 Apprentices: bibliography

Biography Database 1680–1830 (Newcastle, 1998 ongoing)
I Maxted, *The British Book Trades, 1710–1777: an index of Master's and Apprentices' Records in the Inland Revenue Registers at the PRO, Kew* (Exeter, 1983)
Public Record Office, *Alphabetical Guide to War Office & Other Material* (Lists and Indexes, vol. LIII)
W B Stephens, *Sources for English Local History* (Manchester, 2nd edn, 1981)
University of Warwick, *Trade Union and Related Records* (Coventry, 1988)

28 Lawyers

28.1 Lawyers: printed sources

The published *Law Lists*, produced annually from 1775, are the easiest place to start. There is a set running from 1799–1976 in the PRO, and the Guildhall Library also has a good, but incomplete, set, including *Law Lists* for 1787 and 1795. However, they can be difficult to use effectively. Between 1775 and 1789, they contain the names of some men never actually admitted to a court, whereas from 1790 they only give the names of those who had taken out the annual certificate to practise that year. Until 1861 they do not give the date of admission. The entries also give the name of the firm for which the solicitor/attorney worked, together with an indication of its address. Lists of attorneys and solicitors admitted in 1729 and 1730 were printed for presentation to Parliament: a copy is available at the PRO.

For a guide to printed and records sources, consult Holborn's *Sources of Biographical Information on Past Lawyers*.

28.2 Judges and serjeants-at-law

The PRO does hold some records of the appointment of judges and of the creation of serjeants-at-law (who had the monopoly of pleading in the court of Common Pleas until 1846, and from whom, for several centuries, the judges were selected). However, these are widely scattered and not very informative. As there is a great deal of biographical information in print on the judges and the serjeants-at-law, you would be well advised to investigate the published sources first: the main ones are listed in **28.8**.

28.3 Barristers

The term barrister is used, in England and Wales, to describe someone admitted to practise in the superior courts and who is entitled to act as an advocate in those courts. Traditionally, barristers have had a higher level of education and also higher social status than solicitors and attorneys (**28.4**). The PRO is not the place to look for records relating to barristers: entry to the profession was and is controlled by the Inns of Court (Lincoln's Inn, Gray's Inn, the Inner Temple and the Middle Temple). The Inns of Court have published many of their records of genealogical interest: see the printed sources listed in **28.8**. For further information, contact the libraries of the particular Inn of Court: the addresses are given in **48**.

However, the PRO does have records of the oaths of allegiance sworn by barristers: swearing of this oath was required before a barrister could practise in the courts. Signatures to the oath, 1673–1944, are in KB 24, and 1858–1982, in KB 4.

28.4 Solicitors and attorneys: the central courts

The words attorney and solicitor have had a changing meaning not only over the centuries and but also in different parts of the English-speaking world. The word attorney, strictly defined, means a person appointed by another to act in his/her place: often but not necessarily a person who is legally qualified. In the USA and other countries that have a unitary bar, the term attorney-at-law has thus become virtually synonymous with legal practitioner. This was not, and is not, the case in England and Wales. In England and Wales the term was used for lawyers who were admitted to practise in the superior courts of common law and whose function was to deal with the procedural steps of litigation rather than advocacy. They were officers of court and subject to the discipline of the court. Solicitors performed similar procedural functions in courts of equity. Many individuals combined both roles, and in 1873 under the terms of the Judicature Act all solicitors and attorneys became 'Solicitors of the Supreme Court'.

Until 1838, solicitors and attorneys had to be admitted to each of the courts in which they wished to practise. The various central and regional courts regulated the admission of new solicitors and attorneys, and each court kept its own records relating to such admissions. In 1728 an act of parliament required attorneys and solicitors to have served five years as clerks under articles before they could be admitted to a court. Then in 1749 a further act required that a statement to the effect that the articles had actually been carried out (an 'affidavit of due execution') should be filed in the court within three months of admission. Articled clerks were effectively apprentices and so it is also sometimes possible to trace them by using the apprenticeship books in record class IR 1 (see **27.1** for further details).

If you are trying to trace records of a man who describes himself as an attorney, then you should try the records of the common law courts first. Registers and indexes of affidavits of due execution of articles for the King's Bench (formerly in record class IND 1) are now in KB 170. They cover the period 1749–1875. In practice these registers contain most of the details that are in the actual affidavits, so a search of the registers may well be sufficient in itself. The affidavits themselves survive only from about 1775 to 1875 and are in KB 105–KB 107 and KB 109. They usually contain the following details: the name of the clerk, the name, address and occupation of his parent or guardian, the name and address of the master to whom he was bound and the date of the articles and length of the term of the articles. Occasionally they also give the age of the clerk. Similar material for the Common Pleas survives from about 1725 (with a few earlier items going back to 1713) to 1838 in CP 5. Registers of articles (formerly in IND 1) are in CP 71, but they are difficult to use as they are arranged by date of admission rather than by name. Fortunately, there is a personal name index to CP 5 filed with the list in the reading rooms. Since many attorneys practised in both the King's Bench and the Common Pleas, and were therefore admitted to both courts, it is always a good idea to start a search by checking the CP 5 index. Registers of affidavits of due execution for the Exchequer of Pleas survive for 1833–1855 only in E 4/3.

The admission rolls or books themselves are likely to be less useful for family history purposes, since they give at most simply a name, date of admission and address. Rolls of attorneys for the King's Bench (formerly in IND 1) are now in KB 172 (1729–1875); those for the Common Pleas are in CP 11 (1730–1750); those for the Exchequer of Pleas (formerly in IND 1) are now in E 4 (1830–75). Admission books for the Common Pleas (formerly in IND 1) are now in CP 70 (1729–1848) and CP 72 (1740–1853).

Attorneys' admission rolls for Common Pleas are in CP 8 (1838–1860). They record the signatures of attorneys and solicitors who had originally enrolled in other courts, and also give the court to which the individual was originally admitted, together with the date of admission and place of residence both at the time of the original admission and at the time of signing the roll. A contemporary index (formerly in IND 1), covering not only these rolls but others that have not survived, is now in CP 72 (1838–1875). A supplementary admission register (formerly in IND 1) is now in CP 69/1. The admission roll and registers of town and country solicitors, 1832–1883 for the Court of Bankruptcy are in B 2/8–11.

If your man was described as a solicitor then you probably need to look at the records of the equity courts. For Chancery (the main equity court) the main records are the Petty Bag Office Solicitors Rolls in C 216. These cover 1729–1875. They were previously on long-term loan to the Law Society. A nominal roll that partially duplicates these volumes is in IND 1/4613–4614. Various affidavits of due execution of clerkship and other admission papers are also in C 21. There are certificates of admission, giving names and dates of admission and addresses in C 203/7 (1730–1787), which sometimes include admissions to the King's Bench, and also in C 217/21, 22, 181–187 (c1804–1843). Some affidavits of due execution, 1730–1839 are in C 217/23–40, 181–187. Other admission papers are also in C 217/40–54, 182–187. Alphabets of solicitors taking out certificates, 1785–1842, and an address book of attorneys c.1849–1860, are in C 220/11.

Admission papers after 1874 have not survived, but some information can be gained from the indexes to affidavits of due execution in KB 170/13 (formerly in IND 1), IND 1/29729–29733 and indexes to articles of clerkship, 1875–1889, in IND 1/29712–3.

For the equity side of Exchequer there are Solicitors' Certificate Books in E 108 (1785–1843), Rolls of Books of Solicitors in E 109 (1729–1841) and oath rolls for solicitors and commissioners for oaths (1730–1841) in E 200.

28.5 Solicitors and attorneys: the Palatine and Welsh courts

Affidavits of due execution and registers of affidavits of due execution for attorneys admitted to the courts of the Palatinate of Chester, 1728–1830, together with oath rolls, 1729–1830, are in CHES 36; there is also an admission roll (1697–1728) in CHES 35/3/1 and a further admission roll (1777–1806) for the Chester court of Exchequer in CHES 36/3/7. Affidavits of due execution for those admitted to the courts of the Palatinate of Durham, 1660–1843, are in DURH 9, with admission rolls, 1660–1723 and 1730–1843 in DURH 3, and a register of certificates to practise, 1785–1842, in IND 1/10152. Records of attorneys admitted to the Palatinate courts of Lancaster, 1730–1875, are in PL 23: they include affidavits of due execution, 1749–1814, registers of affidavits, 1749–1823, rolls of attorneys, 1730–1785, an oath roll, 1730–1793, a register of certificates to practise, 1785–1871 and minutes of attorneys' assize dinners, 1790–1805.

Before 1830, solicitors and attorneys practising in the Courts of Great Sessions in Wales were enrolled in the records of those courts. These are now at the National Library of Wales (address in **48**). See Parry, *A Guide to the Records of Great Sessions in Wales*. After 1830, attorneys practising in the assize courts in Wales were allowed to enrol in the courts at Westminster. For attorneys enrolled in the court of Common Pleas, 1830–1844, use the supplementary admission register formerly in IND 1 but now in CP 72; for those enrolled in King's Bench, 1830–1834, see KB 172. This privilege was also extended to attorneys and solicitors working in the courts of the Palatinate of Lancaster and the Palatinate of Durham.

28.6 Solicitors and attorneys: records kept by the Law Society

The Law Society has the records of the Registrar of Attorneys and Solicitors, established in 1843. These include lists of admissions from 1845 onwards, with additional lists of admissions back to about 1790. They also have some registers of articles of clerkship from about 1860 onwards. These records are kept at the Law Society, Ipsley Court (address in **48**).

28.7 Civil lawyers

For civil lawyers (i.e. those who practised the civil law used in the church courts and the High Court of Admiralty, and the High Court of Delegates), there is a selective index of advocates and proctors attached to the class list for PROB 39. Civil lawyers were also listed in *Law Lists* (**28.1**). There are short biographies of London advocates (the civilian equivalent of barristers) in the book by Squibb. The admission of proctors (the civilian equivalent of attorneys) in London – that is, those practising from Doctors' Commons – is recorded in the registers of the Archbishop of Canterbury, at Lambeth Palace Library (address in **48**). Records of civil lawyers who practised in provincial church courts are best sought locally, in diocesan record offices. Some papers relating to the admission of proctors to the High Court of Admiralty are in HCA 30 and warrants relating to their appointments are in HCA 50.

28.8 Lawyers: bibliography

J H Baker, *The Order of Serjeants at Law*, Selden Society, Supplementary Series vol. V (London, 1984)

E H W Dunkin, C Jenkins and E A Fry, *Act Books of the Archbishop of Canterbury, 1663–1859* (British Record Society, Index Library, 1929)

E Foss, *A Biographical Dictionary of the Judges of England* (London, 1870)

J A Foster, *Men-at-the-Bar: A Biographical Handlist of the Members of the Various Inns of Court including Her Majesty's Judges etc.* [as at 1885] (London, 1885)

J A Foster, *The Register of Admissions of Gray's Inn, 1521–1889* (London, 1889)

G Holborn, *Sources of Biographical Information on Past Lawyers* (British and Irish Association of Law Librarians, 1999)

J Hutchinson, *A Catalogue of Notable Middle Templars* (London, 1902)

F A Inderwick and R A Roberts, *A Calendar of Inner Temple Records, 1505–1800* (London, 1896–1936)

Law List (London 1775, continuing)

Lincoln's Inn, *Admissions, 1420–1799* (London, 1896)

Lincoln's Inn, *The Black Books, 1422–1914* (London, 1897–1968)

Parliament, *List of Attorneys and Solicitors Admitted in Pursuance of the Late Act for the Better Regulation of Attorneys and Solicitors, 1729–1730* (London, 1729–1731)

G Parry, *A Guide to the Records of Great Sessions in Wales* (Aberystwyth, 1995)

J Sainty, *A List of English Law Officers, King's Counsel and Holders of Patents and Precedence*, Selden Society, Supplementary Series vol. VII (London, 1987)

G D Squibb, *Doctors' Commons* (Oxford, 1977)

C Trice Martin, *Minutes of Parliament of the Middle Temple, 1501–1703* (London, 1904–1905)

29 Medicine and education

29. Doctors' records

In general, the PRO is not the place to look for records of doctors except as they were engaged upon government service. Records of doctors in the Army and Navy, however, are quite extensive: see **18.26** and **19.20–21**. For a guide to the subject, see Bourne and Chicken, *Records of the medical professions: a practical guide to the family historian.*

The *Medical Directory* lists names and addresses from 1845: the PRO Library has copies from 1895 to 1987. From 1858, all doctors had to be registered, with details published in the annual *Medical Register*. The PRO Library has this from 1915 to 1973. For the eighteenth century, look at Wallis and Wallis, *Eighteenth Century Medics (Subscriptions, Licences, Apprenticeships)*, which lists many thousands of individuals, including physicians, surgeons, apothecaries, dentists and midwives.

The Royal College of Physicians was established in 1518, and holds records on its members. Some records of the Barber-Surgeons Company are at the Guildhall Library, including registers of naval surgeons 1705–1745. Physicians and surgeons had to have a licence from the bishop, from 1580 to 1775: records of these will be in local record offices, or at Lambeth Palace Library for the Archbishop of Canterbury. The Bishop of London's records of licensing doctors are at the London Metropolitan Archives and the Guildhall Library. Addresses are in **48**.

29.2 Civilian nurses' records

Before 1919, the individual nurse training schools kept records: these are often still with the hospital records (see **29.4**). The London Metropolitan Archives holds records of some London training schools, including Guy's Hospital, the Nightingale Training School and the Nightingale collection.

The registration of civilian nurses began in 1921, following the foundation of the General Nursing Council in 1919. From 1921, State Registered Nurses were entered on the Register of Nurses (DT 10): the Register included nurses who were currently active, and who may therefore have qualified well before that date. From 1947, State Enrolled Nurses were entered on the Roll of Nurses (DT 11). After 1973, information on various categories of nurses can be found in DT 12. The information given in the Register and Roll includes name and maiden name, qualifications and training, address, change of name, date of marriage, and date of death.

29.3 Midwives' records

For eighteenth century midwives, see Wallis and Wallis. There are registration records of midwives from 1872–1888 and 1904 onwards in DV 7, but many of these are unfit for production.

29.4 Hospital records

The PRO and the Wellcome Institute for the History of Medicine have compiled a computerized database of the location in records offices of the records of over a thousand civilian hospitals in England and Wales. If you are interested in finding the records of a particular hospital you can look at the HOSPREC database at Kew. Administrative records are normally closed for 30 years, and patient's records are closed for 100 years.

The PRO has some hospital records, such as those of the British Lying-In Hospital, 1749–1868 in RG 8, as well as many field hospital records from wartime.

29.5 Teachers' records

The PRO holds policy papers on teacher training and registration, rather than staff records themselves, although some scattered records of staff of district schools, 1848–1910, may be found if you are prepared to tackle MH 27. Detailed information about staff or pupils of individual schools may be found in the appropriate local record office, together with school log books and building plans. For a full discussion, see Morton, *Education and the State*. There are some records of teachers' pensions available for teachers in England, 1899–1930 (PMG 68). Other pension records relate to Army schoolmasters and schoolmistresses, 1909–1928, in PMG 33 and PMG 34.

The registers of the Teachers Registration Council for 1902–1948 are now kept by the Society of Genealogists. They are not open to public inspection, but a search can be made on your behalf.

29.6 School records

Deeds relating to the foundation of schools, and other charitable foundations, were enrolled in Chancery (C 54) until 1902, and then in the Supreme Court (J 18). There are indexes to these trust deeds, arranged by place, covering 1736 to 1904: although most relate to nonconformist chapels, very many concern schools. Much material can be found in the PRO and locally on the history of individual schools: use Morton, *Education and the State*.

29.7 Medicine and education: bibliography and sources

Published works
J Harvey Bloom and R Rutson Jones, *Medical Practitioners in the Diocese of London, Licensed Under the Act of 3 Henry VIII, c.11: An Annotated List 1529–1725* (Cambridge, 1935)
S Bourne and A H Chicken, *Records of the medical professions: a practical guide to the family historian* (1994)
C Hillam, *Brass Plate and Brazen Impudence: Dental Practice in the Provinces 1755–1855* (Liverpool, 1991)
A Morton, *Education and the State from 1833* (PRO, 1997)
W Munk, *The Roll of the Royal College of Physicians of London, 1518–1825* (London, 1861–1878)
J H Raach, *A Directory of English Country Physicians, 1603–1643* (London, 1962)
C H Talbot and E A Hammond, *The Medical Practitioners of Medieval England: A Biographical Register* (London, 1965)
P J Wallis and R V Wallis, *Eighteenth Century Medics (Subscriptions, Licences, Apprenticeships)* (Newcastle-upon-Tyne, 2nd cdn, 1988)

Unpublished finding aids
Indexes to trust deeds, by place, 1736–1904

30 The poor and the Poor Laws

30.1 Introduction

Paupers have attracted the active interest of the state since the Elizabethan Poor Laws of 1601. However, most records will be found locally, as paupers were a charge on their parish of settlement, and local taxes were raised for their support. The parish of settlement was generally the parish of birth, or of the husband's birth. For a brief and lucid guide to the poor relief system, the various Poor Laws, and the idea of settlement, see Herber, *Ancestral Trails*, pp. 285–305. There is little in the PRO about the operation of the Elizabethan Poor Law and its system of outdoor relief for the deserving poor, and Houses of Correction for the undeserving poor. Try the relevant county record office instead, as the records produced in the course of proving settlement can be very informative for family history. See Cole, *An Introduction to Poor Law Documents before 1834*.

30.2 The New Poor Law, 1834, and the workhouse system

Workhouses to supply indoor relief in as repulsive a way as could be designed (in order to put people off from applying for help) were set up by unions of six or so parishes, under the New Poor Law of 1834. The Poor Law Unions continued until 1930. You need to know which union your people may have been under. To find out in which union a particular parish was, see Gibson and Youngs', *Poor Law Union Records: 4. Gazetteer of England and Wales*. The three previous pamphlets in this excellent series give advice on the range of records to be found, and references to documents in local record offices and in the PRO. The records of the Poor Law Commission and the Poor Law Board are in the PRO, in the MH lettercode. They are not particularly easy to use, as the lists are very uninformative, so any search is likely to be lengthy, but it could be very rewarding.

MH 12, the main class of correspondence, is known to contain the names of thousands of individuals. It is listed only by Poor Law Union and covering dates of correspondence, with no indication as to subject. The correspondence is indexed by specialized administrative subjects in MH 15. Many of the records are also in a poor condition.

Local records are easier to use, particularly with Gibson and Youngs' pamphlets to hand.

30.3 Poor Law Union staff

For registers of staff of the workhouses, 1837–1921, see MH 9. The registers give dates of appointment and salary: date of death is sometimes noted. Personal details of people appointed may be found in forms among the mass of papers in MH 12, although virtually all papers after 1900 were destroyed by fire in the 1940s. The forms give full name, age, address, details of previous jobs and reasons for appointment to the present post, and salary. Names of wives and number of children are sometimes given, as are details of religion and qualifications. MH 12 can also contain references for applicants, and correspondence on dismissal.

You may find it worth checking the *Index to Parliamentary Papers* on CD-ROM in the Library, to check on returns of Poor Law Union officials made to Parliament: these can give personal details. The index refers to microfiches seen in the Microfilm Reading Room.

30.4 The poor: bibliography

A Cole, *An Introduction to Poor Law Documents before 1834* (FFHS, 1993)
J S W Gibson, C Rogers and C Webb, *Poor Law Union Records: 1. South-East England and East Anglia* (FFHS, 1993)
J S W Gibson and C Rogers, *Poor Law Union Records: 2. The Midlands and Northern England* (FFHS, 1993)
J S W Gibson and C Rogers, *Poor Law Union Records: 3. South-West England, The Marches and Wales* (FFHS, 1993)
J S W Gibson and F A Youngs, *Poor Law Union Records: 4. Gazetteer of England and Wales* (FFHS, 1993)
M Herber, *Ancestral Trails* (Sutton, 1997)
Index to Parliamentary Papers
E McLaughlin, *Annals of the Poor* (FFHS, 1987)
S Pearl, 'Charities: the forgotten poor relief', *Family Tree Magazine*, May 1991
W Tate, *The Parish Chest* (Cambridge, 1969)
T Wood, 'Workhouse Ancestors', *Family Tree Magazine*, October and November 1995

31 Lunacy

31.1 Introduction

For most of the past, the state has had little interest in the mental health of its subjects, unless they had a sufficient amount of property to require the intervention of the crown as a feudal lord. Pauper lunatics were dealt with locally. For a detailed guide to records on lunacy, read Lappin's thesis, 'Central Government and the supervision of the treatment of lunatics 1800–1913', which can be seen on request in the Research Enquiries Room at Kew. Copies are also available at the Wellcome Institute.

31.2 Chancery lunatics: royal interest in the property of lunatics and idiots

The custody of the lands and persons of idiots ('natural fools from birth') and lunatics ('somctimes of good and sound memory and understanding and sometimes not') belonged to the crown. Idiots and lunatics were the responsibility of the Lord Chancellor, although the Court of Wards took this over for 1540–1646: they were sometimes known as the 'Chancery lunatics'. The king was entitled to administer the lands of an idiot during his life, but of the lunatic only during periods of insanity. The lands or possessions were not generally retained in crown hands, but granted out for the term of the lunacy or idiocy to 'committees' (i.e. those to whose care the lunatic or his estate was committed – possibly the next of kin).

Although the crown's interest was at first paramount, over time the priority appears to have become the proper administration of the lunatic's estate, an issue often of vital importance to the next of kin. The whole point of getting a person declared of unsound mind by a Chancery inquisition was to take away his or her power of independent legal action in the disposition of property: it had nothing to do with committal to an asylum, which was a separate medical procedure. In many cases the alleged lunatic was already in an asylum when the inquisition took place: the only requirement for committal to an asylum was for two doctors to issue a certificate.

Lunatics and idiots were brought to the Chancellor's attention by relatives; by solicitors, or others, acting as the executors of a will or trustees, where one of the beneficiaries was a supposed lunatic; by the Lunacy Commissioners, fearing that the money of an asylum inmate was being misappropriated; or by creditors of the alleged lunatic, who could claim payment from the Master in Lunacy once their debtor had been declared of unsound mind. All petitioners had to support their request for a commission of inquiry with at least two sworn affidavits supporting their opinion of the state of mind of the supposed lunatic. These affidavits do not generally survive, but the gist is given in the abstract of the petition in C 211. About 1,000 affidavits supporting petitions for a lunacy commission are to be found in C 217/55, dating from 1719 to 1733: thcy are not listed individually nor indexed.

The Lord Chancellor had first, to find out (by ordering commissioners to hold an inquisition) whether a person was of sound mind or not; second, to commit the custody of the lunatic and his estate to suitable persons (called 'committees'); and third, to examine the accounts, etc., of the committees.

Commissions and inquisitions are in Latin until the Interregnum, and between 1660 and 1733; for the Interregnum and from 1733 they are in English. Inquisitions of lunacy produced before

1540 are with the inquisitions post mortem in C 132–C 142 (see **41.7**). From 1540 to 1648 they are in WARD 7. Inquisitions from about 1648 to 1932 are in C 211 (or in PL 5 for Lancashire). Disputes ('traverses') on the validity of an inquisition may be found in the common law side of Chancery: see **47.2**. There are few lunacy commissions for England in the twentieth century. The later records, however, do contain copies of inquisitions taken in Ireland, and in some British colonies: the latter are specifically concerned with the mental health of the person, and with getting them transported back to Britain.

Information on the estates and possessions of a lunatic was sent to the Clerk of the Custodies, who granted out the custody of the persons and estates of lunatics and idiots, by the issue of letters patent to the committees. These were not generally enrolled on the patent rolls, but in a separate series of rolls, which unfortunately appear to have been destroyed in the later nineteenth century. However, there is register of bonds given as security by committees, 1817–1904, in J 103. From 1900, registers of bonds by the committees are in J 92. Some bonds given by committees from the eighteenth to twentieth centuries are in J 117.

Accounts were supposed to be submitted annually by the committee to the Chancery Master: these are easy to find (if they survive) by checking the indexes to C 101, the Chancery Masters' accounts, in IND 1/10702. They often give more detail about the tenants than they do about the lunatic, but they can provide some extra information.

The most informative records may be found among the Chancery Masters' reports and exhibits, but there is no guarantee of finding anything. You can pick out lunatics from Chancery litigation, because they are described as *In re Smith, a lunatic*. The reports are in C 38: there are indexes in IND 1, which can be identified from the C 38 list. Some exhibits from cases relating to lunatics will be found in C 103–C 115: in fact, the whole class C 115 exists because of the lunacy of Frances Scudamore, Duchess of Norfolk. There is an index to exhibits in C 103–C 114 filed before the C 103 list. Later exhibits will be found in J 90, but these are kept off site and need to be ordered three working days in advance. If you find that exhibits exist, you may have struck lucky. For example, the exhibits *In re Freeman: a lunatic*, in C 110/164, include extracts from the parish register of St Peter's, Antigua, 1719–1728 and 1752, relating to the lunatic Thomas Freeman's family, several letters from his brother Arthur, and the original letter patent sent out to the family's lawyer committing Freeman to his custody, as well as a further fifty or so papers detailing a legacy of £1,500 by his godfather and namesake to Freeman as an infant, and the difficulty of deciding if it was going to be paid in Antiguan or British currency.

Decrees and orders relating to lunatics may be found in C 33 and J 79 (records from this latter class need to be ordered three days in advance).

Official visitors' reports on Chancery lunatics, from 1879 (with a 75 year closure) are in LCO 10: they give name, address, age, income and allowance.

31.3 Lunatic asylums

People of means had to make private arrangements for any lunatics in the family. The private madhouses were licensed by the justices of the peace, and were examined by several series of government commissioners. One register of admissions to private asylums outside London, for 1798–1812, is in MH 51/735: it includes the names of 1,788 patients, and is indexed by both lunatics (at the front) and keepers of licensed houses (at the back).

Pauper lunatics were dealt with locally under the poor law, vagrancy law or criminal law, and were therefore likely to end up in workhouses, houses of correction or prisons before the establishment of lunatic asylums in the mid nineteenth century. These records would be kept locally, but at the PRO are returns of insane inmates in workhouses and asylums from 1834 to 1909 (MH 12). These give name, age, type of disability and whether considered dangerous. Unfortunately, they are arranged by county and Poor Law Union, and there are subject indexes only (MH 15). Correspondence with asylum districts in MH 17 may be worth looking at. See **30** on how to identify the Poor Law Union, and on guides to what records exist.

There are also returns of insane prisoners in prisons and houses of correction, submitted in March 1858 (MH 51/90–207).

From the early nineteenth century, justices of the peace were encouraged to build county lunatic asylums to house any pauper lunatics in their county: in 1845, this became compulsory. The 1890 Lunacy Act gave them a wider role, and patients with means began to be admitted. Records of the county asylums are likely to be kept locally, as may those of the private asylums: check the HOSPREC database at Kew.

Most patient files have been destroyed. A very few survive in MH 85, MH 86 (with 75 year closures) and MH 51/27–77. However, the registers to the patient files survive in MH 94, for various categories of inmates from 1846 to 1960. The register gives name and sex, name of the institution, and dates of admission, discharge or death. A union card index to all patients admitted (possibly from as early as 1774) was destroyed in 1961: apparently it covered over 2.5 million names.

31.4 Naval lunatics

For naval lunatics, see **19.21**.

31.5 Lunacy: bibliography

J H Lappin, 'Central Government and the supervision of the treatment of lunatics 1800–1913: a guide to sources in the Public Record Office' (unpublished MA thesis, 1995). Ask at the Research Enquiries Desk for this memorandum.

32 The established church

32.1 Introduction

Until the break with Rome in 1534, the established religion of England and Wales was (Roman) Catholic; after this, with the brief exception of Mary I's reign (1553–1558), the established religion was that of the Church of England, covering a wide range from high church to low church, Anglo–Catholic to Calvinist.

The PRO is not the obvious place to look for ecclesiastical records: see Owen's book on the records of the established church, and Bourne and Chicken's guide to Anglican records. In fact, the PRO does have considerable holdings on the administration of the church in relation to the state, and particularly on the monasteries, but relatively little of this contains information of interest to the family historian.

However, there are some sources in the PRO which can provide information on the clergy and the lay members of the church, before and after the Reformation.

32.2 Anglican clergymen

Descent from pre-Reformation clergy, in theory at any rate, should not be possible, as they were vowed to celibacy: however, the Church of England allowed priests to marry.

Before using any documentary sources, you should consult the following printed works, which should be available in a good reference library. *Crockford's Clerical Directory*, published annually from 1858, is the place to start, followed by the lists of Oxford and Cambridge *Alumni* [students] (see Foster, and Venn and Venn, in **32.5**). For the higher clergy, down to archdeacons, try the *Fasti Ecclesiae Anglicanae, 1066–1857*; not all dioceses have been covered up to 1857. There is a card index of clergy, the Fawcett Index, in the library of the Society of Genealogists.

The ordination records in the appropriate diocesan archives can be a very useful source of genealogical information: they usually include a certified copy of the baptismal entry, or a letter explaining why there was none, details of education, and character references. There were several life insurance companies catering solely for the clergy: the Guildhall Library has a collection of London insurance company records, which can provide a wealth of personal details.

Most PRO documents relating to the appointment of Anglican clergymen to benefices are very formal, and do not include any information of great use to genealogists. The bishops' certificates of institutions to benefices, 1544–1912 (E 331) are usually approached through the Institution Books, 1556–1838 (IND 1/17000–17015, on the open shelves). These are arranged firstly by county (1556–1660) or diocese (1661–1838), then by place: they give the name of the clergyman instituted to the benefice, the date, and the name of the patron of the benefice. They can be useful for tracing the ecclesiastical career of the clergyman, but they do not provide any personal details. The Composition Books record payments due by the cleric on taking up his benefice (IND 1/17016–17028, on the open shelves) and refer to the records in E 334.

For the Commonwealth period, the surveys of church livings provide the name of the incumbent, and details of the value of the living as assessed by the parishioners (C 94). Matthews' *Calamy Revised* is a useful source of information about clergy appointed during the Interregnum.

If you have an ancestor who was a clergyman in 1801 or 1851, you may like to investigate two series of records composed of returns made by the parish clergy on conditions in their parish. The Acreage Returns of 1801 (HO 67), although intended to provide factual information on the state of agriculture at a village level, can include some very individualistic comments made by the parish priest on his parishioners. A later survey of places of worship, the Ecclesiastical Census of 1851 (HO 129), can also provide an interesting picture of life at the parish level, and sometimes personal details on the clergy as well.

32.3 Excommunicates, 1280s–1840s

The PRO holds the requests (technically, known as *significavits* or significations) from the bishops for the 'secular arm' (i.e. the power of the state) to be used against people excommunicated by the church: excommunication was a punishment imposed for a wide variety of offences. These significations survive from the 1220s to 1611 (C 85), and again from George II to the 1840s (C 207). It is not clear what has happened to the intervening requests.

The earliest significations usually provide little more than the name of the person excommunicated, but the later ones in C 85 can include reference to occupation, place of residence, father, nature of the offence, etc. About 7,600 significations survive from C 85, and there is a card index to these, first by diocese and then alphabetically by name of the person excommunicated. The documents themselves are in Latin. The significations in C 207 are in English, but have not yet been indexed: as a result, they are less easy to use than the earlier ones.

Significations for the county palatine of Chester were issued by Chester officials, and are in CHES 38. Those for the counties of Flint, Henry VIII to Elizabeth I, and for Pembroke, George II, have been transferred with the rest of WALE 28 to the National Library of Wales.

32.4 Sacrament certificates

From the Test Act of 1672 onwards, various statutes required that office-holders and aliens seeking naturalization should take certain oaths in support of the crown and against papal supremacy; to afforce these oaths, the swearer was required to take the sacrament of the Lord's Supper according to the Anglican rites. Evidence of this was provided by a certificate completed and signed by the minister and churchwardens of the parish with the signatures of two witnesses appended. The certificates were presented when the oath was sworn, at one of the central courts if within thirty miles of Westminster, and at the quarter sessions if further away. As a result, the majority of sacrament certificates in the PRO are from Middlesex, Hertfordshire, Surrey and Kent, within the thirty mile radius of Westminster.

Certificates presented to Chancery, 1673–1778, are in C 224; those presented in the Exchequer, 1700–1827, are in E 196. Certificates presented in King's Bench survive from 1676 and from 1728–1828 (KB 22). Certificates presented in the Cheshire courts, 1673–1768, are in CHES 4: many of them date from the 1715 Jacobite Rising. Sacrament certificates presented to the quarter sessions should be in local record offices.

32.5 The established church: bibliography

S Bourne and A H Chicken, *Records of the Church of England: A Practical Guide for the Family Historian* (Maidstone, 1988)

Crockford's Clerical Directory (Oxford, annually from 1858)

J Foster, *Alumni Oxonienses, 1500–1886* (Oxford, 1891)

J Le Neve and others, *Fasti Ecclesiae Anglicanae* (London, 1716). There is a revised and updated version, covering 1066–1857 (London, 1962 continuing)

F D Logan, *Excommunication and the secular arm in medieval England* (Toronto, 1968)

A G Matthews, *Calamy Revised* (Oxford, 1934)

D M Owen, *The records of the established church in England, excluding parochial records* (British Records Association, 1970)

L F Salzman, 'Sussex excommunicates', *Sussex Archaeological Collections*, vol. LXXXIII, pp. 124–140

J Venn and J A Venn, *Alumni Cantabrigienses, from the Earliest Times to 1900* (Cambridge, 1922–1927)

33 Protestant nonconformists

33.1 Nonconformist church records

The PRO holds the majority of nonconformist registers of births or baptisms, marriages, and deaths or burials for the period before 1837, and also a considerable number after that date: these are discussed in **3**. However, in some cases, these registers contained other records of the church or chapel as well. The General Register Office, to whom they had been surrendered, adopted the practice of tearing out the other records where this could be done easily, and returning them to the church. To discover their present location, you need to consult a guide to the particular denomination's archives (see **33.5**). In a few cases, the information was spread throughout the volume, and this piece of archival vandalism was not carried out, so that some of the registers discussed in **3** still include more general records.

The PRO has published a specialized guide to nonconformist records, *Protestant Nonconformity and Roman Catholicism*, by Shorney.

33.2 Nonconformist chapels and charities

Under the Toleration Act of 1689, Justices of the Peace were made responsible for licensing nonconformist meeting houses: these licences may be found among the quarter sessions records in local record offices. From 1736, deeds involving the inalienable transfer of land for charitable purposes had to be enrolled on the Close Rolls (C 54 and, from 1902, J 18). The great majority of these deeds involved the establishment of nonconformist chapels, schools, burial grounds and charities: between 1736 and 1870 over 35,000 deeds were enrolled. There are two indexes to these deeds, both to places: for 1736–1870 there are volume indexes to trust deeds, and for 1870–1904 there are card indexes. In addition, C 54 and J 18 also have annual indexes to their whole contents. These deeds are a very valuable source for local history and for the involvement of individual nonconformists in establishing their chapels and setting up schemes for self improvement.

33.3 Nonconformists: other records

There are a number of oath or affirmation rolls for nonconformists in the PRO. The Association Oath of 1696, in support of William III, was sworn or affirmed by London and Hampshire dissenters (C 214/9–10), Quakers in Colchester (C 213/473), nonconformist ministers in Cumberland (C 213/60–61) and Baptist ministers in London (C 213/170). There are also affirmation rolls for Quaker attorneys, 1831–1835 (E 3) and 1836–1842 (CP 10).

The Recusant Rolls, 1592–1691 (E 376 and E 377) are annual returns of both Protestant nonconformists and of Catholics, who had property forfeited or who were fined for dissenting from the Church of England.

33.4 Huguenots

Huguenots were French Protestants fleeing from religious persecution from the 1550s onwards, and in large numbers after the Revocation of the Edict of Nantes (which reversed the previous policy of toleration of them) in 1685. It is quite possible, however, for a Huguenot ancestor to appear in England some time after this, as many fled first to Holland or Germany and only later moved to England. The Centraal Bureau voor Genealogie of Holland may be able to assist in these cases: the address is in **48**. There are often strong family traditions of Huguenot descent, and names with a French flavour are usually a good indication of such a background.

The main Huguenot settlements were in London (notably in Spitalfields and Soho), Norwich, Canterbury, Southampton, Rye, Sandwich, Colchester, Bristol, Plymouth, Thorney and various places in Ireland. In the late seventeenth century, it is estimated that some 45,000 Huguenots settled in Britain. There are no known records of any communities in the Midlands or the North of England, and there is little on settlement in Scotland. It is, naturally, more difficult to trace a family which struck out on its own to a new part of the country where no French church existed, and which used the local parish church for baptisms. Huguenot burial records are rare at all times, and by the nineteenth century almost non-existent, except for the records of deaths of the inmates of the London Huguenot Hospital, which are in the Huguenot Library. The Huguenot Library will, for a fee, undertake a brief search in their archive, which includes pedigrees and records about the administration of funds collected for the relief of the refugees. No personal callers can be seen, so you will need to write (address in **48**).

Huguenot material is also to be found in other areas of settlement: in the Guildhall Library of London, the Cathedral Library at Canterbury, the Norfolk County Record Office at Norwich and the Southampton City Record Office, for instance.

Most of the sources for Huguenot genealogy in the PRO have been published by the Huguenot Society in some form, and are available in the PRO Library. The *Calendars of State Papers* are also useful, as are the various lists in print of aliens resident in England, naturalized, or taking oaths of allegiance (see **12** and **15**).

33.5 Protestant nonconformists: bibliography and sources

R W Ambler, 'Enrolled Trust Deeds – A source for the History of Nineteenth Century Nonconformity', *Archives*, vol. XX (1993), pp. 177–186

G R Breed, *My Ancestors were Baptists* (Society of Genealogists, 1995)

D H Clifton, *My Ancestors were Congregationalists* (Society of Genealogists, 1997)

N Currer-Briggs and R Gambier, *Huguenot Ancestry* (Chichester, 1985)

Dr Williams's Trust, *Nonconformist Congregations in Britain* (London, 1973)

N Graham, *The Genealogists' Consolidated Guide to Nonconformist and Foreign Registers in Inner London, 1538–1837* (Birchington, 1980)

Huguenot Society, *Publications* (1885 continuing)

W Leary and M Gandy, *My Ancestors were Methodists* (Society of Genealogists, 1998)

E H Milligan and M J Thomas, *My Ancestors were Quakers* (Society of Genealogists, 1983)

M Mullett, *Sources for the History of English Non-Conformity 1660–1830* (British Records Association, 1991)

P Palgrave-Moore, *Understanding the History and Records of Nonconformity* (2nd edn, Norwich, 1989)

A Ruston, *My Ancestors were English Presbyterians/Unitarians* (Society of Genealogists, 1993)

D Shorney, *Protestant Nonconformity and Roman Catholicism: A Guide to Sources in the Public Record Office* (PRO, 1996)

D J Steel, *Sources of Nonconformist Genealogy and Family History* (London, 1973)
E Welch, 'The Early Methodists and their Records', *Journal of the Society of Archivists*, vol. IV, p. 210

Unpublished finding aids
Indexes to trust deeds, 1736–1904
Index to C 54
Index to J 18

34 Roman Catholics and Orthodox Christians

34.1 Roman Catholic registers

The registers of Catholic churches are either in the PRO (see **3.10**) or with the congregation. The relevant diocesan archivist or the Catholic Central Library may be able to assist in tracing them. *The English Catholic Ancestor* aims at acquiring and disseminating information about Catholic families. The Catholic Record Society has published a great deal of useful material. Burials of Catholics often took place in the parish churchyard and are therefore recorded in the parish registers. For much fuller information on Catholic genealogy, see the book by Steel and Samuel. See also Shorney, *Protestant Nonconformity and Roman Catholicism: A Guide to Sources in the Public Record Office*.

34.2 Records of persecution of Catholics

In the PRO, records of Catholics are largely the records of their persecution, and the bulk of these accordingly varies with fluctuations in anti-popery. The Recusant Rolls (E 376 and E 377) are annual returns of dissenters (Protestant and Catholic) who had property forfeited or were fined, 1592–1691. However, they are large, mostly in Latin, and difficult to use. It is a good idea to check one of the editions produced by the Catholic Record Society first, in order to understand the format of the rolls. Entries are arranged by county, and they record convictions, fines, rentals for forfeited lands and details of chattels seized. There are several 'returns of papists' in the State Papers and records of the Privy Council. For example, there is a printed return for 1625–1642 in SP 16/495; and a return for 1708 in SP 34/26. Try also the manuscript indexes to the Privy Council registers in PC 2, under 'Church affairs'. Most Catholics supported the King in the Civil War, so their estates may be referred to in *Calendars of the Committee for Compounding with Delinquents*. There are many inventories of Catholic possessions in the State Papers for the Interregnum (SP 28). From the reign of George I and the Jacobite risings, there are lists of Catholics who forfeited their estates (E 174, KB 18, FEC 1 and FEC 2).

County record offices hold much material on persecutions of Papists. Between 1715 and 1791, Catholics were required to register their estates with the local Clerk of the Peace.

34.3 Oath rolls

There are lists of Catholic solicitors and attorneys for the period 1790–1836 (CP 10), 1791–1813 (C 217/180/5) and 1830–1875 (E 3). The 'Papists' oaths of allegiance etc. in E 169/79–83 give names and addresses for 1778–1857 (with gaps).

34.4 Records of the Russian Orthodox Church and the Greek Church in London

The archive of the Russian Orthodox Church in London (sometimes known as the Orthodox Greco-Russian Church), 1721–1951, is in RG 8/111–304. Most of the archive is in Russian, with some documents in Greek, English, French and German: there is a descriptive list, in English.

The records are of various kinds to do with the organization of the church, and the Russian community in England, including Russian prisoners of war during the Crimean War. There are also registers and other records of baptisms, marriages and deaths as well as communicants and conversions, dating from 1721 to 1927. Some of these relate to Greeks and other non-Russians.

For a register of marriages in the Greek Church in London, 1837–1865, see J 166.

34.5 Roman Catholics and Orthodox Christians: bibliography

J Bossy, *The English Catholic Community, 1570–1850* (London, 1975)
Calendar of State Papers, Domestic, Committee for Compounding with Delinquents, 1643–1660 (London, 1889–1893)
Catholic Directory (London, annually from 1837)
Catholic Record Society, *Bibliographical Studies*, vols. I–III, changed to *Recusant History*, from vol. IV (Bognor Regis, 1951 to date)
Catholic Record Society, *Publications* (1905, continuing). Vols. 18, 57 and 61 are editions of the Recusant Rolls for 1591–1595.
The English Catholic Ancestor (Aldershot, 1983–1989; Ealing, 1989 continuing)
M Gandy, *Catholic Family History: A Bibliography* (4 vols, 1996)
M Gandy, *Catholic Missions and Registers* (6 vols, 1993)
M Gandy, *Catholic Parishes in England, Wales and Scotland: An Atlas* (1993)
D Shorney, *Protestant Nonconformity and Roman Catholicism: A Guide to Sources in the Public Record Office* (PRO, 1996)
D J Steel and E R Samuel, *Sources for Roman Catholic and Jewish Genealogy and Family History* (London, 1974)
J A Williams, *Sources for Recusant History (1559–1791) in English Official Archives* (1983)

35 Jews

35.1 Jewish genealogy

For specific guides to Jewish genealogy see Mordy, *My Ancestors were Jewish*, and Steel and Samuel, *Sources for Roman Catholic and Jewish Family History and Genealogy*. Mordy gives advice on relevant collections in the UK, research abroad, a list of international research manuals, and a guide to records of the Holocaust.

The registers of the London Spanish and Portuguese Synagogue are partly published. The registers of the Ashkenazim contain a high proportion of entries totally in Hebrew before 1840. Some earlier entries are included in the *International Genealogical Index*. Later records are not easily accessible as most are held by the congregations concerned. The names and addresses of synagogues throughout the British Isles are, from 1896, in the *Jewish Year Book*. For help, apply to the Board of Deputies, Jewish Information Department. There are registers in the archives of the United Synagogue for the three principal London synagogues founded before 1837, and they will search these for a fee. For help on the London Sephardic community apply to the Honorary Archivist at the Spanish and Portuguese Synagogue, where the records are kept.

The London Metropolitan Archives has a large and growing collection of archives on Jewish settlement in London and the UK. The Hartley Library at Southampton University has part of the Anglo-Jewish Archive which used to be in the Mocatta Library University College, London, but the main genealogical collections which used to be part of that archive are now at the Society of Genealogists. These are the collections of Sir Thomas Colyer Fergusson, Ronald D' Arcy Hart and A M Hyamson. However, the PRO holds some records of interest.

Addresses are given in **48**.

35.2 The Jewish community in England and Wales

There were Jews in England in the early Middle Ages, but no line of descent has been traced from members of this early community, which was expelled in 1290. For records relating to this early community, see the *PRO Guide*. The Jewish community was re-established in the mid seventeenth century, from which time there has been a steady rate of assimilation into the gentile population.

The immigrants were two sorts: Sephardim (Portuguese, Spanish and Italian), arriving from 1656 onwards; and Ashkenazim (Central and East European), first coming in the 1680s from Holland and Bohemia. The main influx of Ashkenazim, however, was of Russians and Poles in the last two decades of the nineteenth century (about 120,000 in the period up to 1914).

A good place to start is with the State Papers up to 1782, followed by the Home Office papers, in particular: Correspondence, George III–Victoria (HO 42, 43); Out-letters, 1782–1921 (HO 43, 136, 152); Registered Files (from 1841) (HO 45); and Registered Files, Supplementary (HO 144: some are still under extended closure).

35.3 Colonial Jewish communities

The State papers, Domestic, also contain numerous references to colonial Jews and similar material may be found in Colonial Office records relating to the American and West Indies colonies, including: Colonial Papers, General Series (CO 1) 1574–1757; America and West Indies, Original Correspondence, etc. (CO 5) 1606–1807; British North America, Original Correspondence (CO 6) 1816–1868; Emigration Registers (CO 327 1850–1863); Canada, Original Correspondence (CO 42) 1700–1922; and West Indies, Original Correspondence (CO 318) 1624–1949. There are also similar classes for particular West Indies colonies. Selected papers have been published in the *Calendars of State Papers, Colonial* (to 1738). Try also the

Privy Council, Unbound Papers (PC 1) 1481–1946; Privy Council Registers (PC 2) 1540–1966; and the Plantation Books (PC 5) 1678–1806.

35.4 Foreign Jewish communities

Material on the condition of Jews in foreign countries is occasionally to be found in the various series of State Papers, Foreign, which are arranged by country. These are continued after 1782 in Foreign Office classes. From 1905 such material will be found in the class of General Correspondence: Political (FO 371), though the parallel classes for Commercial (FO 368), Consular (FO 369), News (FO 395) and Prisoners (FO 383) correspondence may also be useful.

35.5 Jewish immigrants and refugees

For material on Jewish immigration in the 1770s , try SP 37. For immigration of German, Polish and Russian Jews, 1887–1905, try HO 45. Foreign Office classes contain material on the conditions of Jews in Europe and sailings of immigrant ships from the German ports in the late nineteenth century. The Correspondence and Papers of the Commissioner of the Metropolitan Police (MEPO 2) contains material on landing of Jewish immigrants, work of Jewish charities and settlement of immigrant Jews in the East End of London, 1887–1905.

The records of the Jewish Temporary Shelter are being transferred from that body to the London Metropolitan Archives in late 1998/early 1999. The records, which start in 1886, include files on Jewish immigrants, and give name on arrival, age, town of origin, destination after leaving the Shelter, and trade or profession.

The London Metropolitan Archives also house administrative records of the Jewish Refugees Committee from the 1930s, as well as some personal files on the children who came on the Kindertransport programme. Other personal files on c.400,000 Jewish refugees (including children) are still kept by the Jewish Refugees Committee: these give date and place of birth, nationality, profession, home address, date of arrival, and address in Britain. Access to all of these different records may be restricted: at the Jewish Refugees Committee, for example, to the person on whom the file was kept, or to their proven next of kin if they have died (write first). The Hartley Library at the University of Southampton also holds material on individual refugees: you need to write to them first. All these addresses are in **48**.

For material on immigration of Jews from central Europe into the United Kingdom in the 1930's, try HO 45 again. AST 1/24 contains details on assistance to about ten Jewish refugees in the 1930s.

35.6 Jewish naturalization

In the eighteenth century, large numbers of Spanish Jews in Jamaica threw off their New Christian identity to become British Jews: Jews in the colonies could get naturalization 85 years or so before they could in Britain. For denization and naturalization. look at **12.5–6**. For changes of names see **17**.

35.7 Settlement

By 1800, there may have been 15,000 to 20,000 Jews in England. Three quarters of these were in London, with significant communities in Bristol and Exeter. Some information of the pattern of Jewish settlement in modern times can be gleaned from the Home Office and Metropolitan Police records referred to above. Clearly the Census Returns of 1841 to 1891 (see **2**) provide the most complete demographic and residential data for the Jewish community; as well as making analysis of the density of settlement in particular districts possible – once identification of Jewish families has been made.

35.8 Economic life

Evidence on the distribution of trades among the Jewish community in London and the provinces in the eighteenth and early nineteenth century might be gleaned from the Apprenticeship Books among the records of the Board of Inland Revenue (IR 1): see Jewish Historical Society, *Transactions*, vol. XXII, for just such a study. Probate records of the Prerogative Court of Canterbury (see **6**) contain wills and related documents of many prominent Jewish families and extracts have been published by the Jewish Historical Society. Further information about the estates of leading Jews may be found in the eighteenth and nineteenth century death duty registers (IR 26) which cover local as well as central probates. Files of Jewish companies occur among the various classes of Companies Files of the Board of Trade Companies Office (BT 41, BT 31, BT 34). Rules and activities of Jewish Friendly Societies, Benefit Societies and Loan Societies are reflected in several classes of records of the Registrar of Friendly Societies (FS 1, FS 3, FS 9, FS 15). Another rich source of Jewish economic and financial activities would be on the records of various royal courts of law, and particularly the Chancery Court which dealt with equity cases and mercantile cases and the High Court of Admiralty dealing with maritime and trading disputes. Detailed records of some Jewish businesses from the seventeenth to the nineteenth centuries may be found as exhibits in Chancery, in C 103–C 114: see the subject index and index to parties held with C 103.

35.9 Trade

The State Papers and the Colonial Office and Foreign Office classes referred to above also contain material relating to trade between England and the colonies and foreign countries, in which Jewish merchants may have been involved. In the West Indies colonies this was certainly the case. In addition to the classes of original correspondence for each colony there are also copies of Acts and Sessional papers of colonial executive councils and legislatures, government gazettes, shipping returns, trade statistics and newspapers. Board of Trade records relating to the colonies include Original Correspondence (CO 388) 1654–1792, Minutes (CO 391) 1675–1782 and Miscellanea (CO 390). Among the State Papers, Foreign, the following are likely to be useful: State Papers, France (SP 78); Holland (SP 84); Germany (Empire) (SP 80); Portugal (SP 89); and Hamburg and Hanse Towns (SP 82). Further material on colonial and foreign trade will be found in the Treasury Board Papers (T 1) 1557–1920, but these are notoriously difficult to use owing to their complicated means of reference. The Port Books (E 190), 1565–1798, survive for the outports, but not for

London, but there are many complementary classes among the records of the Board of Customs which are split between the Public Record Office and the Customs House Library.

35.10 Social life

Sources here are too numerous to cover adequately. But, as examples, the following may serve. Poor Law Board and Local Government Board correspondence with local poor law authorities in areas of Jewish settlement may be expected to yield information on local conditions. Indeed the Clerk to the Whitechapel Guardians was in the late 1880s the chief source of such information for both the Home Office and the Metropolitan Police. The records of the Department of Education and its predecessors are likely to throw light upon Jewish schools and Jewish educational problems. Home Office and Prison Commission files reveal the special arrangements made for the conscientious requirements of Jewish prisoners. Finally, a recent accession to the PRO is HO 239, the records of the Jewish Tribunal under the Shops Act 1936 and 1950 which deals with the licensing of Sunday trading by Jewish traders with conscientious objections to trading on the Jewish Sabbath.

35.11 Jews: bibliography

C Clapsaddle, *Tracing Your Jewish Roots in London* (1988) The addresses given are no longer correct.
Jewish Historical Society of England, *Transactions* .
Jewish Year Book (London, annually from 1896)
I Mordy, *My Ancestors were Jewish* (Society of Genealogists, 2nd edn, 1995)
J M Ross, 'Naturalization of Jews in England', *Transactions of the Jewish Historical Society*, vol. XXIV (1975)
D J Steel and E R Samuel, *Sources for Roman Catholic and Jewish Family History and Genealogy*
   (London, 1974)
C Tucker, 'Jewish Marriages and Divorces in England until 1940', *Genealogists' Magazine*, vol. XXIV, pp.
   87–93, 139–143

36 Prisoners of war

36.1 Introduction

A search of the lists on-line using the keywords 'prisoners' and 'war' will reveal a vast array of documents relating to prisoners of war. However, most of the documentation relates to the cost of feeding, clothing and transporting foreign prisoners or the technicalities of prisoner conventions rather than any biographical information useful to genealogists.

36.2 Prisoners of war to 1793

Before 1793 the few records available relate largely to French or American prisoners in British custody. These include the In-Letters of the Admiralty Medical and Prisoners of War Department in ADM 97, and Correspondence and Miscellaneous Papers in ADM 105, which contain the petitions and complaints of prisoners from 1703, and the State Papers Naval in SP 42. Records concerning the exchange of British prisoners can be found in ADM 97, WO 1/11 and 13, and WO 34/67 and 170. Lists of American seamen made prisoners of war, and removed from the ports to Shrewsbury in the 1770s, are in SP 42/57.

These records cover the period from 1745 but mainly relate to the American Revolutionary War. Other records relating to prisoners of war from these conflicts can also be identified from Andrews, *Guide to the Materials for American History, to 1783, in the Public Record Office of Great Britain*.

36.3 Prisoners of war, 1793–1914

For the period of the wars with France from 1793 to 1815, there are several registers concerning prisoners of war of various nationalities in ADM 103, AO 3, AO 11, AO 16, and WO 25. These registers are completely unindexed. Included in ADM 103 are lists and accounts of British prisoners in France and elsewhere, transmitted by the agent for prisoners in Paris. Registers of French and American prisoners in Britain are also in ADM 103, arranged by depot, prison ship or parole town. Lists of enemy prisoners on parole are contained in HO 28 and there is a register of American prisoners of war in Britain, compiled in 1813, in ADM 6/417. There are also documents relating to the exchange of prisoners of various nationalities in ADM 105/46, WO 1/227, 241–4, 905–16, WO 6/124 and 187.

For the Crimean War from 1853–1855, there is some official material relating to Russian prisoners in British hands in the headquarters papers in WO 28/182 and in naval hospital musters in ADM 102. The records of the Russian Orthodox Church in London in RG 8/180 include lists of Russian prisoners (in Russian) with correspondence in Russian, English and French relating to the distribution of money to them.

For the South African or Boer War from 1899–1902, there are registers of Boer prisoners, recorded in prisoner number order and arranged by area of confinement (e.g. Natal, Transvaal), in WO 108/303–305 and 368–369. Correspondence about their confinement in Ceylon, St Helena and elsewhere can be found in CO 537/403–409 and 453. Correspondence concerning Dutch, German and French prisoners is in FO 2/824–826.

36.4 Prisoners of war, 1914–1919

The International Committee of the Red Cross in Geneva keeps a list of all known PoWs and internees of all nationalities for the First World War. Searches are only made in response to written enquiries, and an hourly fee is charged. Write to the International Council of the Red Cross, Archives Division (address in **48**).

The PRO holds no comprehensive lists of prisoners of war on either side. Lists of prisoners and internees in Britain were compiled but were largely destroyed by bombing in 1940. Two specimen lists of German subjects interned as prisoners of war in 1915–1916 survive in WO 900/45–46. The list is divided into army, naval and civilian prisoners, and gives the regiment, ship or home address of each. For British and Dominion subjects in German hands, there is a list compiled in July 1915 in ADM 1/8420/124. This list is mainly concerned with the Giessen POW camp, including the crews of HMS *Maori* and HMS *Crusader* taken prisoner in May 1915. There are also lists of British and Dominion subjects (mostly army personnel) held in Germany, Turkey and Switzerland in 1916, in AIR 1/892/204/5/696–698.

Deaths of prisoners of war and internees occurring in military and non-military hospitals and in enemy and occupied territory were notified to the British authorities by foreign embassies, legations, registration authorities and American authorities in charge of British internees: these certificates may be found in RG 35.

36.5 Prisoners of war, 1939–1945

The International Committee of the Red Cross in Geneva keeps lists of all known PoWs and internees of all nationalities for the Second World War: searches are only made in response to written enquiries, and an hourly fee is charged. Write to the International Council of the Red Cross, Archives Division (address in **48**).

The documents held in the PRO comprise a few lists of prisoners and a wide range of general administration and policy documents.

WO 392 contains lists of all British and Dominions PoWs held by the Germans and Italians from 1939 to 1945, including the Merchant Navy. An alphabetical list of British and Dominion Air Force prisoners of war in German hands in 1944–1945 can be found in AIR 20/2336. Nominal rolls of Air Force prisoners for certain German camps can be found in AIR 40/258–287, 1488–1491, 2645. A nominal list of all Royal Marines known to have been held in German camps between 1939 and 1945 is in ADM 201/111. Lists of naval personnel interned in enemy camps may be found in ADM 116, code 79, although these are not immediately identifiable from the class list. Escape and Liberation Reports for all services are contained in WO 208/3297–3374, 4238–4276 and 4368–4371. A card index to these records is available in the Research Enquiries Room, together with an annotated manuscript index compiled by David List. Other Escapers and Evader Reports for the period 1940 to 1943 are contained in AIR 20/9159–9161. WO 161 contains details of Officers Repatriation Reports. A series of three volumes, titled *Prisoners of War*, containing the names and service details of 169,000 British and Dominions PoWs in German hands on 30 March 1945, can be consulted in the Research Enquiries Room.

Information concerning PoWs in Japanese hands is more comprehensive than that for PoWs held by the Germans and Italians. The main source is the card index WO 345. This consists of 57,000 cards of Allied PoWs and civilian internees, arranged alphabetically. Registers of Allied PoWs and civilians held in camps in Singapore can be found in WO 367. WO 347 consists of the hospital records for Allied PoWs held in Asia. A further alphabetical list of British PoWs in Japan and Japanese occupied territory can be found in WO 392/23–26, while other nominal lists are in FO 916 and CO 980. Escape and Evasion Reports for the Far East can be found in AIR 40/2462 and WO 208/3493–3494. The Interrogation Reports of liberated PoWs from the Far East are in WO 203/5193–5199, 5640 and WO 208/3499. Nominal rolls of Air Force PoWs for individual camps can be found in AIR 49/383–388. The Imperial War Museum also has an index of all RAF PoWs in the Far East from December 1941 to August 1945.

There is no general index of PoWs held by the British but there are certain lists which may be of assistance. WO 177/1833–1855 contains the War Diaries of selected hospitals, depots and PoW camps. Similarly, other diaries are contained in WO 166, which has a general index at the beginning of the class list. There are nominal lists of PoWs temporarily interned in the Tower of London in WO 94/105. CO 968/33–36 contains correspondence of the Colonial Office Defence Section and includes lists of PoWs in various colonial territories.

There is also a great deal of other material, including camp histories and escape reports, which is detailed in the PRO leaflet *Prisoners of War and Displaced Persons 1939–1953: Documents in the Public Record Office.*

36.6 Prisoners of war, 1950–1953

There are lists of British and Commonwealth servicemen who were known or believed to be prisoners of war in Korea. WO 208/3999 details men captured between January 1951 and July 1953, while WO 308/54 is a list of Commonwealth prisoners of war, compiled in January 1954. General Correspondence concerning PoWs can be found in WO 162/208–264, WO 32/19273 and DO 35/5853–5863.

36.7 Prisoners of war: bibliography and sources

Published works
C M Andrews, *Guide to the Materials for American History, to 1783, in the Public Record Office of Great Britain,* 2 vols (Washington DC 1912–1914).
Prisoners of War: British Army 1939–1945 (Polstead, 1990)
Prisoners of War: Naval and Air Forces of Great Britain and the Empire 1939–1945 (Polstead, 1990)
Prisoners of War: Armies and other Land Forces of the British Empire 1939–1945 (Polstead, 1990)

Unpublished works
There are a number of memoranda concerning PoWs: ask at the Research Enquiries Desk

37 Coroners' inquests

37.1 Introduction

Coroners have been responsible for investigating sudden, unnatural or suspicious deaths, as well as the deaths of people detained in prisons, ever since the twelfth century. Inquests are normally held in public and are regularly reported in the press. As explained below, the survival of coroners' records after 1850 is not good and it is probably easier and more rewarding to search for a newspaper report rather than for the coroner's record. The inquest verdict gives the cause of death: if depositions survive, they are very much fuller. Verdicts were in Latin until 1733, after which English was used.

Most modern coroners' records are held in local record offices rather than at the PRO so before starting your search it is essential that you read *Coroners' Records in England and Wales*, by Gibson and Rogers, which lists the location of records available, by county, and includes a section on sources in the PRO. It is also a good idea to seek the advice of your local record office or reference librarian as inquests for many counties have been published by local record societies; the bibliography below includes only a few of them but these are worth looking at even if you are interested in other counties as they have very good introductions that explain the context of the records and the procedures that created (and kept) them.

If original inquests have not survived, it is sometimes possible to piece basic information (such as the name of the deceased and verdict) together from coroners' bills, which record the coroners' claims for expenses; if they survive at all they will be in local record offices, usually amongst the quarter sessions records. Hunnisett's volume on *Wiltshire Coroners' Bills* will give you a good idea of the quality of information that they can provide. Incidentally, neither a coroner's inquest nor the modern post mortem medical examination are not the same as an inquisition post mortem: the latter is concerned with establishing the identity of the heir, not the cause of death (see **41.7**).

37.2 Coroners' records in the PRO

The PRO has many coroners' rolls for the late thirteenth to the early fifteenth centuries: they are arranged by county (JUST 2). Most coroners' inquisitions in the PRO are filed with the records of the court of King's Bench. This is because, from 1487, coroners were required to bring their inquests to the judges at the twice yearly assizes. Those that did not result in a trial for murder or manslaughter were forwarded to the King's Bench, where they were filed with the indictments according to the law term in which they were handed in: there are no indexes, although some have been published by Hunnisett. For the period 1485–1675, the inquests are in KB 9; after 1675 they are in KB 11 (for the provincial or 'out-counties') and KB 10 (for the City of London and Middlesex). However, the King's Bench clerks stopped filing inquests in the indictment files after 1733 and the general practice of handing in inquests appears to have declined from the mid seventeenth century and to have stopped on most circuits in about 1750. The exception is the Western circuit (Cornwall, Devon, Dorset, Hampshire, Somerset, and Wiltshire) whose inquests survive c.1740–1820 in KB 13.

A coroner's inquisition could act as an indictment, so both they and related depositions are often found amongst assize papers, even if no trial actually took place (see **38**). It is important to note that such inquisitions do not simply relate to obvious cases of murder. They often also include records of inquests in cases we would now consider to be manslaughter, or accidental deaths. From the thirteenth to seventeenth centuries, inquests taken during proceedings that resulted in the granting of pardons can be found amongst Chancery files in C 260. Copies of the proceedings were often included in the pardons themselves, which, if enrolled, are in C 66.

The Palatinates of Chester and Lancaster have extensive coroners' records. The Chester records also include Flint. Inquests from 1714 to 1851, with a few earlier ones, are in CHES 18: from 1798 to 1891 they are in ASSI 66. For the period of overlap, you will need to look in both classes, as the division is an arbitrary one apparently based on some local administrative quirk. Inquests from the Palatinate of Lancaster, 1626–1832, are in PL 26/285–29. For coroners' inquests taken within lands of the Duchy of Lancashire that are outside the county of Lancashire, look at DL 46. This has inquests for certain lands in Middlesex (1817–1884); Surrey (1823–1896); Essex (1821–1822); Halton, in Cheshire (1848–1849); Pontefract, in Yorkshire (1822–1894); and Norfolk (1804–1824, 1853–1875, 1885–1889). There are also very informative depositions about accidental deaths and homicides in PL 27.

Other sources in the PRO relate to the deaths of prisoners. The inquests of prisoners (usually debtors) held in the King's Bench prison, 1747–1750, and 1771–1839 (KB 14), can be informative about previous occupations. There is also a register of deaths of prisoners and of inquests upon them for the Millbank Penitentiary, 1848–1863 (PCOM 2/165). Some deaths fell within the jurisdiction of the High Court of Admiralty (usually those who died on or in the River Thames or who had been prisoners in the custody of the court) and records of inquests therefore survive amongst the records of that court, in HCA 1.

37.3 Coroners' records outside the PRO

Modern coroners' records do not survive very well. Records of individual inquests (other than treasure trove) created after 1875 may be weeded or destroyed, unless they are of significant public interest. Even if they do survive, inquest records are usually closed for 75 years. They are normally held in the local record office, unless they remain in the custody of the coroner. It is most unlikely that they will be indexed by name. *Coroners' Records in England and Wales*, by Gibson and Rogers, is the essential guide.

37.4 Murder

Records relating to murder victims are normally found by searching trial and associated records, published literature (see **38**) and appeals for mercy (see **39.6**). For much of the nineteenth and twentieth centuries many provincial police forces asked the Metropolitan Police Force to assist them in the investigation of murder, so files relating to provincial murders may survive alongside those of London cases in MEPO 3. There are police registers of murders and of deaths by violence (including the deaths of women by illegal abortion) in the Metropolitan Police area, for 1891–1909, 1912–1917, and 1919–1966. These give the name, address and occupation of the victim, date and place of death, and subsequent charges or convictions (MEPO 20).

37.5 Coroners' inquests: bibliography

J S W Gibson and C Rogers, *Coroners' Records in England and Wales* (FFHS, 1992)
R F Hunnisett, *Calendar of Nottinghamshire Coroners' Inquests, 1485–1558*, Thoroton Society, Record Series, vol. XXV
R F Hunnisett, 'Medieval Coroners' Rolls', *American Journal of Legal History*, vol.III, pp. 95–221, and 324–359
R F Hunnisett, *Sussex Coroners' Inquests, 1485–1558*, Sussex Record Society, vol. LXXIV
R F Hunnisett, *Sussex Coroners' Inquests, 1558–1603* (PRO, 1996)
R F Hunnisett, *Sussex Coroners' Inquests, 1603–1688* (PRO, 1998)
R F Hunnisett, *Wiltshire Coroners' Bills, 1752–1796*, Wiltshire Record Society, vol. XXXVI

38 Criminal trials

38.1 Introduction

Are you sure that trial records are what you want? They are not easy to use, and will not necessarily give you good family history information: they do not, for example, normally include transcripts of evidence given in court. For family history purposes, tracing convicts (especially transported ones) is usually easier and more rewarding (see **39, 40**).

The first problem to be overcome is the lack of name indexes. Unless you know when and where your ancestor was tried it will be extremely difficult to track down the trial record. There is no central index of persons tried: some indexes do exist, but they are far from comprehensive.

There are indexes to people who were transported (see **40**). Surviving indictments of people who were tried in the sixteenth and seventeenth centuries at the assizes for the Home Circuit (Essex, Hertfordshire, Kent, Surrey and Sussex) have been published, and indexed, in the *Calendar of Assize Records* by Cockburn. The names of those who were tried in Kent in 1602 are indexed in Knafla's *Kent at Law 1602*. There is a name index in the class list for ASSI 45 for those who made sworn statements on the North Eastern Circuit between 1613–1800. Finally, the microfiche publication *British Trials 1660–1900* is indexed by defendant, victim and location (see **38.3**).

Even if you know roughly when and where the trial took place, you still need to know what kind of court tried the offence. Until the sixteenth century, many manorial courts exercised jurisdiction in cases of petty theft, affray, drunkenness, and other offences (see **41.2**), but from the sixteenth century onwards jurisdiction over minor crimes increasingly passed to justices of the peace (also known as magistrates). Justices of the peace were (then as now) effectively volunteer amateur judges, who were chosen because of their importance in the local community rather than for their legal expertise. Justices of the peace were empowered to try some offences without a jury: this was called summary jurisdiction. They could do this either singly or in groups of two or more. Summary courts with more than one justice were usually called petty sessions. The scope of summary jurisdiction has been steadily widened since the late seventeenth century: far more crimes in England and Wales are tried summarily than by full jury trial. Surviving records of summary trials are held in local record offices, but the survival is generally poor until the mid nineteenth century. The justices also met together, usually four times a year, at meetings that became known as quarter sessions, where until the late nineteenth century, they transacted administrative business of the kind that would now fall to elected local councils and were also empowered to hear certain criminal cases that were to be determined by a jury. With certain limited exceptions (see **38.4**), quarter sessions and other records created by justices of the peace are usually held in local record offices, rather than at the PRO: see Gibson, *Quarter Sessions Records for Family Historians*.

From the thirteenth century, criminal cases could also be tried before professional judges acting as justices of gaol delivery: pairs of judges literally rode through groups or circuits of counties in order to hold their courts, which became known as the assizes. They took their authority from commissions of gaol delivery and (from the 1530s) of oyer and terminer. These enabled them to try or 'deliver' anyone who was imprisoned in the county gaol or who was on bail from it, and also to 'hear and determine' certain other cases such as treason, riot, rebellion, coining, murder, burglary, etc. In most parts of England and Wales, therefore, there were multiple courts able to try criminal cases. Additionally, the King's Bench, which was a central royal court sitting at Westminster, had an overriding jurisdiction over them all. Records of assize courts and of the King's Bench are held in the PRO (see **38.4** and **38.8**).

In some areas of the country the judicial system worked slightly differently. If the case in which you are interested was tried in the City of London, in the ancient county of Middlesex, in Bristol, Wales, or one of the Palatinates of Chester, Durham or Lancaster, read **38.5** and **38.6** below.

It is a fallacy to believe that minor offences were tried in minor courts and that serious offences were tried in the higher courts. Even today there are a number of offences that can be tried with a jury in a county court (the modern equivalent of assizes and quarter sessions) or without a jury in a magistrates court. In the past there was an even greater overlap between the various courts and the kind of cases that they could hear: some offences, such as assault, could be tried at any of the four levels of the court hierarchy. The division of cases between assize courts and sessions was very much a rough and ready one, and depended on convenience and cost as well as on the gravity of the crime. It is possible to generalize only about those crimes for which the penalty was death or transportation.

From at least the sixteenth century, it would have been extremely unusual for capital crimes to be tried anywhere other than assizes (or a court with equivalent power). Anyone who was transported before 1718 or who was transported for 14 years after 1718 must have been tried at assizes (or equivalent). Anyone who was sentenced to transportation for less than 14 years after 1718 could have been tried either at assizes or at quarter sessions. In trying to match the crime to a court, you need to remember that the law kept changing and that some of those changes would influence the kind of trial that could be held. Sheep stealing, for example, was a 'serious' offence in the eighteenth century, normally tried at assizes. But by the middle of the nineteenth century, records of trials for sheep stealing can often be found in quarter sessions or even summary jurisdiction. The reason is simple: the death penalty for sheep stealing was abolished in 1832 with the result that, as far as the law was concerned, it suddenly ceased to be a 'serious' offence.

Scotland has a very different legal system, whose surviving records are in the Scottish Record Office and local record offices in Scotland.

38.2 Using trial records

The second problem is the nature of the trial records themselves. The nature and quality of the assizes records varies considerably from period to period and from circuit to circuit. Trial records consist of a variety of documents: indictments, witness statements, gaol calendars, recognizances (bonds, usually for bail, but sometimes to testify or prosecute), and minute books. With certain limited exceptions, however, they do not contain transcripts of evidence and will not normally give details of the age of the accused or of his/her family relationships.

The indictments set out the nature of the charge against the accused. As with all formal legal records, until 1733 (with a brief interruption between 1650 and 1660) they are in heavily abbreviated Latin and are written in distinctive legal scripts. Even after 1733 when indictments were written in English and in an ordinary hand, the language used is so convoluted and archaic that it can be difficult to understand exactly what the defendant was being charged with. Indictments were not expressed in clear plain English until 1916. Even more disappointing for the family historian is the fact that although the indictments appear to tell you the occupation and parish of residence of the accused, the information given is fictitious. Men are almost always described as labourers, even if they were skilled artisans. The parish of residence is invariably the place at which the crime was committed. If you are prepared to make a thorough search of the indictment and deposition files then you may be able to find more accurate information from some of the associated documents: Knafla has been able to establish correct occupation and place of residence for 87 per cent of the defendants he studied for *Kent at Law 1602*, by doing just this. But remember that a search of this kind is going to be both time consuming and speculative; it will also require a sound knowledge of trial procedures and records as well as palaeographic skills. If you want to attempt it you will need to do a lot of background reading: the works listed in the bibliography below, especially by Baker, Beattie and Cockburn, will get you off to a good start.

Pre-trial witness statements may survive either with the indictments or in a separate series (usually described in the PRO as depositions, but often described in local record offices simply as sessions papers). These are in English and in the ordinary hand of the day, but if you are not familiar with early modern handwriting you may find them difficult to read. From about 1830, the

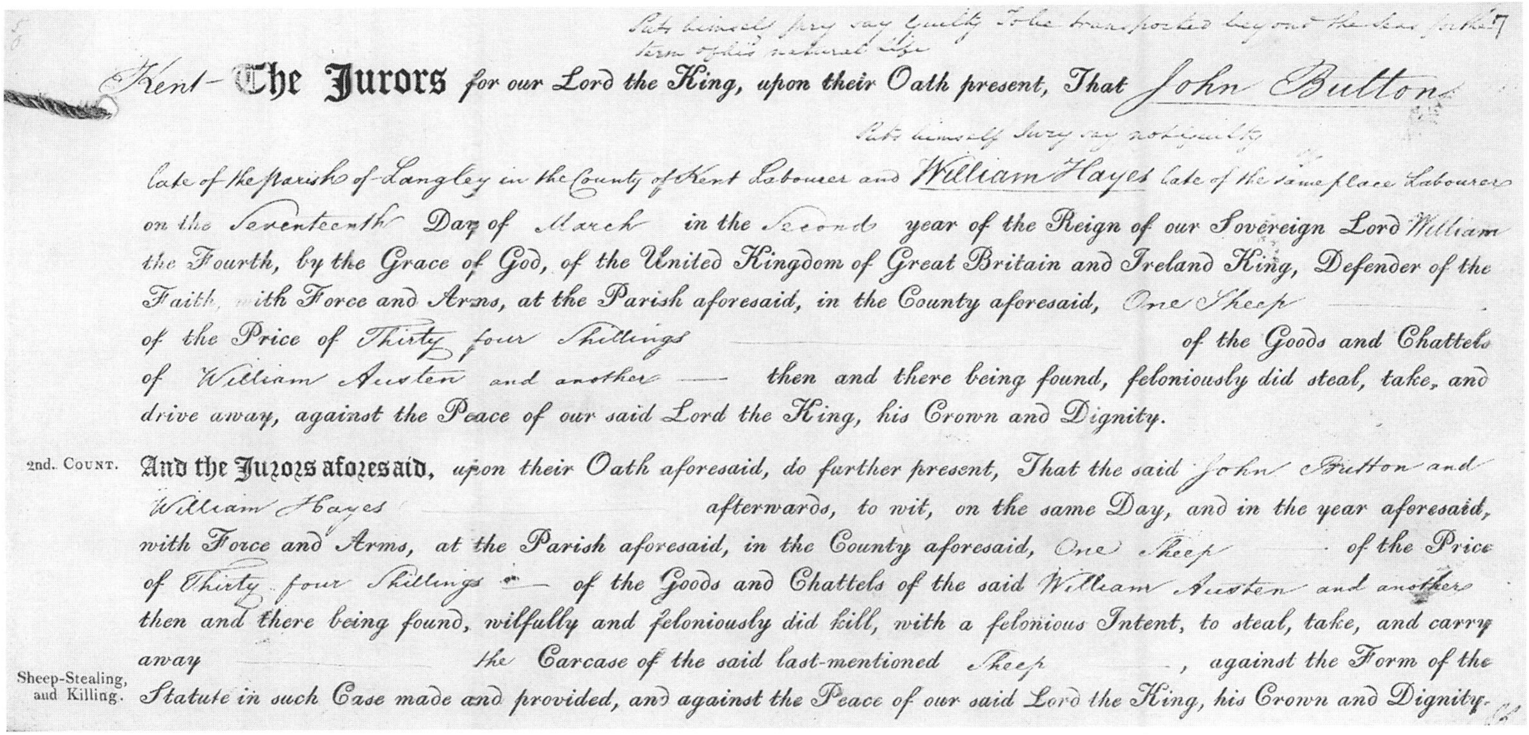

Puts himself jury say guilty To be transported beyond the seas for the term of his natural life

Kent – **The Jurors** for our Lord the King, upon their Oath present, That John Button

Puts himself Jury say not guilty

late of the parish of Langley in the County of Kent Labourer and William Hayes late of the same place Labourer on the Seventeenth Day of March in the Second year of the Reign of our Sovereign Lord William the Fourth, by the Grace of God, of the United Kingdom of Great Britain and Ireland King, Defender of the Faith, with Force and Arms, at the Parish aforesaid, in the County aforesaid, One Sheep of the Price of Thirty four Shillings of the Goods and Chattels of William Austen and another — then and there being found, feloniously did steal, take, and drive away, against the Peace of our said Lord the King, his Crown and Dignity.

2nd. Count. **And the Jurors aforesaid**, upon their Oath aforesaid, do further present, That the said John Button and William Hayes afterwards, to wit, on the same Day, and in the year aforesaid, with Force and Arms, at the Parish aforesaid, in the County aforesaid, One Sheep of the Price of Thirty four Shillings — of the Goods and Chattels of the said William Austen and another then and there being found, wilfully and feloniously did kill, with a felonious Intent, to steal, take, and carry away the Carcase of the said last-mentioned Sheep, against the Form of the

Sheep-Stealing, and Killing. Statute in such Case made and provided, and against the Peace of our said Lord the King, his Crown and Dignity.

Figure 13 The indictment of John Button and William Hayes for sheep stealing, at the Kent assizes, July 1832 entered on a pre-printed form. Space has been left at the top for annotations of the events at trial. Both opted for jury trial ('puts himself') Button was found guilty and sentenced to transportation for life; Hayes was found not guilty. See also Figure 14. (ASSI 94/2130) deposition files have been heavily weeded, so that only depositions in capital cases, usually murder and riot, tend to survive. From the mid twentieth century, depositions survive for a greater variety of cases. The deposition files (especially more modern ones) may also contain items used as trial exhibits such as photographs, maps, appeal papers and in one case even a policeman's pocket book. Some of the exhibits are distressing.

Minute books (usually described by the PRO as crown books or gaol books) may also survive. These usually list the defendants at each session with a brief note of the charges against them and are often annotated with verdicts and sentences. Similar information is contained in sheriffs' assize vouchers (see **38.11**). Trial records are subject to the normal thirty year closure rule; some may be closed for longer periods.

Unofficial transcripts of evidence survive for some early nineteenth century cases in which convicts petitioned for mercy (see **39.6**). Official transcripts of selected criminal trials of special interest, 1846–1931, are held amongst the records of the Director of Public Prosecutions in DPP 4. The records of the Director of Public Prosecutions also include case papers relating to prosecutions (1889–1983) in DPP 1 and DPP 2, and registers of cases (1884–1956) in DPP 3. Most of these records are closed for 75 years.

38.3 Using other sources

Although the formal trial records might be disappointing, it is worth remembering that even quite ordinary trials attracted a lot of journalistic coverage, which sometimes included transcripts of all or part of the evidence, as well as comments on family or occupational background. If you really want to know what happened at the trial, it is probably better to start with published reports of trials rather than with actual trial records. Newspaper coverage became common from about 1750. *The Times*, which has been produced since 1786, is available on microfilm at most major reference libraries, as well as at the PRO, and is indexed. Transcripts, confessions, dying statements of those who were hanged and other 'true crime' accounts have been published in pamphlet, magazine and book form from early modern times to the present day. In the early period such publications were sometimes produced as a one off attempt to break into what was obviously a lucrative market, but local printers sometimes also tried to establish a market of their own by producing a series of pamphlets about local trials. The most famous of these is the *Old Bailey Proceedings* which have been published since at least the 1690s (see below **38.6**), but similar accounts were produced for other parts of the country too: the earliest known copy of the *Surrey Assize Proceedings* dates from 1678 and the series is known to have continued until at least 1780. Surviving pamphlets of this kind can be traced using the British Library's *English Short Title Catalogue* (previously known as the *Eighteenth Century Short Title Catalogue*). A number of these pamphlets have been republished on microfiche by Chadwyck-Healey as *British Trials 1660–1900* together with indexes of defendants, victims and locations; a copy is available at the PRO. To find out more about how to trace printed works on crime, ask for advice at your nearest central reference library.

38.4 Quarter sessions and assizes

Before the assizes were created the judges were sent to try cases in the counties at irregular intervals on what became known as general eyres. The surviving records of these cases, both civil and criminal, are described in Crook's *Records of the general eyre*; Crook also lists those that have been published. The records are in PRO classes JUST 1–JUST 4; their use requires a high level of skill. Few quarter sessions records for the fourteenth and fifteenth centuries survive. Those that do are in the PRO, mostly in JUST 1; they are listed in Putnam's edition, and many have been published by local record societies. From the sixteenth century onwards, quarter sessions survive in increasing quantities, and they are deposited in local record offices; Gibson's *Quarter Sessions Records* gives details and locations, while Ratclif's *Warwick County Records* and Emmison and Gray's *County records* give a very full indication of the nature of the records and the sort of information they contain.

Although a few strays are known to survive in local record offices, assizes records are normally held in the PRO. For the fourteenth and fifteenth centuries they are mostly in JUST 3, with some others in JUST 1, JUST 4 and KB 9. After 1559, they are normally in the ASSI classes. A county by county checklist is given below in **38.7**. Assizes and Quarter Sessions courts were abolished in 1971.

38.5 Anomalous jurisdictions: Bristol, Wales and the Palatinates

In Bristol the right to hear criminal cases was one of the ancient chartered privileges of the Corporation of Bristol. This right was abolished in 1832, after which date assize courts were held for Bristol as for any other county. Surviving trial records before 1832 are held in the Bristol Record Office; those after 1832 are in the PRO amongst the ASSI classes.

Wales and the Palatinates had special jurisdictions serving much the same function as assizes. In Wales, the equivalent jurisdiction was exercised from 1542 to 1830 by the Great Sessions of Wales, whose records are in the National Library of Wales; from 1830 to 1971 the Welsh counties were included among the assizes circuits, so the records are in the ASSI classes at the PRO. Records of the Palatinate of Chester, primarily comprising Cheshire and Flint are held in the PRO in various classes with the lettercode CHES, as are those of the Palatinate of Durham covering County Durham and certain areas beyond (lettercode DURH) and the Palatinate of Lancaster, covering Lancashire (lettercode PL). For a county by county checklist see **38.7**.

38.6 Anomalous jurisdictions: London, the Old Bailey and the Central Criminal Court

Jurisdictions in the London area are even more complex. The area we now know as central London (north of the Thames) was historically part of the county of Middlesex (and its subordinate jurisdiction of Westminster). Those parts of London that had spread south of the Thames were largely in the borough of Southwark. Southwark was normally held to be part of the county of Surrey, although to complicate matters still further, the City of London did occasionally try to claim jurisdiction over parts of it. The City of London was and is a specific administrative area covering approximately one square mile at the heart of modern London. If you are trying to trace the records of a 'London' crime before 1834, it is essential that you first find out whether it took place in the City or in urban Middlesex. You can establish this from the printed *Old Bailey Proceedings*. If your 'London' crime was committed south of the river before 1834, then you need to look at the records of assize courts for the Home Circuit.

Until 1834, sessions of oyer and terminer and of gaol delivery for the City of London were held before the lord mayor and the recorder of London at the Old Bailey. Ordinary sessions cases for the City of London were tried at Guildhall. As part of its privileges, the City of London had also acquired rights over its neighbouring county of Middlesex. These included the right to appoint its own sheriffs to the office of sheriff of Middlesex, and control of the county gaol (Newgate) together with the right to deliver the gaol. This meant that the Middlesex sessions of gaol delivery were also held at the Old Bailey. However, the Middlesex sessions of oyer and terminer were held alongside the sessions of the peace before the Middlesex justices at their sessions house in Clerkenwell.

In 1834 the Old Bailey sessions were abolished and replaced with a court that is officially known as the Central Criminal Court (but which in practice is still called the Old Bailey). The geographical jurisdiction of this new court reflected the continuing spread of London and therefore included parts of Essex, Kent and Surrey as well as the City of London and Middlesex. The court's legal jurisdiction was made equivalent to an assize court as it was given oyer and terminer and gaol delivery functions for both the City of London and for Middlesex. Between 1834 and 1844, it was also given the jurisdiction over crimes on the high seas that had previously belonged to the High Court of Admiralty (**38.10**).

The original records of Old Bailey trials before 1834 are not held in the PRO but *either* at the Corporation of London Record Office (City of London cases) *or* at the London Metropolitan Archives (Middlesex cases). The addresses of both are given in **48**. Records of the Old Bailey or Central Criminal Court after 1834 are held in the PRO in classes with the lettercode CRIM. As a result of the recommendations of the Denning Report, only a two per cent sample of depositions survives.

Trials at the Old Bailey and Central Criminal Court were, and are, particularly well covered by newspapers and other printed sources. Before attempting to use any original trial records you should look for published material. The *Old Bailey Proceedings* were published from the 1690s onwards. These are virtually verbatim reports of the proceedings in court, giving the name of the accused, the charges, the evidence of witnesses, the verdict (often with the prisoner's age if found guilty), and the sentence. The report will also indicate whether the case was a London or a Middlesex one. They are roughly indexed within each volume. Copies of the printed sets are held in many libraries, as well as the PRO in record classes PCOM 1 (1801–1904) and CRIM 10 (1834–1912), but such sets are invariably incomplete. For the period between 1714 and 1834 it would be better to use the microfilm edition, which is also available in many libraries as well as at the PRO. Some additional information, 1815 to 1849, can be found in HO 16 and for 1782 to 1853, in HO 77 (see **38.11**).

The court rooms of the Old Bailey were also used, from about 1660 to 1834, for the trials of individuals accused of offences within the jurisdiction of the High Court of Admiralty. Trial records in these cases, if they survive, are to be found amongst the various High Court of Admiralty classes in the PRO (see **38.10**)

38.7 Assize and similar courts: a county by county checklist of records surviving in the PRO, 1559–1971

(*Records are still being added)

England	Crown & Gaol Books	Indictment files	Depositions
Bedfordshire	1734–1945	1658–*	1832–*
Berkshire	1657–1971	1650–*	1719–*
Buckinghamshire	1734–1945	1642–*	1832–*
Cambridgeshire	1734–*	1642–*	1834–*
Cheshire	1532–51	1831–*	1831–*
Cornwall	1670–1971	1801–*	1861–*
Cumberland	1665–1873	1607–*	1613–*
Derbyshire	1818–1945	1662, 67, 87, 1860–*	1862–*
Devon	1670–1971	1801–*	1861–*
Dorset	1670–1971	1801–*	1861–*
Durham	1753–1944	1582–*	1843–*
Essex	1826–*	1559–*	1825–*
Gloucestershire	1657–1971	1662–*	1719–*
Hampshire	1670–1971	1801–*	1861–*
Herefordshire	1657–1971	1627–*	1719–*
Hertfordshire	1734–*	1573–*	1829–*
Huntingdonshire	1734–*	1643–*	1851–*
Kent	1734–*	1559–*	1812–*
Lancashire	1524–1877	1660–1867, 1877–*	1663–1867, 1877–*
Leicestershire	1818–1945	1653, 6, 1860, 1864–*	1862–*
Lincolnshire	1818–1945	1652–79, 1860–*	1862–*
London & Middlesex	1834–1949	1833–1971	1839–*
Monmouthshire	1657–1971	1666–*	1719–*
Norfolk	1734–*	1606–*	1817–*
Northamptonshire	1818–1945	1659–60, 1860–*	1862, 1864–*
Northumberland	1665–1944	1607–*	1613–*
Nottinghamshire	1818–1945	1663–4, 82, 1860–*	1862–*
Oxfordshire	1657–1971	1661–*	1719–*
Rutland	1818–1945	1667, 85, 1860–*	1862, 1864–73, 1876–*
Shropshire	1657–1971	1654–*	1719–*
Somerset	1670–1971	1801–*	1861–*

Staffordshire	1657–1971	1662–*	1719–*
Suffolk	1734–1863–*	1653–*	1832–*
Surrey	1734–*	1559–*	1820–*
Sussex	1734–*	1559–*	1812–*
Warwickshire	1818–1945	1652, 88, 1860–*	1862–*
Westmorland	1714–1873	1607–*	1613–*
Wiltshire	1670–1971	1729, 1801–*	1861–*
Worcestershire	1657–1971	1662–*	1719–*
Yorkshire	1658–1876	1607–*	1613–*

Wales

Anglesey	1831–1938, 1945–51	1831–*	1831–*
Breconshire	1841–2, 1844–51	1834–*	1837–*
Caernarvonshire	1831–83, 1945–51	1831–*	1831–*
Cardiganshire	1841–2, 1844–51	1834–*	1837–*
Carmarthenshire	1841–2, 1844–51	1834–*	1837–*
Denbighshire	1831–1938, 1945–51	1831–*	1831–*
Flint	1831–1938, 1945–51	1831–*	1831–*
Glamorganshire	1841–2, 1844–1951	1834–*	1837–*
Merionethshire	1831–51	1831–*	1831–*
Montgomeryshire	1831–1938, 1945–51	1831–*	1831–*
Pembrokeshire	1841–2, 1844–1951	1834–*	1837–*
Radnor	1841–51	1834–*	1837–*

There is a leaflet available at Kew that will help you to identify the record class for the county and date that you need. Please note that the covering dates given in the table are meant to give a general indication of survival and that there may be small, unexplained gaps within an otherwise continuous run of records.

38.8 King's Bench

The Court of King's Bench was the highest court of common law in England and Wales until it was absorbed into the High Court in 1875. This section considers only its criminal jurisdiction; for a discussion of the records relating to civil litigation see **47**. The Court of King's Bench evolved from the Curia Regis and had become an established institution by the thirteenth century. The court was not an itinerant one but since it was attached to the person of the King it necessarily moved with the seat of government. By 1422 the court had become settled at Westminster, although the wording of its records still maintained the fiction that it was always held in the presence of the king himself.

The King's Bench gradually developed three separate jurisdictions: original jurisdiction over all criminal matters, supervisory powers over lesser courts, and a local jurisdiction over the county in which it sat (which in practice from 1422 onwards was Middlesex). Like all courts in England and Wales, its formal records were written in heavily abbreviated Latin and in distinctive legal scripts until 1733 (except for a brief period during the Interregnum). Its procedures were elaborate and created complex, interconnected series of records for which there is no single or obvious point of entry. The indexes and finding aids are inadequate. In short these are not records that should be attempted by anyone but the most determined of searchers. As with assize and quarter sessions records, records of King's Bench trials do not contain transcripts of evidence and it may be better to start by looking for a newspaper or other published account of the trial that interests you (see **38.3**).

Despite the received wisdom of traditional legal historians who have assumed that use of this court must have been restricted to the rich and influential, the reality is that the court was accessible to almost all ranks of society. Its wide jurisdiction also meant that cases initiated or referred to the King's Bench (few of which were actually tried) covered a wide range of subject matter, from minor assaults, disorderly houses and obstructed highways to riot, attempted rape, and high treason. The records of the King's Bench are a particularly fruitful source of information about Londoners, but cases also came to the court from all over the country. Occasionally, they even came from the colonies as well.

Records of the King's Bench survive from the thirteenth century until its abolition in 1875. Formal and formulaic narratives of both civil and criminal proceedings are given in the plea rolls: KB 26 (1194–1272) and then in KB 27 until 1702. After 1702 entries for criminal business are found on the Crown Rolls (KB 28). Indictment files, arranged by term, are in KB 9 until 1675. Between 1675 and 1845 there are two series of indictments: KB 10 for London and Middlesex and KB 11 for the provincial or out-counties. From 1845 to 1875 there is once again a single series of indictments (KB 12). Indictments in special cases are in KB 8 (**38.9**). For a description of the kind of information that can be gained from indictments, see **38.2**. Minute books, known as Crown side rule books, survive from 1589 in KB 21. Occasional witness statements survive from the mid seventeenth century, but the survival is particularly good from the eighteenth century onwards (KB 1 and KB 2).

From 1329 the controlment rolls in KB 29 provide references to the entries of criminal business, in KB 27 and KB 28. Some contemporary indexes to indictments exist in IND 1. They are arranged alphabetically by the first letter of the surname of the accused, and then chronologically by term and supply the number of the indictment on the relevant indictment file. There are indexes to London and Middlesex defendants, 1673–1843; to provincial defendants, 1638–1704 and 1765–1843; and to London and Middlesex defendants and some defendants in northern counties, 1682–1699. There is a modern card index to entries on the plea rolls (KB 28), 1844–1859. From 1738, there is also a contemporary listing of the statements in KB 1 in record class KB 39. The great docket books and modern pye books in IND 1 can also be used as finding aids. Both give information about the way cases were processed through the courts, but as they are arranged chronologically they are of limited use unless you already have some information about the date of the trial.

38.9 Sedition and high treason

Records of certain treason trials and other special cases were held in the so-called *'Baga de Secretis'* (KB 8). Unlike the other KB classes, KB 8 is well listed so it is comparatively easy to find cases. Some other records of, or relating to, treason trials, including lists of prisoners and convicts, are in KB 33, PC 1, TS 11 and TS 20; see the PRO information leaflet *The Jacobite Risings of 1715 and 1745*. Many of the most celebrated cases in King's Bench are reported in detail in the published *State Trials*. Trials for seditious libel should be traced through the King's Bench records in the normal way (see **38.8**).

38.10 High Court of Admiralty

The criminal jurisdiction of the High Court of Admiralty was established by act of Parliament in 1535; it lasted until 1834. Commissions of oyer and terminer and of gaol delivery were issued to the Admiral or his deputy authorizing them to try cases of piracy and other crimes committed on the high seas, according to the procedures of common law. Its criminal jurisdiction also included the English havens and the Thames below London Bridge (then the limit of the tidal Thames). Until about 1660 the court usually met at the Guildhall or in Southwark; after 1660 it began also to use the Old Bailey and from 1700 the admiralty sessions were always held there. Published reports of cases are sometimes included in the *Old Bailey Proceedings* (**38.3**). As explained above (see **38.2**), all formal legal records are written in heavily abbreviated Latin and in distinctive legal scripts until 1733, the information given in indictments is often fictitious, and trial records do not normally include transcripts of evidence.

The main series of criminal records is held in HCA 1 which is well listed. It covers the period 1537–1834, with a gap between 1539–1574. The files contain a variety of different kinds of document such as lists of prisoners, bails and bonds, jury panels, as well as indictments and depositions. It also contains material about cases tried by Vice Admiralty Courts in the maritime counties of England (excluding the Cinque Ports) and Wales as well as overseas. An index of persons and ships is available in the Research Enquiries Room; both the list and the index have been published by the List and Index Society (volumes 45 and 46). Criminal examinations for 1607–1609, 1612–1614 and 1661–1674 are in HCA 13/98, 99 and 142. Warrants relating to arrests on ships are in HCA 38 and those relating to executions are in HCA 55. Admiralty out correspondence concerning the court, 1663–1815, is in ADM 2. Records relating to appeals from colonial admiralty courts are in PCAP.

The jurisdiction of the High Court of Admiralty passed to the new Central Criminal Court in 1834. In 1844 the judges of assize were allowed to try offences in any county. For the period 1834–1844, therefore, you should look for the records in the CRIM classes and after 1844 in the relevant ASSI classes.

The High Court of Admiralty also had jurisdiction over instance and prize cases; for a fuller description of instance and prize jurisdiction see **47.9**.

38.11 Criminal trial registers, and other lists of prisoners to be tried, 1758–1892

Most records of criminals and criminal trials are not easy to use, as they are not usually arranged by name. If you have some information, however sketchy, about the date and place of trial then you should try using sheriffs' assize vouchers, the Criminal Registers or the Calendars of Prisoners. Please remember, however, that these sources will only help you to find those who were

KENT.

A CALENDAR

OF

PRISONERS FOR TRIAL

AT

THE SUMMER ASSIZES,

TO BE

HOLDEN AT MAIDSTONE,

On MONDAY, the 30th of JULY, 1832,

BEFORE

The Right Honourable CHARLES, LORD TENTERDEN,

Chief Justice of His Majesty's Court of King's Bench,

AND

The Honourable Sir JOHN BAYLEY, Knight,

One of the Barons of His Majesty's Court of Exchequer,

AND OF THE PRISONERS UNDER SENTENCE.

GEORGE DOUGLAS, ESQ. SHERIFF.

PRISONERS UNDER SENTENCE.

No.	Name.	Age.	Offence.	Sentence.	When Convicted.
1	Ann Tonnick,	60	Privately stealing in a shop	Transported for Life	Summer Assizes 1823
2	Susanna Hopson,	70	Stealing a quantity of Lead	Transported Seven Years	Lent Assizes 1828

PRISONERS FOR TRIAL.

No.	Name and Trade, &c.	Age.	By whom and when Committed.	Offence.	Sentence, &c.
1	John Vant,	43	Rev. J. Poore, D.D.	Stealing two lambs, value two pounds, the property of Thomas Young Greet and others, at Halstow	
2	John Williamson,	20	1832, March 15		
3	Thomas Chambers, alias Challender, *Laborers.*	26			
4	John Green. *Laborer.*	28	T. Day, Esq. ...17 Mayor of Maidstone	Charged on one of the Coroner's Inquisitions, with having at Maidstone, maliciously caused to be taken by Mary Ann Masters, she being then quick with child, a quantity of white arsenic, with intent to procure a mis-carriage.	
5	John Button,	24	J. Jacobson, Esq. ...22	Stealing one wether sheep, value thirty-four shillings, the property of William and John Austen, at Langley.	
6	William Hayes, *Laborer.*	28			
7	Thomas Axton, *Laborer.*	26	I. Espinasse, Esq...22	Breaking the house of William Stoneham, and stealing two silver spoons, two gowns, and a shawl, his property, and a great coat, and other articles, the property of Henry Bird, at Dartford.	
8	John Atkins, *Laborer*	40	Rev. E. Hasted 23	Charged with having a venereal affair with a mare, at Ulcomb.	

Figure 14 Calendar of prisoners awaiting trial at the Kent assizes, July 1892 (ASSI 94/2130)

tried by jury: they will not help for trials held in ordinary magistrates courts without a jury.

Sheriffs' assize vouchers, 1758–1832, give some information about prisoners to be tried at assizes (they do not include those tried at quarter sessions) including their sentences, the length of time they spent in prison and the costs of maintaining them. They are held in E 370/35–51.

The Criminal Registers are returns from the counties, bound up in alphabetical order of county. They show all persons charged with indictable offences, giving the date and result of the trial, sentence in the case of conviction, and dates of execution for those convicted on capital charges. The registers are in two series: HO 26, which covers Middlesex only, 1791–1849; and HO 27, which covers all England and Wales, 1805–1892 (including Middlesex from 1850). For 1807–1811 only, the Middlesex registers in HO 26 relate only to those tried at the Old Bailey; prisoners tried at the Middlesex and Westminster sessions are listed in HO 27.

Printed Calendars of Prisoners, 1868–1971, are held in record class HO 140 and also in CRIM 9 (for London, 1855–1949). Some are closed for 75 or 100 years. The calendars list prisoners to be tried at courts of assize and quarter sessions, and for each one gives age and occupation, level of literacy, the name and address of the committing magistrate, details of the alleged offence, verdict and sentence. Like the Criminal Registers they are arranged by county. Printed calendars of this kind were compiled from at least the early nineteenth century and earlier calendars can sometimes be found in PCOM 2 as well as scattered amongst assizes classes. Copies are also sometimes to be found in local record offices. For the Old Bailey (Central Criminal Court) there are returns of prisoners to be tried, 1815–1849, in HO 16 and printed lists of defendants, 1782–1853, with the results of their trials, in HO 77.

38.12 Criminal trials: bibliography

K R Andrews, *Elizabethan Privateering* (1969)

J H Baker, 'Criminal courts and procedure at common law 1550–1800', in J S Cockburn, ed. *Crime in England 1550–1800* (London, 1977)

J M Beattie, *Crime and courts in England 1660–1800* (Oxford, 1986)

E Berckman, *Victims of piracy: the admiralty court 1575–1678* (1979)

British Trials 1660–1900 (Chadwyck-Healey, 1990)

M Cale, *Law and society, an introduction to sources for criminal and legal history from 1800* (PRO, 1996)

J S Cockburn, ed., *Calendar of Assize Records, Home Circuit Indictments* (London, 1975–1995; Woodbridge, 1997)

D Crook, *Records of the general eyre* (London, 1982)

H Deadman and E Scudder, *An introductory guide to the Corporation of London Record Office* (London, 1994)

F G Emmison and I Gray, *County records (quarter sessions, petty sessions, clerk of the peace and lieutenancy)* (Helps for students of history 62, 2nd edn, Historical Association, 1987)

J S W Gibson, *Quarter Sessions Records for Family Historians: a Select List* (FFHS, 1995)

D T Hawkings, *Criminal ancestors, a guide to historical and criminal records in England and Wales*, (Sutton, 1992)

T B Howell and T J Howell, eds, *A complete collection of state trials . . .* (London, 1816–1826)

L A Knafla, *Kent at Law 1602, The county jurisdiction: assizes and sessions of peace* (London, 1994 continuing)

List and Index Society, *High Court of Admiralty, Oyer and Terminer Records (HCA 1), 1535–1834* (1969, vols 45 and 46)

J McDonell, ed., *Reports of State Trials, New Series* (London, 1858–1898, reprinted Abingdon, 1982)

B H Putnam, ed., *Proceedings before the Justices of the Peace in the Fourteenth and Fifteenth Centuries* (1938)

S C Ratclif and others, eds, *Warwick County Records* (Warwick, 1935–1964)
G O Sayles, *Select cases in the court of King's Bench under Edward I*, 7 Vols (Selden Society, 1936–71)

39 Remanded and convicted prisoners

39.1 Introduction

Today, we are accustomed to regard imprisonment as one of the most likely punishments for criminal behaviour. This was not so in the past. Most offences either carried the death penalty (often commuted to transportation) or were punished by a fine and/or whipping. Each county had its own county gaol which was primarily used to hold prisoners awaiting trial. Many counties also experimented with new prisons where vagrants and later also criminals could be put to work and subjected to disciplines that were intended to reform them. This kind of prison was often called a bridewell or house of correction. However, such initiatives were highly localized and met with varying degrees of success. Most prisons, whether designated as houses of correction or not, were simply used to house prisoners on remand. With certain exceptions (see **39.3**), their records, if they survive, are usually held in the local county record office. A good introduction to the subject is provided by Hawkings's *Criminal Ancestors*, which provides transcripts and facsimiles of a wide range of records relating to imprisonment, not only in the PRO but also in local record offices.

39.2 Conviction and sentence

There is no single central index of either prisoners or convicts. From the early nineteenth century (later eighteenth for London and Middlesex) the criminal trial registers and calendars of prisoners (see **38.11**) will help you to find some information about those who were convicted and sentenced after trial by jury. For prisoners convicted earlier than this, you will have to rely on the information you can gain from trial and associated records: the verdict and sentence are usually noted on the indictment and can also be traced through minute books and sheriffs' assize vouchers (see **38.11**).

Imprisonment was rarely used as a punishment in its own right until the nineteenth century. Those convicted of crimes were more likely to be sentenced to death, to transportation, or to a fine or whipping. Few of those who were sentenced to death actually hanged: most were reprieved, or had their sentences commuted to transportation. Published pamphlet and newspaper literature is the best source for finding out about the lives of those who were hanged (see **38.3**), but the determined searcher may find additional information about the costs of imprisonment and execution amongst the financial papers of sheriffs in E 370 (1714–1832), T 64 (1745–1785), T 90 (1733–1822) and T 207 (1823–1959). These records may also contain information about the cost of administering whippings.

If your convict was sentenced to transportation (or had a death sentence commuted to transportation), then turn to chapter **40**. If you discover or already know that your convict was sentenced to death, or to transportation or was actually transported, you should look at applications for clemency (**39.6**). In fact you should consider looking at these even if your convict received a lesser sentence, as the records created by such applications are often extremely informative, especially about family background and relationships.

Court orders for imprisonment or transfer from one prison to another, with details of the convict's penal history, 1843–1871, are in PCOM 5, with indexes in PCOM 6. They give the name of the convict (and any aliases), age, marital status, trade or occupation, crime, date and place of committal and conviction, sentence, information as to previous convictions and character; name and residence of next of kin, literacy level and religion, together with a physical description. Thereafter you can trace the history and course of their imprisonment via the prison registers (**39.3**).

39.3 Registers of prisoners

Except for a brief period during the nineteenth century, prison records were not collected or retained centrally. Many are still kept by the prisons, or by the authorities who took them over. As a matter of policy, it has been decided that in future prison registers should be deposited in local record offices: essentially this means that most prison registers created after 1878 are more likely to be found in a local record office than in the PRO. Nevertheless the PRO does have various registers, mainly nineteenth century, of some criminal prisons (for debtors' prisons see **46**). These include the prison ships or 'hulks' that were moored in British coastal waters (Woolwich, Chatham, Sheerness, Portsmouth and Plymouth) to house prisoners (usually, but not always, those awaiting transportation), 1776–1857, as well as some of those that were used in Gibraltar and Bermuda until 1875. Lists of those in prison on the night of a census will be included in the census returns from 1841(see **2**).

Registers giving details about convicts in prisons and on the hulks are held in PCOM 2 (1770–1951), and registers of prisoners on the hulks, 1802–1849, are in HO 9. The information given is variable but is likely to include physical description (sometimes with a photograph), as well as details of occupation, marital status, aliases and previous character, as well as an indication of discharge or transfer to another prison. Similar registers, also including detailed descriptions of the prisoners, 1838–1875, are in HO 23 and HO 24, while KB 32/23 has a return of convicts in the Millbank Penitentiary in 1826, which gives name, offence, court of conviction, sentence, age, 'bodily state' and behaviour. The quarterly returns of convicts in prisons and hulks, 1824–1876, in HO 8, can be used to trace details of behaviour, state of health, transfers to other gaols and eventual release. There are quarterly returns relating to the hulks, 1802–1831, in T 38; registers for the *Cumberland* and *Dolphin*, 1819–1834, are in ADM 6, and registers for the *Antelope, Coromandel, Dromedary*, and *Weymouth*, 1823–1828 are in HO 7/3. Some registers and returns of prisoners in the hulks are also found in T 1, but the inadequacy of the lists makes searching extremely difficult. Some useful tips are given in Hawkings' *Criminal Ancestors*, which also has a useful, but now dated, list of prison registers held in local record offices.

39.4 Registers of habitual criminals

Transportation to Australia was effectively stopped in 1857, although it was not formally ended until 1867; this meant that prisoners who would previously have been transported were instead imprisoned and subsequently released back into the community. In an attempt to dispel some of the anxiety this caused, local prisons were asked to compile registers of 'habitual criminals' – that is, prisoners convicted of any of the many crimes specified by the Habitual Criminals Act 1869, or by the Prevention of Crime Act 1871. Printed forms were supplied with these registers: these required name and alias, age, description, trade, prison from which released, date of liberation, offence, sentence, term of supervision, intended residence, distinguishing marks and any previous convictions. In addition photographs were pasted onto the forms. These local registers were supposed to be sent to the central Habitual Criminals Registry, where an alphabetical national register of habitual criminals was compiled of people thought likely to reoffend: the idea was to distribute the printed national register to police stations. The national register did not include the photographs. The first national register of habitual criminals covered December 1869 to March 1876, and included 12,164 people under 22,115 names, out of a total of 179,601 submitted in the local registers (PCOM 2/404).

The PRO does not have a full set of these national registers, but since they were compiled for local distribution, others may survive elsewhere. The registers in the PRO are to be found in PCOM 2/404 (1869–1876) and in MEPO 6/1–52 (1881–1882, 1889–1940); they are closed for 75 years from the date of creation. The PRO also has the local prison registers of habitual criminals for Birmingham, 1871–1875 (PCOM 2/296–299, 430–434) and Cambridge, 1875–1877 (PCOM 2/300). Other local registers are still in the custody of the prisons and constabularies which took over their responsibilities.

There are similarly informative registers of habitual drunkards, 1903–1914 (MEPO 6/77–88).

39.5 Licences

The increased use of imprisonment as a punishment naturally led to increased costs for the criminal justice system, both in terms of the maintenance of individual prisoners and in the costs of prison buildings. By 1853, there were considerable anxieties about the expansion in the prison population that would result from the diminishing numbers of convicts being transported to Australia. A system of licences which enabled convicts of good behaviour to be released before the expiry of their sentences was introduced to prevent this. The licences (popularly known as 'tickets of leave') could be revoked in cases of misbehaviour or reoffending. There are registers of licences to convicts to be at large, annotated with details of subsequent revocation, if any, 1853–1887, in PCOM 3 (male convicts) and PCOM 4 (female convicts), arranged in licence number order. They give name, physical description, age, marital status, educational level, occupation, details of convictions, conduct whilst in prison, name and address of next of kin, religion and health. There are indexes in PCOM 6, which cover 1853–1881 for male licences and 1853–1885 for female licences.

39.6 Pardons, appeals for mercy and other non-trial records

There were well over 300 offences carrying the death penalty by the end of the eighteenth century. However, only a minority of those sentenced to death were actually hanged. By the later nineteenth century, the death penalty had been removed from all but the most serious of crimes.

Pardons were freely granted, either unconditionally, or (from the 1600s onwards) on condition of transportation. Those sentenced to lesser penalties also applied for pardons. Not unnaturally,

Figure 15 These people were committed to Cambridge Gaol in 1875 and 1876, for brief sentences as a punishment for larceny. They were aged between 12 and 60. Much information was also collected about them (PCOM 2/300). From left to right: Alexander Pratt was a soldier in the 6th Dragoon Guards; Caroline Rose was a dustwoman, and blind in one eye; Alice Edwards' occupation was not given; William Plummer was an errand boy; William Lee was a labourer and Selah Chapman was a domestic servant.

those who had influence to call upon, or who were able to claim mitigating factors, were more likely to succeed in having their sentences reduced or commuted. Petitions were based on such things as youth, extreme age, provocation, the existence of dependent relatives who might become a burden to the poor rates, and previous good character. For these reasons, applications for mercy often contain a lot of biographical information and are thus exceptionally useful for family history purposes.

Before 1784, you will need to look at the correspondence of the secretaries of state in the State Papers, Domestic, which continue after 1782 as Home Office General Correspondence (HO 42). Much of the early correspondence of the secretaries of state has been published (and therefore indexed) and should be available to you at a good reference library or via the inter-library loan scheme as well as at the PRO. Records for the reign of Henry VIII have been published as *Letters and Papers . . . of Henry VIII*. For his son, Edward VI and subsequent monarchs, the series is known as the *Calendar of State Papers, Domestic*, and currently extends from 1547 to 1704. Similar records for the period 1760–1772 are published as the *Calendar of Home Office Papers*. For the period 1654–1717, pardons on condition of transportation are entered on the Patent Rolls (C 66) but such enrolments are in Latin, and in any case rarely contain the kind of detail that family historians need.

Separate series of papers relating to applications for mercy start in 1784 (HO 47 is the first.). Even after this, you may find it worthwhile to look at the Home Office General Correspondence in HO 42 (1782–1820) and Home Office Criminal Papers Old Series, 1849–1871, in HO 12 (approached via the registers in HO 14). Similar papers after 1871 are in HO 45 and HO 144.

Surviving petitions for mercy are HO 17 (1819–1840) and HO 18 (1839–1854). They are arranged in coded bundles and you will need to use the registers in HO 19 to identify them. The registers are arranged by date of receipt of petition, and give name of convict, date and place of trial, offence, code number of the bundle in which the petition was filed and, in most not all cases, the outcome of the application. Incidentally, the indexes do not start in 1819 but in 1797. There are also petitions in HO 48, HO 49, HO 54 and HO 56, but the lists are inadequate which makes these classes extremely difficult to search.

Records relating to clemency were also created by the authorities. Letters and statements from trial judges, 1816–1840, are in HO 6. They are somewhat formal, but do include recommendations for mercy together with useful supporting information about the convict and his/her crime. The judges' reports in HO 47 (1784–1829) are a particularly rich source of information as they often include virtual transcripts of the trial evidence (sometimes annotated with the judge's opinion of the veracity of witnesses and the credulity of the jurors) together with character references (both for and against the convict) and other personal information.

Formal records of pardons and reprieves are given by the Home Office warrants in HO 13 (1782–1849) and HO 15 (1850–1871). The modern registers of remissions and pardons, 1887–1960 (HO 188) is far more informative, as details of the cases are given and reasons for the decision are given; each volume has its own rough index.

39.7 Executions

Although most records about condemned persons should be traced as if they were ordinary convicts, there are some additional series of records relating specifically to the hanged, mainly in HO 163 (1899–1921), MEPO 3, and PCOM 9. HO 336 contains the complete records of nine condemned prisoners in order to illustrate the kind of information that was kept on such individuals. Background information on the way the death penalty was implemented can be found in PCOM 8, with more discursive contextual discussion in HO 42 and HO 45. There is no comprehensive list either of those executed or of the men who executed them, but HO 334/1 contains a register of prison burials (1834–1969) which provides the basis of establishing a list of the executed and some personal details about executioners can be found in HO 144 and PCOM 8.

39.8 Remanded and convicted prisoners: bibliography

M Cale, *Law and society, an introduction to sources for criminal and legal history from 1800* (PRO, 1996)
Calendar of Home Office Papers (3 vols, London, 1873–1881)
Calendar of State Papers, Domestic (London, 1856–1972)
D T Hawkings, *Bound for Australia* (Phillimore, 1987)
D T Hawkings, *Criminal Ancestors, a guide to historical criminal records in England and Wales* (Sutton, 1992)
W B Johnson, *The English Prison Hulks* (rev. edn, Phillimore, 1970)
Letters and Papers . . . of Henry VIII (London, 1864–1932)
S McConville, *History of English Prison Administration 1750–1877* (London, 1981)
S McConville, *English Local Prisons, 1860–1900: next only to death* (London, 1995)
S Webb and B Webb, *English Prisons under Local Government* (reprinted, London, 1963)
R Whitmore, *Victorian and Edwardian Crime and Punishment* (London, 1978)

40 Convicted prisoners transported abroad

40.1 Transportation: an introduction

As explained in **39**, the range of punishments open to the authorities for serious criminal offences before the nineteenth century was very limited: it was quite literally a choice between enforcing the death penalty or releasing criminals back into the community. The expansion of Britain's overseas territories added a further possibility: a period of exile during which the convict would be removed from his/her previous criminal associates, be forced to work productively and thereby learn new habits of industry and self discipline and at the same time benefit the development of the colonial economy. Transportation, for the imperial government, was not a question of simply dumping human refuse on the colonies: it was genuinely thought to be effective, efficient and humane. Those who were transported were often quite young: it was after all the young who were most likely to benefit from a new life in a new world, and who were most likely to be fit enough to supply the productive labour that that new world needed. The colonial authorities, not unnaturally, tended to take a more jaundiced view of the benefits of transportation, and bitterly resented it.

After 1615, as a result of an order by the Privy Council, it became increasingly common for a pardon to be offered to convicts who had been sentenced to death, on condition of transportation overseas. In 1718 an act of Parliament standardized transportation to America at 14 years for those who had been sentenced to death and introduced a new penalty – transportation for 7 years – as a sentence in its own right for a range of non-capital offences.

Some 40,000 people had been transported to America when the system came to a halt in 1776 because of the outbreak of the American Revolution. Prisoners who had been sentenced to transportation had to be held in prison instead. The overcrowding that ensued soon resulted in the creation of floating prisons or 'hulks' (see **39**), but of course they too soon became overcrowded. A solution was soon found: in 1787 the 'first fleet' set out to found a penal colony in New South Wales. Transportation to Van Diemen's Land (Tasmania) began in 1803. Transportation was at its height in the 1830s and was probably already in decline when, as a result of the Penal Servitude Act of 1853, it was removed from all but the most serious offences. In 1857 it was effectively abolished, although the Home Secretary retained the right to impose transportation in specific cases until 1867. It is estimated that over 160,000 people were transported to Australia and Tasmania between 1787 and 1867: in the 1830s 4,000 people were being transported every year.

Many of the records relating to voluntary emigration (see **14**) may also contain details of convicts or ex-convicts. For records of trials resulting in transportation, see **38**. For records of prisons and prison hulks, in which convicts were housed for various periods prior to transportation, see **39**.

40.2 Transportation to America and the West Indies

If you are looking for an individual who may have been transported to America or the West Indies, a good starting point is Coldham's *Complete Book of Emigrants in Bondage, 1614–1775*, based on records in the PRO as well as in local record·offices. A supplementary volume, adding about 3,000 further names, was published in 1992. Coldham lists transported convicts and gives, where known, date and place of trial, occupation, month of embarkation and landing, name of ship, and destination. You can move on from this to other published works, since (with the exception of trial records) most of the PRO's original sources relating to transportation in this period have been published. An earlier version of Coldham's research findings, published as *Bonded Passengers to America* (but also covering transportation to the West Indies) includes a readable history of the system and gives a detailed overview of the published sources that are available. Coldham's books will give you enough to start looking for the trial record. If your convict was transported before 1718 or was transported after 1718 for 14 years, then you should look for the trial amongst the records of assize or assize equivalent courts. If your convict was transported after 1718 for a period of 7 years then the trial could have been either at an assize or assize equivalent court, or at quarter sessions (see **38**). Remember that not all those who were sentenced to transportation actually went: perhaps your convict was successful in an application for mercy (see **39.6**). If your convict was involved in a particularly notorious trial then you may find that there are published works available that will save you much time and effort: lists of those transported after the Monmouth rebellion, for example, are included in Wigfield's *The Monmouth Rebels 1685*.

The PRO also holds Treasury money books (T 53) which include details of payments by the Treasury to contractors engaged to arrange transportation between 1716 and 1772. Until October 1744 names of all those to be transported from the home counties are listed, together with names of ships and their captains. Thereafter only totals for each county are given. Until 1742 the colony of destination is usually recorded. Similar information is given in a broken run of transportation lists, 1747–1772, in T 1. Colonial Office correspondence with America and the West Indies (CO 5) includes material on all aspects of transportation to the American colonies. Much of the material relevant to transportation amongst the records of the Treasury and of the Colonial Office has been published (**40.5**), and is therefore available at major reference libraries, as well as at the PRO. For other records relating to the American and West Indian colonies which may include details of convicts or ex-convicts, as well as free emigrants, see **14.6**. For records in the United States see **14.5**.

40.3 Transportation to Australia

As with transportation to America and the West Indies, it is advisable to start your search with published sources. For a general overview of the kind of documents that are available and what sort of information they contain, you will find Hawkings' *Bound for Australia* and *Criminal Ancestors* particularly useful as they provide transcripts and facsimiles of a wide range of records relating to imprisonment and transportation. Readers in Australia should know that microfilm copies of many PRO documents are available in Australia at the National Library in Canberra and at the Mitchell Library in Sydney.

Most family historians start by searching for the trial records, but as explained in **38**, such records are rarely very informative. Remember that no matter how short the sentence, few people would ever be able to return from Australia and that the voyage was long and dangerous: applications for mercy were commonplace and it is far better to start there than with the formal court record. In order to get started you will need to have some idea *either* of the date and place of trial, so that you can trace the convict forward *or* of the date and preferably ship on which the convict arrived in Australia so that you can trace him/her back. You can find this information in a number of ways. The Convict Transportation Registers, 1787–1867 (HO 11) provide the name of the ship on which the convict sailed as well as the date and place of conviction and the term of the sentence. They are not indexed by name of convict, but if you know the name of the ship and preferably also when it either left England or arrived in Australia, it should be relatively easy to find the convict. The names of the convicts on the first fleet which left England in May 1787, reaching Australia in January 1788, are listed by Fidlon and Ryan in *The First Fleeters*. A list of convicts transported on the second fleet of ships, which left in 1789, is in Ryan's *The Second Fleet Convicts*. Censuses or musters were taken periodically in New South Wales and Tasmania between 1788 and 1859. Convicts and former convicts had to identify themselves as such and to supply information about their dates and ships of arrival. Many of these musters are published (see **40.4**) and should therefore be available to you at a good reference library or through the inter-library loan scheme. Once you know when and where the convict was sentenced it is comparatively easy to search for an application for clemency (see **39.6**) and/or for the trial record (**38**).

It was possible for wives to accompany their convict husbands, and some wives applied to do so. Their petitions survive for 1819–1844 (PC 1/67–92) and from 1849–1871 (HO 12, identified via the registers in HO 14). See also C 201 (New South Wales correspondence with the Colonial Office: items marked in the lists as correspondence from individuals may include letters from people wishing to join convict relatives).

Privy Council correspondence, 1819–1844 (PC 1/67–92) contains additional material about transportation as do the Privy Council registers (PC 2), which also give lists of convicts transported for 14 years or less. Contracts with agents to transport the prisoners, with full lists of ships and convicts, 1842–1867, are in the Treasury Solicitor's Department general series papers (TS 18/460–525 and 1308–1361). Reports on the medical condition of the convicts while at sea may be found in the Admiralty medical journals, 1817–1856 (ADM 101), and in the Admiralty Transport Department surgeon-superintendents' journals, 1858–1867 (MT 32).

40.4 Settlement in Australia

Musters or censuses, primarily but not exclusively concerned with the convict population, were taken periodically in New South Wales and Tasmania between 1788 and 1859 (HO 10). The New South Wales census of 1828 (HO 10/21–27) is the most complete, and is available in a published edition by Sainty and Johnson. It contains the names of more than 35,000 people with details of age, religion, family, place of residence, occupation and stock or land held. Whether each settler came free, or as a convict (or was born in the colony) is recorded; and date of arrival and the name of the ship are given. The musters or similar material for New South Wales and Norfolk Island, 1800–1802, for New South Wales, Norfolk Island and Van Diemen's Land, 1811, and for New South Wales in 1822 and 1837 have also been published, full details are given in the bibliography (**40.5**). Copies of all these works are available at the PRO, but you should also be able to find them at a good reference library or via the inter-library loan scheme. Similar material can be found in C 201: the victualling lists for Norfolk Island, for example, are repeated regularly. Papers relating to convicts in New South Wales and Tasmania (IIO 10) contain material about convicts' pardons and tickets of leave from New South Wales and Tasmania, 1835–59. Home Office records also include some information about deaths of convicts in New South Wales, 1829–1834 (HO 7/2).

Colonial Office records relating to Australia sometimes note individual convicts as well as policy decisions, but they are not easy to search for particular named individuals. There are, however, lists of convicts, together with emigrant settlers, 1801–1821, in New South Wales Original Correspondence (CO 201), which contains a wealth of material. Names can also be traced in New South Wales entry books from 1786 (CO 202), and registers from 1849 (CO 360 and CO 369). Records of the superintendent of convicts in New South Wales, 1788–1825, are now held in the State Archives of New South Wales; the PRO holds microfilm copies (CO 207). Some of the lists from these records have been printed in Robson, *The Convict Settlers of Australia*.

For other records which may provide relevant information, see **14.8**.

40.5 Convict transportation: bibliography

C M Andrews, *Guide to the materials for American history to 1793 in the Public Record Office of Great Britain* (Washington DC, 1912–1914)

C Bateson, *The Convict Ships, 1787–1868* (Glasgow, 2nd edn, 1969)

C J Baxter, *Muster and lists of NSW and Norfolk Island, 1800–1802* (Sydney, 1988)

C J Baxter, *General Musters of NSW, Norfolk Island and Van Diemen's Land, 1811* (Sydney, 1987)

C J Baxter, *General muster and lands and stock muster of NSW, 1822*

J M Beattie, *Crime and courts in England 1660–1800* (Oxford, 1986)

N G Butlin, C W Cromwell and K L Suthern, *General Return of convicts in NSW 1837* (Sydney, 1987)

Calendar of State Papers, Colonial, America and West Indies, 1574–1738 (London, 1869–1969)

Calendar of Treasury Books, 1660–1718 (London, 1904–1962)

Calendar of Treasury Papers, 1557–1728 (London, 1868–1889)

Calendar of Treasury Books and Papers, 1729–1745 (London, 1898–1903)

P W Coldham, *Bonded Passengers to America, 1615–1775* (Baltimore, 1983)

P W Coldham, *The Complete Book of Emigrants in Bondage, 1614–1775* (Baltimore, 1987. Supplement 1992)

P W Coldham, 'Felons Transported to America', *Genealogists' Magazine*, vol. 26, pp. 61–65

A R Ekirch, *Bound for America: The Transportation of British Convicts to the Colonies, 1718–1775* (Oxford, 1990)

P G Fidlon and R J Ryan, eds, *The First Fleeters* (Sydney, 1981)

Friends of the East Sussex Record Office, *East Sussex Sentences of Transportation at Quarter Sessions, 1790–1854* (Lewes, 1988)

D T Hawkings, *Bound for Australia* (Chichester, 1987)

D T Hawkings, *Criminal Ancestors, a guide to historical criminal records in England and Wales* (Sutton, rev. edn, 1996)

R Hughes, *The Fatal Shore: A History of Transportation of Convicts to Australia, 1781–1868* (London, 1987)

Journals of the Board of Trade and Plantations, 1704–1782 (London, 1920–1938)

Public Record Office, *Australian Convicts: Sources in the Public Record Office* (Information Leaflet)

L L Robson, *The Convict Settlers of Australia* (Melbourne, 1981)

R J Ryan, *The Second Fleet Convicts* (Sydney, 1982)

M R Sainty and K A Johnson, eds, *New South Wales: Census . . . November 1828* (Sydney, 1980)

W M Wigfield, *The Monmouth Rebels 1685* (Somerset Record Society, 1985)

I Wyatt, ed., *Transportees from Gloucester to Australia, 1783–1842* (Bristol and Gloucester Archaeological Society, 1988)

41 Land ownership and tenancy

41.1 Introduction

In England and Wales, records of the ownership and transfer of particular lands are difficult to locate, as there was no national system of registration before the nineteenth century. Registries of deeds were established in the Bedford Level in the fens, for parts of Yorkshire and in Middlesex early in the eighteenth century; the one in Middlesex closed in 1940, but those in Yorkshire continued to operate until the 1970s. The Bedford Level register can be seen at the Cambridgeshire Record Office; the Middlesex register at the London Metropolitan Archives; and those for parts of Yorkshire in the custody of the West Yorkshire Archives Service in Wakefield (addresses in **48**).

In the City of London and in many other cities and boroughs, transfers of property were often entered on the hustings rolls or in the records of the municipal courts. These should be sought in the relevant local record offices. Although a national Land Registry was established in 1862, registration was voluntary and was little used. Compulsory registration on sale was introduced in London in 1899 and now covers all the major conurbations, although some rural areas are still excluded and there are still many unregistered properties in the compulsory registration areas. The Land Registry does not normally hold original deeds once property has been registered. General enquiries concerning the registration of a property can be made to the Land Registry (address in **48**), by letter or telephone. Personal visits can be made either to the Land Registry headquarters in Lincoln's Inn Fields, or to the relevant district office.

The PRO has hundreds of thousands of property-related records which have come into its custody through one of three reasons. Firstly, if the property in question was at some stage in the possession of the crown or government; secondly, if the property was the subject of litigation and documents were presented as evidence to the courts; and thirdly, if documents were enrolled within a court's records to demonstrate a transfer of ownership or as a means of proving ownership. However, there is no general index to the plethora of documents available for inspection and searching can be difficult without some idea of when, where and why a conveyance took place. Some understanding of the different methods of medieval, early modern and modern land holding (e.g. feudal, copyhold, freehold, leasehold) and of land transfer is also useful.

The records of tithe redemption, enclosures and land valuation, discussed in **42**, can also provide information on landowners in a particular place.

41.2 Court rolls

Before the nineteenth century, a high proportion of people were freehold or customary tenants of a manor. Their landholdings were regulated by the manor court, otherwise known as the court baron, which was responsible for the internal regulation of local affairs as defined in the customs of the manor. A freehold tenant held his land from the lord for the payment of a cash rent, possibly some labour services, and 'suit of court', that is, being obliged to attend meetings of the manor court. When a freeholder died, the heir would normally pay a 'relief' which was a cash payment often of a year's rent. Apart from this, however, the manor court had little authority over their actions and freehold tenants do not appear that frequently in manorial records. On the other hand, customary tenants paid a cash rent, owed 'suit of court', performed more substantial services to the lord of the manor, and were required to pay an entry fine and maintain their lands according to the customs of the manor. Failure to do so would result in punishment by the manor court. By far the most common customary tenants were those who held their land by copyhold tenure. Copyhold land was transferred by surrendering it to the lord of the manor from whom it was held. He then regranted it to new tenants. Conveyances of copyhold property and the admissions of heirs on the death of tenants were entered on the court rolls. More often than not, the tenant was given a copy of the court roll recording the admission which constituted his title of record.

Much litigation took place in the Exchequer which involved the taking of depositions locally about the varying customs (customary law) of individual manors. If you are interested in a particular manor, it may be worth checking the county lists of the depositions in E 134 to see if anything of interest exists.

Court rolls are a valuable source for confirming or expanding information found about individuals in parish registers which, in many cases, they predate. However, there can be difficulties in using court rolls. Firstly, the survival of court rolls has not been good; only a small proportion of rolls survive from before the sixteenth century. Secondly, there might be several manors in one parish or the property of a manor could be scattered through several parishes. It is not always easy to discover of which manor, if any, a man was a tenant. Finally, although English became increasingly commonplace in rolls during the sixteenth century, Latin remained the official language until 1733. Court rolls are held in the PRO and in many other repositories. A register of all known surviving manorial documents is held by the National Register of Archives, at the Historical Manuscripts Commission, and can help with locating court rolls held at the PRO and elsewhere (address in **48**). On-line indexes to the NRA can be consulted at Kew, and on the HMC web site. This also contains information about the Manorial Documents Register.

Most of the PRO's holdings of court rolls come from manors which formed part of the crown lands. Court rolls in SC 2 and DL 30 are included in a published list that includes a place name index: the *List and Index of Court Rolls* (Lists and Indexes, vol. VI). Court rolls in ADM 74, C 104, C 115, C 116, C 171, CRES 5, F 14, J 90, LR 3, LR 11, MAF 5, PRO 30/26, TS 19, and WARD 2 are listed in the 'Union Place Name Index to Court Rolls', available in the Map Room. Other court rolls may be scattered in the following classes: DL 42, DURH 3, E 3, E 32, E 36, E 137, E 140, E 192, E 315, F 16, SC 6, SC 12, SP 2, SP 14, SP 16, SP 17, SP 23, SP 28, and T 1/462.

In the nineteenth century, much copyhold property was converted to freehold, and copyhold was finally abolished by the Law of Property Acts, 1922 and 1924. The PRO holds lists of copyholders who converted to freehold and files relating to such cases are in MAF 9, MAF 13, MAF 20 and MAF 27.

41.3 Fines and recoveries

Other ways to transfer the ownership of land involved the common law and the King's courts: the most usual, fines and common recoveries, were methods of conveying property by means of fictitious legal actions. Conveyancing by fines (also known as final concords) became increasingly common during the late twelfth century. By 1195 the procedure was well established and fines continued to be used until their abolition in 1833. Until the fourteenth century fines were made in the Court of Common Pleas, the Court of King's Bench and the general eyre, a periodic visitation of the English counties by royal justices. From the fourteenth century onwards, all feet of fines made in the central common law courts were made in the Court of Common Pleas.

A foot of fine was the bottom copy of a series of three or more copies of a final agreement, or concord, written on a single piece of parchment. A copy was given to each of the parties to the agreement to retain as their own record while the foot was retained by the court. Fines are very formulaic documents. The intended purchaser, as plaintiff, claimed the property from the vendor; the property was then transferred by a legally sanctioned agreement. The largest series of Feet of Fines are in CP 25/1 and CP 25/2. Other fines are in CHES 31, for the Palatinate of Chester; DURH 12, for the Palatinate of Durham; and PL 17, for the Palatinate of Lancaster. Fines can be located by using the manuscript indexes of fines and recoveries in IND 1/1–6605 and IND 1/17183–17216 arranged by date. Furthermore, certain manuscript indexes to fines from the reign of Henry VIII onwards (CP 25/2) are available on microfilm. Many fines have also been published, mainly by local record societies: it is best to look first in *Texts and Calendars*, by Mullins, to see if any fines for the relevant shire have been printed. Remember that this publication is kept up to date on the Historical Manuscripts Commission's web site, which can be accessed in the PRO Library. For medieval feet of fines, see the article by Kissock, which includes a catalogue of those published.

The recovery was a method of transferring property developed in the fifteenth century. It was used to enable entailed estates to be broken up so that they could be disposed of at will rather than descending within a specific family line. Having already agreed terms beforehand, the individual who wished to acquire the entailed lands would bring a fictitious action against the person wishing to dispose of the land, known as the tenant-in-tail. The tenant-in-tail named a third party to warrant the title to him. This individual became known as the common vouchee. He would appear to defend the tenant's title but would subsequently default (i.e., not turn up in court). This was a contempt of court which allowed the justices to make a judgement against the tenant, thus breaking the entail and enabling the smooth transfer of the property in question.

The majority of Common Recoveries are in CP 40 and CP 43. There are additional recoveries for the Palatinate of Chester in CHES 31. Recoveries can be traced by referring to the manuscript indexes of fines and recoveries in IND 1/1–6605 and IND 1/17183–17216.

41.4 Deeds

There are many original deeds in the PRO, but it is very difficult to find particular deeds. There is no single index, and in many cases their original context has been lost.

The overwhelming majority of original deeds came into the crown's possession either when it acquired property through purchase, forfeiture or other forms of escheat, or when the deeds were produced as evidence in law suits and were not collected by the litigant afterwards. Most deeds are conveyances and other evidences of title, although various other record types, including wills, bonds and receipts, might also be found. A typical deed will contain the name of the vendor, the purchaser, details of the property concerned, the sum paid for the property and the date on which the transaction was conducted. Latin is the language of the overwhelming majority of medieval and early modern deeds, with the remainder written in either English or French. Modern deeds are written in English. In some instances a seal is still attached to the original deed.

The large collections of individual deeds which came from private or monastic sources are primarily in C 146–C 149; DL 25–DL 27; DURH 21; E 40–E 44; E 210–E 213; E 326–E 330; LR 14–LR 16; PL 29; WALE 29–WALE 31; and WARD 2. Many of these have been calendared or descriptively listed. There is also a card index to deeds in C 146–C 148. Some classes of deeds, DURH 21, E 44, E 330, E 355, LR 16 and WALE 31, have not been listed and access to them is currently restricted.

It remained common practice until the nineteenth century to enrol private deeds in the central courts as a way of recording ownership; certain types of deed continued to be enrolled up to 1925 (see **33.2** for trust deeds). The greatest number of deeds was enrolled in the Chancery (C 54); others were enrolled in the Exchequer (E 13, E 159, E 315 and E 368), the Court of Common Pleas (CP 40 before Easter 1583 and 1834–1875 and CP 43, 1583–1834) and the Court of King's Bench (KB 26, KB 27 before 1702 and KB 122, 1702–1875). There are manuscript and typescript indexes and calendars to deeds in C 54, CP 40, CP 43, E 13, E 315, KB 26 and KB 27. Deeds enrolled in E 368 can be traced by referring to IND volumes which must be ordered as original documents.

There are many deeds relating to crown lands amongst the records of the Auditors of Land Revenue and Surveyors General of Woods and Forests (LR), and the Office of Woods, Forests and Land Revenues (LRRO). For deeds in LR 14 and LR 15, refer to the class lists. Deeds in LRRO 13–LRRO 18, LRRO 20 and LRRO 25 can be traced by using the Registers in LRRO 64. There is also a card index to LRRO 16. For deeds in LRRO 37 refer to the class list. Some of these classes of deeds are closed to public inspection: the *PRO Guide* identifies them. There are also some deeds amongst the records of the Crown Estate Commissioners (CRES) in CRES 38. Two small collections of deeds relating to crown lands can be found amongst the records of the Board of Inland Revenue (IR) in IR 10; and the records of the Treasury Solicitor (TS) in TS 21.

In addition, deeds were sometimes used as evidence in law suits and their texts can be found on the plea rolls, the pleadings or as separate classes of documents amongst the records of the relevant court. Deeds used as evidence in Chancery suits exist in large number in C 103–C 115, C 171 and J 90. Deeds used in suits in the Court of Wards and Liveries are in WARD 2, but the list, such as it is, is very difficult to use.

41.5 Rentals and surveys

Information about properties, including the names of owners and tenants, can often be discovered from manorial documents such as custumals, extents, rentals, surveys, terriers and valors. These are more commonly referred to as rentals and surveys. They date from the thirteenth century to the nineteenth century, but most are from the sixteenth and seventeenth centuries. Surveys of property were taken for the purpose of estate management, and private property was sometimes surveyed if it was the subject of litigation. The principal purpose of rentals and surveys was to provide the lord of the manor with up-to-date records of tenants, and the revenues and services that they owed to their landlords. These documents were not intended as records of payments which would normally appear in manorial accounts. Surveys were made by the estate steward or a group of commissioners of survey (specially appointed by the lord of the manor) at special meetings of the manor known as the court of survey. A jury of survey would be empanelled who would answer in open court a series of articles of enquiry about the state and condition of the manor. All tenants were expected to provide documents showing the terms by which they held their lands. These details would be recorded on the survey.

The documents themselves vary considerably in size and scope. Some relate to a single manor; others cover several properties. They might contain one or more membranes, possibly stitched together to form a roll. From the sixteenth century onwards, it is not uncommon to find pages stitched together to form a book. The majority of the records forming this class are written in Latin. During the course of the sixteenth century, however, an increasing number are written in English. There are no rules governing the exact content or precise format of the documents. By the eighteenth century, however, documents such as rentals and rent-rolls are normally set out in regular columns under clear headings.

Rentals and surveys are found among the records of the Crown Estate Commissioners (CRES 39), the Duchy of Lancaster (DL 32, DL 42–DL 44), the Exchequer (E 36, E 142, E 164 and E 315), the Office of the Auditors of Land Revenue (LR 2 and LR 13), the Office of Woods, Forests and Land Revenues (LRRO 1 and LRRO 12), the State Paper Office (SP 10–SP 18 and SP 46) and Special Collections (SC 11 and SC 12). Of special interest are the detailed Parliamentary Surveys (E 317) of the crown lands taken in the Commonwealth period (see **41.9**). Surveys taken as a result of litigation or for other reasons will be found in Depositions by Commission (E 134) and Special Commissions (E 178), which cover the period from the sixteenth century to the nineteenth century.

There are published lists of all the surveys. The principal finding aids for rentals and surveys is the *List of Rentals and Surveys* (Lists and Indexes, vol. XXV) and *List of Rentals and Surveys: Addenda* (Lists and Indexes, Supplementary Series, vol. XIV). These list all documents in SC 11, SC 12, DL 29, DL 42–DL 44, E 36, E 142, E 164, E 315, E 317, LR 2, SP 10–SP 18, and SP 46. Documents in E 178 can be identified by consulting the *List of Special Commissions and Returns in the Exchequer* (Lists and Indexes, vol. XXXVII). For documents in CRES 38, LR 13, LRRO 1 and LRRO 12, please refer to the class lists.

41.6 Ministers' and receivers' accounts

Information regarding the landowners and their tenants can also be found in manorial accounts, commonly known as ministers' and receivers' accounts. The practice of compiling regular and accurate accounts seems to have begun during the early thirteenth century. A variety of local officials were responsible for keeping accounts, particularly bailiffs, beadles (under-bailiffs), keepers, reeves, sergeants, farmers and receivers.

Accounts have a similar appearance to rentals and surveys. Virtually all of the documents were written in Latin, although English was used more extensively as the sixteenth century progressed. One advantage which manorial accounts have over rentals and surveys is that they were made annually and, as a consequence, a greater number of these records have survived. A standard format for accounts was adopted during the thirteenth century and remained in use into modern times. This was the 'charge and discharge' system. The charges section included the revenues accruing to the property; the discharges section comprised payments and expenses made from the property. However, not all accounts are equally useful to genealogists. Those described as rentals and rent-rolls (often confused with manorial surveys) are perhaps the most helpful because they generally lists payments of rents made by tenants.

Most surviving accounts at the PRO are in SC 6 and DL 29. These are listed in the *List of Original Ministers' Accounts, Part I–Henry III to Richard III* (Lists and Indexes, vol. V), the *List of Original Ministers' Accounts: Appendix, Corrigenda, and Index to Part I* (Lists and Indexes, vol. VIII), and the *List of Original Ministers' Accounts, Part II–Henry VII to Henry VIII* (Lists and Indexes, vol. XXXIV). Few original accounts for crown lands survive after the sixteenth century. For the most part, local officials appeared to have delivered their accounts to a receiver-general who in turn submitted his final account to the Exchequer. As a result, there are few details surviving about individual properties and it is unlikely that names of tenants will be included. Nevertheless, some individual ministers' accounts can be found in DL 44, LR 5, LR 6, LR 7, LR 8, LR 12, LRRO 2, LRRO 3, LRRO 12, WARD 8. These are described in the class lists.

41.7 Inquisitions post mortem, homage and wardship: before 1660

Before 1660, on the death of any holder of land who was thought to have held that land direct from the crown (called a tenant in chief by knight service), an inquiry was held by the escheator of the county involved. The escheator was one of the most important royal officials in the localities. It was his responsibility to maintain the crown's rights as feudal overlord. When land was deemed to have no owner, for whatever reason, the property reverted to the king as ultimate feudal lord.

Inquisitions post mortem were conducted according to well-established procedures. A local jury would be summoned by the sheriff and had to swear to the identity and extent of the land held by the tenant at the time of his death, by what rents or services they were held, and the name and age of the next heir. If there was no heir, the land reverted (escheated) to the crown: if the next heir was under age, the crown claimed rights of wardship and marriage over the lands and the heir until he or she came of age. If the heir was adult, livery and seisin of the lands was granted on performance of homage to the king, and payment of a reasonable fine or relief. If the heir's age was in doubt, there might have been a separate inquiry to produce proof of age. These proofs often record memories of other notable events to fix the heir's year of birth. The jury's findings were returned to Chancery as an indenture, along with any associated documentation such as the Chancery writ. A duplicate indenture was kept by the escheator. This system, however, finished in 1660, when feudal tenures were abolished.

The documents produced by inquisitions post mortem, filed with some proofs of age, are a very valuable source for both family and local history: however, not all the information given is reliable.

The inquisitions give details of what lands were held (a separate one was held for each county involved), and by what tenure, and from whom, as well as the date of death, and the name and age of the heir. They are in Latin, in a standard layout. Each inquisition starts with the county, the name of the escheator (the official holding the inquest), and a list of the jurors. The name of the deceased and the date of their death comes next. Then follows a brief description of each landholding, its value (often underestimated) and the tenure by which it is held. This section may include extracts (in English) from a will or an enfeoffment to use (putting the lands into the hands of trustees, in order to avoid the king's claims to livery and wardship, etc, and also to allow lands to be left to people other than the heir at law). At the end, the next heir is identified, and an age given. If the heir was of age (over 21, or over 14 for an heiress), the actual age given may be an estimate. The next heir is usually one male, or one female, or a number of females: lands were split between daughters (who were treated as having an equal claim if there was no male heir), but not between sons.

Sometimes a proof of age was recorded in a separate type of inquisition *(de aetatis probanda)*. Widows also had rights of dower in the lands, which continued long after the deaths of their husbands, and there are inquisitions *(de assignatio dotis)* into this as well. These inquisitions are included with the inquisitions post mortem.

The main series are those returned into Chancery (C 132–C 142): unfortunately they are often illegible. Transcripts of some were sent to the Exchequer (E 149–E 150, E 152) and to the Court of Wards from the reign of Henry VIII (WARD 7), and these are usually in better condition. There are a series of calendars and indexes to inquisitions post mortem (see **41.11**).

The right to wardship was often sold by the crown, by no means always to the next of kin: grants of wardship may be found in the Patent Rolls (C 66). The Close Rolls (C 54) contain writs of livery and seisin, while the Fine Rolls (C 60) include grants of wardship and marriage and writs of livery of seisin.

If you find that the heir was under age and did hold land from the crown in chief, then it is worth investigating the records of the Court of Wards and Liveries, which operated between 1540 and 1660. The records of most potential value are the legal proceedings in WARD 3, WARD 5, WARD 9 and WARD 13: the Court of Wards used equity procedure (see **47.3**), and so the records are full, informative, and in English. The deeds and evidences, in WARD 2, go back as far as the twelfth century: there is a partial index to them in the *Deputy Keeper's Sixth Report*, Appendix II. For more information, consult Bell, *An Introduction to the History and Records of the Court of Wards and Liveries*.

For other legal proceedings about the validity or accuracy of inquisitions post mortem, see the records of the plea side of Chancery. Chancery had a common law jurisdiction over matters affected by the king's prerogative rights, such as royal grants, royal rights over its subjects' lands as discovered through inquisitions post mortem and inquisitions of lunacy, feudal incidents due to the crown, and division of lands between joint heiresses. Pleadings for Edward I–James I are well-listed, in C 43 and C 44; pleadings for Elizabeth I to Victoria are in C 206. There are remembrance rolls in C 221 and C 222, and writs in C 245.

41.8 Chancery enrolments

The records of Chancery contain a lot of useful references to grants of land and conveyances. Evidence of early grants from the crown can be traced on the Charter Rolls (C 53). From 1199 to 1216 they are transcribed, with indexes, in *Rotuli Chartarum*, and thereafter to 1516 in the *Calendars of Charter Rolls*. The principal source of grants of land, however, are on the Patent Rolls (C 66). From 1201 to 1232 they are transcribed with indexes, in *Rotuli Litterarum Patentium* and *Patent Rolls . . . Henry III*; from 1232 to the reign of Elizabeth I they are calendared, with indexes, in *Calendars of Patent Rolls*, except that from 1509 to 1548 they are calendared in *Letters and Papers . . . of Henry VIII*. Draft modern calendars of Patent Rolls for 1584 onwards (ongoing–to 1603 eventually) and contemporary calendars for 1603–1625 have been published by the List and Index Society. There are also contemporary manuscript indexes in C 274 which survive from 1485 (1 Henry VII) to 1946 (10 George VI). They are arranged in letter order of grantees' names: some have indexes. Only those for 17–44 Elizabeth I and 1 Charles I–22 George V are on open access.

The Patent Rolls and Close Rolls were also used to enrol private conveyances. The Close Rolls (C 54) became a popular means of recording private deeds (see **41.4**). The Patent Rolls record licences to alienate. These were used by individuals holding property held by tenure in chief. This could only lawfully be sold with the crown's permission. Copies of the licences were enrolled on the Patent Rolls (C 66). A search through the indexes to the calendars is an easy and sometimes rewarding way of searching for early conveyances. After the printed calendars cease, it is as easy to leaf through the Entry Books of Licences and Pardons for Alienation, 1571–1650 (A 4), as to use the contemporary finding aids to the Patent Rolls.

41.9 Crown lands

Many properties have at some time been in the hands of the crown. Crown lands lacked a system of overall management until the late medieval period. Although a range of officers emerged to manage royal lands during the twelfth and thirteenth centuries, there was no centralized system of control. By the fifteenth century, however, lands were often placed under the stewardship of a senior noble or brought together under a receiver-general and auditors to provide an endowment for a member of the royal family. At the beginning of Henry VIII's reign general surveyors of crown lands were appointed. In 1542 the Court of General Surveyors of the King's Lands was created and given control over all lands coming into crown hands through attainder, escheat, exchange and forfeiture. The dissolution of the monasteries had also seen the establishment of the Court of Augmentations in 1536 to manage the revenues of former ecclesiastical and monastic property. In 1547 both of these courts were abolished and replaced by the single Court of Augmentations and Revenues. Following the abolition of this court in 1554, crown officials presented their accounts to the Auditors of the Exchequer (subsequently known as the Auditors of the Land Revenue). The Auditors were only abolished in 1831: their records went to the new Land Revenue Record Office, which amalgamated with the PRO in 1902. Since then crown lands have been administered by the Crown Estate Commissioners, under various titles.

From 1914–1961, there is a card index (on open access) to the buyers and lessees of crown lands: the actual deeds (in LRRO 16) are closed for 100 years. For 1832–1913, there are indexes to buyers, lessees and places in LRRO 64, to deeds now in LRRO 13, LRRO 16, and other classes:

again the indexes can be seen but documents of more recent date than 100 years ago cannot. For 1786–1830, look at the *Crown Lands Return*, of 1831, available in the Map Room. It may be that other, similar, returns to Parliament exist among the Parliamentary Papers, which can be seen on microfiche in the Library. If it is unclear whether certain lands were part of the crown estates, there is a useful list of crown manors as at 1827 in CRES 2/1613, and the Annual Reports of the various bodies administering the crown lands are in CRES 60 for 1797–1942.

If there is any evidence to suggest that a piece of property was in the crown's hands or that a person was a crown tenant, it is worth exploring, in the *PRO Guide* Part 2, the various lettercodes which contain the bulk of material relating to crown lands – CRES, LR, LRRO, and E 300s. Try also FEC, the Forfeited Estates Commission. The rentals and surveys, ministers' and receivers' accounts and court rolls: CRES 5, DL 30, DL 43, LR 3, LRRO 12, SC 2, SC 6, SC 11 and SC 12 are particularly fruitful sources for identifying crown lands and tenants (see **41.2** and **41.5**).

The Parliamentary Surveys in E 317, recorded in English, can be used to establish both the occupation of lands in the mid seventeenth century as well as providing an indication of the size, extent and layout of the buildings themselves. These surveys were taken by virtue of two acts of 1649 and 1650 which authorized the sale of honors, manors and lands formerly belonging to King Charles I, Queen Henrietta Maria and Prince Charles. The trustees appointed to sell the lands employed local surveyors to conduct surveys of the crown lands. The registrar's books of particulars (based on the surveys) and contracts for sale are in CRES 39/67–74. Individual particulars and contracts for sales of crown lands are in E 320. Many of these sales were reversed following the Restoration of Charles II in 1660.

41.10 Chester, Durham and Lancaster

The palatinates of Chester (CHES), Durham (DURH) and Lancaster (PL) had their own administrations which paralleled those of the central government. Fines and recoveries can be found in CHES 2, CHES 29, CHES 30, CHES 31, CHES 32, DURH 12, DURH 13, PL 15 and PL 17. Deeds can be found in CHES 2, CHES 29, DURH 13, DURH 21, PL 2, PL 14, PL 15 and PL 29. For a description of the nature and format of these types of documents, refer to the relevant subject headings in this chapter.

41.11 Land ownership and tenancy: bibliography

General works
B English, 'Inheritance and Succession in Landed Families 1660–1925', *Genealogists' Magazine*, vol. XXIV, pp. 433–438
M Gandy, *Basic Approach to Latin for Family Historians* (1995)
E Gooder, *Latin for Local History* (2nd edn, 1978)
J H Harvey, *Sources for the History of Houses* (British Records Association, 1968)
E C Mullins, *Texts and Calendars: an Analytical Guide to Serial Publications* (London, 2 vols, 1978, 1983). Continues on the HMC web site.
A W B Simpson, *A History of the Land Law* (Oxford, 1986)
D Stuart, *Latin for Local and Family Historians: A Beginner's Guide* (London, 1995)

Deeds and Feet of Fines
N W Alcock, *Old Title Deeds* (Chichester, 1986)

A A Dibben, *Title Deeds* (Historical Association, 1968)

J Kissock, 'Medieval feet of fines: a study of their uses, with a catalogue of published sources', *Journal of the Society of Archivists*, vol. XXIV (1994), pp. 66–82

F Sheppard and V Belcher, 'The Deed Registries of Yorkshire and Middlesex', *Journal of the Society of Archivists*, vol. VI (1978–1981), pp. 274–286

K T Ward, 'Pre-Registration Title Deeds: The Legal Issues of Ownership, Custody and Abandonment', *Journal of the Society of Archivists*, vol. XVI (1995), pp. 27–39

Manorial records

J Beckett, 'Estate Surveys as a Source for Names', *Genealogists' Magazine*, vol. XXIV (1993), pp. 335–341

J H Betty, 'Manorial Customs and Widows' Estates', *Archives*, vol. XX (1992), pp. 208–216

M Ellis, *Using Manorial Records* (PRO, 1997)

P D A Harvey, *Manorial Records* (Gloucester, 1984)

P B Park, *My Ancestors were Manorial Tenants: How can I find out more about them?* (Society of Genealogists, 1990)

D Stuart, *Manorial Records* (Chichester, 1992)

A Travers, 'Manorial Documents', *Genealogists' Magazine*, vol. XXI (1983), pp. 1–10

Inquisitions post mortem and wardships

H E Bell, *An Introduction to the History and Records of the Court of Wards and Liveries* (Cambridge, 1953)

Calendar of Inquisitions Miscellaneous, Henry III to Henry VII (London, 1916–1968)

Calendar of Inquisitions Post Mortem, Henry III to Henry V, and Henry VII (London, 1898–1995)

Calendarium Inquisitionum Post Mortem (Record Commission, 1806–1828)

R F Hunnisett, 'The Reliability of Inquisitions as Historical Evidence', in eds D A Bullough and R L Storey *The Study of Medieval Records* (Oxford, 1971)

J Hurstfield, *The Queen's Wards* (London, 1958)

R E Latham, 'Hints on Interpreting the Public Records: III, Inquisitions Post Mortem', *Amateur Historian*, vol. I (1952–1954), pp. 77–81

List of Inquisitions Post Mortem, Henry V–Richard III; Inquisitions ad quod damnum and miscellaneous inquisitions, Henry VII–Charles I (C138–C142) (List and Index Society, vols 268–269, 1998)

M McGuinness, 'Inquisitions Post Mortem', *Amateur Historian*, vol. VI (1963–1965), pp. 235–242

Chancery enrolments

Calendar of Charter Rolls (London, 1903–1927)

Calendar of Close Rolls (London, 1892–1963)

Calendar of Patent Rolls, Henry III to Henry VII, and Edward VI to 1582 (London, 1891–1986)

List and Index Society, *Chancery: Patent Rolls Calendar, Elizabeth, 1584–* (vols 241–243, 247, 255 and ongoing)

List and Index Society, *Chancery: Patent Rolls [Contemporary] Calendar and Index, James I* (vols 97–98, 109, 121–122, 133–134, 157, 164, 187, 193, 218, 229 and 233

Letters and Papers . . . of Henry VIII (London, 1864–1932) (This includes a calendar of the Patent Rolls for Henry VIII)

Patent Rolls . . . Henry III (London, 1901–1903)

Rotuli Chartarum (Record Commission, 1837)

Rotuli Litterarum Patentium (Record Commission, 1835)

Crown lands

C D Chandaman, *The English Public Revenue, 1660–1688* (Oxford, 1975)

R Hoyle, *The estates of the English Crown, 1558–1640* (Cambridge, 1992)

W C Richardson, *History of the Court of Augmentations, 1536–1544* (Baton Rouge, 1961)

B P Wolffe, *The Crown Lands, 1460–1536* (London, 1970)

B P Wolffe, *The Royal Demesne in English History* (London, 1971)

42 Surveys of land and house ownership

42.1 Introduction

For most parishes of England and Wales there is either a tithe map and apportionment or an enclosure award and map, which can provide valuable information about land ownership. The tithe maps and apportionments were created in the mid nineteenth century while the enclosure awards and maps relate to a broader time span covering, in the majority of cases, the eighteenth and nineteenth centuries. They give you the opportunity to find out where in a particular parish your ancestors were living, who their neighbours were, what land they owned or occupied, what industries were important locally and a mass of further information. Less well known and equally important are the records of house and land ownership produced by the Valuation Office. This was a survey carried out under the Finance (1909–1910) Act, 1910, which has left behind series of maps and field books which between them provide a detailed record for family and local historians

42.2 Tithe survey records

Tithes were originally a tax of one tenth of all produce, paid to the local clergyman by his parishioners. After the Reformation many entitlements to receive tithes came into the hands of laymen. That is to say, the right to collect tithes came to be 'owned' by non-clerics and could be bought and sold on the open market. Disputes about tithes were a major part of the business of the equity side of the Exchequer: the easiest way to trace them is to use the good list of the county depositions in E 134.

By the nineteenth century there was much popular disenchantment with the system of tithes, and many parishes had local agreements regarding the payment of money in lieu of produce. In 1836 the Tithe Commutation Act set a national framework for all tithes to be fixed as a money payment which was linked to the changing price of wheat, barley and oats. The maps and apportionments created by Tithe Commissioners set out the names of owners and occupiers for the 75 per cent of parishes and chapelries which were still titheable in the 1830s. These records also provide the name and description of the premises and land (for example 'Farm House and Out Buildings'), as well as providing details of the extent of land and the state of cultivation. Copies of tithe maps and apportionments are held in some county record offices, as well as in the PRO (IR 29, IR 30).

For some areas no tithe maps and apportionments were made. This is because satisfactory arrangements for money payments had already been agreed or an award of land in lieu of tithes had been made during an enclosure. There were also some districts where no apportionment was made, even though tithes for the area were commuted under the Tithe Commutation Act. This was because either the amount involved was negligible, or because the landowners were themselves the tithe owners, and the agreement or award of a gross tithe rentcharge was followed by the redemption or merger of the tithe rentcharges. By this procedure the owners of the land/tithe avoided the need (and expense) of producing a map and apportionment. In these cases the result of the proceedings would still need to be recorded as a formal agreement or instrument of merger (in TITH 3), and there should also be a tithe file (IR 18) which will be disappointing for genealogists, although may give valuable information to the regional or local historian.

For detailed advice on using tithe maps, look at Foot's *Maps For Family History*. The easiest way to find out the existence of and document reference for maps and apportionments for a particular parish is to look at Kain and Oliver's *The Tithe Maps of England and Wales*. This is available in the Map Room: it is arranged by county, and each parish entry starts with a number. To order the apportionment add IR 29 to this number: to order the map, add IR 30. For counties in the alphabetical sequence A–M, the maps are seen on microfiche. The original can be seen if absolutely necessary, but at least three working days notice is required. The apportionments are seen on microfilm for all counties. It is a good idea to look at Foot before trying to understand an apportionment, because the arrangement of the information is not easy to grasp on film. Each apportionment contains a key linking plot number on the map to page number in the apportionment, but the key is not immediately simple to use.

42.3 Enclosure maps and awards

The term enclosure, as applied to land, usually refers to either the fencing in of commons for private and exclusive landownership, or the consolidation of plots of land formerly distributed over the shared open fields into compact blocks, linked together and surrounded by hedges or fences and gates. A useful starting point before embarking on research (for enclosures from c.1730) among the surviving records is Tate's book, *A Domesday of English Enclosure Acts and Awards* and Chapman's *A Guide to Parliamentary Enclosure in Wales*.

Enclosures of common lands, pastures and manorial wastes were made from an early period, sometimes arbitrarily and sometimes by agreement. There is a list at the Map Room Enquiry Desk of references to agreements and awards (and early enclosure by parliamentary act) in the PRO, arranged by county and then parish. However this is by no means comprehensive. It should be recognized that some of the earliest enclosures have left no records, although some will be contained within manorial and estate records and are usually deposited with the local county record office.

From at least the middle of the sixteenth century it was common to effect enclosures by decree in the equity courts (especially Chancery and Exchequer). There is no full list of enclosures by this means and they are difficult to find with no preliminary information. From the middle of the eighteenth century (there are a small number earlier than this) it became common to effect enclosure by act of Parliament. These are far easier to trace and to use. The act would name the larger owners of property who had promoted the act. As a result of the enclosure, an award and (in many cases) a map would be drawn up. The award would list the people who were allotted land at enclosure, along with the amounts of land involved. These records can usually be found in the county record offices although others have been listed from several classes in the list referred to earlier. The original acts are held at the House of Lords Record Office (address in **48**).

The General Inclosure Acts of 1801 and 1836 did not specify where the awards were to be kept. Some were enrolled at Westminster and these are now at the PRO in C 54. Where these have been identified they have also been inserted in the list referred to earlier. Others will be found in the county record offices. In 1845 the Enclosure Commission was set up under the Enclosure Act of the same year. The Commission (and its successor departments, the Land Commissioners, the Board of Agriculture, and the Ministry of Agriculture and Fisheries) retained copies of the awards. These awards (which include maps) are now in MAF 1.

Enclosure material varies in the amount of information given. Reference to individuals are restricted to those allotted land and therefore enclosure awards will not list everyone within a particular parish. Where enclosure maps were created (usually from the late eighteenth century onwards) they often cover only that part of the parish or manor affected.

42.4 Valuation Office surveys, 1910–1913

The survey carried out by the Valuation Office under the Finance (1909–1910) Act 1910 saw a comprehensive mapping and valuation of the country. Much of the initial work was done starting from existing Ordinance Survey Maps.

Under the Finance Act of 1910, a tax was attached to the profit of house sales, if part of the profit was judged to have occurred because of the provision of amenities at the public expense. For example, if a park was opened nearby, trees planted in the road, and the road paved, the house price might increase because the site had become more attractive, although the householder had given neither effort nor financial contribution to the improvements.

In order to establish a fixed point from which to measure subsequent increases in value, a huge (and expensive) valuation exercise took place, between 1910 and 1913, the largest since 1086 and Domesday Book. The valuers wrote detailed descriptions and valuations of each house, and details of owners and tenants (but not occupiers) in Field Books (IR 58). To find the right entry in a field book, you have to use the maps (IR 121/1–IR 135/9) to discover the property number. There is guidance available in the form of a leaflet to use at the PRO: you may need to ask for help as well, as actually finding the right map and the right field book can be quite complicated.

A second set of books, known as Domesday Books, was also made: these included the actual occupiers as well as owners and tenants; these are particularly useful as most people lived in rented accommodation. Most of these Domesday Books are to be found in county record offices, which may also have duplicates of the Record Maps. The PRO has the Domesday Books for the City of London and for Paddington (IR 91).

It should be noted that although the valuation was supposed to include all land, even if exempt from payment, there are gaps in the records. Maps covering Portsmouth and Southampton, and an area around Chichester, were all lost during the Second World War. In addition to this many records for around Chelmsford in Essex and for the whole of Coventry appear to be lost. For large properties and estates, the field books may simply have the phrase 'description filed' . This indicates that the information was entered on a separate document in specially created files. These files are not thought to have survived.

As an exercise in raising money, the whole operation proved to be an expensive failure: it was called off in 1920.

42.5 Surveys of land and house ownership: bibliography

G Beech, 'Maps for Genealogy and Local History', *Genealogists' Magazine*, vol. XXII, pp. 197–202
J Chapman, *A Guide to Parliamentary Enclosure in Wales* (Cardiff, 1992)
W Foot, *Maps For Family History, A Guide to the Records of Tithe, Valuation Office, and National Farm Surveys of England and Wales, 1836–1943* (PRO, 1994)
J H Harvey, *Sources for the History of Houses* (British Records Association, 1968)
R J P Kain and R R Oliver, *The Tithe Maps of England and Wales* (Cambridge, 1995)

A Parliamentary Return of Inclosure Awards (House of Commons Sessional Papers, 1904 (50) LXXVIII, 545)

B Short and M Reed, 'An Edwardian Land Survey: The Finance (1909–10) Act records', *Journal of the Society of Archivists*, vol. VIII (1986), pp. 95–103

W E Tate, *A Domesday of English Enclosure Acts and Awards* (Reading, 1978)

43 Taxation

43.1 Introduction

Tax records have always been a fruitful source for historians, and many before 1680 have been published by local record societies. This is one obvious case when it is better to go first to the PRO Library to see what is in print, rather than ordering up original documents. For a list of publications by local societies, ask to see Mullins' *Texts and Calendars*.

Most tax records until the late seventeenth century are in the Subsidy Rolls (E 179). This contains the surviving records of a number of different types of tax that were levied before 1700, the best known of which is the hearth tax (see **43.6**). It includes documents relating to scutage (a feudal payment in lieu of knight service), poll taxes, taxes on land, taxes on goods, taxes on aliens, forced loans, an abortive sheep tax in 1549, etc. Overall sums raised by most of these taxes are enrolled in E 359 and E 360. No tax return can be used as a total census of the population – there were always exemptions and evasions. For full details on the taxes themselves, see Jurkowski, Smith and Crook, *Lay Taxes in England and Wales, 1188–1688*. This invaluable book has been produced as part of the large scale E 179 Project run by the University of Cambridge and the PRO. This has been re-examining the lay tax records, and entering details of tax and place covered (*not* names) into a database which will be made available for public searching.

Many inquisitions and assessments relating to feudal payments based on land, drawing on E 179 and other classes, are printed in *Feudal Aids*, which is indexed by place-name and personal name and is on open access. The original records are mainly in Latin, some are damaged and the handwriting can be difficult to read but lists of names should become legible with practice.

The current E 179 class lists are arranged by (pre-1974) county, for England and Wales, with separate sections for the Cinque Ports; members of the Royal Household (both courtiers and officials) and Divers, Miscellaneous and Unknown counties, that should be consulted by anyone wishing to carry out a complete study of a particular area. There are separate lists for taxes paid by clergy, arranged by diocese – those paid by laymen (i.e. non-clergy) are called lay subsidies. Only those documents described in the lists as including <u>Names</u> actually list the names of tax payers. Within each county, they are arranged by date, using regnal years (e.g. 18 Edward I: these can be converted into a calendar year by using Cheney's *Handbook of Dates*); and then by sub-divisions of the county known as hundreds, or in some areas, wapentakes. To find out the sub-division of the county for the place you are interested in, look at the Gibson's *Hearth Tax Returns*, or at Lewis's *Topographical Dictionary of England*, or his *Topographical Dictionary of Wales*. These dictionaries are very informative, and give a brief history of each town and most villages. You can also use Youings' *Guide to the Local Administrative Units of England*. Once the E 179 database becomes available, you will be able to pinpoint tax records for a particular place immediately.

43.2 Lay subsidies of 1290–1332

The most comprehensive early general tax for which returns survive are the lay subsidies of 1290–1332, a tax on the moveable, personal wealth of individuals, rather than on the land that they owned. They were granted by Parliament in acts which specified what proportion of an individual's wealth was taxable, after agreed exemptions had been made. Exemptions often included equipment necessary to pursue one's occupation, ranging from a knight's armour to a merchant's capital. Apart from in 1301, the grant normally exempted the poorest, e.g. in 1297 those assessed at less than a shilling did not have to pay anything. The heading of the lay subsidy roll will normally state what fraction of assessable property has been granted in tax, ranging from a twelfth to a twentieth. If two fractions are given, the higher one normally applies to more 'urban' areas. After 1334, assessment of individuals was replaced by fixed quotas levied on individual townships, based on a fifteenth on most taxpayers and a tenth on those living in boroughs or ancient crown demesne. Glasscock's *The Lay Subsidy of 1334*, lists the places assessed, giving modern Ordnance Survey grid references. Although the 'fifteenth' continued to be levied intermittently until the seventeenth century, it was fossilized at these 1334 rates, although local or national disasters, such as the Black Death, might lead to reductions being granted to particular places. They are more fully described in Beresford's *Lay Subsidies and Poll Taxes*.

43.3 Poll taxes

In 1377, the first poll tax was granted by Parliament, at a flat rate of 4d a head (one shilling for clergy who had a benefice). All men and women were liable – only those under 14 (possibly one third of the population) and those who begged for a living were exempt. It was also granted in 1379 (on those over 16) and 1381 (on those over 15), but at different rates according to status, thus giving details of occupations, although evasion was widespread. Some returns listed in the E 179 class list as being of 1377 (51 Edward III) are mis-dated as the actual documents record payments at different rates and therefore belong to 1379 or 1381, those also recording occupations probably being of 1379. The failure of this unpopular tax led to its abandonment until the seventeenth century when it was intermittently revived in 1640 and on a number of occasions after 1660 although few detailed returns survive of these later poll taxes.

43.4 Subsidies and other taxes after 1522

After 1522, a fresh attempt was made to assess individual wealth, based on income from freehold land, the capital value of moveable goods and income from wages. The returns list different groups of individuals and record what they were assessed on. Not all categories of wealth were taxed in every subsidy and rates varied – of the four subsidies granted in 1523, the first two levied 1 shilling in the £ on land and houses, with the same on goods over £20 in value (6d in the £ on goods under £20) and 4d in the £1 on wages (only on those earning £1 or more), but the third and fourth only taxed those with more than £50 in land (1526) or goods (1527). Aliens had to pay double rates. Wages were not taxed separately after 1525 and the threshold for payment on goods varied (£5 after 1557, reduced to £3 in 1563). The most informative returns are those of 1524–1527 and 1543–1544, thereafter they only represent a small minority of the population.

They are fully described and illustrated in Hoyle's *Tudor Taxation Records* which also covers the 'Military Survey' of 1522 and other sources for forced loans required from wealthier individuals, such as the privy seal letters to contributors of 1588–1589 in E 34/16–40. He argues that values given in assessments are rough estimates rather than precise valuations – 'they describe reputed wealth rather than real wealth'. Under-assessment was endemic. For more on the use of the 1524/5 lay subsidies for economic and local history, see Sheail, *The Regional Distribution of Wealth in England as indicated in the 1524/5 Lay Subsidy Returns*.

Certificates of residence in E 115, mainly from 1558–1625, were intended to prevent double charging of individuals who resided in more than one county. Each taxpayer was meant to be assessed at his normal place of residence on all his lands and goods throughout the country. The certificates are indexed alphabetically by personal name.

43.5 Seventeenth century: new taxes

In 1642, a new parliamentary tax, the assessment levied on counties, was imposed. It lasted until 1680. County commissioners had to assess and enforce payment, so records of payments by individuals may survive locally. Returns of sums raised are in E 179. In fact, the mid seventeenth century was a time of great experimentation in tax-raising. Details of many previously undescribed taxes, such as have been discovered by the E 179 Project, are presented in Jurkowski, Smith and Crook, *Lay Taxes in England and Wales, 1188–1688*. See also Gibson and Dell, *The Protestation Returns 1641–42 and other contemporary listings: collection in aid of distressed Protestants in Ireland, subsidies, poll tax, assessments or grants, vow and covenant, solemn league and covenant*.

The list of contributors to the 'Free and Voluntary Present' to Charles II in 1662 provides names and occupations or status of the wealthier members of society. About half the numbers who paid hearth tax subscribed to the 'Present'. Returns for Surrey have been published.

The parish lists of contributors to the fund for the relief of Protestant refugees for Ireland in 1642 provide a number of names; but survival is patchy (SP 28/191–195, E 179). The Surrey lists are very good and a typescript list and index is available.

43.6 The hearth tax, 1662–1688

The surviving hearth tax returns and assessments of 1662–1674 relate to the levy of two shillings on every hearth: as such, they are one of the obvious sources for family, local and social history. The hearth tax actually continued until 1688, but the later records were not returned into the Exchequer, and do not survive.

The most complete hearth tax records are those for 25 March 1664. Information supplied includes names of householders, sometimes their status, and the number of hearths for which they are chargeable. The number of hearths is a clue to wealth and status. Over seven hearths usually indicates gentry and above; between four and seven hearths, wealthy craftsmen and tradesmen, merchants and yeomen. Between two and three hearths suggests craftsmen, tradesmen, and yeomen; the labouring poor, husbandmen and poor craftsmen usually only had one hearth. There are many gaps in the records, partly because of the loss of documentation, but partly also because of widespread evasion of this most unpopular tax. Hearth tax returns for particular areas have been published by many local record societies, and some records are to be found in county record offices, among the quarter session records.

The hearth tax consisted of a half-yearly payment of one shilling for each hearth in the occupation of each person whose house was worth more than 20s a year, and who was a local ratepayer of church and poor rates. This actually left out quite large numbers of people, and paupers were not liable at all. Exempt from the tax were charitable institutions with an annual income of less than £100; industrial hearths such as kilns and furnaces (but not smithies and bakeries); people who paid neither church nor poor rate (paupers); and people inhabiting a house worth less than 20s a year who did not have any other property over that value, nor an income of over £100 a year. To prove that you were in the last category, you needed a certificate of exemption from the parish clergyman, churchwardens and overseers of the poor, signed by two JPs. After 1663, the hearth tax return includes lists of those chargeable and not chargeable (exempt), although these may be entered in a block, not necessarily at the end of the parish entry of payers. From 1670, a printed exemption form was used. The certificates of exemption are in E 179/324–351(listed in the standard set of lists): they are arranged by county only. They can give you more detail on why someone was exempt, and for the returns which do not include the 'not chargeables' you may need to look at them to get information about poorer inhabitants, or those engaged in industry.

The British Records Society and the Roehampton Institute London are running an ongoing project to provide a printed edition of at least one hearth tax return for each county (and ideally one from the 1660s and one from the 1670s). If you are an experienced transcriber of seventeenth century documents, you may wish to volunteer for this. If so, please contact The Head of the History Department, Roehampton Institute, Roehampton Lane, London SW15 5PH.

43.7 Land and other taxes from 1689: in local record offices and at Kew

From 1689 to 1830 there are records of land and assessed taxes in local record offices (which list names) and in the PRO (which do not, in general). The accounting records of the taxes are in the PRO, in E 181–E 184. They do not list all tax payers, although defaulters or people whose assessments changed may be listed. Three groups of taxes were administered centrally by the Board of Taxes, and locally by county commissioners. First was the land tax, voted annually from 1692 to 1798, and then made a perpetual charge. Second, the assessed taxes, a group of taxes assessed on the possession or occupation of certain kinds of property, beginning with the window tax in 1696. By 1803, the assessed taxes included taxes on inhabited houses, male servants, carriages, horses for riding and drawing carriages, horses for husbandry, dogs, horse dealers, hair powder and armorial bearings. The third was the income tax, which began in 1799.

Land tax assessments may be found in county record offices: they give owners and occupiers of land. In the PRO are the Land Tax Redemption Office Quotas and Assessments (IR 23). They list all owners of property subject to land tax in England and Wales in 1798–1799. The arrangement is by land tax parish and there is no index of names. In 1798 the land tax became a fixed annual charge and many people purchased exemption from paying. The records of these transactions are also useful and may include maps and plans (IR 22, Parish Books of Redemptions, 1799–1953, and IR 24, Registers of Redemption Certificates, 1799–1963). The arrangement is by parish. See the book by Gibson and Mills for lists of records in the PRO and elsewhere, arranged by county. There is a useful introduction to using local and PRO land tax records, by Pearl, 'Land tax:

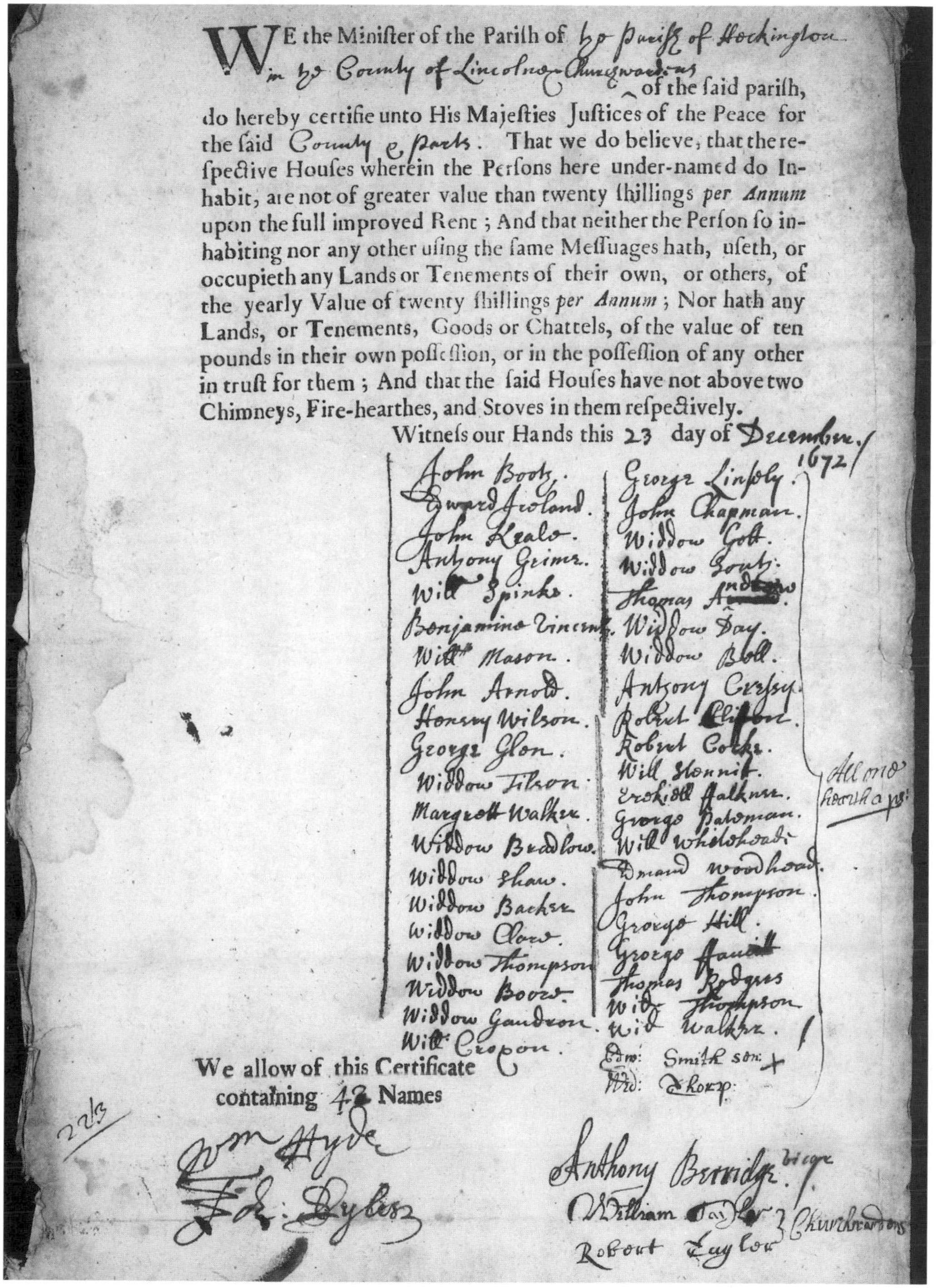

WE the Minister of the Parish of ye Parish of Hockington in ye County of Lincolne Churchwardens of the said parish, do hereby certifie unto His Majesties Justices of the Peace for the said County & parts. That we do believe, that the respective Houses wherein the Persons here under-named do Inhabit, are not of greater value than twenty shillings *per Annum* upon the full improved Rent; And that neither the Person so inhabiting nor any other using the same Messuages hath, useth, or occupieth any Lands or Tenements of their own, or others, of the yearly Value of twenty shillings *per Annum*; Nor hath any Lands, or Tenements, Goods or Chattels, of the value of ten pounds in their own possession, or in the possession of any other in trust for them; And that the said Houses have not above two Chimneys, Fire-hearthes, and Stoves in them respectively.

Witness our Hands this 23 day of December 1672

John Booth.	George Linsly.
Edward Ireland.	John Chapman.
John Keale.	Widdow Gott.
Anthony Grime.	Widdow Youls.
Will Spinke.	Thomas Andrew.
Benjamine Vincent.	Widdow Day.
Willm Mason.	Widdow Boll.
John Arnold.	Anthony Cressy.
Henery Wilson.	Robert Clifton.
George Glen.	Robert Cooke.
Widdow Tilson.	Will Hennit.
Margrett Walker.	Ezekiell ffalkner.
Widdow Bradlow.	George Bateman.
Widdow Shaw.	Will Whitehead.
Widdow Backer.	Edward Woodhead.
Widdow Clowe.	John Thompson.
Widdow Thompson	George Hill.
Widdow Boore.	George ffancill
Widdow Gaudeon.	Thomas Rodgers
Will Cropon.	Wid Thompson
	Wid Walker.
	Edw: Smith sen:
	Wid: Thorp:

All one hearth a pe:

We allow of this Certificate containing 43 Names

223

Wm Hyde

Jo: Dyles

Anthony Berridge vicar

William Taylor } Churchwardens

Robert Taylor

Figure 16 Hearth tax exemption certificates list people too poor to pay, as well as charities and industrial hearths. They are more difficult to find than the lists of tax-payers, also in E 179, and are less well known. This is for Hockington, Lincs, in 1672 (E 179/334) yesterday's electoral register'. For a scholarly study, see Ginter, *A Measure of Wealth*.

If you are a keen explorer of records and have a lot of time, the particulars of Account in E 182 may be the class to investigate. This class comprises supporting documentation to the tax accounts in E 181. The particulars run from 1689 to 1830, and relate to the land tax, the assessed taxes and the income tax. It has an uninformative list giving no descriptions other than county and covering dates, but the introductory note is good. The records do not in general include lists of names, but it can produce the occasional nugget of information. It does not include regular full lists of tax payers, but it does have information on those whose circumstances and therefore taxes change – including those who died, or who got another horse etc. Many payments authorized by central government were made at a local level from the tax revenues and not recorded elsewhere (e.g. rewards to informers leading to the arrest of army deserters, bounties paid to parishes for getting people to enlist in the army). It sometimes has lists of militia volunteers. This is certainly a class ripe for a large-scale listing project. At the moment it is not really a suitable class to recommend to novice researchers.

For death duties, see **6.1**.

43.8 Taxation: bibliography

M W Beresford, 'Lay Subsidies', *Amateur Historian*, vol. III, pp. 325–328 and vol. IV, pp. 101–109

M W Beresford, *Lay Subsidies and Poll Taxes* (Phillimore, 1963)

M W Beresford, 'Poll Taxes of 1377, 1379 and 1381', *Amateur Historian*, vol. III, pp. 271–278

Feudal Aids (London, 1899–1920)

C R Cheney, *Handbook of Dates for Students of English History* (London, 1991)

J S W Gibson, *Hearth Tax Returns, other later Stuart Tax Lists, and the Association Oath Rolls* (FFHS, 1996)

J S W Gibson and A Dell, *The Protestation Returns 1641–42 and other contemporary listings: collection in aid of distressed Protestants in Ireland, subsidies, poll tax, assessments or grants, vow and covenant, solemn league and covenant* (FFHS, 1995)

J S W Gibson, M Medlycott and D Mills, *Land and Window Tax Assessments, 1690–1950* (FFHS, 1997)

D E Ginter, *A Measure of Wealth: English Land Tax in Historical Analysis* (Montreal, 1992)

R E Glasscock, ed., *The Lay Subsidy of 1334* (British Academy Records of Social and Economic History, new series, II, 1975)

R W Hoyle, *Tudor Taxation Records* (PRO, 1994)

M Jurkowski, C L Smith and D Crook, *Lay Taxes in England and Wales 1188–1688* (PRO, 1998)

S Lewis, *Topographical Dictionary of England* (London, 4th edn, 1840)

S Lewis, *Topographical Dictionary of Wales* (London, 1840)

L M Marshall, 'The Levying of the Hearth Tax; 1662–1668', *English Historical Review*, vol. LI, pp. 628–646

C A F Meekings, *Introduction to the Surrey Hearth Tax, 1664* (Surrey Record Society, vol. XVII)

E L C Mullins, *Texts and Calendars* (Royal Historical Society, 2 vols, 1958, 1983: continued on the HMC website)

S Pearl, 'Land tax: yesterday's electoral register', *Family Tree Magazine*, June 1991

K Schurer and T Arkell, *Surveying the people: the interpretation and use of document sources for the study of population in the later 17th century* (Oxford, 1992)

J Sheail, *The Regional Distribution of Wealth in England as indicated in the 1524/5 Lay Subsidy Returns* (List and Index Society, *Special Series*, vols 28 and 29, 1998)

C Webb, *Calendar of the Surrey Portion of the Free and Voluntary Present to Charles II* (West Surrey Family History Society, 1982)

C Webb and East Surrey Family History Society, *Surrey Contributors to the Relief of Protestant Refugees from Ireland, 1642*

F A Youings Jr., *Guide to the Local Administrative Units of England, 2 vols* (Royal Historical Society, 1980, 1991)

44 Tontines and annuity records

44.1 Tontines and annuities

In the late seventeenth and the eighteenth centuries, the government organized several money-raising schemes by selling tontines and annuities. These schemes and the records produced are described by Colwell in *Family Roots*.

There were three English State Tontines, in 1693, 1766 and 1789, and three Irish State Tontines, in 1773, 1775 and 1777. In return for an original investment, participants were guaranteed a yearly income for the life of a living nominee chosen by the investor. People usually nominated their youngest relative. As the nominees died off, the central fund was distributed between fewer and fewer people and the annuity therefore became more valuable as the years passed. There were in all about 15,000 participants. Surviving records often involve proof of identity, or proof of continued existence. The records continue long after the original date of issue: for example, the last surviving nominee of the 1766 Tontine died in 1859. Most of the records are in NDO 1–NDO 3. They may give details concerning the marriages, deaths and wills of contributors and nominees. Contributors were usually substantial people. Many were spinsters. The registers have integral indexes.

Annuities were similar to tontines, in that an original investment paid out an annuity for term of life. However, the annuity did not grow as other annuitants died off. Annuities were offered throughout the eighteenth century. Again, the records obviously extend way beyond the date of issue. NDO 1–NDO 2 are the main record series, but Colwell's *Dictionary of Genealogical Sources in the Public Record Office* includes many other detailed references to tontine and annuity records.

Private, as opposed to government, annuities may be recorded on the Close Rolls in C 54, which have copious indexes.

44.2 Tontines and annuity records: bibliography

S Colwell, *Family Roots: Discovering the Past in the Public Record Office* (London, 1991)
S Colwell, *Dictionary of Genealogical Sources in the Public Record Office* (London, 1992)
F Leeson, *A Guide to the Records of the British State Tontines and Life Annuities of the 17th and 18th Centuries* (Shalfleet Manor, 1968)

45 Business records

45.1 Companies' registration, from 1844

Until 1844, companies could only be incorporated by Royal Charter or special Act of Parliament. From 1844 onwards, various Companies Acts enabled companies to be formed cheaply and easily. Some information about directors and shareholders of registered companies can be found in the companies' registration records,

For records relating to live companies, and to those which have ceased to function within the last 20 years, apply to the Companies Registration Office, at the Cardiff head office, or London, or Edinburgh (addresses in **48**). For a small fee they will produce a microfiche copy which contains all the required documents relating to any one company.

At the PRO are registration records for dissolved companies from 1844 until about twenty years ago. However, you still need to contact to the Companies Registration Offices first, to get the company number, if you are looking for a company dissolved after 1860.

For companies registered under the 1846 and 1856 Acts, and dissolved before 1860, look in BT 41. The records are arranged alphabetically, so this is easy to use.

For registered companies dissolved after 1860, use BT 31 and BT 34, arranged by registration number. The main index to company numbers is, of course, held by the Companies Registration Office. Especially useful (as it relates directly to the files held at the PRO) is the card index to companies dissolved before 1 January 1963 which is held only at the Company Registration Office Cardiff Search Room. Each card indicates whether the file has been destroyed or transferred to the PRO, in which case it will be marked with a BT 31 reference, as well as the company number and the date of dissolution; if the company has been taken over it may also give details of the successor company. This card index is consulted by their staff who take telephone, fax and postal requests from the public for information from the index. There is no equivalent fast finding aid at the Public Record Office.

Records have been kept for only a sample of companies dissolved after 1860 – a large sample at first, dwindling to 5 per cent for modern records. If you do locate a file for your company, you will find that the file itself has been weeded, so that it only contains certain documents. These include memoranda and articles of association, and lists of shareholders, directors and managers, for the first, last and some intermediate years of the company's operation. These give name, address, occupation, sometimes date of death and very rarely change of name. Between 1918 and 1948 they also give nationality if not British.

Notices of receiverships, liquidations and bankruptcies appear in the *London Gazette*, available at Kew in ZJ 1.

45.2 A company's own records

The PRO has the records of canal and railway companies nationalized in 1947 (in RAIL: see **26.1**); other transport undertakings and chartered and commercial companies which have passed into public ownership or whose records have come into public custody; and numerous records of various companies and other commercial undertakings among the exhibits used in litigation in C 103–C 114 and J 90 (see **47.3**) and bankruptcy (see **46**). Otherwise, for records of companies themselves, advice may be obtained from the Business Archives Council, or the Business Archives Council of Scotland (addresses in **48**).

45.3 Business records: bibliography

J Armstrong, *Business Documents: their origins, sources and uses in historical research* (London, 1987)

H A L Cockerell and E Green, *The British Insurance Business, 1547–1970* (London, 1976)

M Davis, 'Business Archives as a Source of Family History', *Genealogists' Magazine*, vol. XIV, pp. 332–341

D J Jeremy, *Dictionary of Business Biography: Biographical Dictionary of Business Leaders active in Britain in the Period 1860–1980* (London, 1984–1986)

Public Record Office, *Registration of Companies and Businesses* (Information Leaflet, giving more detail)

C T Watts and M J Watts, 'Company Records as a source for the Family Historian', *Genealogists' Magazine*, vol. XXI, pp. 44–54

46 Debtors and bankrupts

46.1 Introduction

The court and prison records held in the PRO and locally (see **39** and **47**) include very many references to legal proceedings against insolvent debtors: responsible for their debts but unable to pay them, they remained subject to common law proceedings and indefinite imprisonment, if their creditors so wished. From 1861, insolvent debtors were allowed to apply for bankruptcy.

From 1543 to 1861 debtors who were traders and who owed large sums were usually exempt from the laws relating to debtors and from consequential imprisonment. They were subject instead to bankruptcy proceedings. Until 1841, the legal status of being a bankrupt was confined to traders owing more than £100 (reduced to £50 in 1842). The legal definition of 'trader' came to embrace all those who made a living by buying and selling and by the late eighteenth century, included all those who bought materials, worked on them and then resold them: in other words, most skilled craftsmen. Farmers were specifically excluded but, nonetheless, do appear in the records. Those who wished to qualify as bankrupts, and thus avoid the awful fate of an insolvent debtor, sometimes gave a false or misleadingly general description of their occupations: *dealer and chapman* was very common.

Bankruptcy was a process whereby a court official declared qualifying debtors bankrupt, took over their property, and distributed it to their creditors in proportion to what they were owed: bankrupts could then usually be discharged from their debts and escape imprisonment. Their annual numbers increased from a few hundreds to many thousands between the eighteenth and twentieth centuries. Partnerships of individuals could also declare themselves bankrupt, but companies were not covered until after 1844.

46.2 Published and other sources for debtors and bankrupts

Official notices relating to many bankrupts (from 1684) and insolvent debtors (from 1712) in England and Wales, were placed in the *London Gazette* (ZJ 1), which is indexed from 1790: however before about 1830 the notices include some names not found in the records and omit some names which are. Scottish notices were placed in the *Edinburgh Gazette*, although a few are found in the *London Gazette*. Details were also published in *Perry's Bankruptcy and Insolvent*

Weekly Gazette (later *Perry's Gazette*), from 1827. From 1862 official notices relating to county court proceedings were placed in local newspapers, held by the appropriate local record office or by the British Library Newspaper Library (address in **48**).

These publications (and the records described below) rarely give more than the names, addresses and occupations and sometimes those of their creditors, with formal details of conviction and imprisonment, where appropriate. In most bankruptcy cases, the records held by the Public Record Office are confined to brief, formal entries in various register series that will establish the fact of bankruptcy but will not provide much background detail. Case files, in B 3 and B 9, only survive for a very small sample. Additional information can sometimes be found in the court records of legal actions against them: see **46.1**. From 1842 separate records of bankruptcy proceedings outside the London area were kept by district bankruptcy courts (1842–1869) and by county courts with bankruptcy jurisdiction (from 1861), and they are now held locally. Registers of petitions in bankruptcy in England and Wales from 1912 to date are held in the Royal Courts of Justice, Thomas More Building, where searches may be made on payment of a fee.

Throughout, legal issues relating to bankruptcy were heard separately in local and central courts, and especially in Chancery. Bankrupts guilty of fraud, dishonesty or misconduct remained liable to imprisonment and may be found in the prison records referred to in **46.1**. Records relating to Scottish bankruptcies ('sequestrations') are held in the Scottish Record Office (address in **48**).

Bankruptcy records usually give only the name, address and occupation of the debtors and of their creditors, and a formal summary of court proceedings. In some instances, where case papers survive (B 3, B 9, BT 221, BT 226) or where the proceedings were subjected to legal review (B 1, B 7), they may also provide interesting information about the bankrupts' family and business links, trading activities and economic circumstances.

46.3 Insolvent debtors before 1862

Insolvent debtors were held in local prisons, and often spent the rest of their lives there: imprisonment for debt did not stop until 1869. These will be kept in local record offices. The PRO holds records for the prisons of the central courts, and of the Palace Court. The Palace Court, 1630–1849, was used for the recovery of small debts in the London area (PALA 1–PALA 9). Records of the Fleet, King's Bench, Marshalsea and Queen's prisons for debtors, 1685–1862 are in PRIS 1–PRIS 11, with gaolers' returns of insolvents in certain London prisons, 1862–1869, in B 2. PCOM 2/309 is a register of Lincoln Gaol, 1810–1822, which lists the names of many people imprisoned for debt: other PCOM records may be worth exploration. Try also the returns of imprisoned debtors made to the Court of Bankruptcy, 1862–1869 (B 2/15–32). The periodic passing of Acts for the Relief of Insolvent Debtors allowed for their release, if they applied to a Justice of Peace and submitted a schedule of assets. Records relating to this process may be with quarter sessions records, held by local county record offices: exceptionally, some for the Palatinate of Chester, 1760–1830, are here in CHES 10.

In 1813, the Court for the Relief of Insolvent Debtors was established. After 1847, this court also dealt with London bankruptcies under £300. Petitions for the discharge of prisoners for debt in England and Wales, 1813–1862, were registered by this Court (B 6/45–71: indexes in B 8). Petitions by debtors who were not traders or who were traders owing small amounts, for protection orders against the laws relating to debtors, were registered by the Court of Bankruptcy, 1842–1847, and the Court for the Relief of Insolvent Debtors, 1847–1861 (B 6/88–89, 94–96), and also by local courts of bankruptcy jurisdiction: see **46.4**. Proposals for repayments by insolvent debtors were recorded by the Court of Bankruptcy, 1848–1862 (B 6/97–98).

46.4 Bankruptcy before 1869

Under the Bankruptcy Act of 1571 (13 Eliz. I c.7) commissioners of bankrupts could be appointed to allow a bankrupt to legally discharge his debts to his creditors by an equitable and independent distribution of his assets, and then begin trading again with his outstanding debts wiped out.

The creditors petitioned the Lord Chancellor for a commission of bankruptcy (a fiat after 1832 when the Court of Bankruptcy was established). Registers of commissions of bankruptcy and fiats issued are in B 4 for the period 1710–1849. Entries vary in detail over this period and may give the address and trade of the bankrupt (not between 1770 and 1797), and the names of either the petitioning creditors or those of the bankrupt's agent or solicitor. Entries that have been underlined or ticked mean that a case file on that particular bankrupt should be found in B 3.

The Commissioners published notices in the *London Gazette* (ZJ 1) to inform creditors about their proceedings. Such notices are found from 1684 and are indexed from 1790: before 1832, they include many bankruptcies not included in the surviving B class records. Bankruptcy notices also appear in *The Times* (held here on microfilm). The records of these commissions, in the B record classes, only survive from 1710, and are incomplete until after 1832 (1821 for London). Earlier commissions of bankruptcy can be found enrolled on the Patent Rolls (C 66–C 67); conveyances of bankrupts' estates are enrolled on the Close Rolls (C 54) and relevant petitions are sometimes found in the State Papers (SP).

For the period after 1759, look first at the B 3 class list which contains a sample (about 5 per cent only) of bankruptcy case files, indexed by personal name (*D.C.* stands for *Dealer and Chapman*). Most files date from after 1780 and before 1842. A further sample of case files after 1832 is in B 9 after 1869, most relate to the London area. Case files may contain balance sheets submitted by the bankrupt. These are usually very general statements, rather than itemized accounts, and assignees' accounts. If your bankrupt is not listed in B 3 or B 9, you will have to search various register and enrolment series that will normally only lead to brief formal entries (see **46.5**). These will confirm the fact of bankruptcy, if it took place, but will not provide much detail. Some case files of proceedings under the Joint Stock Company Acts, 1856–57, for 1858–1862, are in B 10. C 217 also contains miscellaneous exhibits in a few bankruptcy cases.

46.5 Bankruptcy procedure before 1869

Enrolments of bankruptcy commissions (after 1758) and fiats may be in B 5. After 1849, creditors petitioned for an Adjudication in Bankruptcy, the registers of which (to 1869) are in B 6. The Commissioners took statements from the bankrupt and his creditors about his debts and the creditors would then elect trustees or assignees to value his assets and distribute them as dividends. Full-time Official Assignees, to prevent fraud, were also appointed after 1831 (appointments made 1832–1855 are in B 5) and thereafter assignees had to pay cash from the sale of a bankrupt's estates into the Bank of England – the class AO 18 contains records of their accounts for the period 1832–1851. Miscellaneous accounts, dating after 1844, are in BT 40.

When sufficient creditors (the proportion varied from three quarters to four fifths, by number and value), were satisfied and had signed a request for a Certificate of Conformity (a statement that the bankrupt had satisfied all the legal requirements), the Commissioners could issue the certificate which effectively discharged him, although dividends might continue to be paid after that date. From 1849 to 1861, there were three classes of certificate: I – where the bankrupt was blameless, II – where some blame could be attributed and III – where it was entirely the bankrupt's fault. Indexed Registers of Certificates of Conformity for 1733–1817 and deposited Certificates for 1815–1856 are in B 6 – entries give the name and address of the bankrupt and the date of the certificate. Enrolled copies of some certificates of conformity, 1710–1846; some assignments of assets to trustees, 1825–1834 and some appointments of trustees, 1832–1855, are in B 5. After 1861, Orders of Discharge were issued instead. Records relating to issues the Commissioners were unable to resolve or appeals in bankruptcy cases are in B 1 and B 7. Actions against individual bankrupts or their assignees may sometimes be found in the records of other courts – Chancery, Exchequer, King's Bench and Common Pleas – many cases coming before the Palace Court (PALA classes) which dealt with small debt cases in the Westminster area.

46.6 District bankruptcy courts, after 1842

District bankruptcy courts were set up after 1842 to deal with cases outside London, sometimes defined as a 20 mile radius from the centre, and after 1869 (in part from 1847, for sums under £20) their jurisdiction passed to the county courts. After 1842, records relating to bankruptcy cases outside London may be held by county record offices and, after 1869, should normally be held there with the records of county courts, although sometimes 'country' cases were heard in London.

From 1849 until 1869, when the London Court of Bankruptcy was established, the two series of London District and Country District General Docket Books in B 6 show the class of certificate awarded or (after 1861) date of discharge, name, address and trade of the bankrupt and sometimes the names of petitioning creditors. For London Court cases, 1861–1870, deeds of composition with creditors or of assignment to trustees are summarized in a series of registers in B 6 (indexes in B 8). Registers of Petitions for protection from bankruptcy process in county court cases, from 1854, are in LCO 28.

46.7 Bankruptcy, 1869–1884

After 1869, routine imprisonment for debt ceased, other than in cases of fraud or deliberate refusal to pay, and the Court for the Relief of Insolvent Debtors was wound up. Creditors who were owed more than £50 could petition for bankruptcy proceedings. Cases in London were dealt with by the London Court of Bankruptcy, the records of which are held at the PRO. London was defined as the City and the areas covered by the metropolitan county courts of Bloomsbury, Bow, Brompton, Clerkenwell, Lambeth, Marylebone, Southwark, Shoreditch, Westminster and Whitechapel. Cases outside London were normally heard by the county courts after 1861 (they had some jurisdiction since 1847) although they could be transferred to the London Court by special resolution of the creditors. County court records are normally held by the appropriate local record office. Registers of Petitions for protection from bankruptcy process in county court cases, from 1854, are in LCO 28. There is a Register of London bankruptcies for 1873–1874 in BT 40/27 and one for County Court bankruptcies for 1879 in BT 40/46.

After 1883, the London Court of Bankruptcy was incorporated into the Supreme Court as the High Court of Justice in Bankruptcy. It subsequently became responsible for the additional metropolitan county court areas of Barnet, Brentford, Edmonton, Wandsworth, West London and Willesden. Bankruptcy petitions were only to be presented to the High Court if the debtor had resided or carried on business within the London Bankruptcy District for six months, if he was not resident in England or if the petitioning creditor could not identify where he lived. A High Court judge could, however, transfer any bankruptcy case to or from a county court. After 1883, official receivers supervised by the Bankruptcy Department of the Board of Trade took over responsibility for the administration of the bankrupt's estate, once a court had determined the fact of bankruptcy and made a receiving order. Its records therefore cover cases dealt with by both the High Court and the county courts.

The Registers of Petitions for Bankruptcy for 1870–1883, held under the references B 6/184–197 and arranged alphabetically by initial letter of the bankrupt's surname, cover both London and Country cases but only give a very brief entry with the case number, bankrupt's name, occupation and address. There are also registers of bankrupts, in both the London Bankruptcy Court and the county courts, for 1870–1886 in the record class BT 40 which give dates of orders of discharge. More detail, for cases heard by the London Court of Bankruptcy, is given in the Registers of Creditors' Petitions (B 6/178–183), the best place to begin a search for cases heard in London 1870–1883. They are arranged chronologically and in alphabetical order of the first letter of the bankrupt's surname. They give his name, address and occupation and that of the petitioning creditor(s), details of what formal act of bankruptcy was committed (e.g. filing a declaration on insolvency or leaving the country), the date (and place if outside London) of adjudication as a bankrupt; the date of advertisement in the *London Gazette*, the names of any trustees appointed, the amount of any dividend paid, as shillings in the £, and the date when proceedings closed. Indexes to Declarations of Inability to pay (London Court cases only after 1854), which were one means of committing a formal act of bankruptcy, give the date of filing and basic details of the name, address and occupation of the debtor and name of his solicitor, 1825–1925, are also in B 6.

46.8 Bankruptcy from 1884

After 1884, the Board of Trade supervised the work of the official receivers, who had the status of court officials and, after a receiving order had been made by the court, held meetings of creditors, investigated the circumstances of the bankruptcy and acted as interim administrators of the bankrupt's assets, pending, or in default of, the appointment of a trustee chosen by the creditors. If the bankrupt's assets were likely to be less than £300, the official receiver normally acted as trustee. When the trustee had realized as much of the bankrupt's assets as possible to pay his debts, he could apply for a release, discharging his responsibility.

For the period 1884–1923, Board of Trade registers in the record class BT 293, which are indexed alphabetically by name, should contain entries for all persons served with a petition for bankruptcy, whether the case was heard in London or locally, although it should be noted that not all petitions resulted in formal bankruptcy. Each entry should give the name, address and occupation of the debtor; the date of filing of the petition for bankruptcy; the dates of orders in case, including final discharge; the names of any trustees and the rate of dividend paid to the creditors. The incomplete set of Estate Ledgers in the record class BT 294, arranged alphabetically by name, may show how the assets were distributed. Official Assignees' accounts, before 1884, are in BT 40.

From 1888, registration of Deeds of Arrangement, made privately between debtors and creditors outside normal bankruptcy proceedings, became compulsory and the registers are in BT 39, with some case files in BT 221. These case files, dating from 1879, may also deal with audits and official releases – there is a card index of names for the official release files on open access. Case files of the Official Receiver relating to High Court cases from 1891 are in BT 226, sampled after 1914. The pre-1914 cases are indexed by name in a card index also on open access. Thereafter, the indexes are in BT 293. Most cases are personal bankruptcies, ranging from comedians to stockbrokers. For information on the winding up of companies see the *PRO Guide* Part 1, 317/1/14.

46.9 Petitions to the High Court, from 1884

Registers of petitions to the High Court, by or against debtors, chronologically arranged by initial letter of surname from 1884, which record the names, addresses and occupations of the debtors and petitioning creditors, the name and address of the solicitor, and the alleged act of bankruptcy committed, are in B 11. The actual petition will only have survived if there is a case file in B 9 on which it has been filed. Registers of receiving orders from 1887 (orders from 1883 are noted in the B 11 Registers), are in B 12 and give the dates of formal court orders including the receiving order, the order of discharge with a note of any conditions attaching to it, and the date of the trustees' release. Names of trustees may also be given, although not if the official receiver was acting as trustee. For London and High Court bankruptcies after 1869, there is a very small sample (less than 5 per cent) of bankruptcy case files, arranged roughly chronologically by date of filing of petition, in the record class B 9. These files may be one or more substantial volumes – those for A W Carpenter, trading as the Charing Cross Bank, run to 152 volumes.

46.10 Bankruptcy appeals

Before 1875, minutes of appeal cases are in B 7, with entry books of orders in B 1. Thereafter, appeals were directed to the Supreme Court's Court of Appeal (classes J 15, J 56, J 60, J 69–70). From 1883, appeals in county court cases went to a divisional court of the High Court (J 60, J 74 and J 95). An incomplete series of Registers of Petitions for protection from process in county court cases, covering the period 1854–1964, is in LCO 28.

46.11 Debtors and bankrupts: bibliography

W Bailey, *List of Bankrupts, Dividends and Certificates, 1772–1793* (London, 1794)
H Barty-King, *The Worst Poverty: A History of Debt and Debtors* (Alan Sutton, 1991)
Edinburgh Gazette (Edinburgh, 1699 continuing)
London Gazette (London, 1665 continuing)
S Marriner, 'English Bankruptcy Records and Statistics before 1850', *Economic History Review*, 2nd
    series, vol. XXXIII, pp. 351–366
Perry's Bankrupt and Insolvent Weekly Gazette (London, 1827–1881)
Perry's Gazette (London, 1882 continuing)

47 Civil litigation

47.1 Introduction: the law and the courts

Civil litigation (legal disputes between two parties) makes up a large part of the PRO's holdings of legal records, covering disputes about land, property rights, debts, inheritance, trusts, frauds, etc. All the legal records held by the PRO now have excellent introductory notes, filed before the list of each class, which should be consulted for detailed and up-to-date guides to the finding aids.

Records of civil litigation differ according to the kind of law and procedure used by the court in which they were heard. Cases heard in the common law courts were usually known as 'actions' and those in equity courts as 'suits'.

The development of law in medieval England was quite different to that of the rest of Europe. Scotland has a very different legal system, whose surviving records are in the Scottish Record Office and local record offices in Scotland.

In England, the common law provided a powerful centralized system of justice which was based on principles derived from the common customs of the country, but was essentially unwritten. This law was used by the ancient royal courts of Common Pleas and King's Bench, in the civil actions heard at the assizes, and in the Exchequer of Pleas and the common law side of the Chancery. The remedies offered by the common law did not always meet litigants' needs. It was difficult, for example, to enforce trusts and wills at common law. In cases of breach of contract the common law remedy would ensure the payment of damages, but it could not compel enforcement of the terms of the contract (a remedy that lawyers describe as specific performance). Courts of equity, which developed alongside the common law courts, were able to provide a different kind of remedy, as they were empowered to give judgements according to conscience and justice, rather than according to law. Courts of equity could (and did) order specific performance (but they could not award damages for non-compliance). The two systems of justice co-existed until the nineteenth century when the Common Law Procedure Acts allowed equitable pleas to be considered in common law actions. The old central courts were abolished in 1875, on the creation of the new Supreme Court of Judicature.

Unfortunately for the family historian, surviving common law records relating to civil litigation (although extensive) are extremely difficult to use. They are very formal and are largely composed of standard legal formulae. It requires considerable expertise to understand the meaning that lies behind the formulae and the records rarely contain useful detail.

In contrast, the records of the equity courts are full and informative and provide a wonderful source for social, family and local history. However, the complexity of the filing procedures of the equity courts and the inadequacy of the available lists and indexes mean that it can be difficult to search for a particular case. This is a problem which will disappear reasonably soon, as the equity finding aids become searchable on-line. The main equity court was the Chancery, where the Chancellor acted as the king's deputy: of lesser, but significant importance was the Equity side of the Exchequer. Other courts, such as the Court of Requests (supposedly for poor plaintiffs) and Star Chamber grew out of the king's council, and used procedures based on those of the equity courts.

In addition to these royal courts, there were similar common law and equity courts in the palatinates of Chester, Durham and Lancaster, and in Wales: the records of Welsh courts are now in the National Library of Wales. The duchy of Lancaster (not the same as the palatinate) had its own courts, available to tenants of duchy lands throughout the kingdom.

Three other systems of law also operated in England. Civil law (a branch of Roman law) was used in the High Court of Admiralty and in the High Court of Delegates; ecclesiastical law (another branch of Roman law) was used in the church courts; and customary law was used in the many local courts based on the jurisdiction of the lord rather than the king.

All these legal systems (except for the ecclesiastical and local courts) were brought together in a series of mid nineteenth century reforms, which resulted, in 1875, in a single Supreme Court of Judicature, with separate Divisions of Chancery, Common Pleas, Exchequer, King's Bench, and Probate, Divorce and Admiralty.

47.2 Records of common law courts

Since the creation of the Supreme Court in 1875, we have become accustomed to the idea that legal business is organized on functional lines: that is, one division of the court deals with matters relating to trusts and real estate, another with personal actions, and so on. Before 1875, the division of business was not by type of case but by type of litigant. Thus, Exchequer dealt with litigation between those who were crown debtors, Common Pleas dealt with actions between subjects of the crown, and King's Bench dealt with actions between crown and subjects. Civil litigation in the King's Bench was heard on the 'Plea Side' (for information about its criminal jurisdiction, known as 'Crown Side,' see **38.8**). Common law actions based on similar subject matter could therefore be heard in any of these courts, so that even if you know that someone was involved in a civil case and what the subject matter was, it will still be difficult to predict the court in which the action took place. Predicting which court a litigant might choose is further complicated by the fact that over the centuries a series of legal fictions were developed which enabled each of the courts to extend its clientele and effectively therefore to poach business from one another. The only exceptions to this are disputes between clergymen and laymen about the right to demand tithes, which were more likely to be heard in the equity side of the Exchequer than in any of the other courts.

These central common law courts were based in Westminster, but it was possible, and indeed usual, for trials to be held locally under a writ known as *nisi prius*. In effect this meant that the cases were heard at the next visit of the circuit judges to hold assize courts, and some records of trials held at *nisi prius* are therefore found amongst the records of the clerks of assize in ASSI classes.

Although much research has been undertaken on the medieval records, the more modern ones have been under-used and are still imperfectly understood. The procedures – and hence the records – of the common law courts were extraordinarily complicated, and the task of understanding how they fit together is not helped by the fact that they were heavily, systematically and unsympathetically weeded in the early twentieth century. You also need to be aware that, with the exception of a short period during the Interregnum of 1649–1660, all formal legal records were written in abbreviated Latin and in distinctive legal scripts until 1733. Even after that date the use of archaic legal phraseology and of legal fictions mean that it can be difficult to interpret the records accurately. There are as yet no published guides to using these records; the lists are inadequate and there are no modern indexes (although there are a number of contemporary finding aids). Researching common law records is not for the faint-hearted and you will have to be exceptionally determined even to attempt it. However, as the article by Watts and Watts shows, determination can occasionally pay handsome dividends.

Since we know that even in the present day most legal actions are compromised or dropped well before any formal legal hearing, the wisest course of action, in theory, would be to attempt to trace cases from the earliest initiation of procedure to the last conceivable entry. However in the current state of knowledge, such an approach is not practical. It is far better, and very much easier, to concentrate on a few major series of records, such as plea rolls, posteas, and judgement books/rolls. Most of these records were not created until the closing stages of cases that were either tried or came very near to being tried, and they will not therefore pick up the many cases that faltered soon after the initial steps of process.

Plea rolls are the formal record of the court's business. They are made up of individual parchment rotuli (a Latin term which literally means 'little rolls') on which are set out, in formulaic language, the nature of the action and an account of the process and final judgement (if any). Those of the King's Bench are in KB 26 (1194–1272), then in KB 27 until 1702, and are continued, for plea side only, in KB 122. These rolls also include the texts of deeds enrolled in the court. Reference to plea side enrolments, 1656–1839, is by means of a contemporary series of dockets now held in IND 1, which give, term by term, alphabetical lists of defendants' names together with the appropriate rotulus numbers in the plea rolls. The practice of filing rotuli on the plea rolls declined after 1760, so much so that by 1841 90 per cent of rotuli went unfiled. For this period therefore, it is essential to use the Entry Books of Judgments, 1699–1875, in KB 168 and J 89, which are arranged chronologically and give the date, county, names of plaintiffs, defendants and attorneys and brief details of the sum in dispute. There are indexes in the same classes.

The plea rolls of Common Pleas, 1273–1874, are in CP 40. Between 1583 and 1838 they include personal and mixed actions only, as pleas of land were enrolled separately on the recovery rolls (CP 43). Although there are no indexes, there are a number of contemporary finding aids that can be used to help a search. These include the prothonotaries' docket rolls in CP 60, 1509–1859 (formerly in IND 1). The docket rolls were probably compiled for the collection of fees, but they do give direct references to the rotuli and so can be useful as a means of reference. From the middle of the sixteenth century the termly entries give the county, the names of the attorney, plaintiff and defendant and the kind of entry made. Until 1770 there are three separate series of docket rolls: one for each of the three prothonotaries. In order to check all the entries for a particular term, you have to use all three rolls. There are gaps in each of the three series. No docket rolls survive for the period 1770–1790. From 1791 onwards there is a single series which ends in 1859. Thereafter similar information, 1859–1874, is contained in the Entry Books of Judgments in CP 64. There are also docket books, 1660–1839, in IND 1, which give the rotulus numbers of cases reaching judgment, and various calendars of entries, also in IND 1.

The plea rolls of the Exchequer of Pleas, 1325–1875, are in E 13. The most useful means of reference to them are the docket books of judgements, 1603–1839, which are in E 46 (formerly in IND 1). These are arranged first by legal term, then alphabetically by name of the defendant against whom judgement was given. They usually give the name of the plaintiff, the type of suit (and sum in dispute in cases of debt), the amount of damages awarded and the resolution of the case. Two series of (selective) calendars of the records down to 1820 have been compiled. The first, arranged by date, is in IND 1; the other, arranged alphabetically by persons and places, is in E 48 and is available on open access in the PRO. Repertory rolls, in E 14, can also be used as a means of reference, but the series is very broken, and covers only the periods 1412–1499, 1559–1669 and 1822–1830. Entry books of judgements, 1830–1875, formerly in IND 1, are now held in E 45. These give the dates of interlocutory and final judgements, but do not give any direct references to the plea rolls.

Chancery also had a common law jurisdiction, called the plea side of Chancery. Its basic jurisdiction covered relations between crown and subject on such matters as royal grants, royal rights over its subjects' lands as discovered through inquisitions post mortem and inquisitions of lunacy, feudal incidents due to the crown, and division of lands between joint heiresses. It also had an increasing role in debt jurisdiction, on actions for recognizances for debt entered in Chancery. Pleadings for Edward I–James I are well-listed, in C 43 and C 44; pleadings for Elizabeth I to Victoria are in C 206. There are remembrance rolls in C 221 and C 222, and writs in C 245.

47.3 The equity courts: Chancery and Exchequer

Equity records of the Chancery run from the late fourteenth century to 1875: after 1875, similar records can be found among the records of the Supreme Court of Judicature. The equity jurisdiction of the Exchequer ran from the mid sixteenth century to 1841, when it was taken over by the Chancery. In contrast to the common law courts, the amount of detail given in equity cases is almost overwhelming. The records abound in vivid sketches of daily life, particularly of disputes among families, often over wills, lands and trusts (including marriage settlements). They are also in English. One of the main problems with using equity records is that the documents relating to a single case were not all filed together, but were in several separate series, so that you have to search many different classes to assemble all the relevant information about a single case. This is made even more difficult by the fact that the names of the parties to the suit may change over time.

47.4 Chancery and Exchequer: the Bernau Index and other finding aids

Searching these records in particular will become much easier when the AD 2001 programme is completed, but at the moment many of them have the advantage of being included in the Bernau Index. The Bernau Index (available on microfilm at the LDS Family History Centres and at the Society of Genealogists) is really the place to start. It has a few minor drawbacks, however. It can be difficult to read, it gives obsolete references, and it makes no attempt to standardize variant spellings of the same surname. It rarely gives any additional information (such as address) that allows individuals with common surnames to be identified without recourse to the original documents.

If you use the Bernau Index, *please* copy the Bernau reference in full, as you will otherwise be lacking vital clues when it comes to translating the obsolete references given into modern PRO references. If you have references to translate, ask at the Map Room desk for Sharp's *How to use the Bernau index*, or use Lawton's articles in *Family Tree Magazine*.

Bernau also compiled a detailed listing of record class C 11 giving both surnames and first names of all parties, together with dates, and often details of their status/occupation and residence. This listing is known as the 'Bernau notebooks', and it is available on microfilm in the Map Room at the PRO, as well as at LDS Family History Centres and the Society of Genealogists.

The PRO holds an extensive collection of indexes to plaintiffs, defendants, deponents, etc. for a large number of classes and parts of classes of equity proceedings: ask in the Map Room for advice as they each have their own problems. There are also excellent guides to the records of these courts by Horwitz, Gerhold and Trowles.

Class	Date range	Title	Bernau Index coverage
		Chancery	
C 1	c.1386–c.1558	Early Proceedings	1386–1538 only
C 2	c.1558–c.1660	Series I, Elizabeth I to Charles I	Elizabeth: ? James I: plaintiffs A–K only (not complete) Charles I: defendants only
C 3	1484–1690	Series II, Elizabeth I to Interregnum	All
C 4	[before 1660]	Answers, etc. before 1660	–
C 5	1613–1714	Pleadings before 1714, Bridges	All
C 6	c.1625–1714	Pleadings before 1714, Collins	–
C 7	c.1620–1714	Pleadings before 1714, Hamilton	–
C 8	c.1570–1714	Pleadings before 1714, Mitford	–
C 9	c.1643–1714	Pleadings before 1714, Reynardson	All
C 10	c.1640–1721	Pleadings before 1714, Whittington	–
C 11	c.1700–1758	Pleadings 1714 to 1758	All: see also the Bernau notebooks
C 12	c.1681–1800	Pleadings 1758 to 1800	All
C 13*	1800–1842	Pleadings 1800 to 1842	–
C 14 *	1842–1852	Pleadings 1842 to 1852	–
C 15	1853–1860	Pleadings 1853 to 1860	–
C 16	1861–1875	Pleadings 1861 to 1875	–
J 54	After 1875	Pleadings from 1875	–
C 21	1558–1649	Country depositions, Series I	Deponents
C 22	1649–1714	Country depositions, Series I	All plaintiffs and defendants Deponents for C 22/1–75 All deponents in cases where the plaintiff's name began with A (Snell)
C 24	1534–1867	Town depositions	Deponents
		Exchequer	
E 112	1559–1841	Pleadings	–
E 133	1559–1841	Depositions before the Barons	–
E 134	1559–1841	Country depositions	Deponents 1559–1800

* These need 3 days' notice to be produced.

The University of Wales has published several catalogues of early modern Welsh cases in these courts: Jones on *Exchequer Proceedings (Equity) Concerning Wales. Henry VIII–Elizabeth*; Jeffreys Jones on *Exchequer Proceedings Concerning Wales in Tempore James I*; and Lewis, *An Inventory of the Early Chancery Proceedings Concerning Wales*. These can all be seen in the PRO Library.

47.5 Equity procedure in Chancery and Exchequer

The normal procedure in all the equity courts was for the plaintiff to submit a written bill of complaint to the court, detailing all the various wrongs alleged to have been committed against him. The defendant would submit a similar document, the answer, refuting the allegations of the bill. The plaintiff would respond with a replication, and the defendant with a rejoinder. This served to identify (and narrow) the main points at issue between the parties. Documents created by this procedure are variously known as 'proceedings' or 'pleadings.' For Chancery, the medieval and early modern proceedings are in C 1–C 10 (reign of Richard II to 1714); then in C 11–C 13 (1714–1842) and C 14–C 16 (1842–1875). For Exchequer they are in E 112 (reign of Henry VIII to 1841), with a few in E 193 (1558–1841). The table makes things clearer.

A series of set questions relating to the points at issue was then drawn up (the interrogatory), which was put to witnesses, by local commissioners if they lived at a distance. Their answers, the depositions, can be very full and helpful. Interrogatories and depositions for Chancery are in C 21–C 25 (reigns of Elizabeth I to Victoria), and for Exchequer in E 133, E 134 and E 178 (reigns of Elizabeth I to Victoria), Calendars of Exchequer actions, in which depositions were taken by commission in the country (E 134), were printed in appendices to the 38th to the 42nd *Annual Reports of the Deputy Keeper of Public Records* for the period 1558–1760, continued in manuscript at the PRO for 1760–1841. The printed calendars exist at the PRO in a county arrangement, as well as in their original date order. Exchequer depositions taken in London are listed in alphabetical order, from Elizabeth I to Victoria, unfortunately without any indication of date (E 133). Cases involving the Crown are given at the back of this list.

Other evidence might include affidavits (voluntary statements made on oath) and exhibits, for a minority of cases. Exhibits consist of documents belonging to the parties that were produced before the Masters and remained unclaimed. They do not necessarily relate to specific points at issue and can contain a wide range of material, including title deeds, court rolls, and correspondence. Although most are poorly listed they are potentially a rich 'lucky dip' for family historians. Chancery affidavits are in C 31 (1611–1875) and Masters exhibits are in C 103–C 114 and C 171 (1234–1860) with Masters documents in C 117–C 126 (17th to 19th centuries). Those in C 103–C 114 are indexed by party (index filed before C 103 list). Similar records for Exchequer are in E 103 (affidavits, 1774–1951); E 140 and C 106 (exhibits, c.1650–c1850); E 185 (Equity petitions, 1627–1841) and E 207 (includes affidavits from the reign of Elizabeth I to 1774). Exhibits in later suits are in J 90: these need three working days' notice to be produced.

In Chancery (the main equity court), pleadings, evidences and exhibits were sent to one of the Masters in Chancery for consideration and a report back to the Chancellor. Masters' reports and certificates for Chancery cases are in C 38 (1544–1875) with supplementary material in C 39 (1580–1892). Similar material for Exchequer in is E 194 (1648–1841).

Orders and decrees made by the Chancellor, or by the judges in the other equity courts, were generally enrolled in some fashion and can be used to identify the subject matter of a case, but be warned: few cases did proceed far enough for this to happen. The Decree Rolls for Chancery are in C 78 (1534–1903) with supplementary rolls in C 79 (1534–1903); entry books of decrees and orders are in C 33 (1544–1875). Contemporary annual indexes do exist in record class IND 1 (on open access in the Map Room), but they are not entirely reliable since the name of the principal plaintiff could change during the course of the case. However, they are often the easiest way into a suit, if you have picked up a clue to its existence. Decrees and orders for the Exchequer are in

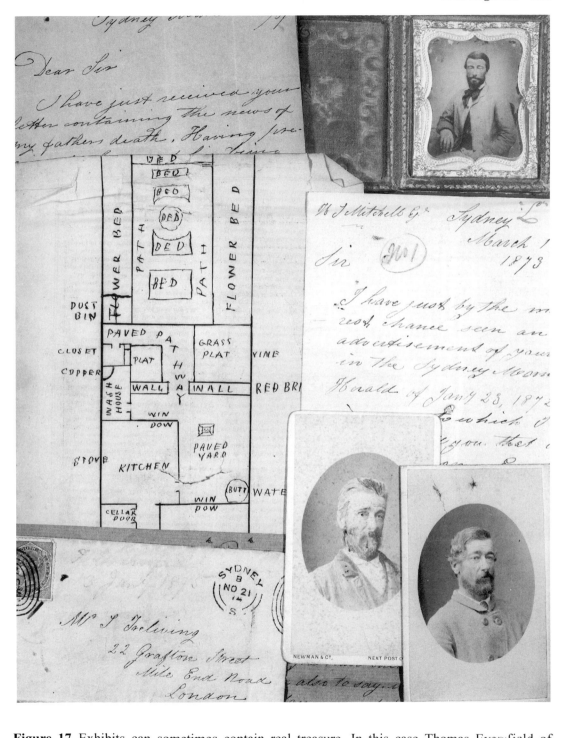

Figure 17 Exhibits can sometimes contain real treasure. In this case Thomas Eversfield of Sydney had responded in 1873 to an advertisement of the death of his father, back in England, and had to prove his identity. (J 90/1576)

E 128 (1580–1662), with supplementary material in E 129 (c.1350–c.1840); original decrees are in E 130 (1660–1841) and original orders are in E 131 (1660–1841); entry books of decrees and orders are in E 123–E 127 (1558–1841).

You may also find material in the Masters' Accounts in C 101: these are accounts of the administration of property in dispute, or in the control of the court because of lunacy etc. These are straightforward to find once you have the name of the suit, as they are indexed by plaintiff in IND 1/10702.

47.6 The Court of Star Chamber, 1485–1641

Star Chamber (named after the room in the Palace of Westminster in which it met) was effectively the King's Council sitting as a tribunal to enforce law and order. It became a separate court of law after 1485. Its business expanded significantly throughout the sixteenth century, but its success brought enmity from practitioners in the traditional common law courts and it was abolished in 1641. Although cases brought to Star Chamber were ostensibly about offences against public order, many of them were actually private disputes about property rights. The Court used procedures like those of the equity courts, so the main series of records are in English.

The case papers or proceedings are well listed.

Assigned to	Actual date range	Class	Finding aids
Henry VII	1485–1509	STAC 1	Listed in the standard list set, giving plaintiffs, defendants, subject and county (with appendices for stray and newly listed documents). Name index in *Lists and Indexes Supplementary Series IV*. Included in the Bernau Index.
Henry VIII	c.1450–1625	STAC 2	As above
Edward VI	Hen VII–Eliz I	STAC 3	As above
Mary	Hen VII–Eliz I	STAC 4	As above
Elizabeth I	1558–1601	STAC 5	Listed in an eighteenth century 4 volume manuscript list, in several sequences of letter bundles, by first plaintiff's surname. Name index in *Lists and Indexes Supplementary Series IV*.
		STAC 7	Manuscript list giving parties, subject and county
James I	1601–1625	STAC 8	Listed as above: indexed by the Barnes index
Charles I	1625–1641	STAC 9	Listed as above: cases begun under James I will be in STAC 8

For STAC 8 (James I), Barnes has produced three volumes of indexes, indexing parties, places, offence, and counties in considerable detail, using a numeric code system which is explained in each volume. Copies are available in the Map Room. These indexes are quite difficult to get used to, but very helpful for local history, or for the history of offences, as well as for people searching for particular parties. You will need to read the introductory material, explaining the codes used, and you have to identify which index and which column to look in.

The records of Star Chamber do not survive in entirety. There are large numbers of proceedings, but no decree or order books survive. You can find out a great deal of detail about a case, but with little chance of discovering its final outcome. Barnes has argued that every Star Chamber case in which at least one defendant was convicted resulted in a fine, and that notes of these fines were recorded on the Exchequer Memoranda Rolls in E 159. Another computer print-out in the Map Room lists these for 1596–1641. The classes E 101 and E 137 also contain some accounts of fines.

A list of cases relating to Wales is in Edwards, *A Catalogue of Star Chamber Proceedings Relating to Wales* (Cardiff, 1929). It is also worth exploring the publications of local record societies as many cases have been published by them. For more information, try Guy's handbook to Star Chamber and Barnes' article.

47.7 The Court of Requests, 1483–1642

The Court of Requests was an offshoot of the king's council, intended to provide easy access by poor men and women to royal justice and equity. It was established in 1483, when the chancery official responsible for sorting petitions from the poor became clerk of the council of requests. A cheap and simple procedure attracted many suitors (not all of them poor, but particularly including women). The Court used procedures like those of the equity courts, so the main series of records are in English. For a general overview, see Leadam, *Select cases in the Court of Requests*.

The records of the court cease in 1642. Its privy seal was removed during the Civil War. Although the court was never formally abolished, much of its caseload eventually passed to local small claims courts. Types of case heard included title to property, annuities, matters of villeinage, watercourses, highways, wilful escape, forgery, perjury, forfeitures to the king by recognizance and dower, jointure and marriage contracts.

Monarch	Date range	Bundles in REQ 2	Finding aids
Henry VII–Henry VIII	1485–1547	1–13	Listed in *List and Index, XXI, Proceedings in the Court of Requests* (gives parties, subject and place): 1–40 also listed with a little more detail, and some dates, in the lists marked 'Hunt's series'. Indexed in *List and Index Supplementary, VII, vol. 1*. Included in the Bernau Index.
Edward VI	1547–1553	14–19	As above
Mary I	1553–1558	20–25	As above
Elizabeth I	1558–1603	26–136	As above
		137–156	Listed in the manuscript 'Atkin's Calendar', and indexed in *List and Index Supplementary, VII, vol. 1*.
		157–294	Listed in a further unnamed manuscript list, and indexed by person, subject and location in: bundles 157–203 in *List and Index Supplementary, VII, vol. 2*; bundles 204–294 in *List and Index Supplementary, VII, vol. 3*
		369–386	None
James I	1603–1625	295–311	Listed in a further unnamed manuscript list, and indexed by person, subject and location in *List and Index Supplementary, VII, vol. 4*
		387–424	Bundles 387–409 are listed in a further unnamed manuscript list, indexed by person, subject and location in *List and Index Supplementary, VII, vol. 4*
		425–485	None
Charles I	1625–1649	486–806	None
?	various dates	807–829	None

Unlike the Star Chamber, the judicial and administrative records (in English and Latin) of the Court of Requests have survived fairly well: most are in REQ 1, but there may be some unsuspected material in REQ 2/369–386. REQ 1 includes:

REQ 1			
order and decree books	Hen VII–Chas I	1–38, 209	orders, decrees, final judgements and, before 1520, appearances
order books	Eliz I–Chas I	39–103	draft orders, decrees and memoranda
appearance books	Hen VIII–Chas I	104–117	records of appearance by defendants, usually by attorney
contemporary indexes to affidavits	1637–1641	118, 150	incomplete
affidavit books	1591–1641	119–149	signed affidavits (by servers) that process, especially writs of summons, had been served
note books	1594–1642	151–170	outline records of the progress of suits
process books	1567–1642	171–197	recording the issue of writs of privy seal, attachments for arrest, appointment of commissions, injunctions, and orders for appearances
witness books	Eliz I–Chas I	198–206	
register of replications	1632–1636	207	
commission book	1603–1619	208	recording return dates of depositions by commission

47.8 Records of equity courts: Chester, Durham and Lancaster

In the palatinates, the Chancery of Durham and the Chancery of the County Palatine of Lancaster lasted from the fifteenth century to 1971: the Chester equity court, known as the Exchequer, lasted from the fifteenth century to 1830. The equity court of the Duchy of Lancaster, known as the Duchy Chamber, started in the fourteenth century and still exists in theory. The Duchy of Lancaster is not co-extensive with the county of the same name: the Duchy holds lands in many other parts of the country. The record-keeping practices of these courts were very similar to those of the central equity courts. Pleadings in cases relating to real property (i.e. land) in the Palatinate of Chester are in CHES 15 (Henry VIII to 1830) and for debts and personal property in CHES 16 (1559–1762); for Durham they are in DURH 2 (1576–1840); for the Duchy of Lancaster they are in DL 49 (1502–1853), with draft injunctions in DL 8 (1614–1794). For the Palatinate of Lancaster the bills are in PL 6 (1485–1853), the answers are in PL 7 (1474–1858) and the replications in PL 8 (1601–1856).

Chester depositions are in CHES 12 (Elizabeth I); Durham interrogatories and depositions are in DURH 7 (1557–1804); Duchy of Lancaster depositions are in DL 3 and DL 4 (Henry VII to 1818) and DL 48 (1695–1739). and those of the Palatinate are in PL 10 (1581–1854). Affidavits, exhibits and other miscellaneous papers for Chester are in CHES 9 (1501–1830), CHES 11 (Henry III to Charles II). For Durham they are in DURH 7 (1557–1804). For the Duchy of Lancaster they are in DL 9 (1560–1857) and DL 49 (1502–1853) and for the Palatinate they are in PL 9 (1610–1678, 1793–1836) and PL 12 (1795–1860), with reports and certificates in PL 30 (1813–1849).

Decrees and orders for Chester are in CHES 13 (1559–1790) with entry books in CHES 14 (1562–1830). For Durham they are in DURH 5 (1613–1778) with drafts in DURH 6 (1749–1829). Duchy of Lancaster entry books of decrees and orders are in DL 5 (1472–1872), draft decrees are in DL 6 (Henry VIII to 1810). Entry books of decrees and orders for the Palatinate are in PL 11 (1524–1848).

47.9 Records of the civil law courts: Admiralty, Delegates and Privy Council Appeals

There were also various civil law courts (generally applying Roman or 'civil' international law). Civil disputes (concerning commercial disputes, wages, salvage and damage to ships or cargoes) were normally heard in the High Court of Admiralty (which also had a common law criminal jurisdiction, see **38.10**). The civil business of the High Court of Admiralty was conducted from about 1660 in a separate Instance Court. The records of the Instance jurisdiction are extensive, but like other legal records they can be difficult to use. The records most likely to interest family and social historians are the examinations and answers in HCA 13 (1531–1768), and the instance papers in HCA 15–HCA 19 (1586–1874). The examinations and answers are in English and contain detailed accounts of evidence tendered by witnesses; they also include information about the witness's name, age, address, occupation and age. Instance papers contain a variety of papers including affidavits, allegations, answers, decrees, petitions and exhibits. If you know the name of your ancestor's ship, the indexes to ships' names in HCA 56 (1772–1946) can be useful.

The High Court of Delegates was established during the reign of Henry VIII to hear appeals from the ecclesiastical courts which, before the break with Rome, would have been made to the Pope. It also had appellate jurisdiction from the Instance court of the High Court of Admiralty, the Court of Chivalry and the courts of the chancellors of Oxford and Cambridge Universities. Every appeal necessitated the appointment of a special commission under the great seal directed to judges delegate appointed by the Lord Chancellor. Its records are in the DEL lettercode, and have been well listed. The Court was abolished in 1833 and its jurisdiction in ecclesiastical and maritime causes was transferred later that year to the Judicial Committee of the Privy Council which retained responsibility for appeals until 1858 (1879 for maritime cases): see its records in the PCAP lettercode.

A useful overall means of reference to the records of the High Court of Delegates is provided by the *Return of all appeals in causes of doctrine or discipline made to the High Court of Delegates* (Sessional papers, House of Commons, 1867–1868, vol. LVII: available on the open shelves). This does not give direct references to particular documents but it does give sufficient information to enable cases to be traced through the records. It gives a description of the nature of the cause, the names of the parties to the cause, the date of appeal, the court or courts from which the cause was appealed, details and date of sentence together with the names and offices of the judges delegate on the commission. It is indexed by names of causes and by subject.

47.10 Records of the Supreme Court of Judicature

In 1875, the existing superior civil courts were amalgamated into a new Supreme Court, consisting of a High Court of Justice and a Court of Appeal, which was able to apply either common law or the rules of equity as needed. The High court consisted of five divisions: King's (or Queen's) Bench, Common Pleas, Exchequer, Chancery, and Probate, Divorce and Admiralty. In 1881, the Common Pleas, Exchequer and Queen's Bench Divisions were amalgamated. Theoretically all jurisdiction belongs to all divisions alike, but in practice the exercise of jurisdiction in particular matters is assigned to particular divisions. The Queen's Bench Division deals with actions founded on contract or tort (causing harm or injury to a person without legal justification), and in commercial cases. The Chancery Division deals with actions relating to land, trusts, mortgages, partnerships and bankruptcy. In 1971 the Probate, Divorce and Admiralty Division was renamed the Family Division; its Admiralty business was transferred to the Queen's Bench Division and contentious probate actions were transferred to the Chancery Division.

The records of the High Court are filed by type rather than by case, so it can be extremely difficult and time consuming to trace and assemble all the surviving material for any particular action. You also need to be aware that it is rarely possible to gain detailed information about the cases after 1945. Specimen judgement books are in J 89. The entry books of decrees and orders (J 15) can be useful in tracing cases heard in the Chancery Division; there are contemporary annual indexes to these orders under the name of the first plaintiff in record class IND 1. If you are tracing a case heard in the Queen's Bench Division you should start with the cause books in J 87 and J 168. Exhibits, which are always a source of fascinating information, are in J 90.

The Appeal Court, which was also created as part of the Supreme Court in 1875, heard civil appeals only until 1966. Its surviving records are in J 83 and J 84 with judgements (1907–1926) in J 70. Such records are rarely informative, since the cases were argued verbally, usually on points of law rather than on new evidence.

47.11 Chancery: unclaimed money (dormant funds)

Many families have stories of money 'in Chancery'. This may refer to money deposited by solicitors (from 1876) when they were unable to trace legatees or next of kin. Since 1876, annually-prepared accounts have been produced: they can be inspected, free of charge, at the Court Funds Office (address in **48**). Evidence of beneficial interest is required. Lists of funds published as supplements to the *London Gazette* (1893–1974), can be consulted in the PRO. Successful claims are extremely rare.

47.12 Civil litigation: bibliography and sources

Published works
W P Baildon, *Select cases in the court of Chancery 1364–1471* (Selden Society, 1896)
J H Baker, *An Introduction to English Legal History* (London, 1990)
T G Barnes, 'The archives and archival problems of the Elizabethan and early Stuart Star Chamber', *Journal of the Society of Archivists*, II (1963)
C G Bayne and W H Dunham, *Select cases in the council of Henry VII* (Selden Society, 1958)
P W Coldham, 'Genealogical Resources in Chancery Records', *Genealogists' Magazine*, vol. XIX, pp. 345–347 and vol. XX, pp. 257–260
G I O Duncan, *The High Court of Delegates* (Cambridge, 1971)
I Edwards, *A Catalogue of Star Chamber Proceedings Relating to Wales* (Cardiff, University of Wales, Board of Celtic Studies, *History and Law* series, 1929)

K Emsley and C M Fraser, *The courts of the County Palatine of Durham* (Durham County Local History Society, 1984)

R E F Garrett, *Chancery and Other Legal Proceedings* (Shalfleet Manor, 1968)

D Gerhold, *Courts of equity – a guide to Chancery and other legal records* (Pinhorn handbook 10, 1994)

J A Guy, *The court of Star Chamber and its records to the reign of Elizabeth I* (HMSO, 1984)

H Horwitz, *Chancery Equity Records and Proceedings 1600–1800, a guide to documents in the Public Record Office* (rev. edn, PRO, 1998)

H Horwitz, *Samples of Chancery Pleadings & Suits: 1627, 1685, 1735 and 1785* (List and Index Society, vol. 257, 1995)

H Jenkinson and B E R Fermoy, *Select cases in the Exchequer of Pleas* (Selden Society, 1932)

T I Jeffreys Jones, Exchequer *Proceedings Concerning Wales in Tempore James I* (Cardiff, University of Wales, Board of Celtic Studies, *History and Law* series, 1955)

E G Jones, *Exchequer Proceedings (Equity) Concerning Wales. Henry VIII–Elizabeth* (Cardiff, University of Wales, Board of Celtic Studies, *History and Law* series, 1939)

G Lawton, 'Using Bernau's Index', *Family Tree Magazine*, vol. VIII, 1991–2 (3 parts)

I S Leadam, *Select cases in the Court of Requests* (Selden Society, 1898)

I S Leadam, *Select cases . . . in Star Chamber* (Selden Society, 1903)

E A Lewis, *An Inventory of the Early Chancery Proceedings Concerning Wales* (Cardiff, University of Wales, Board of Celtic Studies, *History and Law* series, 1937)

E A Lewis and J Conway Davies, *Records of the Court of Augmentations relating to Wales and Monmouthshire* (Cardiff, University of Wales, Board of Celtic Studies, *History and Law* series, 1954)

R G Marsden, *Select pleas in the Court of Admiralty* (Selden Society, 1897)

M J Prichard and D E C Yale, *Hale and Fleetwood on Admiralty Jurisdiction* (Selden Society, 1992)

H Sharp, *How to use the Bernau index* (Society of Genealogists, 1996)

R Somerville, 'The palatinate courts in Lancaster', *Law and law makers in British History, papers presented to the Edinburgh Legal History Conference 1979* (Royal Historical Society Studies in History Series, XXII)

T Trowles, 'Eighteenth century Exchequer records as a genealogical source', *Genealogists' Magazine,* vol. 25, pp. 93–8

C T Watts and M J Watts, 'In the High Court of Justice . . .', *Genealogists' Magazine*, vol. 20, pp. 200–206

D E C Yale, *Lord Nottingham's Chancery Cases* (Selden Society, 1957, 1962)

Unpublished finding aids
Bernau Index (at the Society of Genealogists and LDS Family History Centres)
Bernau notebooks (at the Society of Genealogists and the PRO)

48 Useful addresses

Alderney, Clerk of the Court, Queen Elizabeth II St, Alderney GY9 3AA, Channel Islands   01481 822817

Army Medal Office, Government Buildings, Droitwich Spa, Worcestershire Rd, Worcestershire WR9 8AU   01905 772323

Army Museums Ogilby Trust, 85 The Close, Salisbury, Wilts SP1 2EX

Association of Genealogists and Record Agents, 29 Badgers Close, Horsham, West Sussex RH12 5RU

Association of Jewish Refugees in Great Britain, 1 Hampstead Gate, 1A Frognall, London NW3 6AL   0171 431 6161

Association of Scottish Genealogists and Record Agents, 51/3 Mortonhall Rd, Edinburgh EH9 2HN   0131 667 0437

Australasian Federation of Family History Organisations, c/o Western Australian Genealogical Society Inc., 6/48 May St, Bayswater, Western Australia

Australian Genealogists, Society of, Richmond Villa, 120 Kent St, Observatory Hill, Sydney, NSW 2000, Australia

Baptist Historical Society, Secretary, 60 Strathmore Ave., Hitchin, Hertfordshire SG5 1ST   01462 431816

Black Genealogical Society, 40 Hey Park, Liverpool, Merseyside L36 6HR

Borthwick Institute of Historical Research, St Anthony's Hall, Peasholme Green, York YO1 2PW   01904 642315

British Association for Cemeteries in South Asia (Secretary), 76½ Chartfield Ave., London SW15 6HQ

British in India Museum, 1 Newtown St, Colne, Lancashire BB8 0JJ   01282 870215/613129

British Library, 96 Euston Rd, London NW1 2DB   0171 412 7677

British Library, Newspaper Library, Colindale Ave., London NW9 5HE   0171 412 7356

British Woman's Land Army Society (Chairperson), 50 Church Lane, Marple, Stockport, Cheshire SK6 7LA

Business Archives Council of Scotland, University of Glasgow, Glasgow G12 8QQ

Business Archives Council, The Clove Building, 4 Maguire St, London SE1 2NQ   0171 407 6110

Cambridgeshire Record Office, Shire Hall, Cambridge CB3 0AP

Canterbury Cathedral, City and Diocesan Record Office, The Precincts, Canterbury CT1 2EG

Carmarthenshire Archives Service, County Hall, Carmarthen, Carmarthenshire SA31 1JP   01267 224184

Catholic Central Library, Lancing St, London NW1 1ND   0171 383 4333

Centraal Bureau voor Genealogie, PO Box 11755, NL-2502 AT, The Hague, The Netherlands

Central Criminal Court, Courts' Administrator, Old Bailey, London EC4M 7EH

Channel Islands Family History Society, PO Box 507, St Helier, Jersey JE4 5TN, Channel Islands

Chapel Royal, St James's Palace, London SW1

Church of England Record Centre, Galleywell Rd, London SE16 3PB   0171 231 1251

City of London Police Record Office, 26 Old Jewry, London EC2R 8DJ

Civil Service Commission, Management and Personnel Office, Treasury Chambers, Parliament St, London SW1P 3AG

College of Arms, Queen Victoria St, London EC4V 4BT

Commonwealth War Graves Commission, Information Office, 2 Marlow Rd, Maidenhead, Berks SL6 7DX   01628 34221

Companies Registration Office (Isle of Man), Finch Rd, Douglas, Isle of Man

Companies Registration Office (Northern Ireland), IDB House, 64 Chichester St, Belfast BT1 4JX

Companies Registration Office (Scotland), 102 George St, Edinburgh EH2 3DJ

Companies Registration Office, Crown Way, Maindy, Cardiff CF4 3UZ   01222 380801

Companies Registration Office, London Search Room, Companies House, 65–71 City Rd, London EC1Y 1BB   0171 253 9393

Corporation of London Record Office, PO Box 270, Guildhall, London EC2P 2EJ   0171 332 1251

Court Funds Office, 22 Kingsway, London WC2B 6LE

Dr Williams's Library, 14 Gordon Square, London WC1II 0AG   0171 387 3727

Family History Library, 35 North West Temple, Salt Lake City, Utah 84150, USA

Family Records Centre, 1 Myddelton St, London EC1R 1UW   0181 392 5300

Family Welfare Association (administrators of the Women's Land Army Benevolent Fund), 501–505 Kingsland Rd, Dalston, London E8 4AU

Federation of Family History Societies, Administrator, c/o Benson Room, Birmingham and Midland Institute, Margaret St, Birmingham B3 3BS

Foreign and Commonwealth Office, Records and Historical Service Unit, Hanslope Park, Hanslope, Milton Keynes MK19 7BH (for medal entitlement for Palestine Police)

Friends House Library, Euston Rd, London NW1 2BJ   0171 388 1977

Friends of the Public Record Office, Public Record Office, Ruskin Ave., Kew, Richmond, Surrey TW9 4DU   0181 876 3444 ext. 2226

Genealogical Office, 2 Kildare St, Dublin 2, Republic of Ireland

Genealogical Publishing Company, 1001 North Calvert St, Baltimore, Maryland 21202, USA

Genealogical Research Institute of New Zealand, PO Box 36–107, Moera, Lower Hutt, New Zealand 6330

Genealogical Society of South Africa, Suite 143, Postnet, X2600, Houghton 2041, Republic of South Africa

Genealogical Society of Utah, 50 East North Temple, Salt Lake City, Utah 84150, USA

Genealogical Society of Utah, British Isles Family History Service Centre, 185 Penns Lane, Sutton Coldfield, West Midlands B76 8JU

General Register Office (Northern Ireland), Oxford House, 49–55 Chichester St, Belfast BT1 4HL   01232 252020

General Register Office (Scotland), New Register House, Edinburgh EH1 3YT   0131 334 0380

General Register Office of England and Wales
    CA Section, Segensworth Rd, Titchfield, Fareham, Hampshire PO15 5RR
    Adoptions Section, Trafalgar Rd, Southport PR8 2HH   0151 471 4313
    Family Records Centre, 1 Myddelton St, London EC1R 1UW   0181 392 5300
    Certificate enquiries, PO Box 2, Southport, Merseyside PR8 2D   0151 471 4816

General Register Office of Ireland, 8–11 Lombard St, Dublin 2, Republic of Ireland   003531 6711000

General Registry (Isle of Man), Finch Rd, Douglas, Isle of Man   01629 673358

Gray's Inn Library, 5 South Square, Gray's Inn, London WC1R 5EU

Guernsey, Ecclesiastical Court of the Bailiwick of Guernsey, Bureau des ConnÈtables, Lefebvre St, St Peter Port, Guernsey, Channel Islands   01481 721732

Guernsey, Priaulx Library, St Peter Port, Guernsey, Channel Islands   01481 721998

Guernsey, The Greffe (HM Greffier), Royal Court House, St Peter Port, Guernsey, Channel Islands   01481 725277

Guild of One Name Studies, Box G, c/o 14 Charterhouse Buildings, Goswell Rd, London EC1M 7BA

Guildhall Library, Aldermanbury, London EC2P 2EJ   0171 332 1863

Hartley Library, Special Collections, University of Southampton, Highfield, Southampton SO17 1BJ   01703 592 721

Historic Ship Collection, East Basin, St Katherine's Dock, London E1 9AF

HMS *Belfast*, Symons Wharf, Vine Lane, Tooley St, London SE1 2JH

HMS *Victory*, HM Naval Base, Portsmouth, Hampshire PO1 3PZ

Home Office, Immigration and Nationality Department, Lunar House, 40 Wellesley Rd, Croydon CR9 2BY   0181 686 0688

House of Lords Record Office, House of Lords, London SW1A 0PW   0171 219 5316

Huguenot Library, University College, Gower St, London WC1E 6BT   0171 380 7094

Hyde Park Family History Centre, Church of Jesus Christ of Latter Day Saints, Hyde Park Chapel, 64–68 Exhibition Rd, London SW7 2PA   0171 589 8561

Imperial War Museum Duxford, Cambridgeshire CB2 4QR

Imperial War Museum, Department of Documents, Lambeth Rd, London SE1 6HZ   0171 416 5221

India Office Collections, British Library, 96 Euston Rd, London NW1 2DP

Inner Temple Library, Inner Temple, London EC4Y 7DA. Postal enquiries only

Institute of Commonwealth Studies, 28 Russell Square, London, WC1B 5DS   0171 580 5876

Institute of Heraldic and Genealogical Studies, Northgate, Canterbury, Kent CT1 1BA   01227 768664

International Council of the Red Cross, Archives Division, 19, Ave. de la Paix, CH-1202 Geneva

International Society for British Genealogy and Family History, PO Box 3115, Salt Lake City, Utah 84110-3115, USA

Irish Genealogical Research Society, 82 Eaton Square, London SW1W 9AJ

Irish Midlands Ancestry, Laois & Offaly History Centre, Bury Quay, Tullamore, Co. Offaly, Ireland   003531 506 21421

Jersey, Judicial Greffe, Morier House, Halkett Place, St Helier, Jersey JE1 1DD, Channel Islands   01534 502300

Jersey, Société Jersiaise, Lord Coutanche Library, 7 Pier Rd, St Helier, Jersey JE2 4XW, Channel Islands   01534 730538

Jersey, Superintendent of Births, Marriages and Deaths, The States Building, St Helier, Jersey, Channel Islands

Jewish Genealogical Society of Great Britain, PO Box 13288, London N3 3WD
Jewish Museum, 80 East End Rd, London N3 2SY; Raymond Burton House, 129–131, Albert St, London NW1 7NB   0171 284 1997
Jewish Refugees Committee, Drayton House, Gordon St, London WC1H   0171 387 4747

Lambeth Palace Library, Lambeth Palace Rd, London SE1 7JU   0171 928 6222
Land Registry, H. M., Lincoln's Inn Fields, London WC2A 3PH   0171 917 8888
Law Society Archives, Ipsley Court, Redditch, Hereford and Worcester   0171 242 1222
Library of Congress, Washington DC 20540, USA
Lincoln's Inn Library, Lincoln's Inn, London WC2A 3TN   0171 242 4371
London Metropolitan Archives, 40 Northampton Rd, London EC1R 0HB

Manx National Heritage Library, Kingswood Grove, Douglas, Isle of Man IM1 3LY   01624 648000
Maritime Archives and Library, Merseyside Maritime Museum, Albert Dock, Liverpool L3 4AA   0151 478 4418/4424
Maritime History Archive, Memorial University of Newfoundland, St John's Newfoundland, Canada A1C 5S7
Methodist Archives and Research Centre, John Rylands University Library, Manchester University, 150 Deansgate, Manchester M3 3EH   0161 834 5343
Metropolitan Police Archives, New Scotland Yard, Victoria St, London SW1 0BG
Metropolitan Police Museum c/o Room 1334, New Scotland Yard, Victoria St, London SW1 0BG
Middle Temple Library, Middle Temple Lane, London EC4Y 98T
Ministry of Agriculture, Fisheries and Food, Records Review Section, Lion House, Willowburn Trading Estate, Alnwick, Northumberland NE66 2PF
Ministry of Defence
   Air Historical Branch, 3/5 Great Scotland Yard, London SW1A 2HW   0171 218 5452
   Army Personnel Centre, Secretariat, Public Enquiries, Room 424, Kentigern House, 65 Brown St Glasgow G2 8EX   0141 224 8883
   CS(R)2a (Royal Naval Records); CS(R)2b (Army Personnel Records); CS(R)2c (Polish Service Personnel Records); CS(R)2e (Navy Personnel Records); Bourne Ave., Hayes, Middlesex UB3 1RS 0181 573 3831
   Royal Marines, Commandant General, Ministry of Defence (Navy), Main Building, Whitehall, London SW1A 2HB
Modern Records Centre, University of Warwick Library, Coventry CV4 7AL   01203 524495

National Archives of Canada, 395 Wellington St, Ottawa, Ontario K1A 0N3, Canada
National Archives of Ireland, Bishop St, Dublin 8, Ireland   003531 4072300
National Army Museum, Department of Records, Royal Hospital Rd, London SW3 4HT   0171 730 0717
National Genealogical Society, 4527 17th St North, Arlington, Virginia 22207-2399, USA
National Library of Australia, Parkes Place, Canberra, ACT 2600, Australia
National Library of Ireland, Kildare St, Dublin 2, Republic of Ireland   003531 6618811
National Library of Scotland, George IV Bridge, Edinburgh EH1 1FW   0131 226 4351
National Library of Wales, Aberystwyth, Dyfed SY23 3BU   01970 623816
National Maritime Museum, Maritime Information Centre, Romney Rd, London SE10 9NF   0181 858 4422
National Railway Museum Library, Leeman Rd, York YO2 4XJ   01904 621261
National Register of Archives (Scotland), West Register House, Charlotte Square, Edinburgh EH2 4DF   0131 535 1314
National Register of Archives, Royal Commission on Historical Manuscripts, Quality House, Quality Court, Chancery Lane, London WC2A 1HP   0171 242 1198
Naval Dockyards Society, c/o 44 Lindley Ave., Southsea PO4 9NV   01705 787263
New Zealand Society of Genealogists Inc., PO Box 8795, Symonds St, Auckland 3, New Zealand

Office for National Statistics see General Register Office of England and Wales
Oriental Office Collections, British Library, 96 Euston Rd, London NW1 2DP   0171 323 7353

Presbyterian Historical Society of Northern Ireland, Church House, Fisherwick Place, Belfast BT1 6DW

Principal Registry of the Family Division, First Ave. House, 42–49 High Holborn, London WC1V 6NP 0171 936 7000

Probate Searchroom, Principal Registry of the Family Division, First Ave. House, 42–49 High Holborn, London WC1V 6NP 0171 936 7000

Public Record Office, Ruskin Ave., Kew, Richmond, Surrey TW9 4DU 0181 876 3444

Public Record Office of Northern Ireland, 66 Balmoral Ave., Belfast BT9 6NY 01232 251318

Registry of Deeds, King's Inn, Henrietta St, Dublin 1, Republic of Ireland 003531 6707500

Registry of Shipping and Seamen, Anchor House, Cheviot Close, Parc-Ty-Glas, Llanishen, Cardiff CF4 5JA 01222 747333

Royal Air Force Association, 43 Grove Park Rd, London W4 0181 994 8504

Royal Air Force Museum, Department of Aviation Records (Archives), Hendon Aerodrome, London NW9 5LL 0181 205 2266

Royal Air Force, Personnel Management Agency, RAF Innsworth, Gloucester GL3 1EZ. PMA(CS)2a(2)a for officers; PMA(CS)2a(2)b for airmen 01452 712612 ext. 7906

Royal Archives, Windsor Castle, Windsor, Berkshire, SL4 1NJ 01753 831118 ext. 260

Royal Commission on Historical Manuscripts see National Register of Archives

Royal Courts of Justice, Room 81, Strand, London WC2A 2LL (for recent changes of name) 0171 936 6221

Royal Marines Museum, Eastney, Southsea, Hampshire PO4 9PX 01705 819385

Royal Marines, Drafting and Record Office, HMS Centurion, Grange Rd, Gosport, Portsmouth PO13 9XA 01705 822351

Royal Military Police, Roussillon Barracks, Chichester, Sussex PO19 4BL 01243 786311 ext. 237

Royal Naval Museum, HM Naval Base, Portsmouth, Hampshire PO1 3NH 01705 727577

Royal Navy Medal Office, Room 3103, Centurion Building, Grange Rd, Gosport, Hants PO13 9XA 01705 702204

Rural History Centre and Museum of English Rural Life, The University of Reading, Whiteknights, PO Box 229, Reading RG6 2AG

Salvation Army, Family Tracing Service, 117–121 Judd St, London WC1H 9NN

Sark, Registrar, La Vallette, Sark, Channel Islands

Scots Ancestry Research Society, 134 Thornhill Rd, Falkirk FK2 7AZ 01324 622429

Scottish Genealogy Society, Library and Family History Centre, 15 Victoria Terrace, Edinburgh EH1 2JL 0131 220 3677

Scottish Record Office, HM General Register House, Edinburgh EH1 3YY 0131 535 1314

Scottish Tartan Society, Port-na-Craig Rd, Pitlochry PH16 5ND 01796 474079

Society of Genealogists, 14 Charterhouse Buildings, Goswell Rd, London EC1M 7BA 0171 251 8799

Spanish and Portuguese Jews' Congregation, Honorary Archivist, 2 Ashworth Rd, London W9 1JY 0171 289 2573

St Anthony's College, Middle East Centre, Oxford OX2 6JS

Thomas Coram Foundation, 40 Brunswick Square, London WC1N 1AZ

Ulster Historical Foundation, 12 College Square, East Belfast BT1 6DD 01232 332 288

United Reformed Church History Society, Westminster College, Cambridge CB3 0AA

United Synagogue, Office of the, Adler House, 735 High Rd, London N12 0US 0181 343 8989

Wapping Police Museum, 98 Wapping High St, London E1

West Yorkshire Archives Service, Wakefield Headquarters, Registry of Deeds, Newstead Rd, Wakefield WF1 2DE 01924 305980

Women's Land Army Benevolent Fund see Family Welfare Association

Index

Bold type indicates major references.

Abbreviations: b.m.d = births, marriages and deaths; CI = Channel Islands; IOM = Isle of Man